The
Female
Hero in American
and British
Literature

The Female Hero in American and British Literature

Carol Pearson
Katherine Pope

R. R. Bowker Company
New York & London, 1981

Published by the R. R. Bowker Company
1180 Avenue of the Americas
New York, N.Y. 10036
Copyright © 1981 by Xerox Corporation
Printed and bound in the
United States of America

Library of Congress Cataloging in Publication Data
Pearson, Carol, 1944–
    The female hero in American and British literature.

    Bibliography: p.
    Includes index.
    1. American literature—History and criticism.
2. English literature—History and criticism.   3. Heroes
in literature.   4. Women in literature.   5. Heroines in
literature.   6. Feminism and literature.   I. Pope,
Katherine, 1939–   . II. Title.
PS169.H4P4   823'.009'352042   81-10939
ISBN 0-8352-1402-8   AACR2
ISBN 0-8352-1466-4 pbk

Contents

Contents

Preface

The Female Hero in American and British Literature is a work of myth criticism that explores patterns of female heroism in American and British literature with emphasis on nineteenth- and twentieth-century novels. The great works on the hero—such as Joseph Campbell's *The Hero with a Thousand Faces,* Dorothy Norman's *The Hero: Myth/Image/Symbol,* and Lord Raglan's *The Hero: A Study in Tradition, Myth and Drama*—all begin with the assumption that the hero is male. This prevailing bias has given the impression that in literature and life, heroism is a male phenomenon. This work begins with the assumption that women are and have been heroic, but that the culture has often been unable to recognize female heroism. For this reason, this book uses the term "hero" rather than the diminutive "heroine" to refer to fictional subjects. As we have previously explained:

> Patriarchal society views women essentially as supporting characters in the drama of life. Men change the world, and women help them. This assumption has led to inaccurate literary terminology and criticism. For some time critics have called male protagonists "heroes" or "villains," and female protagonists "heroines." However, in classifying female protagonists, we discovered a conceptual difficulty. It is misleading to speak of Antigone, Hester Prynne, and Alice as heroines, and of Creon, Dimmesdale, and the Cheshire Cat as heroes. Like the traditional hero, the three women venture out on the path to self-discovery, while the male characters function in supporting roles.*

The conclusion of this study, which is supported by numerous references to sympathetically portrayed heroes by both female and male authors, is that on the

---

* Carol Pearson and Katherine Pope, *Who Am I This Time? Female Portraits in British and American Literature* (New York: McGraw-Hill, 1976), pp. 4–5.

archetypal level the journey to self-discovery is the same for both the male and female hero. The nature of the female hero's plight, and the degree and kind of liberation she achieves, vary widely according to historical period and according to the politics, philosophy, and gender of the author. Nevertheless, whatever these differences of emphasis and interpretation, the archetypal *stages* of the journey are the same. As defined by Joseph Campbell in *The Hero with a Thousand Faces*, the three stages of the archetypal journey of the hero are the departure, the initiation, and the return. The successful completion of the journey requires the hero to overcome a variety of obstacles, or "dragons," that may appear at any stage.

Although the experience of male and female heroes is the same on the archetypal level, it differs in important particulars because of the roles and opportunities afforded each sex in western society. This book traces the stages of the journey of the female hero, concentrating on those elements of the female hero's quest that differ from those of her male counterpart. In doing so, it makes the female hero visible and thereby contributes to our knowledge of the psychological and spiritual life journeys of women in western society. It also supplements traditional literary and cultural theories of the hero so that they might more accurately reflect the archetypal patterns of human life.

The arrangement of parts and chapters in *The Female Hero in American and British Literature* reflects the structural parallels in the male and female heroic experience. The content of each chapter, however, focuses on those aspects that are unique to the female hero's experience. Part I, The Hero and Her World, explores the reasons that the female hero has been neglected as a subject for cultural and literary study, and defines briefly the way that the female hero embodies the true heroic ideal. Part I also identifies those dragons that are the result of patriarchal myths and institutions that oppress women. (Because negative myths about women are internalized through the socialization process, the first task of the female hero is to slay the dragons within.) Part II, The Journey, explores the psychological journey in which she slays the inner dragon and wins the treasure—that is, the liberation of her true, vital, and powerful self. Part III, The Return, focuses on the hero's return to the kingdom. It delineates the various forms of community she discovers or creates, and describes her confrontation with the external dragons of patriarchal society.

The female's actual heroic journey is more complex, more abbreviated, and less linear than the chronological arrangement of stages suggests. For example, all female protagonists experience some of the archetypal events, but few experience them all, and individual literary works about the female hero tend to emphasize only one of them. Furthermore, female heroes vary as much as male heroes. Women may be warriors and slay dragons, like Joan of Arc in George Bernard Shaw's *Saint Joan*; they may rise from rags to riches, as do Samuel Richardson's Pamela and Theodore Dreiser's Sister Carrie; or, like Joan Didion's Maria in *Play It as It Lays,* they may be existential heroes who confront the void as the heart of experience. Female and male protagonists often begin as orphans and search for a new family and a new place in the world, for example, Charles Dickens's David Copperfield and Charlotte Brontë's Jane Eyre. Or they may begin in a seemingly secure place, as do Sophocles' Oedipus and Henrick Ibsen's Nora, and leave or be cast out as they come to understand its true nature. *The Female Hero in American and British Literature* codifies a basic pattern and accordingly stresses the correlations between literary works, but it also explores the rich variety at the source of the female hero's problems, the nature of her guides and antagonists, and the quality of her heroic action.

For their assistance in preparing the manuscript in various capacities we gratefully acknowledge Jane Carter, Julie Hambrook, Gloria Moldow, Denise Moore, Jane Murray, Abby Penenburgh, and Cindy Swinburne. Katherine Pope also wishes to thank her husband, Will Marshall, her brother, Kenneth S. Pope, and her parents, Kate and Kenneth Pope, for their encouragement. Carol Pearson warmly thanks her colleagues and friends Debora Carver, Liv Estrup, Rosemary Rocco, and Anne Wilson Schaef for their support.

Part I
The Hero
and Her World

Chapter 1
The Female Hero

*I long to speak out the intense inspiration that comes to me
from the lives of strong women. They have made of their lives a
great adventure.*

Ruth Benedict

The classical works on the hero—such as Joseph Campbell's *The Hero with a
Thousand Faces,* Lord Raglan's *The Hero: A Study in Tradition, Myth and Drama,*
Jessie Weston's *From Ritual to Romance,* and Dorothy Norman's *The Hero:
Myth/Image/Symbol*—conclude that the basic heroic pattern in all cultures can be
reduced to a monomyth.[1] Dorothy Norman states in *The Hero:* ". . . the myths of
the hero pertain to our most essential struggle with ourselves. . . . It is the hero in
man who both reacts most sensitively to challenge, and courageously pays the
price for performing whatever deed is necessary to his or our evolution."[2] Carl Jung
sees the journey of the hero as dramatizing the human being's inner development
toward maturity and psychological wholeness. "The only real adventure that remains for each individual is the exploration of his own unconscious and the
ultimate goal of this search is to form a harmonious and balanced relationship with
the self."[3] Furthermore, Jung, Norman, and others believe that the single heroic
archetype and its subpatterns, or stages, are repeated in the various disciplines that
deal with human experience—anthropology, history, philosophy, psychology,
literature, and art. For example, the psychologists Jung and Freud find analogues
for their patients' dreams in classical heroic myths. Freud's theory of the Oedipus
complex is perhaps the best-known example of the tendency to look for corres-
pondences between literature and human psychology. Scholars Jessie Weston and
Mircea Eliade find striking parallels between myths about the hero and ritual
practices in primitive societies.

According to Joseph Campbell, in *The Hero with a Thousand Faces,* the
archetypal journey of the hero occurs in three stages: the departure, the initiation,
and the return. Each of these in turn has several parts. The departure, for example,
includes the call to adventure, the refusal of the call, the intervention of supernatural aid, the crossing of the first threshold, and the entry into the world of
chaos. The initiation phase incorporates the road of trials, the encounter with the
tempter figure of the same sex, the reconciliation with the parent of the same sex,
and the ultimate boon. In the process of journeying through all of these stages, the

hero approaches, confronts, and slays or is slain by the paralyzing inner dragon, and either is defeated or wins the ultimate boon of inexhaustible life, joy, and wholeness. Upon the hero's return, the kingdom is rejuvenated.[4]

Our understanding of the basic spiritual and psychological archetype of human life has been limited, however, by the assumption that the hero and central character of the myth is male. The hero is almost always assumed to be white and upper class as well. The journey of the upper-class white male—a socially, politically, and economically powerful subgroup of the human race—is identified as the generic type for the normal human condition; and other members of society—racial minorities, the poor, and women—are seen as secondary characters, important only as obstacles, aids, or rewards in his journey.

Even when theorists endeavor to interpret the heroic archetype as inclusive and nonelitist, the attempt usually is doomed to failure because of the patriarchal habit, which uses the male pronoun to indicate the generic and which refers to the human experience as the male experience. Joseph Campbell, in *The Hero with a Thousand Faces,* begins by saying that the hero may be either male or female. He then proceeds to discuss the heroic pattern as male and to define the female characters as goddesses, temptresses, and earth mothers. He declares: "The hegemony wrested from the enemy, the freedom won from the malice of the monster, the life energy released from the toils of the tyrant Holdfast—is symbolized by a woman—if his stature is that of the world monarch, she is the world, and if he is the warrior, she is fame. She is the image of his destiny which he is to release from the pressure of enveloping circumstances" (p. 342). Jung, too, is bound by dualistic assumptions, according to which he identifies the conscious with masculinity, and by extension with men, and the unconscious with femininity and women. He concludes that the male in his life journey explores the unconscious, a task facilitated by an archetypal female anima figure; in contrast, the female moves out of unconsciousness into consciousness with the help of the male animus figure. Female supporting characters teach feminine qualities to the male, and male supporting characters teach masculine qualities to the female. Furthermore, when Jung is discussing the human experience in general, he reverts to describing what he defines as the male experience: "The exploration of *his* own unconscious" (emphasis added) is "the real adventure" of "each individual." Freud assumes that males should achieve heroic self-definition. If women attempt to do so, he insists, they are afflicted with penis envy.[5]

The assumption that the male is subject and hero and the female is object and heroine injects patriarchal sex-role assumptions into the discussion of the archetypal hero's journey; this confuses the issue and obscures the true archetypal elements of the pattern. For example, in arguing that the hero must leave and replace the parent figure to achieve independence, Campbell notes that conflict erupts between parent and child. "There is a new element of rivalry in the picture: the son against the father for the mastery of the universe, and the daughter against the mother to be the mastered world."[6] If one conceives of women as heroic, or even human, Campbell's statement makes no sense. How can a human being "be the mastered world"? This lapse into stereotypical thinking about male and female behavior translates heroism into "macho" terms: The hero "masters" other people as well as the natural world. It certainly is true that the male hero from Homer to Hemingway often demonstrates his heroic power by killing or dominating others; but it is not accurate to assume that this macho heroic ideal is *the* archetypal human pattern. An exploration of the heroic journeys of women—and of men who are relatively powerless because of class or race—makes clear that the archetypal hero masters the world by understanding it, not by dominating, controlling, or owning the world or other people.

Even works about privileged male heroes, especially works in the romantic or transcendental tradition, frequently express ambivalence about the macho ideal of heroism. American novels often have two males who exemplify different heroic modes. Typically, characters such as Coverdale in Nathaniel Hawthorne's *The Blithedale Romance,* Huck Finn in Mark Twain's *Huckleberry Finn,* and Nick Carraway in F. Scott Fitzgerald's *The Great Gatsby* learn the folly of the masculine heroic ideal by observing the behavior of men like Hollingsworth, Tom Sawyer, and Jay Gatsby, respectively. In Herman Melville's *Moby Dick,* Ahab asserts, "I'd strike the sun if it insulted me."[7] Ishmael observes this arrogant and destructive behavior and learns from it, and his triumph ultimately comes not through attempting to control the world, but through understanding himself to be part of its natural processes.

The contrast between Ahab and Ishmael illustrates the struggle between the forces of life and death, which Norman, Campbell, and other theorists recognize to be central to the heroic archetype. Norman writes, "Myths of the heroes speak most eloquently of man's quest to *choose life over death.*"[8] Because death, the ultimate adversary of the hero, is not so much physical as spiritual and psychological, one who dehumanizes, dominates, or owns another human being is an agent of death. The hero, by contrast, is the agent of life. According to Campbell, the hero is "the champion not of things become but of things becoming; the dragon to be slain by him [her] is precisely the monster of the status quo: Holdfast the keeper of the past."[9] In defeating the dragon of conventional thinking and behavior, the hero makes it possible for people to be spontaneous, to think freely and creatively, and to act in accordance with their deepest feelings and their innate humanity. The hero's achievement, in short, is to affirm life.

Freeing the heroic journey from the limiting assumptions about appropriate female and male behavior, then, is an important step in defining a truly human—and truly humane—pattern of heroic action. The macho hero represents in only an inadequate and distorted way the archetypal heroic ideal; for this reason, the recognition of female heroism is important, not only as a way of reclaiming women's heritage, but also as a corrective to the male bias implicit in traditional discussions of the hero. Until the heroic experience of all people—racial minorities and the poor as well as women—has been thoroughly explored, the myth of the hero will always be incomplete and inaccurate.

One of the major themes in Bertolt Brecht's well-known German drama *Mother Courage and Her Children* is that people who are not recognized by the society as noble or heroic often slay dragons out of necessity. The protagonist describes her own heroic feat by saying, "They call me Mother Courage because I was afraid I'd be ruined. So I drove through the bombardment of Riga like a madwoman, with fifty loaves of bread in my cart. . . . They were going moldy. . . ."[10] She speaks for all those who face obstacles so severe that just continuing to live reflects immense heroism: "The poor need courage. They're lost, that's why. That they even get up in the morning is something—in *their* plight. Or that they plough a field—in wartime. Even their bringing children into the world shows they have courage, for they have no prospects" (p. 392). The poet Alta writes in "#29" of *Theme and Variations*: "there are many kinds of courage."[11]

There are many historical reasons why the study of female heroes has been neglected. With the rise of individualism, democracy, and secularism, men were expected to develop their individual identities. Women, on the other hand, continued to be taught a collective myth: They should be selfless helpmates to husband and children. Men increasingly were encouraged to achieve in the secular, pragmatic world; women were to be spiritual and not to corrupt themselves with dealings in the marketplace. In general, female independent selfhood was and still is defined by the traditional patriarchy as theologically evil, biologically unnatural, psychologically unhealthy, and socially in bad taste. Literature, therefore, tends to portray the woman who demonstrates initiative, strength, wisdom, and independent action—the ingredients of the heroic life—not as a hero but as a villain. For example, virtually all strong women in the novels of Hemingway, Mailer, and Lawrence, if they are not mastered by the male hero, are depicted as villains or bitches.

When female heroism is not condemned, it often is simply ignored. It may be seen as less interesting than male heroics, such as killing bears and Germans, rescuing women from other men, and scoring touchdowns. This point of view exists despite the repeated instances of bravery, strength, and wisdom by women in their roles as wives, mothers, protectors, and bread-winners. An obvious example in American history is the women who homesteaded in the West. These women performed the same heroic feats as men, as well as the tasks designated to women; yet western literature generally portrays them as damsels in distress or as unwilling and inadequate companions and victims of the men who conquered the frontier. According to Sheryll Patterson-Black's article "Women Homesteaders on the Great Plains Frontier," "an average of 11.9 percent . . . of homestead entrants were women. . . . 37 percent of the men succeeded in making final claim to the land, while 42.4 percent of the women succeeded, a percentage which discounts the [prevailing] theory of women as helpless, reluctant pioneers."[12]

The scarcity of female heroes in contemporary literature and film also results from the conservatism of popular literary and media forms: Such forms are based not on life, but on popular belief. They seem realistic precisely because they confirm what we already believe. In this way, popular literature often perpetuates such limiting myths. Lenore J. Weitzman and Diane M. Rizzo's classic study "Images of Males and Females in Elementary School Textbooks in Five Subject Areas," undertaken in 1974, illustrates this phenomenon. The study found that, although "women comprise 53% of the U.S. population, . . . females are only 31% of the textbook total—while males are 69%; and, as grade levels become higher, the percentage of pictures including women decline." "Men are shown in over 150 occupational roles—they are doctors, chefs, farmers, chemists, waiters, carpenters, pilots, etc. The illustrations of adult men are glamorous and exciting—and they stimulate young boys to dream about a wide range of occupational choices. In contrast, *choice* is almost nonexistent for girls because the adult women in textbooks are all the same. Although adult women in our society do many things, almost all women in textbooks are housewives." Weitzman and Rizzo determined that in textbooks "there are two kinds of roles in which females predominate. First, more women than men are shown as mean or evil characters. It is women who are overrepresented among the witches and villains of the textbooks. . . . The second role in which there are more females than males is among people who are shown as clumsy or stupid, and as the foolish objects of a joke."[13]

Unless the heroism that women demonstrate in the world is reflected in the literature and myth of the culture, women and men are left with the impression that women are not heroic; that their heroism, when it occurs, is a reaction to the moment and that they ultimately revert to dependence on a man; and that the woman who elects a life of courage, strength, and initiative in her own behalf is an exception, a deviant, and doomed to destruction. Molly Haskell concludes *From Reverence to Rape: The Treatment of Women in the Movies*, by asking, "Where is the mechanism for turning autobiography into the new myths, the new narrative forms? . . . Where are the women to create the new fictions to go beyond the inner space—as women are doing every day in real life—into the outer world of invention, action, imagination?"[14]

While conventional literature, as a document of social propaganda, does perpetuate the status quo, the best literature often challenges the culture's assumptions. Nathaniel Hawthorne's *The Scarlet Letter* and Thomas Hardy's *Tess of the D'Urbervilles*, for example, expose the hypocrisy and injustice of society's treatment of the "fallen woman." Such literature testifies to the destructive effects of traditional social behavior. It also documents women's revolutionary courage to risk change, and thus provides us with a positive alternative to social norms, similar to those we find in the diaries and autobiographies and real lives of women. Such a model is Clara Middleton, in George Meredith's late-nineteenth-century novel *The Egoist*, who finds herself betrothed to an ignorant and complacent man whose character is defined in the title of the book. She is described by her creator as "a girl desperately situated and not a fool."[15] Clara is typical of the female hero who has a will that refuses to be either hidden or destroyed, and who knows or learns what all women, real or fictional, eventually discover—that she is her own hero on her own journey to selfhood. (See Chapter 4 for an analysis of Meredith's story.) Elizabeth Barrett Browning, in her long poem "Aurora Leigh," warns those who would be so blind and points out that the view of women "as the complement" of the "male sex merely" obscures the heroism of traditional women: "You forget too much / That every creature, female as the male, / Stands single in responsible act and thought. / As also in birth and death."[16]

Occasionally, an author is blinded by a patriarchal point of view and thereby fails to understand the heroism of a woman character. In the case of the obtuse author, it is the job of a critic or subsequent author to rediscover the lost or hidden hero. For example, in her novel *Shirley*, Charlotte Brontë reinterprets Milton's Eve. Brontë has the protagonist Shirley Keeldar explain to her friend, Caroline Helstone, "Milton was great; . . . He saw heaven: he looked down on hell. He saw Satan; and Sin his daughter, and Death their horrible offspring . . . Milton tried to see the first woman; but . . . he saw her not. . . . It was his cook that he saw; or it was Mrs. Gill."[17] Shirley redefines Eve as a hero: "The first woman's breast that heaved with life on this world yielded the daring which could contend with Omnipotence" (p. 256).

In *Beyond God the Father*, a contemporary study of women and Judeo-Christian theology, Mary Daly explains the fundamental significance of the redefinition of Eve: "In a real sense the projection of guilt upon women *is* patriarchy's Fall, the primordial lie." Daly argues that as long as men can use women as scapegoats, they never will face their true metaphysical and psychological realities. For women to become heroes, they too must refuse to see themselves as the guilty or inadequate Other. Furthermore, "Women's eradication of the 'sin' of complicity in self-destruction is basically redemptive for the whole society, since oppression is dehumanizing for both the subordinate and the superordinate groups."[18]

The present book is itself an example of literary criticism that reclaims the female heroes of traditional literature and reinterprets them in the light of feminist analysis. In the process, the authors expose as fallacious the major traditional assumptions about women in literature. One such assumption is the traditional belief that the female protagonist and her real-life counterpart seldom travel beyond the protective environment of the home. In fact, the female protagonist frequently ventures as far beyond her childhood environment as her male counterpart. Geoffrey Chaucer's Wife of Bath, for example, makes numerous trips to the shrine at Canterbury. Saints such as Judith and Joan lead armies. Rosalind, in William Shakespeare's *As You Like It,* is by far the most active and adventuresome of the exiles in the Forest of Arden. Daniel Defoe's Moll Flanders is the typical picaresque hero who is continually on the move in England and in the colonies. Lucy Snowe, in Charlotte Brontë's *Villette,* travels to France and works in a strange boarding school, and eventually establishes a school of her own. Thomas Hardy's protagonist in *Tess of the D'Urbervilles* wanders from her home to the D'Urberville estate and then to the dairy; across inhospitable and deserted areas of the Wessex countryside; to a small village where Angel Clare finds her and where she kills her rapist Alec D'Urberville; and finally to Stonehenge, where she is apprehended. Myra Henshaw, in Willa Cather's *My Mortal Enemy,* elopes and spends the rest of her life among strangers in various hotels. Ibsen's Nora elects to move out from her married life with Torvald into a world that offers little or no satisfactory place for the woman on her own, a fact to which the experience of her friend, Mrs. Lundt, testifies.

In twentieth-century literature, Doris Lessing's Martha Quest, in *The Four-Gated City,* leaves Africa, goes to London, and after the apocalypse lives on a small, isolated island. Margaret Atwood's protagonist in *Surfacing* leaves Toronto to go to her parents' remote cabin and ultimately into the dark core of the Canadian woods. Maria in Didion's *Play It As It Lays* and Oedipa in Thomas Pynchon's *The Crying of Lot 49* take to the California freeways. Sissy Hankshaw, in Tom Robbins's *Even Cowgirls Get the Blues,* having left home and family and then her husband, travels back and forth across the United States as the country's greatest hitchhiker. Joanna Russ takes advantage of the freedom of the science fiction genre and creates Janet, in *The Female Man,* who travels to earth from the planet Whileaway. In the world of fantasy literature, Dorothy flies through the air to Oz, and Alice falls down a rabbit hole and then goes through the looking glass.

As with the male, the journey offers the female hero the opportunity to develop qualities such as courage, skill, and independence, which would atrophy in a protected environment. Such qualities do not spring full blown from the hero's head, but are developed as responses to the demands and challenges of experience. Many female heroes, then, are active in the world in the same ways as male heroes. Sophocles' Antigone defies Creon's law to bury her rebel brother, and her commitment to the appropriateness of her courageous deed is unswerving even in the face of death. Charles Portis's *True Grit* opens with the statement, "People do not give it credence that a fourteen-year-old girl could leave home and go off in the wintertime to avenge her father's blood but it did not seem so strange then, although I will say it did not happen every day."[19] This girl's heroism resembles that of the typical male western hero. She maintains her courage and emotional control in the most trying and dangerous circumstances. Eliot Fremont-Smith in the *New York Times* describes the protagonist's particular brand of heroism:

> True Grit is when you are a 14-year-old girl from Yell County, Ark., and you've just shot a dangerous outlaw and the gun's recoil has sent you backward into a pit, and you are wedged in the pit and sinking fast into the cage below where bats are brushing against your legs, and you reach out for something to hold on to and find a rotting corpse beside you and it's full of angry rattlers, and then it turns out you didn't kill the outlaw, he's up at the rim of the pit laughing at you, about to shoot—and you don't lose your nerve. That's True Grit.[20]

Elizabeth Gaskell portrays several female characters who are strong, wise, and courageous. In *North and South,* Margaret Hale confronts a mob of starving cotton workers athirst for her father's blood, and Mary Barton searches for a witness to prove Jim Wilson innocent of the murder of Mr. Carson's son. Both the conservative Hale and the revolutionary Barton act with courage and competence. Similarly, Shirley Keeldar in Charlotte Brontë's novel *Shirley* owns a mill, supervises the farm on her estate, loves to talk business, and rides horseback fast and well. Like Jane Eyre and Rochester, Shirley and Louis Moore, whom she eventually marries, both exhibit the independence, spirit, and rationality associated with masculinity, combined with an equal degree of compassion and intuition. Occasionally, the spirited nature and the courageous acts of the female hero transform not only her immediate world but the larger social order. The biblical Queen Esther convinces King Ahasuerus to liberate her people and destroy those in power who would persecute the Jews. The warrior-saint Judith kills the king of the opposing army and wins the battle for Israel.

Women, like men, may attain heroism through their wisdom or through their commitment to a truth beyond that recognized by social convention. Molly Haskell, in *From Reverence to Rape,* lists a handful of female heroes, including Charlotte Brontë's Lucy Snowe, Charles Dickens's Ada, and E. M. Forster's Margaret Schlegel, whom she describes as "women who were neither beautiful nor especially charming, who did not abide by sex-role definitions, and who (more scandalous than having a child out of wedlock) pursued knowledge and truth for its own sake."[21]

Often, the female hero is in tune with spiritual or natural values that the society advocates but does not practice. The reader comes to see characters such as Sophocles' Antigone, Shaw's Joan of Arc, Cordelia in Shakespeare's *King Lear,* and Little Nell in Dickens's *The Old Curiosity Shop* as superior to the society and to the individuals who destroy them. Sometimes, however, the hero's association with the qualities the society lacks makes her better able to survive than more conventional characters. Lena Grove in William Faulkner's *Light in August* and Molly Bloom in James Joyce's *Ulysses,* for example, are in touch with prolife, natural values, which keep them from being destroyed by the death-aligned philosophies and habits that kill Joe Christmas and spiritually paralyze Leopold Bloom and Stephen Dedalus.

The hero who is an outsider because she is female, black, or poor is almost always a revolutionary. Simply by being heroic, a woman defies the conditioning that insists she be a damsel in distress, and thus she implicitly challenges the status quo. If she and the author of her story are aware that sexism is not ordained by God or nature but that it is a social phenomenon that can be changed, the work will be explicitly feminist. In either case, her heroic action often results from the superior knowledge the outsider possesses. Many female heroes, for example, see the follies of political, military, or economic conquests, which force people to sacrifice their lives or their happiness for glory or material gain. In Jean Giraudoux's modern French play *The Madwoman of Chaillot,* the protagonist lures into her basement the greedy men in power who would dig up the streets of Paris to secure the oil purported to lie beneath. These men, with their assumption of an "us" or "them" relationship to the world, feel justified in stealing the oil to make money and war. Because they assume that the "madwoman" is crazy and harmless, she is able to lock them in the sewer below her basement.

The female hero's powerless position in patriarchal society and her freedom from the negative effects of male socialization may cause her to be more realistic and less destructive than her male counterpart. Called out on a dare on his wedding day, the Virginian, in Owen Wister's novel of the same name, runs the risk of losing the woman he loves because it would be unmanly not to duel with the drunkard who accuses him of vile behavior. In contrast, when Owen Rooster, in Portis's *True Grit,* gets drunk and says, "A man will not work for a woman, not unless he has clabber for brains," Mattie Ross refuses to fight with him. She explains, "I could have confounded him and his silliness right there by saying, 'What about me?' What about that twenty-five dollars I have given you?' But I had not the strength nor the inclination to bandy words with a drunkard. What have you done when you have bested a fool?"[22]

It is axiomatic that the tragic hero falls from power because of hubris. An excess of pride is a characteristic of those bred to have power and accordingly to believe in their superiority. The white male tragic hero experiences a tragic fall when his inflated ego encounters experience. The destruction of the oppressed more often occurs because they accept the role of victim. Women, educated to be inferior and agreeable, are more often destroyed through insecurity than through pride. Harriet Arnow's Gertie Nevels in *The Dollmaker* has a vision of a full, humane, and creative life. However, because she underestimates her own heroic qualities, and does what her husband and her mother think best, she and her family are destroyed.

The difference between the female and the male heroic pattern usually results from the cultural assumption that strong women are deviant and should be punished. Female heroes such as Daniel Defoe's Moll Flanders, Samuel Richardson's Pamela, and Edith Wharton's Lily Bart in *The House of Mirth* have to be strong, wise, and courageous to survive in the world. In addition, they have to disguise these qualities because, to win the treasure of love and social position, they have to play the role of the passive, dependent, innocent young thing. Thus, both male and female writers often portray women as secret heroes. Because society punishes deviation from a sex role or racial stereotype, women, blacks, and others out of power express those heroic qualities traditionally associated with the white upper-class male only when members of that group are not present. Jim and Huck in Mark Twain's *Huckleberry Finn,* for example, are fully self-expressive only when they are alone on the raft. A female character often expresses her independent views only in the company of a woman friend. Ainsley in Margaret Atwood's *The Edible Woman* pretends to be childlike and dependent when she is with men.

She confides to her roommate, however, that her real goal is to have a child and to raise it herself. The traditional role she plays is a device to find a man who is "co-operative" and "who will understand and not make a fuss about marrying me." Her roommate explains to the reader that Ainsley uses her role-playing to "go about getting what she wants with a great deal of efficiency."[23] Other female characters, such as Moll Flanders, do not feel free to confide in anyone but the reader.

The camouflage practiced by the hero may also be used by those writing about her. Annis Pratt, in "The New Feminist Criticism: Exploring the History of the New Space," suggests that women authors especially hide their tracks when demonstrating female heroism and criticizing sexism. She shows how, in traditional novels by women, "sexist norms are criticized in the middle of the action but the critical hero gets it in the end; [in] comic plots . . . patriarchal misbehavior on the part of unsuitable suitors is mocked and then the hero marries somebody less ridiculous in the end. . . . [and] in both genres a pattern emerges in which feminist consciousness is raised but society has its way in the end." Pratt explains this phenomenon as characteristic of oppressed people, and she uses the analogy of "a little black church in the marsh":

> Every now and then . . . the members of the congregation want to break loose and sing "Oh Freedom" with its chorus of "Before I'll be a slave / I'll be buried in my grave / and go home to my lord / and be free." Whenever they sing that, they've got this big old black pot in the vestibule and as they sing they pound the pot. That way, no white folks are going to hear. The drowning effect, this banging on the pot to drown out what they are actually saying about feminism, came in with the first woman's novel and hasn't gone out yet.[24]

In prefeminist literature, the conventional narrative frame for a portrait of the hero may also result from a very real ambivalence in the author's mind about women and the female role. The author may portray a heroic woman, demonstrate the problems she encounters by virtue of being unconventionally heroic and female, and still be unable to imagine a narrative framework in which to resolve the dilemma. Myths about female behavior, moreover, make it difficult for authors to find suitable plots for the exploration of female heroism. Realistic literature, in order to seem credible, must conform to people's beliefs about reality. It matters little that Isabella Bird of *A Lady's Life in the Rocky Mountains,* a small, sickly Victorian "lady," traveled alone on horseback in the Rocky Mountains in winter because she enjoyed it.[25] People do not associate this kind of behavior with women. The great adventure of woman's life, according to the culture, is courtship and marriage. Thus, most works with women as central characters are versions of the love story. In "What Can a Heroine Do? or Why Women Can't Write" Joanna Russ bemoans this paucity of plots:

> The tone may range from grave to gay, from the tragedy of Anna Karenina to the comedy of Emma, but the myth is always the same: innumerable variants on Falling in Love, on courtship, on marriage, on the failure of courtship and marriage. How She Got Married. How She Did Not Get Married (always tragic). How She Fell in Love and Committed Adultery. How

She Saved Her Marriage but Just Barely. . . . How She Loved a
Vile Seducer and Eloped, and Died in Childbirth.[26]

Authors who have written about female heroes have been challenged to use
traditional plots in creative and unconventional ways. Dorothy Sayers in *Gaudy
Night* writes a feminist mystery story in which Harriet Vane overcomes her guilt
about being a liberated woman by discovering that the murderer is not a liberated
woman like herself but a traditional woman who spouts clichés about women's
roles. Erica Jong in *Fear of Flying* employs the conventional love story to show how
Isadora Wing becomes liberated from her self-destructive dependence on men.
Charlotte Perkins Gilman uses the gothic mode in *The Yellow Wallpaper* to show
how women are driven mad by the dissonance between their experience and
society's interpretation of that experience.

In works about more traditional women, authors get around the scarcity of
credible plots by having their protagonists kill dragons, save others, and embark on
journeys in interesting, symbolic ways. Virginia Woolf, in *To the Lighthouse*,
develops an elaborate conceit in which Mrs. Ramsay's activities as a hostess are
symbolically associated with a sailor's adventure on the high seas. Emily Dickinson
skirts nineteenth-century prohibitions against women's writing about sexuality by
having her poetic personae initiated into sexual experience in symbolic ways. Their
initiations always are stated in metaphysical terms.

The restrictions placed on the female hero's life and, thereby, on plots have a
positive aesthetic effect, which is to make the female hero's story both more
complex and interesting. An awareness of the psychological and social mine field
through which the female hero moves also gives the reader an increased appreciation of her courage and ingenuity. Mary Wilkins Freeman praises the hero of "The
Revolt of Mother" for the ways she found to express her heroism even in a limited
and constrained life, writing, "Nobility of character manifests itself at loopholes
when it is not provided with large doors."[27]

In fact, any author who chooses a woman as the *central* character in the story
understands at some level that women are primary beings, and that they are not
ultimately defined according to patriarchal assumptions in relation to fathers,
husbands, or male gods. Whether explicitly feminist or not, therefore, works with
female heroes challenge patriarchal assumptions. In addition, both traditional and
contemporary works with a female hero typically depict her primary problems as
outgrowths of the culture's attitudes about women and of women's economic and
social powerlessness.

Often, literature recounts the complicated stages by which a woman comes
to recognize her own heroism for the first time. Works such as Ibsen's *A Doll's
House* reveal the courage, strength, and wisdom that it takes for a woman to do so
and to risk affirming that heroic selfhood in a world that denies female heroism. In
the process of Ibsen's narrative, Nora renounces the mask of the silly, childish
heroine-housewife, and emerges as the fully responsible, heroic woman she has
been all along. Florida Scott-Maxwell, the American-born actress, writer, political
activist, mother, and Jungian psychologist, writes in her notebook (published in
1968 as *The Measure of My Days*) of the joys and rewards of such an emergence. She
also points out to her readers that in order to assume the role of female hero, "you
need only claim the events of your life to make yourself yours. When you truly
possess all you have been and done, which may take some time, you are fierce with
reality."[28]

The author presenting a feminist hero cannot assume that the reading audience will necessarily sympathize with a feminist point of view. This artistic difficulty has given rise to a new form of the traditional *bildungsroman,* which combines literary elements with essayistic ones; that is, the novel is part story and part argumentative essay. This is especially true of novels discussed in Chapters 4 and 5. The essayistic element of such novels (consider those of Erica Jong and Charlotte Brontë) is often criticized. Even Virginia Woolf argues that Brontë's feminist speeches cause awkward breaks in her novels and keep her from being a truly great writer: Woolf writes that Charlotte Brontë "had more genius in her than Jane Austen; but if one reads them over and marks that jerk in them, that indignation, one sees that she will never get her genius expressed whole and entire. Her books will be deformed and twisted. . . . She will write of herself where she should write of her characters. She is at war with her lot."[29] Readers who make conventional assumptions about the ideal form of a novel may criticize the works of many feminist writers for being polemical. But it might make more scholarly sense to recognize the form as legitimately that of an essay/novel. Whatever the critical justification, the structural and stylistic principles used by such works make it possible for other readers to empathize with a hero who challenges the assumptions of the culture.

The female hero's very heroism calls into question the metaphysics of much of contemporary literature. The male central characters of contemporary literary works usually are anti-heroes in a hopeless and meaningless world; they view themselves and all humanity as powerless victims of metaphysical nothingness and technological, bureaucratic society. In contrast, female characters are increasingly hopeful, sloughing off the victim role to reveal their true, powerful, and heroic identities. George Gissing, in his novel *The Odd Women,* credits the feminist movement with enabling women to be gloriously heroic in a modern industrial age in which male anti-heroes are more common than heroes. Furthermore, it is the belief of Gissing, and of the other authors who treat the same subject, that the emancipation of women will transform society. In *The Odd Women* Rhoda remarks to Barfoot:

> "There's one advantage in being a woman. A woman with brains and will may hope to distinguish herself in the greatest movement of our time—that of emancipating her sex. But what can a man do, unless he has genius?" . . .
>
> Miss Barfoot mused, and her face lighted up with a glad thought. "You are right. It's better to be a woman, in our day. With us is all the joy of advance, the glory of conquering. Men have only material progress to think about. But we—we are winning souls, propagating a new religion, purifying the earth!"[30]

By definition, the true hero shatters the established order and creates the new community. Dorothy Norman in *The Hero* points out that a "birth of consciousness" in the ancient cultures was always accompanied by myth in which the laws of the gods were broken.[31] According to Joseph Campbell in *The Hero with a Thousand Faces,* "The ogre tyrant is the champion of the prodigious fact, the hero is the champion of creative life." The hero achieves "a transmutation of the whole social order . . . so that through every detail and act of secular life the vitalizing image of the universal godman who is actually imminent and effective in all of us may be somehow made known to consciousness."[32]

Jessie Weston in *From Ritual to Romance* discusses the idea that the hero's transformation of society serves to redeem it; she traces this back to the fisher-king myth, which assumes an identity between king and land. The old king becomes wounded or ill—usually he has some kind of sexual dysfunction—and the kingdom becomes sterile: Babies are not born; crops do not flourish. Either the king or a younger surrogate goes on a quest for a fish, grail, or other sacred object representing the mystical power of fertility and creativity. When the quest is successful, the king is made young or well again, or is replaced by the budding hero, and fertility returns to the kingdom.[33]

Thus, the hero returns to the original state of health and wholeness by regaining his creative powers. One might assume—as Jung does—that if the hero is a woman, the treasure she seeks or wins at the end of her quest would require the development of qualities associated with the male rather than the generative, nurturing qualities traditionally associated with the female. In fact, the study of the heroic pattern reveals that the treasure of wholeness and selfhood is the same for both the male and female hero and encompasses both "male" and "female" qualities. However, because society denigrates "feminine" qualities, a woman is not likely to value her female attributes, and, therefore, women—like the fisher-king—are envisioned as wounded: In Freud's theory of penis envy and Germaine Greer's study of "the female eunuch," women are castrated men rather than whole, powerful, vital, human beings.[34] Because Freud believed that women are inadequate males, he advised them to seek a surrogate penis by marrying and having sons. This attitude has been shared by the culture, which labels the feminine as inadequate, trivial, and in some cases even evil, and therefore encourages women to remain passive, dependent, and childlike and to find a man to complete and guide them. When the hero develops adult male and female qualities, she learns that the "wounding" was a hoax. Even more important, she discovers a whole, integrated self that transcends limiting sex-role patterns.

The applicability of the fisher-king myth to the relationship between women and the culture is clear. When women discover that their femaleness is not a wound, the kingdom—or society—is miraculously transformed. In the past, isolated female heroes such as Antigone played the transforming role. However, frequent modern portraits of the female hero, by their very number, promise a more complete transformation of society than the classical hero achieved. The modern female hero comes to realize that even previously forbidden qualities must be assimilated into the self in order to achieve the ultimate boon of wholeness. When she integrates those attributes that are, in society's terms, intrinsically evil and inappropriate to women, she does not, like the macho hero, feel the need to kill, subdue, conquer, master, dominate, or marry a symbol of those values. Furthermore, her experience in a sexist society makes a woman less likely to envision heroism in traditional elitist terms. Unacknowledged as a cultural leader, she does not presume to kill dragons for others, and therefore they are not expected to become her followers or subjects. Others are both actually and potentially her equals, and she encourages them to undertake their own journeys.

The fact that the female hero does not martyr herself for others and that she undergoes the journey for her own benefit absolutely violates female sex-role conditioning, which teaches a woman to be selfless. Yet fundamental to the new consciousness she embodies is a paradox: Undertaking a heroic quest to discover the true self is less selfish than the more traditional role of selfless helpmate.

Because the hero does not give up her life for others, she has no reason to entrap them, make them feel guilty, or dominate them. When she refuses to sacrifice her own self to others, she becomes more rather than less able to aid others in their search for fulfillment.

Indeed, the female hero learns a series of paradoxical truths. Self and other, mind and body, spirit and flesh, male and female, are not necessarily in opposition to one another. The hero's reward for violating the sex-role taboos of her society is the miracle of combining inner wholeness with outward community. Such a shift of consciousness cannot be taught; it can only be achieved. Therefore, the kingdom can be transformed only when others join the hero in her quest.

The hero learns about paradox by journeying through duality. She embarks on the quest when she chooses herself and rejects or is rejected by the captors and dragons that tell her she is naturally unheroic. The motivation for her journey is a search for someone to save her and that "savior" is implicitly defined in opposition to a tempter who seeks to destroy her. The stage is set for the return and the attendant transformation of the kingdom when the hero recognizes that the tempter and the savior are not opposites and not ultimately external to her. When she fully claims responsibility for the savior and the tempter within her she can affirm both herself and her world. This is the return consciousness that transforms the kingdom.

For male heroes not devoted to the macho heroic ideal, the experience is analogous. Both male and female heroes begin the quest for wholeness and selfhood by risking the violation of conventional norms, including conventions about appropriate sex-role behavior; both learn not to manipulate and restrain other people; and both reach accommodation with the best qualities associated with men and with women, integrating strength with humility, independence with empathy, rationality with intuition, and thought with emotion.

Because society divides human qualities into categories of male and female, the symbols for the final state of wholeness usually are androgynous. Weston points out that the grail is often depicted with the phallic sword and that their proximity suggests erotic union. The sword and cup suggest a psychological ideal of the complete self, which is powerful, creative, fertile, and alive because it is whole. Having found the grail, male and female heroes recognize that they are fully human and fundamentally alike. This humane and egalitarian heroic vision is the ethical foundation for the transformed kingdom.

Chapter 2
The Mirror and the Cage

The mythic hero typically encounters a force in the world that threatens to bring destruction or imprisonment. Whatever form the antagonist assumes, it represents an aspect of the hero's own psyche that must be overcome in order for the hero to gain a free, whole, and joyful life. According to Joseph Campbell in *The Hero with a Thousand Faces*, "the dragon to be slain" is "the monster of the status quo: Holdfast, the keeper of the past."[1] The status quo includes a system of assumptions that go largely unquestioned by the culture. These assumptions are embodied in myths, which oversimplify the nature of the social, physical, and metaphysical world and hide the truth about the hero's identity. The hero, by definition, departs from convention and thereby either implicitly or explicitly challenges the myths that define the status quo. In so doing, the hero exposes the truth regarding society's distorted vision of the world and of the hero's own potential. The restrictive myths, which are potentially destructive forces, thus become a source of wisdom.[2]

The tyranny of these myths is a major theme in Doris Lessing's contemporary novel *The Four-Gated City*. The novel begins with Martha Quest's realization that her society obscures the fact of the class system. Everyone is extremely status conscious and some people are extremely rich while others are poor, yet the society as a whole pretends—and to some extent even believes—that differences have disappeared. Such falsification governs all areas of life. Furthermore, those with heroic insight, which conflicts with the myths of the status quo, are severely punished. Martha comes to recognize that Lynda, the wife of her friend, employer, and sometimes lover, Mark, was driven mad because she had extrasensory experiences, and according to everyone Lynda knew, ESP was impossible. Martha comments,

> Soon, probably in the next decade, the truth would have to be admitted. It would be admitted with bad grace, be glossed over, softened. And just as we now say, "They burned and drowned witches for a couple of centuries out of a primitive

and ignorant terror," soon we will be saying, "When they stopped torturing and killing witches, they locked people with certain capacities into lunatic asylums and told them they were freaks, and forced them into conformity by varieties of torture."[3]

Such people were brainwashed and given shock treatment and drugs, which "deprived the victims of their moral stamina and ability to fight back" (p. 516).

This kind of oppression, Lessing argues, confirms the status quo and makes people afraid to go beyond the understanding of their contemporaries: "The mechanisms were always exactly the same, whether political, religious, psychological, philosophic. Dragons guarded the entrances and exits of each layer in the spectrum of belief, or opinion; and the dragons were always the same dragon, no matter what names they went under. The dragon was fear; fear of what other people might think; fear of being different; fear of being isolated; fear of the herd we belong to; fear of that section of the herd we belong to" (p. 524). A failure to act according to the values of conventional society may result in social ostracism, poverty, madness, or death. In less dramatic instances, it may simply mean being disliked. For a woman, socialized to please and to court love and marriage as her highest ambitions, the fear of rejection may be enough to prevent her from acting on her knowledge. If no one validates her perceptions, she may well believe she is stupid, crazy, or even evil, and therefore decide to repress her own vision and conform to society's guidelines. Indeed, she is likely to be paralyzed by the phalanx of interrelated, oppressive forces that restrict her life. Maria, in Joan Didion's novel *Play It As It Lays*, for example, is faced with a whole raft of obstacles to self-actualization and fulfillment—among them, the misogynistic attitudes of men, the physical and psychological horrors of an illegal abortion, self-hatred, alienation, and a total lack of any information about how to construct a meaningful life in the midst of the depersonalized, artificial world of Hollywood. Maya Angelou's protagonist in *I Know Why the Caged Bird Sings* learns during her childhood in Stamps, Arkansas, that to be female, black, and poor "is [to be] caught in the tripartite crossfire of masculine prejudice, white illogical hate and Black lack of power."[4]

As discussed in Chapter 1, the potential for self-actualization and the heroic life is obscured from men as well as from women by society's restrictive myths regarding sex roles. Contemporary writers such as Joseph Heller in *Something Happened* are just beginning to point out the harmful effects of male sex-role conditioning. On the other hand, virtually every serious work in English and American literature that portrays a woman as a major character points out in some way the deleterious effect of the feminine role. Nevertheless, despite the authors' recognition of the destructive effects of traditional womanhood, most works largely take for granted the forces that circumscribe women's lives. Others may criticize to only a limited degree the imbalance of power between the sexes. In *Pamela* and *Clarissa*, Samuel Richardson implicitly criticizes the doctrine of the inferiority of women and of the nonaristocratic middle class, but does not go so far as to attack the double standard or the doctrine of wifely obedience. Writers like Henry James in *The Portrait of a Lady* and Thomas Hardy in *Jude the Obscure* call our attention to the myths and conventions that are destructive to women by dramatizing how a worthy hero is slain by them. Explicitly feminist works are those that clearly identify the traditional myths about femininity as dragons to be slain, and portray female heroes engaged in the battle.

Quite often, authors who are critical of women's plight cover their tracks by deferring at some point to the myths of the status quo. In extreme examples, like Fanny Burney's *Evelina*, feminist sentiments may be stated by a minor character and then severely criticized by the narrator. In this case, the criticism seems sincere, but in others it is merely a distraction from the real message. Daniel Defoe, for example, demonstrates how poverty, the insistence on female purity, the double standard of sexual freedom, and the lack of a means of economic autonomy for most women force Moll Flanders to lie, to steal, and to prostitute herself. Even though he rhetorically condemns her actions and she appends a token repentance to her confessions, the dominant impression Defoe conveys through characterization and plot is that Moll Flanders is a strong and basically admirable character. At the end of the novel, Defoe depicts Moll as rich and happy, and living a socially respectable life with a man she loves.

However, most authors who are sympathetic with "fallen women," like Elizabeth Gaskell in *Ruth* or Thomas Hardy in *Tess of the D'Urbervilles*, usually kill them off at the end. Alternatively, writers who portray women as initially too unconventional, vital, and energetic for the traditional female role—for example, Dorothea Brooke in George Eliot's *Middlemarch*—tend to conclude by disposing of them through marriage. Such was the standard plot of movies of the 1930s and 1940s, in which screen stars like Bette Davis and Joan Crawford played unconventional, liberated women who enjoyed careers until the last few minutes of the film—the final scene, in which they give up "all that" for the "happy ending" of marriage and convention.

British and American literature reveals four societal myths that are most likely to destroy or imprison the female hero, and to prevent her from discovering either her true identity or a home in the world. The enemies—the dragons that she therefore must challenge in order to free herself—are the myth of sex differences; the myth of virginity; the myth of romantic love; and the myth of maternal self-sacrifice. These conspire to leave the potential hero content with being a heroine only—that is, a secondary, supporting character in a man's story, who is unworthy and unable to do anything other than self-destruct for the sake of others. The following four sections in this chapter show how pervasive is the understanding in literature that these four myths repress and destroy women. The final section discusses portraits of women who reconcile the dichotomy between the stereotypes and their own identities, a reconciliation they achieve by consciously hiding their true selves behind conventional female roles.

A Woman's Place

If we have come to think that the nursery and the kitchen are the natural sphere of woman, we have done so exactly as English children come to think that a cage is the natural sphere of a parrot—because they have never seen one anywhere else.

George Bernard Shaw

From the moment of birth, when the conventional first question is asked regarding the gender of the child, a female is constantly bombarded with social images, rewards, and punishments that are designed to ensure that she does not develop any quality associated with the other half of humanity. She must, in other words, be "feminine," and restrict herself to "a woman's place." The classic doctrine of separate spheres and complementary qualities is succinctly summarized in Alfred Lord Tennyson's *The Princess:*

> Man for the field and woman for the hearth;
> Man for the sword and for the needle she;
> Man with the head, and woman with the heart;
> Man to command, and woman to obey;
> All else confusion.[5]

In truth, the "confusion" anticipated in Tennyson's poem is found to exist at the very heart of the myth of a dualistic universe.

First of all, the tendency to see men and women as inherently opposite—as respective embodiments of head and heart, conscious and unconscious, adventurousness and nurturance, aggression and passivity—has led each sex to denigrate the other because it represents the negative half of all human characteristics. Women repeatedly find themselves the objects of hostility and ridicule from men who fear and hate qualities identified as feminine. Many works of serious literature are built around situations in which a male hero confronts a projection of the attributes he identifies as female but cannot internalize in a positive form. The countless "temptresses" are examples of such projections. So, too, are characters like Big Nurse in Ken Kesey's *One Flew over the Cuckoo's Nest.* This work, in typical Western style, identifies culture and civilization with women; it then blames a woman for the "emasculation" of men by a bureaucratic, technological state. This kind of scapegoating has existed since Eve first was blamed for the original fall of humanity, and it continues in the modern world, regardless of the universal understanding that women have had almost no power over the development of the technological state. In every period of British and American literature, in fact, whatever qualities are out of favor are identified as female. In the Middle Ages, for example, an age of literature written mostly by unmarried clerics, lechery is represented in female characters such as Chaucer's Wife of Bath and Criseyde. In the eighteenth-century Age of Reason, female characters like Belinda in Alexander Pope's *The Rape of the Lock* are satirized for their irrational behavior. In the American West, where nature has been valued over society, the male protagonists of classics like Mark Twain's *Huckleberry Finn* and James Fenimore Cooper's *Leatherstocking Tales* seek to escape the restrictive elements of civilization that they associate with women.

Repression and oppression are elements typically found in the development of a social framework based on a dualistic set of values. The less-valued qualities are repressed by the dominant group (males, whites, the upper class, etc.), and this repression creates a shadow phenomenon in which the dominant group projects these "lesser" qualities onto the subordinate group (women, minorities, the poor, etc.). To some degree, the culture's fear of oppressed groups results from this projection—from the attempt to deny in ourselves half the qualities natural to human beings.

In Emily Brontë's nineteenth-century novel *Wuthering Heights,* repressed passion in both its erotic and violent aspects is associated with the heath and with the destructive love of Catherine and Heathcliff. Lockwood, the narrator, has a dream, in which he is cruel to Catherine because he is terrified of the passion, sexuality, and vulnerability that she represents and that he cannot admit in himself. In his dream, she is a small child, wandering the heath. When she attempts to enter the window of his sleeping compartment, he reacts hysterically: "Terror made me cruel; and, finding it useless to attempt shaking the creature off, I pulled its wrist on the broken pane, and rubbed it to and fro till the blood ran down and soaked the bed-clothes: still it wailed, 'Let me in!' and maintained its tenacious grip, almost maddening me with fear."[6]

The Shadow identity that the hero must confront and integrate into his or her psyche always has attributes associated with the other sex. Yet the female hero in turn finds that she has been taught to repress, to hate, and to fear precisely those qualities that society identifies with heroism—adventurousness, independence, self-actualization, courage, and inquisitiveness—because they are considered to be male qualities. If the female hero never understands that the Shadow is within herself and is positive, she may well become obsessed with an external being who manifests the projected attributes. In the Gothic novel, the female psyche is symbolically envisioned as a house, and the Shadow appears as the woman in the tower, the ghost that haunts the halls, or the monster in the cellar. In Charlotte Brontë's *Jane Eyre*, Bertha Mason, Rochester's mad wife imprisoned in a tower, is clearly a projection of Jane's own repressed passionate nature. When the repressed characteristics manifest themselves in positive form, the Shadow is destroyed: When Jane integrates passion into her psyche, Bertha dies. At the end, Jane is able to feel sexual passion for Rochester and yet still remain sane and in control of her life.

The woman possessed by an unacknowledged Shadow often will project her monstrous image of the repressed attribute onto another woman. It is a staple of comic literature that the most frigid matron will be the first to condemn the "fallen woman," and the most obedient, docile wife may viciously attack the bluestocking or feminist. Women who have not yet confronted the Shadow within may have a vested interest in pretending that the inner dragons that limit their heroic potential do not exist. Edna Stumpf writes in an article on the gothic genre, entitled "You're Beautiful When You're Scared," that appeared in *Metropolitan* magazine,

> A person becomes liberated when she knows that she is strong. Strength comes in stages. When you are weak, you pretend that there is no threat, and you comply with the wishes of others in order to retain this illusion. The weak heroine lives in the pages of *Woman's Day* and the *Ladies' Home Journal*. These characters have "happy problems." . . . There are no concerted threats, there are no villains, but circumstances sometimes go awry—the stuff of mild melodrama. There is anguish in these stories but no focus for it, just an implication of guilt on the part of the heroine. This is the heroine as victim.[7]

The female hero finds herself unable to feel whole; furthermore, she is psychologically dependent on another person who is a source of psychological pain. She also finds herself in a world of equally repressed men. Finally, she discovers that the separate-but-equal myth not only causes fragmentation in the self; it actually masks a radical imbalance of power between men and women. In fact, patriarchal society views all of life dualistically, and every dualism masks a hierarchy. In every set of dualisms—mind/body, spirit/flesh, head/heart, individualism/collectivism—the qualities associated with men are judged to be superior to their feminine counterparts. In *Women in Love*, D. H. Lawrence, a twentieth-century apologist for the subjugation of women, contrasts Gudrun and Gerald's destructive passion with the ideal love of Birkin and Ursula. Birkin teaches Ursula that their relationship should be "an equilibrium, a pure balance of two single beings:—as two stars balance each other." This superficially egalitarian metaphor, however, turns out to be only an updated version of John Ruskin and Tennyson's separate-but-unequal doctrine. Birkin's idea of the appropriate relationship between lovers is dramatized when Mino the cat boxes a female cat into submission, and then stands "in pure superiority," in "statuesque young perfection." Ursula protests that the cat is a bully, but Birkin explains, "He is only insisting to the poor stray that she shall acknowledge him as a sort of fate, her own fate: because you can see she is fluffy and promiscuous as the wind. I am with him entirely. He wants superfine stability."[8] Birkin's arguments echo those of John Milton, who saw the fall of humankind as a result of Eve's wandering. Had she only remained at Adam's side where he could keep an eye on her and tell her what to do, the world would have remained perfect.

A number of literary works describe a woman's discovery that she has less power and less freedom than her husband. In Ibsen's *A Doll's House,* Nora is the "ideal" wife, sacrificing her own interests to those of her husband. She even embezzles money to save his life. Nevertheless, when he elects not to protect her from criminal charges, she realizes that he is free to disregard the traditional marital bargain. When Tess Durbeyfield, in *Tess of the D'Urbervilles,* confesses to Angel Clare that she also had a premarital sexual experience, he leaves her. In a number of stories, a traumatic event, or a fleeting comment, forces a character to confront the fact that her relationship with a man is the sole source of her status, desirability, affluence, or right to respect. Maria in Didion's *Play It As It Lays* realizes that men give her looks of "sexual appreciation, meant not for Maria herself but for Carter Lang's wife." When no one knows she is the wife of a powerful and successful man, she is treated with condescension or contempt. After one particularly humiliating episode, an actor exploits her sexually and then has her arrested for taking his car. Later, he apologizes, saying, "You never told me who you were."[9]

Tennyson's dictum "Man to command, and woman to obey" makes it clear that conventional marriage is based not on equality, but on a master-servant relationship. Henry James's *The Portrait of a Lady* compares the marriage contract to a property owner's title to a piece of prized land. Gilbert Osmond is fond of talking to his wife, Isabel Archer, about their "indissoluble union," but any sign of a separate opinion on her part is seen by him as a threat to that union. He ends up "hating" her for having a "mind of her own" because he assumes that her "mind was to be his—attached to his own like a small garden-plot to a deer-park. He would rake the soil gently and water the flowers; he would weed the beds and gather an occasional nosegay. It would be a pretty piece of property for a proprietor already far-reaching."[10]

In the common view, women are expected to be obedient, yet they also are held morally responsible for their actions. A standard eighteenth-century theme is the dilemma of the young girl whose parents, husband, or employer tells her to do something self-destructive or immoral. Central to Clarissa's plight in Richardson's novel is whether she must obey her parent's order to marry Solmes for his money. Richardson's Pamela often does not know quite what to do when Mr. B——, her master, tries to rape her. Fanny Burney's Evelina is convinced that her grandmother is immoral and will not only disgrace her but ruin her chance for a good marriage. Nevertheless, she feels compelled to obey her when they travel together. Having walked a tightrope between self-protection and at least token obedience, she resolves her plight in a conventional manner by marrying the virtuous Lord Orville, whom she can obey with good conscience because of his moral superiority. According to societal myth, women are to be obedient; they are also to be restricted. Conventional society assumes that women will be wives and mothers, and will spend all their time serving others. Bonanza Jellybean, in Robbins's *Even Cowgirls Get the Blues*, notes that a little boy can look forward to being "a fireman or a cop . . . or a deep-sea diver or a quarterback or a spaceman or a rock 'n roll star or a cowboy." If a little girl is not delighted with her "doll babies, tea sets and toy stoves" and the future of "housewifery, desk-jobbing or motherhood," which these childhood playthings portend, a child psychologist must be called in to "force her to face up to reality."[11]

The cage and the mirror are the symbols commonly used to express the limiting and oppressive effects of the traditional female role. It is not unusual for women in fairy tales to be imprisoned, like Rapunzel, or sleeping, like Sleeping Beauty. Villains like Lovelace in Richardson's *Clarissa* assume that women enjoy captivity. He imprisons and finally rapes Clarissa Harlowe, and is convinced until her death that, in keeping with the sex-role myths of the culture, she will ultimately accept and find happiness through being his slave—"I have known a bird actually starve itself, and die of grief, at its being caught and caged, but never did I meet with a woman that was so silly. . . . How do I know, except I try, whether she may not be brought to sing me a fine song, and to be as well contented as I have brought other birds to be, and very shy ones too."[12]

Anne Brontë in "The Captive Dove" and Maya Angelou in *I Know Why the Caged Bird Sings* compare women's lot with a bird in captivity, an association so common as to border on the cliché. When a work presents the circumscribed nature of a woman's life positively rather than negatively, the cage becomes a "garden." John Ruskin, who defended male supremacy in his debates with John Stuart Mill, argues in "Of Queen's Gardens" (1865) that though the sexes are equal, "they are nothing alike, and the happiness and perfection of both depends on each asking and receiving from the other what the other only can give." The woman's sphere is the garden of the home: "By her office and place, she is protected from all danger and temptation. The man, in his rough work in the open world, must encounter all peril and trial—to him therefore must be the failure, the offense, the inevitable error; often he must be wounded or subdued, often misled, and always hardened."[13]

Female characters typically discover that the "queen's garden" is a cage and the supposed "natural" female role too restrictive for their talents. George Eliot, in *Daniel Deronda*, writes a particularly moving scene in which Deronda is reunited with his mother, who tells him about the pain an exceptional woman feels when she is forced into the feminine role:

> You may try; but can never imagine what it is to have a man's force of genius in you, and yet to suffer the slavery of being a girl. To have a pattern cut out . . . this is what you must be; this is what you are wanted for: a woman's heart must be of such a size, and no larger, else it must be pressed small like Chinese feet; her happiness is to be made as cakes are, but a fixed recipe![14]

Eliot's allusion to bound feet may remind the reader that all the women in Cinderella's land had feet too large for the glass slipper—save one. Charlotte Brontë suggests in *Jane Eyre* that all women have hearts and minds too large for the female role:

> Women are supposed to be very calm generally: but women feel just as men feel; they need exercise for their faculties, a field for their efforts as much as their brothers do; they suffer from too rigid a constraint, too absolute a stagnation, precisely as men would suffer; and it is narrow-minded in their more privileged fellow-creatures to say that they ought to confine themselves to making puddings and knitting stockings, to playing on the piano and embroidering bags.[15]

Marge Piercy forcefully argues in her poem "A Work of Artifice" that the "female role" is so unnatural that women are carefully socialized from birth to remain small and limited enough not to outgrow it. She compares the socialization of women to the Japanese bonzai tree, which is artificially dwarfed to present a fine appearance, and suggests the tragedy of "the bound feet / the crippled brain / the hair curlers / the hands you / love to touch."[16] Society has required that, in Rousseau's words, women be "relative to men. To please them, to make themselves loved and honored by them, to educate them when young, to care for them when grown, to counsel them, to make life sweet and agreeable to them—these are the duties of women at all times, and what should be taught them from their infancy."[17] Patriarchal institutions have ensured that a woman must depend on a man for her economic and social welfare. Therefore she is seen, and often sees herself, as an object who exists only in relation to the subject, man.

Because a woman learns early that it is her destiny to gain the treasures of financial support, love, and social acceptance by pleasing others rather than by heroically acting and changing the world, she focuses not on what she sees, but on how she is seen. To the degree that she does so, her cage is a mirror. Sleeping Beauty and the Wicked Witch both are concerned about the mirror's answer to "Who is the fairest one of all?" In fairy tales a woman's worth comes from her youth and beauty; old women usually are witches. Even in realistic literature, the attempt of the aging woman to appear young is almost always either pathetic or comic. Blanche du Bois, in Tennessee Williams's *A Streetcar Named Desire*, struggles to maintain the illusion of youth and chastity, and when she fails, she is castigated and humiliated. Sarah Orne Jewett's short story "The Durham Ladies" tells of two women who have never married; they go to town to purchase two elaborate French wigs to make themselves look younger, but merely succeed in appearing ridiculous.

The poet Alta ridicules the woman of any age who is more seen than seeing. She comments: "Who wants men watching them constantly? / What's the opposite of a voyeur? a voyee?"[18] In effect, the woman entrapped in a mirror polices herself so that those in power will be attracted to her and care for her. Erica Jong writes in "Alcestis on the Poetry Circuit," "The best slave / does not have to be beaten / She beats herself."[19] Margaret Atwood emphasizes the dangers of living a life in the mirror. In *Surfacing,* Anna is the epitome of the traditional woman who lives to please men. Atwood describes her gazing into the mirror, compulsively putting on makeup, "a seamed and folded imitation of a magazine picture that is itself an imitation of a woman who is also an imitation, the original nowhere, hairless lobed angel in the same heaven where God is a circle captive princess in someone's head."[20] Mary Elizabeth Coleridge's nineteenth-century Gothic poem "The Other Side of a Mirror" uses the same image to explore the horror of the hidden life. In it she tells of a woman who always wore a mask, who sat "in silence and in secret bled / No sigh relieved her speechless woe, /She had no voice to speak her dread."[21]

Both boys and girls learn appropriate behavior and appraise their own self-worth in response to what they are told about ideal behavior and about how others treat them. Both learn to hide their true selves and to conform to a sex-role ideal. One of the first lessons a female child learns, however, is that she is somehow inadequate. This lesson of male superiority and female inferiority causes self-doubt, or in many cases even self-hatred, and leads women to commit themselves to the self-denying myths of virginity, romantic love, and maternal self-sacrifice. Marie, the central character of Agnes Smedley's *Daughter of Earth,* recalls her father's elation when her brother is born: "A *son* has been born! I felt neglected, and when I ran to my father and threw my arms around one of his pillarlike legs, he shook me off and told me to go away. There seemed something wrong with me . . . something too deep even to cry about." Both of Marie's parents, she notes, "made me believe I was an evil creature." She accepted her parents' view of her because in her words, "they seemed infallible. Still there are tears I have never forgotten . . . childish tears that are said to have no meaning, and pain that children are said to forget."[22]

After being told she is defective, a woman is encouraged to be "perfect" rather than heroic; but when she compares herself to the women the society sets up as models, she feels doubly inadequate—as a person and as a woman. Maggie Tulliver in George Eliot's *The Mill on the Floss* feels inferior when she is compared with her pretty cousin Lucy: "Everything about her was neat—her little round neck, with the row of coral beads; her little straight nose, not at all snubby; her little clear eyebrows, rather darker than her curls, to match her hazel eyes, which looked with shy pleasure at Maggie." Mrs. Tulliver says Maggie is "naughty," but "Lucy Deane's such a good child—you may set her on a stool, and there she'll sit for an hour together, and never offer to get off."[23] Del Jordan, in Alice Munro's *Lives of Girls and Women,* compares herself with her contemporaries, who appear to fulfill the modern adolescent ideal of female perfection—" the 'well-groomed girls' with 'cool hands,' neat arranged hair, and dry underarms. Even their periods were 'discreet'; nature served and did not betray them."[24]

The woman who most fulfills the ideal also is likely to experience rejection. Alison Murray in Margaret Drabble's *The Ice Age* is cruelly and repeatedly rejected by a jealous sister who finds her too beautiful and too talented. She sets out to "undo herself. She had stripped herself, leaving only her body, a clotheshorse." She gives up a flourishing acting career because her success threatens her husband. She gives all her attention to the care of her cerebral palsied daughter, Molly, and to raising money for research into a cure for the disease, but she is still disliked. People are threatened by her because she is beautiful, and apparently a perfect, selfless mother. She ends up believing there is something horribly wrong with her. She rejects her lover when he is kind and affectionate to her and to Molly, and only returns to him when he lapses into a self-destructive bout of drunkenness. She disowns her healthy but rather obnoxious daughter, who is imprisoned in a foreign country. At the close of the novel, Drabble foretells the future of each character. Of

Alison she writes, "Alison Murray, no leaving . . . her life is beyond imagining. . . . Britain will recover, but not Alison Murray."[25]

Female characters then, are caught in a double bind: If they cannot be "perfect women," they are inadequate; but if they appear to be perfect, they are threatening and alienated. It is unlikely, however, that any woman will absolutely conform to the culture's image of the ideal, because such images are based on mutually exclusive ideas. The traditional model for women is the Virgin Mother. Not less impossible to emulate is the current ideal of the superwoman. Joanna Russ writes in her contemporary novel *The Female Man,*

> I know that somewhere, just to give me the lie, lives a beautiful (got to be beautiful), intellectual, gracious, cultivated, charming woman who has eight children, bakes her own bread, cakes and pies, takes care of her own house, does her own cooking, brings up her own children, holds down a demanding nine-to-five job at the top decision-making level in a man's field, and is adored by her equally successful husband because although a hard-driving, aggressive business executive with eye of eagle, heart of lion, tongue of adder, and muscle of gorilla (she looks just like Kirk Douglas), she comes home at night, slips into a filmy negligee and a wig, and turns instantly into a *Playboy* dimwit, thus laughingly dispelling the canard that you cannot be eight people simultaneously with two different sets of values.[26]

Scott-Maxwell concludes in her diary, "It may be the contrast between the ideal and the real that makes so many women hate being women."[27]

The culture bombards the female hero with the message that she is woefully inadequate, unlike the more privileged male; then it provides her with a series of myths for her emulation that promise to transform her into a praiseworthy being. However, the pursuit of each ideal serves only to further confirm her sense of inferiority and despair, and thereby to increase her dependency on others.

The Good Angel

> To be totally innocent . . . would be to be utterly unknown, particularly to one's self.
>
> Djuna Barnes, *Nightwood*

The prefallen, preconscious, purely innocent virgin is the first model a young girl is expected to emulate. Whether seen in high mimetic form as in the Virgin Mary or in the low mimetic, in Little Nell, the virgin is expected to be not only chaste, but selfless. Associated with the Apollonian and Platonic ideals of pure spiritual form, the virgin exists outside of time and process, without an ego. Bram Dijkstra in "The Androgyne in Nineteenth-Century Art and Literature" attributes the modern reemphasis on this otherworldly ideal to the rise of bourgeois industrial society.

Woman was forced to gather into herself all humanistic qualities, all sweetness and light, all softness and compassion; she
became the passive component in a dualism which allowed
the male to arrogate to himself all active, aggressive (and
hence economically progressive and lucrative), qualities of
personality. . . . A pure, virginal woman represented all the
humanistic and moral universals the male needed to prove his
value before God, but with which he could not be expected to
concern himself in the realm of purely male affairs. . . . Only
virginity presented a guarantee that woman's redemptive
power was intact. Hence the pathological emphasis on virginity in the bourgeois literature of the eighteenth and
nineteenth centuries. . . . Virginity and the passive "femininity" implied by that condition gave moral absolution to the
male for his immorality in the economic and social realm. As
such it became one of the cornerstones of the developing
capitalist system.[28]

Dijkstra's point is nowhere more clearly exemplified than in the sentimental,
even melodramatic response in the eighteenth and nineteenth centuries to the
suffering and ultimate death of a pure girl child. Thousands of people sobbed
openly, for example, when they read or heard that Little Nell, in Dickens's *The Old
Curiosity Shop,* had died. In Chapter 69, Dickens describes the stereotype he is
employing: "If you have seen the picture-gallery of any old family you will remember how the same face and figure—often the fairest, slightest of them all,
comes upon you in different generations; and how you trace the same sweet girl
through a long line of portraits—never growing old or changing—the Good Angel
of the race—abiding by them in all reverses—redeeming all their sins."[29] The
impious comment of Oscar Wilde that "one would have to have a heart of stone to
read the death of Little Nell without laughing"[30] satirizes the ridiculously sentimental portrait of the pure virgin and the denial of moral responsibility by a culture that
makes women its scapegoats.

The aging, selfless virgin is rather condescendingly portrayed as a virtuous
dupe in works like Flaubert's "A Simple Heart" and James Joyce's "Clay," but the
woman who lives for others and remains essentially a child may also inspire
generous comment. Jane Austen in *Emma,* for example, holds out Miss Bates as an
ideal of human goodness:

Miss Bates enjoyed a most uncommon degree of popularity
for a woman neither young, handsome, rich, nor married. She
stood in the very worst predicament in the world for having
much of the public favour; and she had no intellectual
superiority to make atonement to herself; or frighten those
who might hate her into outward respect. She had never
boasted either beauty or cleverness. Her youth had passed
without distinction, and her middle of life was devoted to the
care of a failing mother, and the endeavour to make a small
income go as far as possible. . . . It was her own universal
good will and contented temper which worked such wonders.
She loved everybody, and was interested in everybody's happiness, quick-sighted to everybody's merits.[31]

Models like Little Nell and Miss Bates, selfless and innocent though they may be, do not encourage heroism. Emily Dickinson ridicules the woman whose purity resides in mediocrity and conventionality, and mocks these "soft, cherubic creatures."[32]

In *A Room of One's Own*, Virginia Woolf discusses how the ideal of virginity itself limits women's achievement and psychological growth. The chief task of the virgin is not to learn all she can about the world, but to be protected from physical, emotional, and intellectual knowledge—indeed, from even the appearance of experience. Thus, in service of the virginity myth, women have been discouraged from seeking the experiences necessary to be good writers or thinkers. Even in the twentieth century, Woolf says, chastity has "a religious importance in a woman's life, and has so wrapped itself round with nerves and instincts that to cut it free and bring it to the light of day demands courage of the rarest."[33]

Any deviation from the ideal of virginal perfection is evidence that a woman is truly inferior and worthy of punishment and suffering. The complacent Mary Bennet, in Jane Austen's early nineteenth-century novel *Pride and Prejudice*, comments on Lydia's elopement and subsequent disgrace by pronouncing "that loss of virtue in a female is irretrievable; that one false step involves her in endless ruin; that her reputation is no less brittle than it is beautiful; and that she cannot be too guarded in her behaviour towards the undeserving of the other sex."[34] In Alice Munro's contemporary novel *Lives of Girls and Women*, Del Jordan's mother tells her to use her brain and not get "distracted, over a man." Del understands that this message means not that she should fulfill herself, but that she should keep herself pure by living the cerebral life: "I felt that it was not so different from all the other advice handed out to women, to girls, advice that assumed being female made you damageable, . . . whereas men were supposed to be able to go out and take on all kinds of experiences and shuck off what they didn't want and come back proud."[35]

Nonetheless, experience always intrudes, and because of this advice, women are ill prepared for it. George Meredith, in his novel *The Egoist*, speaks of the worthlessness of innocence to women, and he criticizes the way women continue to encourage that useless tool in each other: "Women do not defend their younger sisters for doing what they perhaps have done—lifting a veil to be seen, and peeping at a world where innocence is as poor a guarantee as a babe's caul against shipwreck."[36] Henry James often focuses on the destruction of a female innocent whose virtue is no match for the world of experience. In *Daisy Miller*, he is critical of the society that ostracizes a woman for the appearance of unchastity, but he also warns of the dangers to the woman who is too innocent to take care of herself. Daisy dies because she is too innocent to understand her environment adequately. Similarly, Isabel Archer, in *The Portrait of a Lady*, finds her search for knowledge ended by her husband and his former lover, Madame Merle, who have "made a convenience" of her. Isabel's sister-in-law tells her how she has been used, and with shock says, "the things, all around you, that you've appeared to succeed in not knowing" are astounding. She offers her "aid to innocent ignorance."[37]

Paradoxically, when a woman transcends innocence, when she develops a self, opinions, or sexual feelings, literary portraits suggest that she is likely to feel guilty for her failure to fulfill completely the ideal of female purity. Guilty feelings about a willful self permeated the diaries of young girls like Anne Frank, as well as the thoughts of young fictional characters like Jane Eyre. In most cases, the protagonist's inability to attain the goal of total purity and selfless innocence, coupled with her ongoing hatred for the persistent imperfect self, leads her to settle for self-denial, suffering, or even self-destruction as an alternative. In many instances, her efforts to achieve perfection and her efforts to destroy or repress herself are indistinguishable. Dickens's Little Nell and Shakespeare's Cordelia in *King Lear* fulfill the myth of virginal purity by dying. Rosamund Stacey, in Margaret Drabble's *Thank You All Very Much*, recalls punishing herself in order to be a good girl: "As a child, I used to endure any discomfort rather than cause offense. I would eat things I loathed, freeze to death in underheated sitting rooms, roast under hair dryers, drink in cafes from chipped and filthy cups, rather than offend hosts, waitresses, hairdressers. To me the pain of causing trouble was greater than anything that I myself within myself could endure."[38] Elena, in Joyce Carol Oates's *Do with Me What You Will*, was taught to be a "living doll" by her mother. A child model, Elena would sit without complaining even when the lights were burning and damaging her eyes. When her alcoholic father kidnaps her, she docilely stays in a lice-ridden hotel room, and becomes virtually catatonic.

Psychologist R. D. Laing's *The Divided Self: An Existential Study in Sanity and Madness* sheds some light on the interactions among the myths of female inferiority, selfless virginity, and self-destruction. One of his patients, Joan, found that because her parents wanted her to be a boy, she could be only nothing. She explains,

> With my parents I couldn't be a boy and they never made it clear what else they wanted me to be except that. So I tried to die by being catatonic. . . . I had to die to keep from dying. I know that sounds crazy but one time a boy hurt my feelings very much and I wanted to jump in front of a subway. Instead I went a little catatonic so I wouldn't feel anything. (I guess you had to die emotionally or your feelings would have killed you.) That's right. I guess I'd rather kill myself than harm somebody else.[39]

In George Eliot's *The Mill on the Floss*, Maggie Tulliver's virginity, which is emphasized throughout the work, includes both chastity and self-sacrifice. To the degree that her selflessness is motivated by insecurity, it finds its logical end in martyrdom. As a child, she is told she is unattractive. When her unruly hair is criticized, she cuts it off, and is then ridiculed for being more unattractive and silly than ever. The cutting of the hair symbolizes her continuing denial of her passionate nature and her attempts to win love and social acceptance.

Maggie's family is most approving when she acknowledges the secondary status and serves and supports her "superior" brother and her cousin. Although she is much more intelligent than her brother, it is he the family sends to school, and she is ridiculed because of her inappropriate love of learning. Her vivacious, spirited nature, moreover, is often compared negatively with the passivity and good manners of her "perfect" cousin Lucy. The message she gets is very clear: By virtue of being female, she is inferior to her brother, and by virtue of her personal defects, she is inferior to the ideal woman represented by her cousin.

When her family loses its money, Maggie's options are even further circumscribed, and her major problem is a total lack of intellectual or emotional stimulation. At this point in her life, she comes across *Thomas a Kempis* in her brother's schoolbooks, and reads, "All things pass away, and thou together with them. Beware thou cleave not unto them, lest thou be entangled and perish. . . . If a man should give all his substance, yet it is nothing. . . . That having left all, he leave himself, and go wholly out of himself, and retain nothing of self-love. . . . I have often said unto thee, and thou shalt enjoy much inward peace."[40] Eliot makes certain the reader sees the parallel between this religious philosophy of self-denial and Maggie's cutting her unruly hair. As she reads the book, "Maggie . . . pushed her heavy hair back as if to see a sudden vision more clearly" (p. 305).

As an adult woman, Maggie falls in love with Lucy's fiancé, Stephen. When he declares his love, the narrator comments:

> Such things, uttered in low broken tones by the one voice that has first stirred the fibre of young passion, have only a feeble effect—on experienced minds at a distance from them. To poor Maggie they were very near; they were like nectar held close to thirsty lips; there was, there *must* be, then, a life for mortals here below which was not hard and chill, in which affection would no longer be self-sacrifice. (p. 492)

The handsome and rich Stephen offers her "something like the fulness of existence—love, wealth, ease, refinement, all that her nature craved" (p. 480). To gain this treasure, however, she has to overcome her belief that she is not worthy of happiness, and that her redemption can come only by suffering. Eliot makes it clear that in this case there are no external dragons to slay. Had Maggie married Stephen the whole world would have loved her, for everyone appreciates success; even Lucy would have forgiven her.

Maggie gives up the green world of fulfillment in deference to Lucy and to Phillip, the hunchback she feels it her duty to marry. While Eliot admires Maggie's selflessness, she also demonstrates how she was a victim, sacrificed on the twin altars of ideal womanhood and male supremacy. The novel ends when Maggie dies saving her "superior" brother's life. One might note that Eliot did not practice such self-sacrifice in her own life. She left home, lived with George Lewes for twenty years without marrying him, and devoted her life to writing novels. Writing *The Mill on the Floss* may well have helped her slay the dragon of her own fear of success and the guilt she felt for deserting her family and defying convention of love and work.

Elizabeth Gaskell's Hester in *Sylvia's Lovers* is reminiscent of Maggie. Like Maggie, Hester is morally superior to the other characters. A purely unselfish Christian, and the purest of virgins, she loves Sylvia's husband, Phillip. She demonstrates the purity of her love when she attempts to reconcile Phillip with Sylvia, only to learn that she has arrived too late: The reconciliation has occurred without her. The sense of unworthiness that accompanies her purity is revealed when she exclaims: " 'Oh, Lord God Almighty! . . . was I not even worthy to bring them together at last?' And she went away slowly and heavily back to the side of her sleeping mother. But 'Thy will be done' was on her quivering lips before she lay down to her rest."[41]

Mary Daly explains the theological basis for this voluntary self-sacrifice on the part of women in *Beyond God the Father:* "The qualities that Christianity *idealizes,* especially for women, are also those of a victim: sacrificial love, passive acceptance of suffering, humility, meekness, etc. . . . Moreover, since women cannot be 'good' enough to measure up to this ideal, . . . this is an impossible model. Thus doomed to failure even in emulating the Victim, women are plunged more deeply into victimization."[42] The hero who fails to measure up to the ideal of virginity learns from her culture that the fault is her own. She may then declare war on herself. If she can also understand the injustice of women's lot, she may use tranquilizers, alcohol, or other drugs to punish the self and to dull the rage her knowledge brings. Or, like the central character in Sylvia Plath's *The Bell Jar,* she may attempt suicide or go mad. The central character in Dorothy Parker's "Big Blonde" depends on male "friends" to pay her bills. She becomes immensely depressed, primarily because in her role as mistress she is a sex object only. When she finds herself less and less able to play the part of the happy-go-lucky support to the male ego, she is torn between her sexual guilt, her failure in maintaining the mistress role, and her anger that none of the men she has lived to please are willing even to hear about her despair. After numbing herself with alcohol for years, she finally commits suicide.

Despite herself, the hero develops both sexual feelings and a will of her own, which she identifies as equal in seriousness and somehow related. Lady Elizabeth Tanfield Cary, a Jacobean poet and playwright, warns that a woman not only must be chaste, "but from suspicion she should free her life, / And bare herself of power as well as will."[43] To the degree that a woman accepts the myth of virginity, she is cut off from her sexuality. It becomes an outside force, perhaps even a visitation from the devil, which she may be willing to suffer pain and death to rid herself of. In Hawthorne's "The Birthmark," the scientist Aylmer concocts a potion for his wife to drink in order to remove her birthmark, the symbol of her sexuality and her one sign of imperfection. Georgiana is concerned only that Aylmer finds her repulsive; she tells him, "Danger is nothing to me; for life, while this hateful mark makes me the object of your horror and disgust—life is a burden which I would fling down with joy. Either remove this dreadful hand [the mark] or take my wretched life!"[44] She drinks the antidote and dies.

Negative attitudes toward female sexuality may be translated, in more realistic literature, into a female protagonist's shame about her own body. In Munro's *Lives of Girls and Women,* the younger hero's mother tells her about Mary Agnes, whose humiliation stemmed not so much from being raped as from being seen naked. They "left her lying on the cold mud, and she caught bronchitis and nearly died." After hearing this story, Del feels shame even in taking off her clothes at the doctor's office; and she imagines that if she were to be seen naked, like Mary Agnes was, she "could not live on afterwards."[45] The protagonist who has sexual experience, even when it is forced on her, is ruined; she is undesirable for marriage and subject to social exile, hardship, and death. Hardy, in *Tess of the D'Urbervilles,* questions the harshness with which Tess is treated after her sexual encounter with Alec: "The recuperative power which pervaded organic nature was surely not denied to maidenhood alone?"[46] Two well-known stanzas from Oliver Goldsmith's eighteenth-century novel *The Vicar of Wakefield* advise the betrayed woman that her first concern should be the redemption of her male betrayer, even if it requires her death.

> When lovely woman stoops to folly,
>   And finds too late that men betray,
> What charms can sooth her melancholy,
>   What art can wash her guilt away?

> The only art her guilt to cover,
>   To hide her shame from every eye.
> To give repentance to her lover,
>   And wring his bosom—is to die.[47]

The counterpart of the "good angel," sacrificed to redeem an unregenerate world, is the "ruined woman," a major figure in eighteenth- and nineteenth-century literature by Richardson, Gaskell, Smollett, Hardy, Wordsworth, Hawthorne, and others. Even in twentieth-century novels, a young girl is likely to feel guilt about the most involuntary of sexual experiences. Kate Millett recounts such an experience in her autobiography, *Flying*. At thirteen, Kate is waiting for the bus when a man opens his car door and offers her a ride. Believing he is one of her father's employees, she gets in. He drives to a secluded spot, begins to molest her, and when she tries to escape, calls her "little bitch. Slut." She finally escapes into the dark, but the experience haunts her. She believes, "It is my fault. They must never know how. Telling on him is telling on me. . . . It's a sin. A sin to have gotten in his car. I have been touched by him. Did I lose my virginity? What does it mean really? Not a sin if I escaped. Even if I ran away, was it a sin?"[48] In Maya Angelou's *I Know Why the Caged Bird Sings,* Marguerite is raped at a very young age by her mother's lover, Mr. Johnson. Afterward she feels guilty and is specifically concerned about losing the affections of her beloved and, in her eyes, superior brother. "What he did to me, and what I allowed, must have been very bad if already God let me hurt so much. . . . And . . . if I told him [her brother Bailey], would he still love me?"[49] The narrator of Joanna Russ's *The Female Man* describes rape as "one of those shadowy feminine disasters, like pregnancy, like disease, like weakness; she was not only the victim of the act but in some strange way its perpetrator." A woman is guilty, for being simultaneously sexual and female, and to the degree that she has succeeded in hiding her sexuality, rape convicts her by revealing her "secret inadequacy" and "wretched guiltiness."[50] Furthermore, it exposes her weakness, vulnerability, and victimization.

A female character's guilt may make her accept even unreasonable criticism or punishment. Gertrude Stein's Melanctha in *Three Lives* becomes ill and dies because her boyfriend Jeff cannot accept her earlier sexual experience. When Angel Clare rejects Tess Durbeyfield because she confesses to a premarital relationship, Tess accepts isolation, poverty, and homelessness as her just desert.

Because female sexuality is associated biologically with pregnancy, conventional society is inclined to see the second as punishment for the first. Del, in Alice Munro's *Lives of Girls and Women,* is told by her friend, whose mother is a nurse, that women who have sex before marriage always suffer and sometimes die: "Because if a girl has to get married, she either dies having it, or she nearly dies, or else there is something the matter with it."[51] Even methods of self-abortion become forms of self-brutalization. Joyce Carol Oates, in her novel *Wonderland,* describes how

> women showed up at the hospital, bleeding. All the time.
> Trying to dislodge the flesh inside their wombs, feverish with
> the need to scrape themselves out. What a mess they made for
> someone else to mop up. . . . The doctors said they were

crazy. Why so wild? So vicious? Savage as animals turning upon themselves, but also very sly and imaginative. The doctors said they were crazy but Jesse did not think it was that simple.[52]

Del Jordan remembers reading about the use of "hatpins, knitting needles, bubbles of air," and "about a poor farmer's wife in North Carolina throwing herself under a wagon when she discovered she was going to have her ninth child."[53] These acts suggest the rage women may come to feel toward their sexual organs, which, because of societal myths, contribute to and justify their guilty victim status.

Thomas Hardy's portrait of Sue Bridewell in *Jude the Obscure* brings home the way even the most courageous and liberated woman will have difficulty escaping the destructive hold of the virginity myth on her life. Sue, who is by temperament not only virginal but celibate, wants to live a dignified, independent, free life. She walks out on her husband to be with Jude, but refuses to marry him: "Fewer women like marriage than you suppose," she argues, "only they enter into it for the dignity it is assumed to confer, and the social advantages it gains them sometimes—a dignity and an advantage that I am quite willing to do without."[54] She braves social disapproval and poverty, but her punishment is classic: the loss of her children. Pregnant for the third time, she complains to Father Time (the son of Jude and the passionate Arabella) about having so many children to support when the father is too poor. The misguided child decides to solve the problem and kills himself and the other children. Hardy portrays Sue's capitulation as tragic martyrdom. She leaves the man she loves to return to her husband, explaining: "My children—are dead—and it is right that they should be! I am glad—almost. They were sin-begotten. They were sacrificed to teach me how to live! Their death was the first stage of my purification. That's why they have not died in vain" (p. 403). In returning to her legal husband, she is denying herself. When he agrees to take her back, her response to his will expresses her martyrdom: "Sue imperceptibly shrank away, her flesh quivering under the touch of his lips" (p. 403).

According to conventional thinking, pregnancy and the restricted life of the selfless wife and mother—especially when the wife receives no joy in the marriage—are simultaneously punishment for sexuality and will, and penance that paves a woman's road to redemption. In the earliest myth of the Judeo-Christian culture, God tells Eve after she has eaten the apple, "I will greatly multiply thy sorrow and thy conception; in sorrow thou shalt bring forth children; and thy desire shall be to thy husband, and he shall rule over thee."[55] Eve's sinful disobedience is only secondarily sexual. Her first sin is undertaking an independent search for knowledge—tasting the apple in defiance of the orders of a male God and male companion. Her punishment and redemption, therefore, come from obedience to her husband, who, in turn, promises to protect her from further evil. In secular terms, this means that the woman who fails to fulfill the ideal of virginal perfection, who falls into the world of intellectual or sexual experience, is provided with another myth for transcending the inadequate self: the myth of romantic love, which promises to redeem the inferior woman through union with a superior male.

All for Love

From a very young age, the female protagonist hears fairy tales like Sleeping Beauty and Snow White, which promise that she will be awakened by the kiss of a handsome prince. He offers her the green world of vitality, love, and prosperity. Donald Barthelme's contemporary novel *Snow White* gently satirizes the romantic love myth and exposes its negative effects, which even modern women experience. Barthelme's sexually liberated Snow White lives with seven men, and yet she still waits for the ideal prince to come along and transform her life:

> *The psychology of Snow White:* What does she hope for? "Some day my prince will come." By this Snow White means that she lives her own being as incomplete, pending the arrival of one who will "complete" her. That is, she lives her own being as "not-with" (even though she is in some sense "with" the seven men, Bill, Kevin, Clem, Hubert, Henry, Edward and Dan). But the "not-with" is experienced as stronger, more real, at this particular instant in time, than the "being-with." The incompleteness is an ache capable of subduing all other data presented by consciousness.[56]

Because Snow White feels incomplete and inadequate without a man, the dominant mode of her life is bored anticipation, the "sleep" of the fairy tale. "Waiting," Barthelme comments, "as a mode of existence" is a "darksomemode" (p. 177). Similarly, in "Waiting," a poetic monologue by Faith Wilding, waiting is a woman's central activity, partially because a man is expected to initiate the romantic moments that provide the focus and meaning for her life. A woman sums up her life this way: "Waiting for him to notice me, to call me / . . . Waiting for my great love / Waiting for the perfect man / . . . Waiting to get married."[57]

Women who see themselves as damsels in distress do not act to improve their own situations. They remain helpless victims and await the arrival of a male rescuer. Dorothy Richardson's *The Long Day* tells the story of girls who work grueling, long hours in a factory, but who will not unionize because each awaits her prince. They have no faith in their own ability to change their environment because they have been taught that women cannot make it through life—economically, socially, emotionally, or sexually—without a man. Their only choice is to take a relationship on his terms.

Because she believes in her inferiority and inadequacy, the female character may consider herself to be real only when reflected in the mirror of a loving man's gaze. Sylvia Ashton Warner, a novelist and a teacher of Maori children in her native New Zealand, confesses how her lack of self-esteem makes her dependent on others' loving her: "I cannot breathe without love in the air. I'd cease to exist when not in love. . . . I can quite truthfully say that I never lifted a hand unless *for* someone; never pursued a thought without the motivation of trying to make someone love me." Even when her husband grows cold to her, she continues to care more for him than for herself: "My work loses its value unless you are happy. Everything loses its value. Your contentment comes before my work."[58]

Theoretically, the myth of romantic love affects women and men equally. Male characters in literature certainly romanticize their loved ones. From the courtly love tradition to F. Scott Fitzgerald's depiction of the smitten Gatsby, men govern their lives by a desire to please a mythic goddess. However, even when male and female characters love each other with the same commitment and intensity, there is an inherent imbalance of power in the relationship. At least the courtly lover embarks on a crusade to prove his love. The courtly lady merely waits. Marguerite Johnson, in Angelou's *I Know Why the Caged Bird Sings,* reads Horatio Alger stories, which tell her that boys who "were always good, always won." She longs to embark on the quest to win the American dream of excellence and prosperity, but, although she knows she can be good and has ability, all the stories are about boys. Thus, she reasons, she cannot achieve the Horatio Alger ideal by herself: "What I needed was a boyfriend. A boyfriend would classify my position to the world, and even more importantly to myself."[59]

Beth, in Marge Piercy's *Small Changes,* also finds that her status comes from male approval, even as a teenager; boys, on the other hand, are judged by their achievements, so that their relationship with her carries less weight:

> A girl needed a boy a lot more than he needed you; your rating
> depended on him. He might be good at any one of a number
> of things and that would win him points. But no matter what
> else a girl did well, no matter what they said once a year on
> Honors Day, what counted was pleasing boys. . . . The con-
> stant message in the air was that, if you didn't attract boys, you
> must change your body, rearrange your head, your personal-
> ity, your ideals to fit in with what was currently wanted. Or else
> you were a failure. You were a dog.[60]

Isadora Wing, the narrator and central character of Eric Jong's *Fear of Flying* and *How to Save Your Own Life,* cannot face life without a man because she has internalized virtually all of the dragon myths regarding "being a woman." Psychologically paralyzed as she is, Isadora is nevertheless able to articulate with accuracy and wit the conventional attitudes that do her in. Jong points out, for example, that conventional women so fear the social judgment, harassment, and isolation inflicted on the single, independent woman that they "gladly embrace even bad marriages."[61]

Historically, in literature, man is presented as woman's sole source of status and approval. Her only avenue to material and social advantage in the world, he has the power to judge her and, according to his whim, to damn her to poverty, disgrace, and disregard. In *Pamela,* Samuel Richardson's Mr. B—— can seduce Pamela and then cast her off. As Pamela says, "Those Things don't disgrace Men that ruin poor Women."[62] Mr. B—— also rewards Pamela for her chastity with marriage, but even then she must obey him or lose the advantages he provides. Her perfect obedience after marriage is almost ludicrously manifested during the marriage ceremony, when she curtsies, calls him master, and thanks him for condescending to marry her.

One of the few well-known myths with a female protagonist, the story of Psyche and Eros, epitomizes the traditional male-female relationship. Psyche is married to a god, but she is forbidden to look at him. For her disobedience in sneaking a peek, she is banished. She attempts through a series of labors to redeem herself and return to his side, but fails. It is only through his intercession on her behalf that the chastened and grateful Psyche is reunited with him. The Christian doctrine of wifely obedience comes from the biblical metaphor likening Christ's relationship with his Church to a man's relationship to his wife. In Chaucer's *The Canterbury Tales* patient Griselda illustrates the ideal. She obeys her husband perfectly even when he claims to have killed her children.

Such blanket affirmation of male supremacy and female obedience appears only in literature that is devoted to promoting the status quo. Increasingly in modern literature, which tends to examine the values of the society it describes, there is an implicit or explicit acknowledgment that this concept conflicts with a woman's humanity and potential for happiness and even with her true spiritual salvation. For example, Charlotte Brontë's *Jane Eyre* points out how idolatrous it is to worship a man as a god. Jane's very love for Rochester cuts her off from God and from herself: "He stood between me and every thought of religion, as the eclipse intervenes between man and the broad sun. I could not, in those days, see God for this creature of whom I had made an idol."[63] She flees from him to save herself and her soul.

Today, it is generally understood that the romantic and spiritual man-god—the male ideal worthy of a woman's self-sacrifice and worship, for whom she is expected to set aside herself and her life—simply does not exist, except in myth. Emily Carr, the Canadian artist, writes in her diary of finding some love letters from a man who, years earlier, had asked her to marry him. She has refused because "he demanded *worship*" and because "he would have bored me until my spirit died."[64]

In spite of this general recognition in the twentieth century that the man-god is dead, however, the preheroic female protagonist continues to dream. In *Slouching toward Bethlehem*, Joan Didion writes a love letter to John Wayne, mourning the absence of a man capable of bringing her the green world of continuity, happiness, and security. As a young girl on a barren army base, she recalls, she amused herself by watching endless movies.

> It was there, that summer of 1943 while the hot wind blew outside, that I first saw John Wayne. Saw the walk, heard the voice. Heard him tell the girl in a picture called *War of the Wildcats* that he would build her a house "at the bend in the river where the cottonwoods grow." As it happened I did not grow up to be the kind of woman who is the heroine in a Western, and although the men I have known have had many virtues, and have taken me to live in many places I have come to love, they have never been John Wayne, and they have never taken me to that bend in the river where the cotton-woods grow. Deep in that part of my heart where the artificial rain forever falls, that is still the line I wait to hear.[65]

The male narrator and the other male characters in Barthelme's *Snow White* repeatedly try and fail to be the romantic ideal that Snow White wants, and the narrator recounts that she was not satisfied. "I don't know what to do next." Paul, the prince, fails her also, and she laments, "Paul is pure frog. He is frog through and through. I thought he would, at some point, cast off his mottled wettish green-and-brown integument to reappear washed in the hundred glistering hues of princeliness. But is he *pure frog*. So. I am disappointed. Either I have overestimated Paul, or I have overestimated history. In either case I have made a serious error." The dilemma is resolved when Paul is poisoned, and Snow White can now pretend that he was indeed a prince. Barthelme explicitly criticizes the antilife nature of this romanticism: "Snow White continues to cast chrysanthemums on Paul's grave, although there is nothing in it for her, that grave. I think she realizes that. . . . She was fond not of him but of the abstract notion that, to her, meant 'him.' I am not sure that that is the best idea."[66]

While the romantic lover's power to save the female hero is seriously undercut in modern literature, his power to destroy women becomes more obvious, as does the general connection between romantic love and death. In Joyce Carol Oates's "Where Are You Going? Where Have You Been?" a teenage girl is picked up at a drive-in restaurant by a middle-aged rapist and murderer who is dressed like another teenager. Even when she knows he will kill her, she does not resist. She is debilitated by terror, but she is also paralyzed by her training to please and obey men. Erica Jong's less exaggeratedly passive and obedient protagonist, Isadora Wing, also discovers that her quest for sex with an anonymous man is a courting of annihilation. The lover is "no man at all, but . . . a specter made of our own yearning." He is the rapist, the "man under the bed. . . . Maybe he was really death, the last lover." She both fears and desires him because she believes he will free her from her inadequate self by either completing or killing her, or both. "If we haven't the power to complete ourselves, the search for love becomes a search for self-annihilation; and then we try to convince ourselves that self-annihilation is love."[67] The nineteenth-century hero Jane Eyre describes St. John Rivers's proposal of marriage as a temptation "to rush down the torrent of his will into the gulf of his existence, and there lose my own."[68]

Denis de Rougemont, in *Love in the Western World*, analyzes the connection between love and the urge for self-annihilation. He explains that the myth of romantic love is a secular equivalent of pagan fertility cults:

> A myth is needed to express the dark and unmentionable fact that passion is linked with death, and involves the destruction of any one yielding himself up to it with all his strength. For we have wanted to preserve passion and we cherish the unhappiness that it brings with it; and yet at the same time both passion and unhappiness have stood condemned in the sight of official morals and in the sight of reason. Hence, thanks to the obscurity [of myths such as the stories of Tristan and Isolde and Eloise and Abelard], we have been able to receive and enjoy imaginatively the disguised content of the myth, and yet have not grown sufficiently aware of the nature of this content to be confronted by the contradiction.[69]

Because marriage has been defined by convention as separate from passion, the experience of being married can entail as much death-in-life as the sexual-romantic existence it is designed to supersede. For women, who surrender separate names and separate selves, the traditional marriage is a sacrificial act, and women many times find themselves trapped or destroyed by it. Anne Finch, Countess of Winchelsea, complains in "The Unequal Fetters" (1702), "Marriage does not slightly tye men / Whil'st close Pris'ners we remain."[70] Sasha, in *Memoirs of an Ex-Prom Queen*, feels at her wedding "like a sacred virgin, chosen for an elaborate initiation rite, prepared and purified according to ancient rule."[71] In Dorothy Parker's "Story of Mrs. W——," a housewife likens her bed to a coffin where "at night I stretch my length / And envy no one but the dead."[72]

Sylvia Plath's poem "The Applicant" is based on an elaborate conceit in which the perfect wife is a lifeless, servile robot: "A living doll, everywhere you look / It can sew, it can cook." The ironic speaker in the poem urges a man to "marry it / marry it / marry it."[73] Tom Robbins writes in *Even Cowgirls Get the Blues,* "Marriage is when a girl gives up the fight, walks off the battlefield and from then on leaves the truly interesting and significant action to her husband, who has bargained to 'take care' of her. What a sad bum deal. Women live longer than men because they really haven't been living."[74]

The woman who tries to emulate the traditional model of the wife's role may become an object of scorn. Major Brutt, in Elizabeth Bowen's *The Death of the Heart,* is repulsed when Portia attempts to demonstrate her wifely potential.

> With a quite new, matter-of-fact air of possessing his room, she made small arrangements for comfort—peeled off his eiderdown, kicked her shoes off, lay down with her head into his pillow and pulled the eiderdown snugly up to her chin. By this series of acts she seemed at once to shelter, to plant her and to obliterate herself—most of all that last. Like a sick person, or someone who has decided by not getting up to take no part in a day, she at once seemed to inhabit a different world.[75]

Piercy's *Small Changes* shows how marriage profoundly changes the way women are perceived by their husbands, by society, and by themselves. Before marriage, Miriam is vibrant, outspoken, intelligent, and seemingly liberated. After marriage, she gives up her career to have a baby, and then realizes that she has lost her autonomy and independence. She begins to feel useless and dependent, and the world agrees with her. When she acts in the old energetic and vital way at a party, the other guests look on her with condescension and embarrassment.

Some works show that men who feel guilty or inadequate unleash their anger and frustration on their wives. In Eugene O'Neill's *The Iceman Cometh* and Robert Browning's *The Ring and the Book,* men who cannot assuage their own sense of guilt kill their suffocatingly virtuous wives. Marie, the narrator and central character of Agnes Smedley's *Daughter of Earth,* tells how the men around her beat their wives, treating them as scapegoats for their poverty and blaming them for having too many children. Yet these same wives selflessly continue sacrificing their own lives for husbands and children. Marie concludes, "In my hatred of marriage, I thought that I would rather be a prostitute than a married woman. I could then protect, feed, and respect myself, and maintain some right over my own body. Prostitutes did not have children, I contemplated; men did not dare beat them; they did not have to obey. The 'respectability' of married women seemed to rest in their acceptance of servitude and inferiority."[76]

The evidence of literature is that women remain in the most boring and dehumanizing marriages because they believe they are partial and inadequate and can be fulfilled only by serving a superior male. Sasha, in *Memoirs of an Ex-Prom Queen,* attempts her own emergence from a stifling marriage but cannot rid herself of her fear of living without a man. In the final scene, she returns home and changes her hairstyle instead of her life. Erica Jong's Isadora Wing, on the verge of leaving her husband, Bennett, in *Fear of Flying,* is still agonizing over her decision in *How to Save Your Own Life.* To her, the phrase "my husband" "was a seal, an imprimatur, an endorsement that I was a *bona fide* woman." However unhappy she is with him, her leaving him will be taken by herself and others as a failure. In order to make the break, she has to recognize that her plight is shared by many other, basically strong women:

> All my life I had known women who supported their families, did their own work, did most of the housework—yet needed to be married, often to men they clearly did not enjoy. I knew rich women who had husbands as baubles, career women who treated their husbands as sort of extra children in the family, frenetic housewives who raised kids and cooked and also kept their husbands' stores, businesses, or medical practices from sinking into total confusion. There was no doubt about the strength of these women. Except perhaps in their own eyes. Did every one of them need the phrase *my husband* as badly as I did?[77]

Isadora Wing's life history demonstrates how the most talented women live under the shadow of the myth of female inferiority. Taught to be selfless, Isadora feels guilty when she leaves her first husband, Brian, in *Fear of Flying*, to save herself. She also feels inadequate because she cannot make a success of her marriage and does not have the courage to leave it. She is paralyzed because she believes she is a failure as a poet and as an adventurer. When we last see her in *How to Save Your Own Life*, she has finally left her husband, but she has not shed her belief in the romantic love myth. She leaves Bennett only when she finds another man. As she and Josh make love, she muses that "all her feminism, all her independence, all her fame had come to this, this helplessness, this need." He "slides in and out of her" as if he "owned her soul." Having found Mr. Right, she yearns to have "his baby, their baby, she wanted to feel that pain, that pleasure" (pp. 284–285).

The theme of a woman who cannot leave her husband because of feelings of inadequacy and lack of courage is not new. In the eighteenth century, Defoe's Moll Flanders patronizingly explains that the fear of being without a man is "nothing but a lack of courage."[78] James's Isabel Archer, in *The Portrait of a Lady*, admits to her friend Henrietta Stackpole that her marriage is so unhappy that she is "wretched," and yet she will not leave her husband, Gilbert Osmond: "I can't publish my mistake. I don't think that is decent. I'd much rather die."[79] Her fear, however, is more complicated than Isadora's. Isabel sets out to fulfill her aristocratic ideal, "the union of great knowledge with great liberty," which gave one respectively "a sense of duty and a sense of enjoyment" (p. 361). She sets out as a young woman, determined to be both free and responsible. "I try to judge things for myself," she explains to her suitor, Caspar Goodwood; "to judge wrong, I think, is more than not to judge at all. . . . I wish to choose my fate and to learn about life" (p. 143).

Isabel's circumstances are conducive to making free choices. Ralph Touchett talks his father into leaving her money because Touchett notices that unlike most women who "waited, in attitudes more or less gracefully passive, for a man to come that way and furnish them with a destiny," Isabel "gave one an impression of having intentions of her own" (p. 64). But although the bequest allows her to be the mistress of her fate, Isabel is not able to make heroic choices. Her tragic flaw is innocence and a failure of imagination. Instead of gaining knowledge of the world, she marries a man who epitomizes culture and experience. The result is not the ennobling wisdom she sought, but cynicism and resignation. This man—the self-

styled first gentleman of Europe—is an egotist. "Under all his culture, his cleverness, his amenity, under his good nature, his facility, his knowledge of life, his
egotism lay hidden like a serpent in a bank of flowers" (p. 360). As in many of
James's finest novels, an innocent American's encounter with the continental
world of "experience" becomes a fall from paradise. Her husband values traditions
for their own sake, and he defines the aristocratic life as "altogether a thing of
forms, a conscious, calculated attitude." He sees the world as "base" and "igno-
ble," but he lives for it "not to enlighten or convert or redeem it, but to extract from
it some recognition of one's own superiority" (p. 360). To this end, he divides
people into three categories: "some three or four very exalted people" whom he
envies; the vulgar whom he despises and assumes should envy him; and those
close to him—his wife and daughter—whom he assimilates into part of his aristocratic display. His fondest hope for his daughter is that she will marry a Lord, so that
the marriage will do *him* credit. He decides to marry Isabel for her money and
because she promises to be a good possession: "What could be a happier gift in a
companion than a quick, fanciful mind which saved one repetitions and reflected
one's thought on a polished, elegant surface? . . . His egotism had never taken the
crude form of desiring a dull wife; this lady's intelligence was to be a plate, not an
earthen one—a plate that he might heap with ripe fruits, to which it would give a
decorative value, so that talk might be for him a sort of served dessert" (p. 295). In
short, he epitomizes the static, hierarchical, dehumanizing attributes of the dragon
of convention.

After learning that Osmond has used her in the most cold-blooded and
hypocritical ways, Isabel defies his orders for the first time, but she cannot leave
him. She simply assumes that the alternative to her husband is another man. The
most obvious choice is Caspar Goodwood. He responds to her so passionately that
she recognizes she "had never been loved before"; yet if Osmond's proprietary,
egotistical love is the "serpent," Goodwood's overwhelming passion is "the hot
wind of the desert, at the approach of which the other dropped dead, like mere
sweet airs of the garden" (p. 360). She is tempted to give up responsibility for her
own life and go with him: "She believed just then that to let him take her in his arms
would be the next best thing to her dying," but when he kisses her, "like white
lightning . . . she felt each thing in his hard manhood that had least pleased her,
each aggressive fact of his face, his figure, his presence, justified of its intense
identity and made one with this act of possession" (p. 482). She rejects
Goodwood's love because he would possess and destroy her more completely
than Osmond, with his commitment to form rather than substance, ever could.

To his credit, Goodwood argues that "a woman deliberately made to suffer is
justified in anything in life." In returning to Osmond, Isabel rejects this idea.
Earlier, when confessing her unhappiness to Harriet, she says, "One must accept
one's deeds. I married him before all the world; I was perfectly free; it was
impossible to do anything more deliberate" (p. 407). Isabel's resolve to live respon-
sibly and morally is intensified by her discovery of her husband's depravity. She
discovers that Osmond's daughter, Pansy, is the product of his illicit liaison with
Madame Merle, and that Madame Merle has cold-bloodedly arranged her marriage
to Osmond for the benefit of the daughter she never acknowledged. Although we
do not see Isabel after her decision to return to Osmond and Pansy, it is clear she is
adopting a life of self-sacrifice and penance to atone for the sin of making the
wrong choice, and that her actions are not so much moral and responsible as
self-destructive. She cannot reject the person who victimized her because she feels
guilty about becoming a victim.

The myth of romantic love is held out to women as their version of the heroic quest. It promises them vitality, freedom, and fulfillment, but, as literary works show, the end of the quest is either annihilation or imprisonment. In Ralph Touchett's words, Isabel Archer's story is "so pitiful"; instead of growing and experiencing life as an autonomous individual, she is "ground in the very mill of the conventional!" (p. 478). Like Isabel, the female character who does not recognize the pernicious effects of the myth of romantic love on her life, and thereby believes her marriage was freely chosen, assumes all of the guilt for the marriage's failure. She is a failure either by choosing the wrong man or by her inability to transform him into a prince. Typically, she will spend the rest of her life doing penance for her mistake by adopting the role of the self-sacrificing mother.

The Giving Tree

> [Women] weren't born to be free, they were born to have babies.
>
> Norman Mailer, Deer Park

The perfect mother embodies selflessness and nurturance. Jane Lazarre in The Mother Knot invokes this paragon of virtue: "Mother, goddess of love, to whom we all can go for protection and unconditional love, perfect human being we have all been taught to believe in, whom poets have compared to the earth itself, who kneels down, arms outstretched, to enclose us and fend off the rains."[80] This mother gives continually without expecting any reward but the joy she receives from making others happy.

John Steinbeck's The Grapes of Wrath celebrates this mythic figure. In Steinbeck's novel, the life-perpetuating, selfless ethic of motherhood acts as a force countering the dominant impulse of a capitalist society toward greed and exploitation. Ma, a human embodiment of Mother Earth, takes care of everyone else even when the strongest men are crumbling around her. Her strength is godlike and eternal, and she is able to give continually to others without being diminished. The novel ends as Rose of Sharon, with Ma's encouragement, saves the life of a starving man by offering him milk from her breast. Her action transforms her into a Madonna-like, quasi-mystical being. While she strokes the stranger's hair, she looks up and smiles "mysteriously."[81]

The role of mother-goddess offers a woman power, admiration, and in many cases even worship. Virginia Woolf's Mrs. Ramsay, in To the Lighthouse, is compared with a queen, a Greek goddess, and a fountain of "delicious fecundity."[82] Charles Tansley, a young man who escorts her to town, expresses the awe people feel in her presence when he notes that although she is fifty years old, she is "the most beautiful person he had ever seen. With stars in her eyes and veils in her hair, with cyclamen and wild violets" (p. 58). In a reversal of the myth of romantic love, Mrs. Ramsay is a goddess, who has not only her eight children but "the whole of the other sex under her protection" (p. 13).

The Giving Tree, a well-known and much praised children's story by Shel Silberstein, uses the male-child/female-mother relationship without criticism as the metaphor for a celebration of man's relationship to nature. In doing so, the story lays bare the underlying tenets of the myth of maternal self-sacrifice. A tree, which is the mother figure, allows a man she loves to cut off and take away parts of her that he needs—limbs for his house, lumber for a boat—until she is only a stump on which he sits. However, she is a happy stump, for although she has given him everything she has, and although he has given her nothing in return, she has the satisfaction of knowing that she has been useful to him. Margaret Atwood in *The Edible Woman* and Marge Piercy in *Small Changes* exposes the cannibalistic nature of this relationship. The narrator of Henry James's *The Sacred Fount* likens it to vampirism. He discovers a series of "love" relationships in which either the man or the woman plays this maternal role. In one instance, he hears of a woman of intelligence and grace who is increasingly diminished and subdued, while the man she loves takes on her attributes. The narrator is told, "whoever she is, she gives all she has. She keeps nothing back—nothing for herself." He responds knowingly, "I see—because *he* takes everything. He just cleans her out."[83] The exploitation at the heart of this relationship is the secret horror masked by the beautiful, evocative term "love." Woolf implies that Mrs. Ramsay dies of exhaustion; she is sucked dry because the fountainlike spray of her nurturing love is "drunk and quenched by the beak of brass, the arid scimitar of the male, which smote mercilessly, again and again, demanding sympathy."[84]

Anaïs Nin warns women against assuming the maternal role with men they love, lest they encourage male irresponsibility and destructiveness:

> The woman accepts the maternal role, and then she can for-
> give anything. The child does not know when he is hurting the
> mother. A child does not notice weariness, pain. He gives
> nothing and demands everything. If the mother weeps he will
> throw his arms around her, then he will go on doing what hurt
> her before. The child never thinks of the mother except as the
> all-giving, the all-forgiving, the inexhaustible, eternal love.
> The child devours the mother.[85]

Once a woman is cast in the role of mother, she takes the blame for her "child's" actions and feelings—even his hatred or mistreatment of her.

Janet, an alien from the all-female planet Whileaway in Joanna Russ's *The Female Man*, has not internalized the myth of female responsibility for the mis-behavior of men, and therefore she innocently challenges its assumptions. A man at a party heaps misogynistic insults on her when she rejects his sexual advances, and she responds in kind and defeats him. The other men and women at the party are shocked because they believe that a "man's bad temper is woman's fault. It is also the woman's responsibility to patch things up afterward."[86]

The myth of the perfect mother is an extension of the virginity myth; both images are asexual, both require selflessness, and both cast the woman in a scapegoat role. Like Christ, the virgin and the mother are spotless lambs that take on the sins of the world. Rosamund Stacey, in Margaret Drabble's *Thank You All Very Much*, understands that it is presumptuous, perhaps even blasphemous, for a mortal to undertake this role. Such willing self-sacrifice is also a symptom of a negative self-image. Rosamund remembers that "when I was young . . . I used to see the best in everyone, to excuse all faults, to put all malice and shortcomings down to environment: in short, to take all blame upon myself."[87]

The self-image of a woman whose ego is already besieged by the harmful effects of the myths of virginity and romantic love is not likely to be improved by taking responsibility for the sins, improprieties, and mistakes of others. However, until the twentieth century, women at least were praised for their nurturing, care-taking function. Indeed, according to conventional thinking, motherhood was the only positive role for an aging woman. Aging virgins or sex objects were usually the objects of ridicule or scorn, but they could escape that fate if they devoted their lives to serving others. Jane Austen's Miss Bates in *Emma* and the stereotypical whore-with-a-heart-of-gold in numerous other stories avoid censure because they are selfless. Traditionally, feminine work—housecleaning, cooking, sewing, caring for children in the home, and schoolteaching, nursing, social work—are not seen by the culture as work, but as proper expressions of woman's mothering role. The execution of these tasks, therefore, does not count as an achievement; rather it is proof of womanliness.

Charlotte Brontë, writing to Robert Southey, demonstrates that despite the criticism of the boredom and limitations of the female role found in her fiction, and her personal penchant for the life of the mind, she assumes an obligation to do women's work out of a deep-seated sense of duty. Although she did not marry until late in life, she kept house for her father and was rewarded by his praise: "I have endeavoured not only attentively to observe all the duties a woman ought to fulfill, but to feel deeply interested in them. I don't always succeed, for sometimes when I'm teaching or sewing I would rather be reading or writing; but I try to deny myself; and my father's approbation amply rewarded me for the privation."[88]

In the twentieth century, the mothering role becomes denigrated. Not only do child psychologists begin holding mothers responsible for every misdeed and complex their children develop, but Philip Wylie, in *A Generation of Vipers,* charges the American "Mom" with ultimate blame for all the ills besetting America. When mothers are not thus castigated for their creation of all the evils of society, they are dismissed as trivial and boring. Alta explains in an autobiographical novel, *Momma: A Start on All the Untold Stories,* "People hate housewives. Youve probably noticed jokes about us: we couldn't have any brains or we wouldnt be doing this. & the women themselves . . . say 'o, i'm just a housewife.' " She remembers an article in a ladies' magazine about a housewife who had the blues until her husband assured her that her job was more important than his—for she was raising sons who would influence the world. Alta notes the story would not have been published in *Esquire,* for "even the men who do that to their wives would see her as stupid for going along with it. & nobody wants to read what stupid people do. being a wife is one of those games you lose even if you win."[89] Jane Lazarre notes that the mother-goddess is outmoded in a society that values only money. "A mother goddess cannot make a living . She is merely tolerated in the adult world."[90]

The charge of triviality, however, has always been implicit in the definitions of male (important) and female (secondary) spheres, and women of many periods have worried that they might be wasting their lives. In 1851, Elizabeth Stuart Phelps wrote an autobiographical short story called "The Angel over the Right Shoulder," in which a mother who is also a writer is torn between the belief that it is her duty to take ample care of her children and her sense that the housewife role is "frivolous and useless." She yearns to "see some results from her life's work. To know that a golden cord bound her life-threads together into some unity of purpose."[91]

She wants to be a hero, not a supporting character, until she has a dream in which an angel explains that God "requires of her no great deeds, but faithfulness and patience to the end of the race which was set before her" (p. 29). She will be judged on her kindness toward or neglect of the "little ones" in her charge. At the end of the story, the protagonist accepts her plight, but there is a built-in irony in the story. Earlier, she puts her daughter to bed, and recognizes the insanity of giving up her life for a daughter who will, in turn, be expected to sacrifice for others: "Most earnestly did she wish, that she could shield that child from the disappointment and mistakes and self-reproach from which the mother was suffering; that the little one might take up life where she could give it to her—all mended by her own experience. It would have been a comfort to have felt that, in fighting the battle, she had fought for both" (p. 23). Her decision to sacrifice her talent and inclination for her children makes it unlikely that her daughter will escape the chain of inherited martyrdom.

A woman may be hindered in her desire for self-expression and achievement by a belief in her own inferiority, a belief that she is fit only for the lesser sphere. Rebecca Harding Davis's "The Wife's Story" concerns a woman who, like Davis, wants "work fit for me."[92] Davis's ambivalence about her own conflicting needs to be a "good woman" and to achieve are reflected in her negative treatment of the housewife. Her ambitions are seen as inappropriate, Faustian, and deserving of punishment. She is protected from disgrace because she is warned in a dream of the final results of such grandiosity. In it, she is the star of an opera she has written, but when the curtain drops, the audience laughs and hisses. When she awakes, her baby is put in her arms and, relieved to be "free from the vacuum of death and crime" (p. 17), she concludes that "a woman has no better work in life than . . . to make herself a visible Providence to her husband and child" (p. 19). In other words, since she is convinced that she would be a failure in her chosen career and that her wickedness in following the career would merit punishment, she is grateful that she can win some social acceptance through the second-best role of wife and mother.

Whether a woman chooses achievement or motherhood, conventional attitudes label her guilty and inadequate as a woman and as a human being. The only way to win acceptance is to combine achievement with mothering, but the traditional demands of the maternal role leave little time for accomplishment. Virginia Woolf explains that women need rooms of their own, because mothers are unlikely to write masterpieces on the dining room table with children underfoot. The woman in Phelps's short story has a retreat where she tries to write, but she has no uninterrupted time. She complains to her husband, "What would you think, if you could not get an uninterrupted half hour to yourself, from morning till night? I believe you would give up trying to do anything."[93]

Phelps's protagonist and the welfare mother and writer who is the hero of Alta's *Momma* find that they are prevented from sustained thought because of the demands of their children and because of their own nagging guilt about conventional maternal tasks left undone. Each mother is unable to resolve the situation because she loves her children and because traditional society's "experts" insist that mothers need to be at home and to be infinitely interruptable for their children's sake.

Like many husbands, the wife who works outside the home does not necessarily have the satisfaction of achievement or self-expression, because often she works at a menial job. She then ends up with two menial, time-consuming jobs and even less time for herself. On the top of this, she feels guilty because she cannot be a "good"—i.e., full-time—mother to her children. Alta writes about being poor and a single parent:

> what is it like to be a mother in this country. what is it like to
> love ur children. to want to be good with them & to be too
> frantic to have the patience. what is it like to raise children with
> no help. 10 million mothers each alone, raising their children.
> its crazy, thats obvious, . . . for days we dont leave our cage.
> what is it like if, like some of us, you must work outside the
> home & then come home & work & love ur children & stories
> are clawing yr heart to get out but you have no time, no time.[94]

The very love the mother feels for the child ties her down to a web of duties
and responsibilities. Even if she doubts the necessity of her sacrifice, she would
rather deny herself than run the risk of hurting her children. Grace Paley, in "A
Subject of Childhood," describes a mother who tells her child how much she loves
him. But when we move inside the mother's thoughts, we recognize that for her
that love means entrapment and pain: "I held him so and rocked him. I cradled
him. I closed my eyes and leaned on his dark head." The sun shines on them
suddenly, and she sees in the shadow a representation of her condition. "Through
the short fat fingers of my son, interred forever, like a black and white barred king
in Alcatraz, my heart lit up in stripes."[95]

Nathaniel Hawthorne's Hester Prynne, in *The Scarlet Letter*, is punished for
adultery by having to live at the edge of Puritan Salem and wear a scarlet *A*. She
identifies the daughter who is the product of the illicit union as "my happiness and
my torture": "Pearl keeps me here in life" for she "is the scarlet letter, only capable
of being loved, and so endowed with a millionfold the power of retribution for my
sin." She is allowed to keep Pearl because God has confided "an infant immortality, a being capable of eternal joy or sorrow . . . to her care—to be trained up by her
to righteousness—to remind her, at every moment, of her fall—but yet to teach
her, as it were by the Creator's sacred pledge, that, if she bring the child to heaven,
the child also will bring its parent thither." Without Pearl, Hester notes, she would
gladly have joined the witches in the forest. When she removes the scarlet *A* and
plans to leave Salem to live a happy life with Dimmesdale, Pearl refuses to come to
her without the token of her guilt. When Hester again "fastens it to her bosom . . .
there was a sense of inevitable doom upon her." Hester ultimately cannot escape
her fate because of her love for her daughter and because of her belief that Pearl's
redemption and her own depend on her playing the part of a visible symbol of sin.[96]
Although Edna Pontellier, in Kate Chopin's *The Awakening*, is not concerned
explicitly with the souls of her children, she commits suicide rather than inflict on
them an unconventional, "immoral" mother.

Literature shows us that the conventional selfless love women have for their
children imprisons them in the sacrificial role the society says is "natural," and in
many instances it causes them to resent their children. The central character in Jane
Lazarre's *The Mother Knot* finds that she can feel her love for her son fully only after
she has arranged for him to stay in day care. She has been prevented from leaving
him because she is afraid that the "experts" are right: It would do him irreparable
harm. Her sense that her own life and talent are going down the drain creates
ambivalence in her feelings for him. Tillie Olsen's "Tell Me a Riddle" is the story of
an old immigrant woman who is dying a painful death, and who is full of anger at
her husband and children for the waste of her life. On her deathbed, she cannot
bring herself to embrace her infant grandchild. Wondering whether she is an
"unnatural grandmother," she muses that it "was not that she hadn't loved her

babies, her children. The love—the passion of tending—had risen with the need like a torrent; and like a torrent drowned and immolated all else."[97] She likens her conventionally defined maternal love to a river, which when the children grow up must be dammed up: "O the power that was lost in the painful damming back and drying up of what still surged, but had nowhere to go." She refuses however to live in a "desert" riverbed, "a memoried wraith." She looks to "the springs" that were the source of that river of life and love, but this time to take the "journey herself" (pp. 117–118). She finds the self she wanted to be, that she believed she would be, singing of a "loftier race" with "freedom in their souls" and "knowledge in their eyes" and of a time of peace when "every life shall be a song" (p. 150). Her bitterness is not only for the loss of her own life, but for the universal failure of humankind to bring about this utopian world, a failure that results from the sacrifice of their vision and their potential selves to the demands of poverty and male and female roles. She faces the ultimate irony that in sacrificing herself for her children, she brought them prosperity, but not freedom, peace, or an end to the inherited ethic of self-sacrifice.

Literary portraits of women who are traditional mothers are almost always tragic when sympathetically drawn. To some degree this results from the discrepancy between society's myth that mothers can totally control their children and the reality that women have little control over their own lives, let alone their children's. Both are continually affected by the society as a whole. To a greater or lesser degree, the maternal sacrifice is futile. Tillie Olsen writes powerfully in *Yonnondio* about the tragedy of bringing up children in poverty, where a parent can do so little for the children and where even a good mother is likely to take out her own frustrations and angers on the children. In "I Stand Here Ironing," in *Tell Me a Riddle and Other Stories,* Olsen's narrator muses about the life of her eldest daughter and fears that "nothing will come of" her potential.

> She was a child seldom smiled at. Her father left me before she was a year old. I worked her first six years when there was work, or I sent her home to his relatives. There were years she had care she hated. She was dark and thin and foreign-looking in a world where the prestige went to blondness and curly hair and dimples, slow where glibness was prized. She was a child of anxious, not proud love. We were poor and could not afford for her the soil of easy growth. I was a young mother, I was a distracted mother. There were the other children pushing up, demanding. . . . She is a child of her age, of depression, of war, of fear.[98]

To see one's child wasted is painful in itself. An attendant problem, moreover, is that the mother may feel guilty because she could not stem the forces that repress and limit the child's life. The guilt further undermines her sense of worth and ability.

Further, even the most confident traditional mother is likely to experience self-doubt when her children no longer need her continual care. Frances Wingate, in Margaret Drabble's *The Realms of Gold,* rather easily combined motherhood with her career as an archaeologist. Even she, however, is at a loss when the youngest of her four children reaches school age. The ultimate irony of the myth of maternal self-sacrifice is that there is no subsequent model for womanhood. At a relatively young age, women get the message that they no longer have a role. In a visit to a laboratory, Frances discovers that the female octopus inevitably dies shortly after giving birth. She wonders if women, too, are expected to cease to exist: "Perhaps, her children now so old, and no longer needing her care so much, there was nowhere else for her to go. What were women supposed to do, in their middle years . . .?"[99]

Children are likely to repudiate their mothers just about the time that the woman's confidence is at a low ebb. Children do so partly as a normal part of the maturation process. If they are to become fully mature adults, they must dissociate themselves from the parents or remain forever under their protection and control. But they also may reject their mothers because they begin to share the culture's assumption that father and his work are more valuable. George Bernard Shaw, in *Major Barbara*, writes: "That is the injustice of a woman's lot. A woman has to bring up her children; and that means to restrain them, to deny them things they want, to set them tasks, to punish them when they do wrong, to do all the unpleasant things. And then the father, who has nothing to do but pet them and spoil them, comes in when all her work is done and steals their affection from her."[100]

The father, in addition, is apt to share the children's contempt for the housewife role, and to the degree that he was jealous of the tight bond between wife and children there may be an element of revenge in his efforts to win over the children from her. Since the maternal role of all-powerful goddess conflicts with that of the helpless, adoring woman expected by the myth of romantic love, the husband may feel that he has been rejected by the wife. Likewise, when the husband fails in his role of godlike provider and dragon-slayer and the wife does not manage to be a selfless, all-nurturing goddess, each is likely to project the failure onto the spouse and to engage in the battle for the allegiance of the children. In Edward Albee's *Who's Afraid of Virginia Woolf?* the struggle seems all the more vicious and poignant because George and Martha are actually childless, and have imagined a child to fill the void in their lives.

Both George and Martha are victims of their expectations about appropriate sex-role behavior. Martha viciously attacks George for his failure as a college professor, and he, with equal vigor, attacks her for being whorish, loudmouthed, and castrating. To justify themselves, they attack each other, and George strikes the final blow, which symbolizes his victory in the power struggle and his assumption of full authority over their "child": He announces that their imaginary son has been killed in a car accident, and thus he destroys the illusion that had given Martha her strength to fight.

Sasha Davis, in Alix Kates Shulman's *Memoirs of an Ex-Prom Queen,* also loses the sense of power that she initially feels from the role of earth mother in her family. Unlike Martha, she initially is able to give a convincing performance of the role of female perfection. Having been a prom queen, she becomes a supermother who is obsessed with the care of her children, and in doing so she excludes her husband Willy from their special bond: "How could he possibly learn on Sundays the intricate rhythm we had established during the week? How could he relieve me if he left us in the morning and returned late at night, or if he were away, as the omniscient Spock book had divined, on a business trip."[101] By the second child, however, she is not only feeling trapped, but she also senses that she is losing Willy because of her nesting instincts. Whether her husband wins the allegiance of the children, moves out, dies, or simply becomes distant, the self-sacrificing maternal figure is likely to find herself alone and unappreciated.

Many literary works demonstrate that women get revenge on those for whom they sacrifice. The numerous unsympathetic portraits of the "American Mom" and the "Jewish Mother" (Philip Roth's *Portnoy's Complaint,* for example) suggest that women who give their lives for their children get back at them one way or another. A woman may cripple her children by nagging or making them feel guilty, or she may not acknowledge even to herself that she is angry with her children and may get revenge by destroying the mother they love. Most often, she either acts out an exaggerated form of the maternal sacrificial role and becomes a martyr, or she withdraws emotionally and does her duty lifelessly. Sophia Tolstoy, a selfless helpmate to her husband Leo, writes of his coldness toward her. In spite of all she does to make his life comfortable and to support his work, he makes her feel invisible. She resolves: "Gradually I shall retreat into myself and shall poison his life."[102]

Janet, a young housewife in Margaret Drabble's *The Realms of Gold,* is urged by her husband's mother to take a night class to prevent her from "turning into a cabbage." She is going to be allowed to expand her life but only as he directs and only for the purpose of becoming entertaining to him. Her only hope for maintaining her own identity is to refuse to do his bidding: "The main reason why she did not want to get into an evening class was that she did not want either her husband or her mother . . . [to] make any inroads on her misery. . . . Her only hope lay in total resistance."[103] Joyce Carol Oates's characters generally, and her female characters in particular, often get revenge by refusing to live. Nada, in *Expensive People,* maintains a consciousness untouched by reality or relationships. She defines herself as "out of history . . . clean of its stink and crap, and there is no one to thank for it, no one but myself and good luck you son-of-a-bitch, to criticize me for not suffocating in it!"[104]

The withdrawal from life may also be a desperate bid for freedom, and a retreat into an inner world. The female character who experiences years of brutalized feelings, dismissal, and disapproval retreats from the messages of her unworthiness. Maria, in Joan Didion's *Play It As It Lays,* for example, is institutionalized and refuses to talk to anyone. Helene, at the end of Oates's *Wonderland,* realizes that her involvement with anything outside herself has ended, and she is ecstatic: "Good! It was good! Her heart was pounding fiercely. The erotic glow in her loins, so teasing and warm, had spread lightly through her body now, light as May air, harmless. She was fulfilled. She was free of the man who hurried beside her, who could not love her now, and she was free of her husband, her daughters, the people in the park, her own youth. It was over: the tyranny of her body, the yearning for other bodies, for talking and touching and dreaming and loving. She had freed herself. It was over for her."[105]

These women initially strive to fulfill society's ideals of wife- and motherhood in order to gain the promised rewards—a sense of fulfillment, the love of one's family, and the respect of society. Each discovers the myths to be, in fact, unrealistic and destructive. This discovery occurs even when the story deals with the most modern of marriages, if the people involved try to fulfill an appropriate social image at the expense of their true natures. The conventional myth, however *avant-garde,* when given preference over the validity of one's own vision, becomes a dragon. Doris Lessing in her short story "To Room Nineteen" calls this preference for the socially appropriate "a failure in intelligence: the Rawlings' marriage was grounded in intelligence." They married in their late twenties; they had fallen in love after knowing each other quite a while and after having a number of affairs.

They lived in their charming flat for two years, giving parties and going to them, being a popular young married couple, and when Susan became pregnant, she gave up her job, and they bought a house in Richmond. It was typical of this couple that they had a son first, then a daughter, then twins, son and daughter. Everything, appropriate, and what everyone would wish for, if they could choose. But people did feel these two had chosen; this balanced and sensible family was no more than what was due to them because of their infallible sense for *choosing* right.[106]

Supremely conscious, they carefully observe their friends' mistakes in order to avoid them, and they work to be both friends and lovers to each other. Every night "he told her about his day and what he had done, and whom he had met, and she told him about her day (not as interesting but that was not her fault both knew)" (p. 301). She stays home while the children are young, and both of them decide that "when these four healthy wisely brought-up children were of the right age, Susan would work again, because she knew, and so did he, what happened to women of fifty at the height of their energy and ability, with grown-up children who no longer needed their full devotion" (p. 308).

But something goes wrong. Much earlier than fifty, when the children first enter school, Susan begins frantically acting the superhousewife, making clothes and cakes. Then she stops, having discovered that "I never feel free. There's never a moment I can say to myself: There's nothing I have to remind myself about, nothing I have to do in half an hour, or an hour, or two hours" (p. 316). Her husband reminds her that he is not free either; he is a slave to a job he does not enjoy. The Rawlings' married life is "like a snake biting its tail. Matthew's job for the sake of Susan, children, house and garden—which caravanserai needed a well-paid job to maintain it. And Susan's practical intelligence for the sake of Matthew, the children, the house and the garden—which would have collapsed in a week without her" (p. 306).

Specifically, the Rawlings' intelligence never took into consideration how far the role of housewife and mother systematically undermines a woman's identity. Susan cannot see any viable alternative to her role because she has lost not only her confidence, but her power to choose what she would like to do. She begins to go alone to a fleabitten hotel, neglecting family responsibilities, just to sit in room nineteen. She does not "find herself" in the traditional sense, for she cannot understand what has happened to her in any terms other than her own inadequacy. When she is at home, she feels split, believing that her true self remains in the lonely hotel room. Her husband suspects her of an affair—in fact, he hopes she is having an affair, because he would like some rational explanation for her unaccounted absences and her vacant stares. Finally, when she cannot conceive of another thing to do or say that does not falsify her position, she escapes to room nineteen for the last time, turns on the gas, and fades rather pleasantly out of life.

Conventional literary portraits of women tend to celebrate and encourage the life-denying myths of female inferiority, virginity, romantic love, and maternal self-sacrifice; others—such as the ones discussed in this chapter—demonstrate that the logical extension of each myth is a psychological prison of increasing self-distrust and self-denial. But in every period of literature there have been major female characters who have understood, at least initially, that they are valuable and responsible beings, and that the traditional female role is too restrictive and limiting to accommodate their heroic potential. The following section explores portraits of heroic women who seek to fulfill both the requirements of society and the needs of the self. These characters do so by assuming the mask of the heroine.

Stranger in a Strange Land

> I have been all my life in hiding.
>
> Kate Millett, Flying

All people wear social masks, which hide to some degree a secret, more authentic self. However, the dichotomy between a woman's inner self and the facade that she presents to the world often is greater than a man's because the conventional female role so thoroughly precludes independence, strength, and individual achievement. Indeed, the selfless role by definition implies that a woman should not have a self. Thus, a woman who lives in accordance with traditional patriarchal society must find a separate, private world in which she can at least occasionally be her more dynamic, creative, and wise self. Beth, in Marge Piercy's contemporary novel Small Changes, daydreams, listens to music, and reads in order to counter the deadening effects of the boredom and self-effacement that result from her efforts to be a good wife. The music "was a messenger from another place, some level where people lived more fully, felt more strongly, reached out and experienced in a way that no one about her ever did."[107] Music reinforces her curious and adventurous nature, so that she can play the part of the submissive housewife without succumbing to the role, until she ultimately can refuse the role entirely. Lucy Snowe, the central character of Charlotte Brontë's Villette, is expected, as a governess, to serve others under the most desolate conditions with little reward. In order to fulfill the needs of her true self, she must maintain "two lives—the life of thought, and that of reality"; and, she explains to the reader, "provided the former was nourished with a sufficiency of the necromantic joys of fancy, the privileges of the latter might remain limited to daily bread, hourly work, and a roof of shelter."[108]

In a number of stories, the female protagonist discovers for the first time that she has a separate, heroic self, which conflicts with her conventional self-image, and she subsequently decides, at least for a time, to keep the authentic self hidden and to continue to speak and act according to the conventional script. Ella Price, the middle-aged hero of Dorothy Bryant's contemporary novel Ella Price's Journal, returns to college and begins to notice, as a result of keeping a journal in her English class, that her true feelings are different from those that society has told her she should have. She writes in her journal, "Sometimes I feel bitter about being a woman. Maybe it's just these books I am reading, but I don't think so. I think I've always felt that way. But I never said anything because I was afraid of what people would think." She knows that such opinions will threaten her husband and daughter and she resolves to "keep smiling and nodding" and "avoiding any subject that would lead to trouble."[109]

In George Eliot's Daniel Deronda, Daniel's mother hides her real feelings because she is too talented and strong to be considered a "good woman." "Every woman is supposed to have the same set of motives," she has learned from conventional society, "or else to be a monster. I am not a monster, but I have not felt exactly what other women feel—or say they feel, for fear of being thought unlike others." The end result of her disguises is an inability even to tell the truth without appearing to perform. When she tells her son about her life and why she made the decision to part with him, she engages in "a piece of what may be called sincere acting: this woman's nature was one in which all feeling—and all the more when it was tragic as well as real—immediately became matter of conscious representation: experience immediately passed into drama, and she acted her emotions."[110]

Many literary works show how women use stereotypically feminine behavior as a survival tactic. This female version of the "shuffle" that blacks used to survive slavery may be consciously employed, in order to avoid threatening those in power, to win social approval, to gain financial support, or even to make deviant behavior seem harmless. Phoenix Jackson in Eudora Welty's short story "A Worn Path" acts out the stereotypes associated with being black, female, and old when she encounters a younger, white male on the road to town. She stands passively while he carries on about the absurd behavior of "niggers" at Christmas, until the moment when she can take advantage of his complacent self-absorption and snatch up the nickel that he has dropped on the ground. Martha Quest, in Doris Lessing's The Four-Gated City, plays the fool to gain exemption from the feminine role. By making others laugh, she avoids threatening them with her unconventional behavior. "When the point was reached when conformity might be expected," she gains "exemption in an act of deliberate clumsiness—like a parody, paying homage as a parody does to its parent-action. An obsequiousness, in fact, an obeisance." Likening herself to the jester and the slave, she recognizes that the comic persona, Matty, "had been created by her as an act of survival. However, the mask not only hides her heroic potential from others, it also prevents her from manifesting that potential, so she resolves to be 'Martha,' not 'Matty.' "[111]

Defoe's Moll Flanders is an expert role-player: "Let them say what they please of our sex not being able to keep a secret," she comments, "my life is a plain conviction to me of the contrary."[112] Born in Newgate prison to a mother who is transported to "the plantations" shortly after giving birth, Moll is functionally an orphan, "left a poor desolate girl without friends, without clothes, without help or helper in the world." She complains, "I was not only exposed to very great distress, even before I was capable either of understanding my case or how to amend it, but brought into a course of life which was not only scandalous in itself, but which in its ordinary course tended to swift destruction both of soul and body" (p. 159).

Like many classic works of literature, the novel exposes the conflict between social expectations and a woman's actual situation. The culture requires Moll to be chaste, passive, and innocent—to be a "good woman." However, to survive, she must be strong and aggressive, and she must gain experience in the ways of the world as quickly as possible. She wants love, social respectability, and financial security, and she believes that she can achieve her goal only through marriage. In the house where she first finds work as a seamstress, she falls in love with a man who offers undying affection and the promise of marriage, and then seduces her. Thereafter, she is referred to in the story as a "whore," even though she wants to be the faithful wife of her betrayer. Moll comments, "Thus I finished my own destruction at once, for from this day, being forsaken of my virtue and my modesty, I had nothing of value left to recommend me, either to God's blessing or man's assistance" (p. 160). Moll's confessions of an evil nature serve to heighten the reader's sense that such self-criticism is unjustified and that her later virtual prostitution and thievery are not so much a result of innate wickedness as they are realistic survival tactics.

Her fear that she cannot make her own way in the world motivates her to marry her seducer's brother. However, after she has borne two children, her husband dies, and she decides: "I had been tricked once by that cheat called love, but the game was over; I was resolved now to be married or nothing, and to be well married or not at all" (p. 60). She wishes to be a loving and faithful wife, but she "knew nothing how to pursue the end by direct means" (p. 135). Instead, she plays a part in order to land a series of husbands, but she is troubled by the discrepancy between her role and her previous experience. Later, when she is about to re-encounter a man she had known earlier, she describes herself as "one that has lain with two brothers, and has had three children by her own brother! one that was born in Newgate, whose mother was a whore, and is now a transported thief! one that has lain with thirteen men, and has had a child since he saw me! . . . Well, if I must be his wife, and love him suitably to the strange excess of his passion for me; I will make him amends if possible, by what he shall see, for the cheats and abuses I put upon him, which he does not see." After five happy years, this husband dies of melancholy because he loses his money, and Moll is left at forty-eight with her children to support. She is too old to be a mistress, cannot find honest work, and has no friends who can aid her. Like her mother before her, she resorts to stealing. She keeps her own name and lodgings secret, and she takes her marks off guard by supporting their illusions. By this strategy she becomes "the richest of the trade in England" (p. 274), but she finally slips up and is sent to Newgate. There she meets a husband of years back whom she truly loved, but who had left her because of their poverty. When they are transported together to the plantations, she discovers that her mother left her "a sum of money," and she and her loving husband live in "the greatest kindness and comfort imaginable" and "both of us in good heart and health." A token repentance accompanies this happy ending, but overall, the work undercuts the virginity myth by cynically suggesting that by their pretense to chastity and selflessness, women may actually gain sexual love, social prestige, and wealth.

Fictional women much more conventional than Moll understand (either implicitly or explicitly) that when a woman is dependent on a man and must appear to merge her will with his, the only possibility for autonomous action, as Elizabeth Janeway explains, "is to do what's expected, but to feel in opposition to the behavior expected."[113] Clara Middleton, in George Meredith's *The Egoist*, contemplates a conventional marriage and wonders if a woman could maintain her identity by having "an inner life apart from him she is yoked to."[114] Because the traditional wife lives constantly under the scrutiny of her husband, her disguise is likely to be subtle and her mask unlikely to be dropped even for a moment. Emily Dickinson's "She Rose to His Requirement" describes the wife who successfully camouflages her dissatisfaction beneath an appropriate facade:

> She rose to his requirement, dropped
> The playthings of her life
> To take the honorable work
> Of woman and of wife.[115]

Among the duties expected of the traditional wife is her physical participation
in sexual intimacies, even if she does not desire them. In order to endure, she may
choose to retreat emotionally into herself. In Anne Sexton's poem "The Farmer's
Wife," the bored woman goes through the motions of being a good wife, including
"that old pantomime of love," but it "leaves her still alone." She lives "her own self
in her own words," hating her life and the alienation of lying in bed with a man,
"each in separate dreams."[116] Pendarin, in Evangeline Walton's fantasy novel *The
Children of Llyr*, has a sexual relationship with her husband's enemy to secure her
husband's freedom. As he pulls her down on the bed, "suddenly something inside
her shrank and scurried back, sick, into the innermost recesses of herself." She
attempts to "leave the body there upon the bed; let him have it. You are separate
from that; you must be. You must stay away, hiding in some inner space. . . . Oh,
be very far away."[117]

When a husband or lover is easily deceived, a woman often feels superior
toward him and bitter about being dependent on such a dull-witted man. She may
often long to reveal the truth and thereby to demonstrate how deceived and
ignorant he has been. Raina, in George Bernard Shaw's play *Arms and the Man*,
initially endeavors to embody the expected romantic feminine image and to cast
her fiancé, Sergius, in the role of Prince Charming. Later she confesses to her
mother in private conversation: "I always feel a longing to do or say something
dreadful to him [Sergius]—to shock his propriety—to scandalize the five senses
out of him. . . . I don't care if he finds out about the chocolate cream soldier [the
man Raina found hiding in her bedroom] or not. I half hope he may."[118]

Such women rarely reveal their actual thoughts or experiences to their men,
however, and much of their energy is drained by the constant effort to repress their
wisdom, vitality, strength, and independence. One of Jane Howard's interviews in
A Different Woman is with a woman who, in spite of her own capabilities, endeavors to reinforce the myth of male supremacy and female inferiority. "*My
constant fear is that I'll show my husband up. It's a real effort not to, because by the
time he's up and dressed I've cleaned the house and made ten phone calls and put
everything in order and gone off to work.*"[119] Florida Scott-Maxwell writes in her
diary of the way wives deal with the "weak, tired, shadow side" of a man that he
brings home from work: "We indulge him, restore him, and though we exploit him
(that is a mutual game) it often seems to us our role and fate to deal with his
inferiority, and conceal it from him."[120] Anaïs Nin comments, "Men are like the
earth and we are the moon; we turn always one side to them, and they think there is
no other, because they don't see it—but there is."[121]

It is the atmosphere of secrecy that makes women seem mysterious and
mythic. James Joyce's Molly Bloom in *Ulysses*, Addie Burden in William Faulkner's
As I Lay Dying, and Lena Grove in Faulkner's *Light in August* are less human beings
than mythic embodiments of the energy and creativity that the male character
attempts to deny. Daisy in F. Scott Fitzgerald's *The Great Gatsby*, for example, is
seen from afar by Gatsby as beautiful, mythic and evocative of splendor; viewed up
close by the narrator Nick Carraway and by the reader, she is exposed as a rather
shallow, immoral, "careless" woman.[122] The mythic role is only powerful, then, if
others believe, and often such belief requires distance.

The consciously mythic woman therefore must devote all her energies to
sustaining the illusion and to repressing the self that threatens to destroy it: She

must keep the king, the giant, the patriarch from waking up and learning that she is not a creature of his dreams but a separate human being with feelings and ideas separate from his. John Galsworthy's Irene, in *The Forsyte Saga*, has power over men because she does not react to them. To reveal any fallible human identity would threaten her power. Fitzgerald's "The Last of the Belles" shows how Ailie Calhoun fears being close to others because they will see the truth behind her mask, and she will lose her power: "Beneath this mask, her mask of an instinctive thoroughbred, she had always been onto herself and she couldn't believe that anyone not taken into the point of uncritical worship could be real."[123] Georgia Douglas Johnson's early 20th-century poem "A Paradox" describes her discomfort in playing hard-to-get. She wishes to "fling this robe aside" to show her passion for him, but she is convinced that he will lose interest if she does:

> Alas! You love me better cold
> Like frozen pyramids of old
> Unyieldingly?[124]

As a result of her hidden or undeveloped selfhood, the mythologized woman is often a tragic or pitiable figure. Esther Harding, in *The Way of All Women*, says that the woman who merely reflects men's anima projections is "doomed to be a child to the end of her days."[125] Adrienne Rich in "Snapshots of a Daughter-in-law" alludes to John Dryden's idealized portrait of the artist Corinna, for whom "neither words nor music are her own." Even her beauty is "adjusted in reflections of an eye."[126] The woman herself may become convinced that she exists only as another's projection. Dr. O'Connor in Djuna Barnes's *Nightwood* describes Robin as saying, " 'Remember me.' Probably because she has difficulty in remembering herself."[127]

Anaïs Nin is fascinated by the ever-changing, ever-acting, beautiful June, but realizes she does not know who June is.

> She invents dramas in which she always stars. I am sure she creates genuine chaos and whirlpools of feelings, but I feel that her share in it is a pose. That night, in spite of my response to her, she sought to be whatever she felt I wanted her to be. She is an actress every moment. . . . The extent of her falsity was terrifying, like an abyss. Fluidity. Elusiveness. Where was June? Who was June? There is a woman who stirs others' imagination, that is all. She was the essence of the theatre itself, stirring the imagination, promising such an intensity and heightening of experience, such richness, and then failing to appear in person, giving instead a smoke screen of compulsive talk about trivialities.[128]

Nin concludes that "it is feminine to be oblique. It is not trickery. It is a fear of being judged" (p. 58).

Thus, the mythic illusion of the ideal woman completely swallows up the self. Isadora Wing, in Jong's *Fear of Flying*, is so anxious for male attention and so overawed by a belief in the superiority of male opinion that she confesses, "Men have always liked me because I agree with them. Not just lip service either. At the moment I say it, I really do agree."[129] Some literary characters explicitly assert that their success in the world depends on a refusal to acknowledge the existence of a separate self even to themselves. The mysterious Sara in John Fowles's *The French Lieutenant's Woman* insists: I am not to be understood even by myself. And I can't tell you why, but I believe my happiness depends on my not understanding."[130]

Protagonists in realistic novels may appear to be totally oblivious to their own motivations. Samuel Richardson's Pamela, for example, is a servant girl who loves the aristocratic, rakish Mr. B——, and it is certainly in her economic and emotional interest to marry him. She does not, however, consciously set out to "land him" as Defoe's Moll Flanders or Henry Fielding's Shamela would. Her conscious goal is to be passively obedient to her "master," to serve others unselfishly, and to remain chaste. It becomes clear through the course of the novel that it is her unconscious goal to marry him. Continually, she finds excuses to stay in the house where she is subject to his attempts at seduction and rape, although she falls on her knees before him and clasps his legs, and so on in protest. In short, the virginity ideal and her best interest do not coincide. She believes in the myth of the passive virgin, but, in self-contradiction, she actively uses it to win him, oblivious to her own duplicity. George Meredith notes in *The Egoist* that women must learn to "read the masters of their destinies" to survive. Yet

> total ignorance being their pledge of purity to men, they have to expunge the writing of their perception on the tablets of the brain; they have to know not when they do know. The instinct of seeking to know, crossed by the task of blotting knowledge out, creates that conflict of the natural with the artificial creature to which their ultimately-revealed double-faced, complained of by every-dissatisfied man, is owing. Wonder in no degree that they indulged their craving to be fools, or that many of them act the character.[131]

As in the case of Richardson's Pamela, the undeveloped, invisible, or unrecognized self may be a constant from the very beginning of the story. In other literary works, the author recounts a long and painful struggle between the true self and the conventional mythic image. Joanna Field, in *A Life of One's Own,* tells how the conflict between her conscious and unconscious beliefs keeps her from knowing quite what she really thinks. She learns about opinions beneath her conscious, rational ones by automatic writing. The "discrepancy between the views of my deliberate and automatic selves gave me an ideal of what might be the reason why I found it so difficult to make up my mind what I liked or what I thought about a thing." Because she did not listen to her inner feelings, she writes, "I never quite felt sure of my conclusions and was liable to reverse them on the slightest provocation."[132]

In her diary, Sophia Tolstoy at times records her intense suffering and, at other times, insists that no conflict exists: "It makes me laugh to read over this diary. It's so full of contradictions, and one would think I was such an unhappy woman. Yet is there a happier woman than I? It would be hard to find a happier and more friendly marriage than ours. Sometimes, when I am alone in the room, I just laugh with joy, and making the sign of the cross, say to myself, 'May God let this last many, many years. . . .' "[133] Eventually, her psychological pain and conflict led to a mental breakdown.

Beth, in Marge Piercy's *Small Changes,* recognizes that she "had lied to the diary" she kept as a teenager "just as she lied to her mother." She realizes that she was not afraid anyone else would read her diary. She lied to herself, and did not write of the way things had been; instead it "was the record of how it was all supposed to be."[134]

Nin's narrator in the *House of Incest* looks "with chameleon eyes upon the changing face of the world," reflecting rather than initiating reality. She describes herself as "wrapped in lies . . . like costumes." The conflict between the persona and the repressed and unacknowledged self creates a bizarre, terrifying existence. She reports, "I am a woman with Siamese cat eyes smiling always behind my gravest words, mocking my own intensity. I smile because I listened to the OTHER and I believed the OTHER: I am a marionette pulled by unskilled fingers, pulled apart, inharmoniously dislocated; one arm dead, the other rhapsodically in mid-air. . . . I see two women in me freakishly bound together, like circus twins."[135]

Kate Wilhelm's science fiction novel *Abyss* is a powerful symbolic treatment of the theme of a woman's split life. In it the two parts of the self are represented respectively by two alternative universes. Tippy comments, " 'No one believes in ghosts, and yet, there is something that we can't see, something horrible, completely terrible and loathsome. We are all so sane, so quietly, dependably, self-assuredly sane,' she said, almost mockingly. 'But something here isn't sane at all.' " Dorothy, the protagonist, is susceptible to the otherworldly forces because she already feels the supposedly real physical world around her—the objects in her house—to be somehow foreign to her and because the two universes parallel her inner, dual, and confused identity: "Sometimes none of this seems real," she wonders, "or if it is, then I can't be."[136]

Eventually, the conflict between the true self and the conventional images may become intolerable. Alienated from others and without positive support for what she really feels, a woman is likely to become convinced that she is evil, or mad. In Doris Lessing's *The Golden Notebook,* none of the myths of the culture apply to the protagonist's actual experience. In five different notebooks, she tries in five different ways to order and interpret her life. In each case, she attempts to fit her experience into the conventionally appropriate narrative framework for women—the love story—but each notebook is a distortion, a lie. By the end of the work, she goes temporarily mad, staying alone in her room, ordering and reordering newspaper clippings in an attempt to make some sense of the world around her.

At this point, in order to overcome the chaos and confusion at any price, a woman may turn on her own heroic self, which social requirements and the unbearable pain of the conflict finally convince her to destroy. Such is the tragedy of Edith Wharton's *The House of Mirth,* a direct result of the opposition between Lily Bart's spontaneous heroic nature and conventional society, which sees her heroic spirit as immoral.

Like Defoe's Moll Flanders, Lily wants the good life. Her father lost his money, and her mother bitterly charges her with the ability to regain wealth through pretense: "You'll get it all back," she notes, "with your face."[137] In addition to her beauty, Lily's weapons are charm and virtue. With them, she hopes to capture a wealthy husband, but her ambitions are "not as crude as Mrs. Bart's." Like her father, she has a touch of the poet, and likes to "think of her beauty as a power for good, as giving her the opportunity to attain a position where she should make her influence felt in the vague diffusion of refinement and good taste" (p. 40). Her enemy is "dinginess . . . and to her last breath she meant to fight against it, dragging herself up again and again above its hold till she gained the bright pinnacles of success which presented such a slippery surface to her clutch" (p. 45). Lawrence Selden loves her for her beauty but even more for the glimpses of her heroic spirit, which has been debased by her straining after wealth and status. The impetus behind her social climbing is a heroic determination to live a truly beautiful life. Wharton shows that the perversion of Lily's heroism is predictable: "She was so evidently the victim of the civilization which had produced her, that the links of her bracelet seemed like manacles chaining her to her fate" (p. 8). Her fate is to live in the mirror of others' opinions. To become a sought-after dinner guest, she learns to anticipate others' moods and needs, to charm them, to support their illusions, to do little tasks for her hosts. When she occasionally drops the mask, she ruins her pose. Although she refuses to marry Selden because he is poor, she loves him. She loses a chance to marry "well" because she chooses at a key moment to be with him, and she ruins her reputation in protecting his.

Lily is not ultimately willing to sell herself for status or for wealth. She chooses poverty rather than pay her debt to Guy Trenor with sexual favors. Time after time she discourages a dull but rich suitor, just as he is considering marriage to her. When the gossips charge her with promiscuity, she does not answer them initially because "the truth about any girl is that once she's talked about she's done for; and the more she explains her case the worse it looks" (p. 262). Later, however, when she has lost any chance of recovering her reputation except through using the letters that would vindicate her, she still does not do so because of her love for Selden and because she does not want to sink to the moral level of her accusers.

The society that Lily lives in does not provide her with a way to reconcile her desire for both aethestic and moral beauty. Her desire for the wealth necessary for beautiful surroundings conflicts with her desire for goodness and honor. Further, having learned to live in the mirror of others' opinions, she sees not only with her own, but with the world's eyes. Having chosen the path of honor, she nevertheless sees herself in the world's eyes as tarnished and fallen and no longer worthy of wealth and love. She explains to her cousin Gertie, "Can you imagine looking into your glass some morning and seeing a disfigurement—some hideous change that has come to you while you slept? Well, I seem to myself like that—I can't bear to see myself in my own thoughts—I hate ugliness, you know" (p. 191). Frantically attempting to win back social acceptance, she pulls on the mask ever tighter to hide this unworthy self. Selden laments the fading of a "transparency through which the fluctuations of the spirit were sometimes tragically visible." This heroic transparency is replaced by "a process of crystallization which had fused her whole being into one hard substance" (p. 221).

Lily's conviction regarding her unworthiness and Selden's evident disillusionment with her keep her from telling him how she has protected his good name. She destroys the letters that could prove her innocent to guard against her temptation to act dishonorably to clear her name. Only his belief in her, she believes, "kept her moral." When he no longer loves her, still "something lived between them . . . it was the love his love had kindled, the passion of her soul for his." This passion allows her to destroy the letters, but without them she is destined for the "dingy" life she struggled to avoid.

She further recognizes that although "it was indeed miserable to be poor—to look forward to a shabby, anxious middle-age, leading by dreary degrees of economy and self-denial to gradual absorption in the dingy communal existence of the boarding-house, . . . there was something more miserable still." The cost of hiding the self for social advantage is rootlessness and alienation. She has "a sense of deeper impoverishment, of an inner destitution compared to which outward conditions dwindled into insignificance" (p. 371). Partly she is disappointed and disillusioned with herself. More than that, she is lonely:

> It was the clutch of solitude at her heart, the sense of being swept like a stray uprooted growth down the heedless current of the years. That was the feeling which possessed her now—the feeling of being something rootless and ephemeral, mere spindrift of the whirling surface of existence, without anything to which the poor little tentacles of self could cling before the awful flood submerged them. (p. 371)

Even her parents had been "rootless, blown hither and thither on every wind of fashion, without any personal existence to shelter them from its shifting gusts" (p. 371). Because Lily has always lived in the mirror of others' opinions, she cannot interpret her experience in a genuinely individual way. Even her heroism is based on Selden's point of view. When the world and the man she loves seem unified in their condemnation of her, she seeks to escape her own internal condemning voices by taking an overdose of sleeping potion. Although Selden reconsiders and runs to her side to affirm his love for her, he arrives too late. She dies, therefore, not so much because of his rejection of her, but because she condemns herself.

Charlotte Perkins Gilman, in *The Yellow Wallpaper*, also describes the terrifying experiences of a woman struggling to understand her situation and yet distrusting at every moment the understanding that could save her sanity. This nineteenth-century protagonist is suffering from depression and is ordered by her doctor and her husband to remain in a room and rest. Although she is forbidden to write, she needs the outlet and so she writes in secret. "I must say what I feel and think in some way—it is such a relief,"[138] she explains to her journal. She also confides that she does not agree with the ideas of her husband, John, or her brother, but by and large, she follows their advice because they are both physicians "of high standing." The cultural consensus is that they know more than she does about what is good for her, and she does not trust herself enough to act on her own knowledge. She is told that she is staying in a nursery, but it quickly becomes apparent to the reader that it is a room used to lock up the insane: The windows are barred; the bed is bolted down. An inmate of this room, she hates the wallpaper, and as she begins to study it (for she has nothing else to do), a subpattern emerges. Behind the wallpaper is a woman who alternately "creeps about" and attempts to free herself. Before long it becomes clear to the reader that the protagonist's hallucination is a symbolic representation of her situation. One night she tears off all the paper to free the entrapped woman, but she feels continuing ambivalence about her act. She goes mad rather than leave her husband because she cannot reconcile her divided feelings.[139] She "sees" women who have "escaped" crawling around outside, and she repudiates their example, for "a step like that is improper and might be misconstrued" (p. 34).

At the same time, the symbolic action of freeing the woman trapped behind the wallpaper is recognized by the protagonist as a way of liberating herself. Seeing all the creeping women, she wonders whether "they all" came "out of that wallpaper as I did" (p. 35). However, she sees no hope of acting according to her own vision. Her madness does free her from the traditional female role, but only in the sense that it only allows her to get revenge. She anxiously awaits the moment when her complacent, loving, but somewhat simpleminded husband finds her creeping around the edges of her cage. It is with joy and some rather spiteful self-satisfaction that she tells him—all the time creeping around the room—"I've pulled off most of the paper, so you can't put me back!" When he faints, she continues around the room, "creeping over him every time!" (p. 36).

Harriette Arnow's *The Dollmaker* describes how one woman's distrust of her own heroic perceptions and impulses destroys not only herself but also her family. Gertie Nevels is a poor rural woman who is six feet tall and as strong as any man in the community. She is brave enough to stop a car by riding in front of it on her mule and forcing a reluctant and condescending army officer to give her a ride to town. When she realizes she will not make it to the doctor in time, she performs a tracheotomy on her infant son with her whittling knife and saves his life. Her heroism in a crisis is matched by her patience and endurance. She has, over fifteen years, saved enough money—by cutting corners and by making and selling jam—to escape tenant farming and buy the idyllic Tipton Place, thus ensuring prosperity and felicity to her family.

Gertie is also an artist. She carves wooden dolls, and plans to sculpt a bust of a "laughing Christ" out of a huge block of cherry wood. She is not verbally articulate, but this sculpture is intended to express her wise and humane vision. Even though she was taught from birth a philosophy based on a harsh, puritanical, judgmental God, she affirms an alternative, life-perpetuating vision in accord with her own nature. Gertie always thinks of the figure in the block as a male, but the words of her wise daughter Cassie direct the reader to see the block and the entrapped figure in it as a symbol of Gertie's state. Cassie begs, "Take her out, Mom. It's Sunday—she wants out. She's been a waiten there so long—so awful long, ever since I was little."[140]

Gertie fears, however, that her laughing Christ, made in the image of her secret, repressed self, is blasphemous. From birth, Gertie's mother taught her that she was wrong, evil, and inadequate, and that she was to be damned by a judgmental Christ. When Gertie's brother Henley dies, her mother accuses her of contributing to his damnation by encouraging his dancing.

Gertie also learns from her mother to be ashamed of her strength, because the perfect lady is passive and weak. As a result, she never tells anyone, not even her husband, that she—not the doctor—saved her son's life. When her mother convinces John, the owner of the Tipton Place, not to sell it to her because it is her duty to follow her husband, she does not resist. There is evidence that Gertie's father, her husband, and his mother would all have supported her had she enlisted their aid but she does not fight because she believes she does not really deserve good fortune. At the break of day, she looks over the land that was to be her reward for years of poverty, hard work, and perseverance:

> She stood there staring out across the ridge top, and saw the sun had risen. It poured red light upon the north-western side of the ridge. The beeches lower down, and the sugar maples, were shadowed still, but higher up, toward the cove top, the trunks of the tall young poplars were pink in the rising light. It came to her that maybe she had always known those other trees would never be her own—no more than the fireplace

with the great slab of stone—just as she had always known that Christ would never come out of the cherry wood. (p. 145)

In forsaking her dream, like Judas, Gertie betrays Christ, the Christ within her. She contemplates carving Judas, sorrowful after his betrayal and giving away the thirty pieces of silver.

In Detroit, Gertie becomes a stranger in a strange land. She embodies in her physical being the plight of all female heroes entrapped in a restrictive role. Her home is too small for such a large woman, and she is always bumping into things. Instead of the natural free life the Tipton Place promised, the center of her house is the "Icy Heart" refrigerator her husband Clovis went into debt to purchase, but she does not voice her objections to the urban, mechanistic ideology, which believes that owning an "Icy Heart" is the ultimate female fulfillment. Consistently she identifies the villain not as the external society or her own insecurity, but her unconventional, heroic qualities. When her son Reuben is miserable in school, she blames herself for encouraging nonconformist views. "She knows that most of the trouble with Reuben was herself" (p. 368). "If she had taken her mother's Christ and Battle John's God and learned to crochet instead of whittle, and loved the Icy Heart" everything would be all right. Against her own better judgment, she advises him to "try harder to be like the rest—to run with the rest—it's easier, and you'll be happier in the end—I guess" (p. 340). Reuben leaves the family, but Gertie's insecurity ultimately destroys her daughter Cassie's life. Cassie is a loner, and plays only with her imaginary friend, Callie Lou. Like her mother, she has a split life. The neighbors say she should adjust and play with the other children. When Gertie forbids Cassie to play with Callie Lou, part of her secretly roots for Cassie to stick to her guns. The result of this double message is tragedy. Playing with her "friend" by the railroad tracks, Cassie is struck by a train, while Gertie, attempting to warn her or get to her, is prevented by the fence and the noise from saving her.

Gertie remains heroic in many ways. After the death, a neighbor gives her a drug to numb her pain and Gertie overcomes the temptation to continue to take it. She fights for her family's physical survival, as always, but is less and less likely even to try to assert her own values. Finally, she chops up the cherry block to make cheap, garish crucifixes. They violate her aesthetic and moral framework, but they sell and help feed the family. The description of the sacrifice of the figure in the block—the final act of self-immolation in the novel—suggests murder and suicide: "She brought the great hammer hard down upon the wedge, again on the ax. The wood, straight-grained and true, came apart with a crying, rendering sound, but stood for an instant longer like a thing whole, the bowed head, the shoulders; then slowly the face fell forward toward the ground, but stopped, trembling and swaying, held up by the two hands" (p. 599). Articulate with her knife but not with words, Gertie destroys the only means she has to share her superior wisdom with others and thereby to heal the split between her inner and outer selves. The power of Arnow's tragic novel, like that of Sophocles' *Oedipus the King,* rests in the sense of inevitability that pervades the novel. In this case, however, it is not the gods that make Gertie's fate inevitable, but the socialization to female inferiority, which keeps her from trusting her own superior knowledge.

The destruction of the cherry block is accompanied by a tragic moment of enlightenment. Gertie's excuse for never completing the statue is that she could never find the right face for Christ, or the Judas that betrayed him. She realizes that she and all her neighbors represent both figures: Each potentially is a "laughing

Christ," but each—because of sex roles, poverty, and insecurity—has betrayed that vision: "They was so many would ha done. . . . Why, some of my neighbors down there in the alley—they would ha done" (p. 599).

In all three stories—*The House of Mirth, The Yellow Wallpaper,* and *The Dollmaker*—the theme is the betrayal of the inner vision for the sake of convention. Wharton, Gilman, Arnow, and other authors understand that the choice of the split life—in which the protagonist hides her heroic self beneath the appropriate social mask—leads not to happiness or to social success or even to survival but to eventual, tragic self-destruction. Some writers explicitly refer to the imprisoning isolation and psychological damage that results from the hidden self, which the conventional woman accepts as inevitable. The anthropologist Ruth Benedict and the Canadian artist Emily Carr, for example, complain in their diaries that their true feelings are locked away from themselves and from others. Benedict notes, "My real me was a creature I dared not look upon. . . . No one had ever heard of that *me*. If they had, they would have thought it an interesting pose. The mask was tightly adjusted."[141] Carr speaks of the pain of being locked in a "yourself shell": "You can't break through and get out; nobody can break through and get in." She longs for an "instrument strong enough to break the 'self-shell.' "[142] However, the preheroic woman dreads social reprisals, which she is convinced would result from the honest revelation of her true self, more than she fears the alienation and the injury to the self that she hides. Anaïs Nin anticipates, in *House of Incest,* that "only the fear of madness will drive us out of the precincts of our solitude, out of the sacredness of our solitude. The fear of madness will burn down the walls of our secret house and send us out into the world seeking warm contact."[143]

In fact, as we shall see in Part II of this book, numerous fictional women leave the "secret house"—the life of the hidden or denied heroic self. These heroic characters have the courage to remove the conventional mask and to successfully defy the dragons that would destroy them or imprison them forever in the images of traditional womanhood.

Part I I
The Journey

Chapter 3
Slaying the Dragon

I'm convinced that there are whole areas of myself made by the kind of experience women haven't had before. . . . What is happening is something new in my life . . . a sense of shape, of unfolding . . . the beginning of something I must live through.
Doris Lessing, *The Golden Notebook*

The heroic journey is a psychological journey in which the hero escapes from the captivity of her conditioning and searches for her true self. As in the classic version of the story, she descends into the underworld of her psyche to encounter the life-denying forces, or "dragons," within. These are the forces of fragmentation, self-loathing, fear, and paralysis. When she slays the dragons, she becomes, or is united with, her true self.

In realistic literature, dragon slaying is not always a single event occurring in a clearly defined "underworld." However, the realistically portrayed hero often leaves the conscious world in order to confront life-denying forces. The hero's mythic descent is often depicted as a retreat into a state of temporary madness; as an adventure in the world of dreams, fantasy, and science fiction; or as a psychological return to childhood. In Joan Didion's *Play It As It Lays,* Sylvia Plath's *The Bell Jar*, and Margaret Atwood's *Surfacing*, for example, the hero courts insanity in order to discover the deeper reality that the myths that dominate her conscious mind have obscured. In *The Four-Gated City,* Doris Lessing explains: "Perhaps it was because if society is so organized or rather has so grown, that it will not admit what one knows to be true, will not admit it, that is, except as it comes out perverted, through madness, then it is through madness and its variants it must be sought after."[1]

The Four-Gated City presents clearly many of the basic aspects of the hero's encounter with the dragon. The novel's hero, Martha Quest, deliberately sets aside times during which she descends into her own heart of darkness, into induced insanity, in order to confront the negative messages she received from her parents and from society at large. Every day she "worked on her own mind, with her mind. . . . each scene fought back into memory against lethargy, pain, reluctance. Afterwards she crawled into bed, worn out" (p. 257). Later, during one of these retreats into her self, "she encountered head-on and violently the self-hater. . . . how powerful an enemy he was, how dreadfully compelling, how hard to fight" (p. 535).

Martha Quest learns that to gain freedom from this inner enemy, she must first give in to it, rather than fight it. "She was completely in the grip of this self-hating person, or aspect of herself. Remorse? No, it was more that her whole life was being turned inside out, so that she looked at it in reverse, and there was nothing anywhere in it that was good; it was all dark, all cruel, all callous, all 'bad' " (p. 535).

The inner monster is an internalization of the outer society's negative messages about her self-worth. As Martha gradually comes out of her self-induced insanity and isolation, she realizes, gratefully, that what enabled her to free herself from the inward devouring monster was the ability to confront him by herself:

> The central fact. If at any time at all I had gone to a doctor or to a psychiatrist, that would have been that . . . without knowing what I know, through Lynda, I'd not have been able to hold on. Through hints and suggestions in all the books, through my own experience, through Lynda—but without these, a doctor or a psychiatrist would have needed only to use the language of the self-hater and that would have been that. Finis, Martha! Bring out your machines. Bring out your drugs! Yes, yes, you know best doctor, I'll do what you say: I'm too scared not to. (p. 553)

Lynda, who becomes Martha's mentor, lives by turns in mental institutions and in the basement of the house. Martha learns from Lynda's example the danger of being "worsted in that battle . . . because of having to confront that buried self-hater when one was not strong enough" (p. 520). In Lynda's head is a quieter and older voice that might have countered the message of the self-hater, but she has lost touch with it. "It was as if she had an enemy who hated her in her head, who said she was wicked and bad and disobedient and cruel to her father. Before it had been as if she had had a friend close to her who had 'told her things and kept her company.' But now she tried to behave well because of this cruel tormentor in her head. She kept quiet, paid a great deal of attention to her clothes (for she noted that 'they' took this as a good sign), was beautiful and lived in a state of terror" (p. 523). The voice that "told her things" is associated with Lynda's extrasensory powers—powers that prove, she is taught, her insanity and worthlessness. Thus, the self-hater obscures both the true self and the rescuing voice that might link her to a world beyond herself.

The recognition that the dragon exists as both an external and an internal force may occur in a visionary moment, as it does for Anna in Lessing's *The Golden Notebook*. Anna is cutting out articles from the newspaper, trying to make some sense out of the world, when she grasps the full horror of the chaos that underlies her society: "That evening sitting on the floor, playing jazz, desperate because of her inability to 'make sense' out of the bits of print, she felt a new sensation, like an hallucination, a new and hitherto not understood picture of the world. This understanding was altogether horrible . . . this illumination . . . was beyond the region where words can be made to have sense."[2]

In Lessing's later novels, when the hero faces the horror of the dragon's reality she may then have a vision of rescue. Here is our last sight of Martha Quest before the apocalypse.

> She walked beside the river while the music thudded, feeling herself as a heavy impervious insensitive lump that, like a

planet doomed always to be dark on one side, had vision in front only, a myopic searchlight blind except for the tiny three-dimensional path open immediately before her eyes in which the outline of a tree, a rose, emerged, then submerged in dark. She thought, with the dove's voices of her solitude: Where? But *where*. How? Who? No, but *where*, . . . Then silence and the birth of a repetition: *Where*? Here. Here? Here, where else, you fool, you poor fool, where else has it been, ever. (p. 591)

After Martha Quest's personal vision, the reader is plunged into a postapocalyptic vision. Both human and animal life is dying off or becoming mutated. Yet just as things seem their worst, the survivors with whom Martha Quest lives experience a transformation:

During that year we hit the depths of our fear, a lowering depression which made it hard for us not to simply walk into that deadly sea and let ourselves drown there. But it was also during that year when we became aware of a sweet high loveliness somewhere, like a flute played only just within hearing. . . . It was as if all the air was washed with a bright promise. Of what? Love? Joy? It was as if the face of the world's horror could be turned around to show the smile of an angel. (p. 643)

They begin talking "to people who were not of our company, nor like any people we had known—though some of us had dreamed of them. It was as if the veil between this world and another had worn so thin that earth people and people from the sun could walk together and be companions" (p. 643). New mutant children are born who have extrasensory powers of "hearing" and "seeing" and who commune with both the "old" and the "new" people. Martha Quest explains that even as children "they all carry with them a gentle strong authority. . . . It is as if—can I put it like this?—they are beings who include that history in themselves and who have transcended it. They include us in a comprehension we can't begin to imagine. These seven children are our—but we have no word for it. The nearest to it is that they are our guardians" (p. 647).

Although the journey is predominantly within the self, external figures sometimes appear as realistic analogues to the inner dragon and rescuer. They may either symbolize or simply reinforce the destructive and nurturing messages within. The new mutant children in Lessing's novel, for example, are the external embodiments of Lynda's inner friend who "told her things and kept her company." Among works with a female protagonist there is little consensus about the identity of the external figures. The Judeo-Christian God, for example, may be portrayed as a judgmental patriarch who condemns the hero and tells her she must be redeemed by a male savior. Yet in Shaw's *Saint Joan*, that same God sends Joan of Arc voices that confirm her sense of power and mission beyond the traditional female role. A husband or lover, mother or father, female friend or stranger, may be a captor figure if he or she reinforces the myths of female inferiority, virginity, and romantic love; yet any of these may be a rescuer if he or she reinforces the hero's sense of worth and power.

The inner self-hater may be personified as either male (the Ogre Tyrant) or female (the Wicked Witch), depending on the hero's experience. The slaying of the inner dragon may occur as a result of a journey into the self, as in Lessing's novels, or it may involve the injuring or killing of the external embodiment of the self-hater in the hero's life, as previously internalized rage is expressed. Such a killing, prompted by rage, may heal the split in the female hero's psyche. In certain literary works, homicide or the fantasizing of the death of the external captor figure is seen as a liberating experience.

In Joanna Russ's science fiction allegory *The Female Man*, the slaying of the inner di *gon is dramatized as the killing of a male chauvinist. The narrator, Joanna, is divided into three characters who live in alternative worlds and who are each referred to as "Everywoman."[3] The division of the protagonist into fragmented parts is explicitly seen as a result of the split between the self and personae characteristic of women in patriarchal society. Jeannine is the traditional woman who lives on a world very like ours. She is contemplating marriage to a man she does not love or respect—in fact, she does not even enjoy his company—because she believes that she must marry to please her mother and to attain a "brand name." She must find a deified male to give her a home in the patriarchy. She confesses that her whole life has been controlled by the dragon myths and dedicated to pleasing men:

> All I did was
> dress for The Man
> smile for The Man
> talk wittily to The Man
> sympathize with The Man
> flatter The Man
> understand The Man
> defer to The Man
> entertain The Man
> keep The Man
> live for The Man. (p. 29)

Jeannine is rescued from her impending marriage by the appearance of Janet, a fantasy figure who comes from a nonsexist utopia on the planet Whileaway. Russ has explained that she could not unify Janet and Jeannine into one character until she introduced a third character, Jael, alias Alice Reasoner, who is an allegorical embodiment of rage.[4] Jael lives on a planet that has been torn by a war between men and women for years, and her mission is that of a secret assassin. The dragon to be slain is a parody of the patriarch, a stereotyped male chauvinist, who blatantly spouts the messages of the captors. He declares Jael inferior and of value only because of her ability to serve men sexually: "It doesn't matter what you say. You're a woman, aren't you? . . . This is what God made you for. . . . You want it. You want to be mastered" (p. 181). At the end of his speech he lunges at Jael who, it turns out, has talons for fingernails and metal teeth. She kills him with her teeth and claws and arises "clean and satisfied from head to foot." She then reports on the response of the other three characters: "Jeannine is calm. Joanna is ashamed of me. Janet is weeping. . . ."

> "Look, was it necessary?" says one of the J's, addressing to me
> the serious urgency of womankind's eternal quest for love,

> the ages-long effort to heal the wounds of the sick soul, the
> infinite, caring compassion of the female saint. . . .
> "I don't give a damn whether it was necessary or not," I said.
> I liked it." (p. 181)

The male chauvinist is an aspect of the narrator's psyche as clearly as are Jeannine, Janet, and Jael; his death marks the slaying of an inner dragon, the internalized negative myths about women. Jael's attack and her offer to bring the male-female war to Earth produce different responses in the other protagonists. These responses represent the typical reactions of the other aspects of a woman's self to her own rage. The traditional woman, Jeannine, is all for it. Janet is saddened because she is accustomed to the freedom and humanity of the all-female community on Whileaway. She believes that her paradise is the result of a plague that killed all the men, but Jael says it was actually created by means of a war in which the women destroyed the men, and that rage is unavoidable in the heroic journey. The novel implies that Jeannine and Joanna have to kill the male chauvinist within and challenge him without before they can respond to life as fully and as humanly as Janet does.

As *The Female Man* illustrates, the hero who confronts the inner dragon characteristically experiences a series of three emotions—fear, then rage, and then joy. The approach to the dragon is marked by fear. Like Lynda in *The Four-Gated City* and Maggie Tulliver in George Eliot's *The Mill on the Floss*, the female hero has been socialized to express her rage toward herself. Self-doubt has caused her to feel weak and afraid of the forces that oppose her. When she identifies and slays the inner dragon, the rage turns outward. At the moment of actual confrontation and slaying, the hero suddenly recognizes that she is not what "they" say she is, and that she is in fact valuable and strong. At this moment, she is likely to be overcome by a sense of outrage.

Accordingly, Joanna in *The Female Man* moves through rage and sadness to exhilaration and laughter. She ends her narration with a comic speech to the book itself, instructing it to go and take its place "bravely on the book racks of bus terminals and drugstores": "Do not scream when you are ignored, for that will alarm people, and do not fume when you are heisted by persons who will not pay, rather rejoice that you have become so popular. Live merrily, little daughter-book. . . . Recite yourself to all who will listen; stay hopeful and wise" (p. 213). She anticipates the day when "I, Janet . . . I, Joanna . . . I, Jeannine, I Jael, I myself" will be unified and free in a new world where the female hero is not an alien; and she counsels her daughter-book, "Do not get glum when you are no longer understood. . . . Do not reach up from reader's laps and punch the reader's noses. . . . For on that day, we will be free" (p. 214).

It is appropriate that the rescue figures in both *The Four-Gated City* and *The Female Man* have mystical or supernatural dimensions, because the slaying of the dragon and the recognition of the rescue figure always involves a profound change in consciousness. Previously, the hero's vision has been defined by the limiting assumptions of her society. As she slays the dragon, the scales fall from her eyes. In a feminist equivalent of the Zen experience, the dragon slayer changes from perceived to perceiver, from object to subject, and this shift in point of view overturns her entire perception of reality. Suddenly, she is no longer saying no to the old vision but yes to herself and to her own vision. In the light of this new vision, the dragons are revealed as mythical beasts: the power to destroy disappears when the belief that sustains them goes. Ultimately, then, the hero learns that there is no need to "slay" dragons except with the white light of truth. Exposed, they fade away. Ursula Le Guin, in *The Left Hand of Darkness*, explains this treasure that is won at the end of the heroic journey as not merely a rebellion against society's reality, but an entirely new frame of reference. "To be sure, if you turn your back on Mishnory and walk away from it, you are still on the Mishnory road. To oppose vulgarity is inevitably to be vulgar. You must go somewhere else; you must have another goal; then you walk a different road."[5]

Stages of the Journey

The heroic journey to self-fulfillment has three primary stages, which are here called The Exit from the Garden, The Emperor's New Clothes, and A Woman Is Her Mother. In each stage, the protagonist is faced with a powerful figure to interpret, a dragon to slay, and a treasure to win. In the first stage, the hero exits from the garden when she comes to realize that people she had previously seen as guides for her life—parents, husbands, religious or political authorities—are her captors. To free herself, she must leave the garden of dependency on these captor figures, slay the dragon of the virginity myth, and assume the role of spiritual orphan. Her treasure at this stage is freedom and unlimited possibility. During the second stage, her powerful figure is the seducer. Through encountering him she is symbolically awakened into the world of experience. The seducer, however, turns out to be another captor. The hero finds she must slay the dragon of romantic love and demythologize the seducer. Discovering that the qualities society has defined as male—sexuality and independence—are hers also, she achieves the treasure of wholeness and autonomy. In the third stage, the hero either literally or symbolically journeys to her ancestral home in search of her father, and discovers instead that it is her mother with whom she seeks to be rejoined. In this stage, a rescue figure aids the hero in freeing herself from the myth of female inferiority and in identifying a viable female tradition.

In *The Female Man*, the three stages of the heroic journey occur virtually simultaneously because Russ organizes the book spatially rather than temporally. Each stage occurs on a different planet. Jeannine, Joanna's persona on Earth, is a traditional woman who is in the process of escaping from the captor messages of her parents and her culture. Jael comes from a world in which men and women are engaging in a protracted and brutal war. Janet, finally, is a fantasy rescue figure from the planet Whileaway who is the woman Joanna could be in a nonsexist world. Through Janet, Joanna gets in touch with female potential strength.

In all three stages of the journey, the hero learns to trust her full humanity in a world that sees men and women as incomplete complements to each other. In the first stage, authorities fail her and she draws on her own inner resources for the first time. In the second, she learns that the qualities she believed were masculine and therefore looked for outside herself are also hers. In the third, she learns that these human heroic qualities can be seen within a female tradition. The recognition that she is a hero in a tradition of female heroes is the prerequisite for the reward of community. (See Part III: The Return.)

L. Frank Baum's *The Wizard of Oz*, Dorothy Sayers's *Gaudy Night*, and Margaret Atwood's *Lady Oracle* are three examples from fantasy literature that demonstrate the uniformity and diversity of the myth of the female hero. They also

shed light on the traditional popularity among women of children's fantasy literature and of detective and gothic fiction. In the children's story, for example, the
hero is often an orphan or alien who searches for her true family or society as
opposed to the unsympathetic one in which she finds herself. The detective story
and the gothic romance emphasize the female hero's role as a sleuth, who discovers the truth behind deceptive appearances.

The primary stages of the hero's journey can be seen in allegorical form in
Baum's children's story.[6] Like most heroes, Dorothy is an orphan, living with foster
parents in a limiting and dull environment. In the one-room cabin in "the midst of
the great Kansas Prairies" where she lives with her Aunt Em and Uncle Henry,
everything—house, prairie, uncle, aunt—is grey. In fact it is only her dog, Toto,
who makes Dorothy laugh and thus saves her from "growing as grey as her other
surroundings" (p. 12). Her Aunt Em was not always grey. She was once a "young,
pretty wife," but the prairie and the difficulty of her life "had taken the sparkle from
her eyes and left them a sober grey; they had taken the red from her cheeks and
lips, and they were grey also. She was thin and gaunt, and never smiled now"
(p. 10).

The first stage of the journey is the flight, escape, or expulsion from the
garden or cage. For Dorothy, it is clearly an expulsion, but one with overtones of
rebirth: A cyclone picks up Dorothy, Toto, and her house and blows them away to
Oz, but as she is carried by the wind she feels "as if she were being rocked gently,
like a baby in a cradle." When the house lands, she discovers that it has killed the
Wicked Witch of the East, who "has held all the Munchkins in bondage for many
years," and that she is therefore the hero.

In the first stage of Dorothy's journey, she kills the obvious dragon, the
Wicked Witch, seemingly by accident. Yet it may be that the true dragon is
"greyness," which she "slays" simply by leaving. By starting her journey, the
female protagonist becomes a hero—although she may not yet recognize herself as
such. It is significant that the house—the traditional symbol of women's
confinement—is destroyed by the cyclone that frees Dorothy. She can never return
to the same cage. This suggests that she may escape greyness for good. Oz is lush,
colorful, and fertile, with a "small brook, rushing and sparkling along between
green banks, and murmuring in a voice grateful to a little girl who had lived so long
for the dry, grey prairies." The landscape suggests the promise of a rich, full,
adventurous life. The hero's first response, like Dorothy's, may be terror and the
desire to return to the old life. It is this feeling of being lost and alone that
necessitates her journey.

At this stage, the hero often meets a supernatural or human mentor who
directs her on her way. In Dorothy's case it is the good Witch of the North, who
gives her the Wicked Witch's magic shoes and advises her to seek the Wizard in the
City of Emeralds. Almost always at this stage, the savior is seen as male. Dorothy
goes to find the Great Wizard, who the Witch of the North says "is more powerful
than all the rest of us together." He, and he alone, they believe, can save her. While
searching for this father-rescue figure, she encounters three characters who represent the qualities she needs to be a hero—courage, intelligence, and compassion. These qualities are embodied in male characters. Ironically, the characters
who embody these virtues think they lack them. The Cowardly Lion proves to be
most brave; the Tin Man, who wishes to ask the Wizard to give him a heart, is most
compassionate; and the Scarecrow, who bemoans his lack of a brain, makes all the
clever plans. The message for the reader and for Dorothy is that each hero has the

necessary qualities, but needs the opportunity to develop and express them. As the Wizard explains to the Scarecrow, "A Baby has brains, but it doesn't know much. Experience is the only thing that brings knowledge, and the longer you are on earth the more experience you are sure to get" (p. 180). In dealing with frightening and dangerous events, Dorothy develops her intelligence and courage. She develops her capacity for love through her affection for her companions and through her longing for Aunt Em.

The budding hero has all the capacities she needs, but they are latent. Furthermore, the conditioning that teaches women to find men to slay their dragons for them interferes with the development of these qualities. The Wizard of Oz knows that he is only pretending to be a wizard, and that he cannot give anyone heroic qualities. Indeed, the Emerald City looks green only because he insists that everyone wear green glasses to protect their eyes from the glare. To stall for time he refuses to aid Dorothy and her friends until they have killed his archenemy, the Wicked Witch of the West. The Witch takes Dorothy prisoner, but melts "away to nothing" when Dorothy, trying to save the burning scarecrow, gets angry and throws a bucket of water on her. In this case, the life energy symbolized by the water flows from Dorothy's love for her friend and her resulting outrage at injustice to him. Having killed the second wicked witch, Dorothy and her companions return to the Wizard to demand their rewards. They discover that he is just "a little old man, with a bald head and a wrinkled face, who seemed to be as much surprised as they were" (p. 173). In a delightful parody of the myth of romantic love and the patriarchal tendency to inflate the image of men to twice their normal size, Dorothy unmasks the Wizard, the symbol of the father-lover-savior, who she thought could solve all of her problems. The Wizard confesses that he is "just a common man," "a humbug," who formerly worked in a circus. In this allegorical rendition of the female hero's journey, the hero kills the Wicked Witch—society's negative image of the powerful woman—and discovers that the patriarch cannot save her, because the greater-than-life image of the ideal male is an illusion. Dorothy's immediate response is to attack the Wizard and call him a bad man; but he is not evil, he is simply not magic. He explains, "I'm really a very good man; but I'm a very bad Wizard."

In this second stage of the journey, Dorothy learns that qualities society sees as male—intelligence, courage, and greatness of heart—are hers. She is the hero and is whole, needing no wizard either to complete or to save her; she has learned that she can kill the witch herself. However, she still does not know how to go home, and she still feels lonely and in need of a community. The Wizard explains that "while I had no magical powers at all I soon found out that the Witches were really able to do wonderful things" (p. 178). He advises her to visit Glinda, the good Witch of the South. At this point, it should be clear that the witches of the north and south represent elements of Dorothy's own power and are her rescuers; the witches of the east and west are her dragons. The Wicked Witch of the West (a fairy tale version of the self-hater) asserts, "I could make her my slave, for she does not know how to use her power" (p. 145). The good Witch of the South tells Dorothy that she has the power to rescue herself. "If you had known their power [the magic shoes she gained in killing the Wicked Witch of the East], you could have gone back to your Aunt Em the very first day you came to this country" (p. 234).

In the third and final stage of the journey, the hero meets a female rescue figure who tells her that she can save herself. She has discovered female power, and she can now go home. What becomes apparent at this point is that the heroic journey affects not only the microcosm (the self of the hero), but the macrocosm (the hero's world) as well. Back on the Kansas prairie, Dorothy finds not greyness and hostility, but new life, fertility, and love. Uncle Henry has built a new farmhouse, and he is milking the cows when she arrives; and, instead of looking horrified and pressing "her hand to her heart" in fear of the girl's exuberance, Aunt Em holds her in her arms and covers her face with kisses. Because she has become a hero, the world to which she returns is transformed.

Detective stories and gothic romances traditionally have been popular with women because women have had to search out the truth behind societal myths in order to survive. In both the gothic tale and the detective story, society tells the hero that the crimes apparently committed against her are not crimes at all; they are either her just punishment for failing to fulfill the traditional female ideal, or the products of her diseased imagination. In the examples of both genres discussed here, the hero slays the dragon when she learns that she is not the villain, and that the villain is real and outside herself. In Dorothy Sayers's *Gaudy Night*, Harriet Vane replaces Lord Peter Wimsey (the hero of most of the novels in the series) as Sayers's central character and crime fighter. She is called back to her alma mater—a women's college at Oxford—to help discover the identity of a criminal who threatens to discredit the college (and by extension women's education) by creating a scandal. A series of poison-pen letters and cases of vandalism soon escalates into attempted murder.[7]

Harriet Vane has trouble discovering the villain, however, because of her predilection to see herself as the guilty party. In Lessing's terms, she is dominated by the self-hater. She met Lord Peter Wimsey when she was being tried for the murder of her lover. Wimsey saved her life (in Sayers's *Strong Poison*) by proving her innocence, but in the process of the trial the illicit relationship was made public. The public convicted her of being a whore and a murderer. She feels guilty for sowing her wild oats in public and also for deserting her former lover shortly before he was murdered.

Because she feels guilty about sex and about not being a totally devoted helpmate, she believes that she is not good enough to marry the illustrious Peter Wimsey, who fell in love with her virtually at first sight. She feels guilty also because she is living a celibate life and depriving Wimsey of happiness. Harriet assumes that the villain would naturally have the qualities that she condemns in herself and therefore imagines the murderer to be a "sex crazed spinster" and an unconventional, intellectual woman. Wimsey cautions her that her own guilt and fears are distorting her judgment, but she is unable to rid herself entirely of the belief that her previous "fall" into sexuality and knowledge was sinful rather than liberating and that her redemption could occur only through the sacrifice of her life to her seducer.

The criminal turns out to be not a liberated woman but a traditional bitter, self-sacrificing woman, who hates other women. She is a widow who preaches clichés about a woman's duty to serve a man; and she accuses Harriet Vane with the words of Harriet's own self-hater: "You had a lover once, and he died. You chucked him because you were too proud to marry him. You were his mistress and you sucked him dry, and you didn't value him enough to let him make a honest woman of you. He died because you weren't there to look after him. I suppose you'd say you loved him. You don't know what love means. It means sticking to your man through thick and thin and putting up with everything" (p. 373). As soon as the criminal is discovered and Harriet realizes that *she* is not guilty, the second and third stages of the hero's journey occur simultaneously. When she likes herself, she can marry Peter Wimsey, and she can unashamedly feel kinship with the women of Oxford.

There is one more interesting complication to the plot, without which the "happy ending" would be no more than a concession to the myth of romantic love. Harriet's sense of unworthiness is intensified by the debt to Wimsey. Because he saved her life, she sees him as her superior. As long as he plays the part of the classical knight and she the damsel in distress, she cannot be his equal. Wimsey recognizes this fact. When she risks her life in the course of discovering the murderer, he resists the temptation to save her. By not intervening even to save her life, he gives her the message that he knows she is a hero capable of saving herself. When she succeeds, she sees herself, as he does, as his equal, and the classical happy ending promises the reward of an egalitarian marriage.

The discovery that the villain is outside the self is also at the heart of the gothic genre. Classically, the crazy woman in the attic, the skeleton in the closet, and similar figures are believed only to be products of the hero's inflamed imagination. She is told that no crime has been committed. The discovery of the crime and the villain confirms the hero's sanity or (more moderately) her view of reality. In Margaret Atwood's *Lady Oracle*, the protagonist, Joan Foster, writes gothic novels under the pseudonym Louisa K. Delacourt.[8] She also recounts her life in terms of the gothic, and the metaphors for her heroic journey within have all the gothic trappings: a trip into a mirror, a visit into the maze, and death by drowning, followed by a period of contemplation and suffering and then a rebirth into a new, transfigured life. Her increasing understanding of her situation is reflected in the gothic plots she writes. To the degree that these plots are products of her fantasy life, they reflect her true vision more adequately than do her rational ideas. For example, in the traditional gothic, the hero is saved from death by the romantic male figure. However, Joan remembers tales—"The Lady of Shalott," "The Little Mermaid," and "The Red Shoes"—in which the price of love is the hero's death. Joan feels she must sacrifice her exuberant, spontaneous, natural self to gain the love of a man. She tries to dance and "wings grew from" her shoulders, but then she steps on glass. She sees the blood on her feet as "the real red shoes, the feet punished for dancing. You could dance, or you could have the love of a good man. But you were afraid to dance, because you had this unnatural fear that if you danced they'd cut your feet off so you wouldn't be able to dance. . . . Finally you overcame your fear and danced, and they cut your feet off. The good man went away too, because you wanted to dance" (p. 335).

The long poem she writes during experiments with automatic writing is a true—and to her embarrassing—reflection of her own situation. She does not know if the romantic hero is a rescuer or a murderer. It was "like a gothic gone wrong. . . . There were the sufferings, the hero in the mask of a villain, the villain in the mask of a hero, the flights, the looming death, the sense of being imprisoned, but there was no happy ending, no true love" (p. 232).

The entire novel is a flashback, which occurs after Joan's staged "death" and before her resurrection. The literal events of her life are similar to elements of the gothic. They also reflect more adequately than any of the works discussed thus far the primary elements of each of the three stages of the heroic quest.

Joan escapes from the cage of her mother's dominance when she leaves home and loses weight. She had been fat to thwart her mother, her captor, and she had used obesity also as "an insulation, a cocoon . . . a disguise." At this initial step in the journey, she leaves the cage; but "without my magic cloak of blubber and invisibility, I felt naked, pruned as though some essential covering was missing" (p. 141).

Her mother is a typical, intensely bitter product of sexism. She had married because she was pregnant. Joan analyzes the situation: "It wasn't that she was aggressive and ambitious, although she was both these things. Perhaps she wasn't aggressive or ambitious enough. If she'd ever decided what she really wanted to do and had gone out and done it, she wouldn't have seen me as a reproach to her, the embodiment of her own failure and depression, a huge edgeless cloud of inchoate matter which refused to be shaped into anything for which she could get a prize" (p. 67). Two women give Joan the initial encouragement necessary to escape from her mother. Aunt Lou encourages her to have faith in herself and always says, "You can handle it." When Aunt Lou dies, she leaves Joan money on the condition that she lose weight. Thus, her aunt's legacy motivates her to shed her protective "cocoon" and also gives her the confidence and the financial power to leave her childhood home. Her aunt also took her to occult meetings led by Leda Sprott, who told Joan, "You have great gifts. . . . Great powers" (p. 112). Sprott's advice leads to the experiments with automatic writing, through which she begins to understand the true nature of the myth of romantic love.

Her mother's most direct legacy is a sense of female inferiority and a belief that she must hide her real self. Even after leaving home, she is controlled by her mother's messages of female monstrousness, which she has internalized. Joan envisions her mother sitting at her three-mirrored vanity: "As I watched, I suddenly realized that instead of these reflections she had three actual heads, which rose from her toweled shoulders on three separate necks. This didn't frighten me, as it seemed merely a confirmation of something I'd always known" (p. 66). She sees her mother and herself as monstrous because of their fragmentation, and their monstrousness as a shameful secret that must be hidden from men. The dream continues: "Outside the door there was a man, a man who was about to open the door and come in. If he saw, if he found out the truth about my mother, something terrible would happen, not only to my mother but to me" (p. 66).

Joan is increasingly aware that women's monstrousness is a product of their victimization, as her obesity was a way of dealing with her overbearing mother. She further realizes that she has been socialized to see the victim—rather than the oppressor—as guilty and shameful. As an adult, Joan meets Marlene Pugh, who once led a group of Brownies who consistently ridiculed and persecuted her. One day they tied Joan to a bridge and left her for the "bad Man" to find. "Marlene the ingenious inquisitor. She hadn't recognized me, but when she did I knew what would happen: she would have a smile of indulgence for her former self, and I would be overcome with shame. Yet I hadn't done anything shameful; she was the one who'd done it. Why then should I be the one to feel guilt, why should she go free? Hers was the freedom of the strong; my guilt was the guilt of those who lose, those who can be exposed, those who fail" (p. 229).

It is because of the myth of female inferiority—of the monstrousness of victimization—that Joan governs her behavior by what people will think, and hides and distrusts her own perceptions. Even after escaping from her obesity and from her mother's domination, Joan is still trapped in the mirror of convention. Her experiment with automatic writing—the description of which is reminiscent of Lewis Carroll's *Through the Looking Glass*—reveals to her the implications and effects of the conventional myths, or dragons, that she has internalized. This revelation enables her to slay the dragons and discover her true perceptions and her true self. Going into a trance in front of the mirror, she has "the sense of going down a narrow passage that led downward, the certainty that if I could only turn the next corner or the next . . . I would find the thing, the truth or word or person that was mine, that was waiting for me" (p. 221). A female figure appears, who "lived under the earth or inside something, a cave or a huge building; sometimes she was on a boat. She was enormously powerful, almost like a goddess, but it was an unhappy power" (p. 221). This woman, whose "tears are the death you fear," is reminiscent of the protagonist's mother. The male figure who appears combines elements of a Byronic hero and those of Joan's prosaic husband, Arthur, who delivers "some rather boring prosy sermons about the meaning of life" (p. 222).

Through this and other gothic encounters, Joan continually confronts the tyranny of her mother and of the men who dominate her and perpetuate her split life. She experiences the division between the public and the personal self as a literal one: "I was two people at once, with two sets of identification papers, two bank accounts, two different groups of people who believed I existed. I was Joan Foster, there was no doubt about that. . . . But I was also Louisa K. Delacourt" (p. 213). The imaginative literary world Louisa Delacourt creates is a product of women's collective fantasies gleaned from Joan's long years of being "a good listener." She differs from other women, who "wanted their husbands to live up to their fantasy lives," and she "kept Arthur in our apartment and the strangers in their castles and mansions, where they belong. I felt this was quite adult of me" (p. 215). She also must keep separate her two gothic secrets: her shameful past as a fat girl—a secret associated with the traditional gothic—and her secret identity as the author of gothic romances. The split widens when, in addition to writing the gothics, she begins to live them in her imagination. For example, she imagines herself having an affair with the "Royal Porcupine," who sports capes, who loves to waltz and to do wild, unpredictable things, and who is associated (as the romantic gothic male hero often is) with death; his art work includes the frozen carcasses of small animals.

Joan's husband, Arthur, is an immature radical who says he wants a wife whose mind he can respect. She is certain he would disapprove of her gothic fantasy life, and she discovers that he actually dislikes her strength and talent. He is threatened when her piece of automatic writing (called *Lady Oracle*) turns her into a celebrity. In working through his conflicting messages, she recognizes that "there were as many of Arthur as there were of me" (p. 211). "It wasn't that Arthur was dishonest: what he thought and what he said he thought were the same. It was just that both of these things were different from what he felt" (p. 210). She tries to "turn into what Arthur thought I was, or . . . should be," but then realizes that in spite of his stated encouragement to "exercise my intelligence constructively," he really "enjoyed my defeats. . . . My failure was a performance and Arthur was the audience. His applause kept me going" (p. 210).

The impulse to lie about herself comes from her need for love and approval and her feeling that if she revealed her shameful secrets she would be rejected and unloved, and thereby destroyed. Like her three-headed mother, she is destined to remain a monster because "if I brought the separate parts of my life together (like uranium, like plutonium, harmless to the naked eye, but charged with lethal energies) surely there would be an explosion" (p. 127).

Appropriate to the gothic mode, she is literally haunted by her mother, who appears in an astral body before, at the moment of, and after her death. She also appears to Joan in dreams, "menacing and cold" or "sitting in front of her vanity table . . . crying" (p. 214). Joan speaks of carrying her mother "around my neck like a rotting albatross" (p. 213), as she carries around the "outline of my former [fat] body . . . like a phantom moon" (p. 214). The gothic elements the protagonist experiences—"the looming death, the sense of being imprisoned"—are also associated with the mother who haunts her (p. 232). These versions of the internalized self-hater must be slain if she is to unify her separate selves.

To reach the "happy ending," she also discovers the secret identity of "the hero in the mask of a villain, the villain in the mask of a hero" (p. 232). To see the truth about each man, she frees herself from dualistic thinking, because the terms do not adequately describe the complex, human, and individual identities of the men she knows. Her fantasy life includes only men who are rescuers or villains—who, her mother told her, either did things for you or did things to you. In actuality she finds she cannot clearly distinguish the bad villain from the good rescuer.

When she was a Brownie, Joan met a man on the bridge who gave her daffodils and "exposed" himself to her. Later when the malicious Brownies tie her up to leave her at his mercy, he appears again (is he the same man? she is not sure) and kindly unties her: "Was it the daffodil man or not? Was the man who untied me a rescuer or a villain? Or, an even more baffling thought: was it possible for a man to be both at once?" (p. 64). Later she recognized that "every man I'd ever been involved with, I realized, had had two selves: my father, healer and killer; the man in the tweed coat, my rescuer and possibly also a pervert; the Royal Porcupine and his double Chuck Brewer [a perfectly ordinary man]; even Paul, who I'd always believed had a sinister other life I couldn't penetrate" (p. 292).

She initially sees the two sides of each man as analogous to the gothic hero and villain, who respectively "saved" or threatened to kill the heroine. The ordinary appearance of all the men she knows seems a disguise for the larger-than-life qualities. She envisions her father as "a conjuror of spirits, a shaman. . . . He'd killed people [in the war] and raised the dead [as a doctor]" (p. 77). She looks to him to be the wizard who will provide meaning to her journey. In her search for these two stereotypes in her father and in Arthur, she learns that the male lead in the myth of romantic love is neither a hero nor a god. She makes the same discovery in her writing. In the gothics she has written, the man with the cloak is always the rescuer, as she hoped her father, Arthur, and the Royal Porcupine would be, and the wife is the villain, as she believes her mother to be. In her traditional plot, in her book within the book, Felicia, the adulterous and jealous wife, attempts to kill the young, virtuous Charlotte; but Redmond, the romantic, cloaked figure, appears, casts aside his wife, and expresses his love for Charlotte. Redmond, who seemed to be the villain-seducer, turns out to be the rescuer who loves her and saves her life. The rakish husband is transformed from villain to rescuer by his admiration and love for the young maiden. The real villain is another woman.

Something about this traditional gothic plot line seems wrong to Atwood's protagonist, and when she goes home after her mother's death, she begins the process of understanding and altering it. She initially assumes that her mother is the villain who has kept her and her father apart. She goes home in search of a father: "I wanted him to tell me the truth about life, which my mother would not tell me, which he must have known something about, as he was a doctor and had been in the war, he'd killed people and raised the dead. I kept waiting for him to give me some advice, warn me, instruct me, but he never did any of these things" (p. 77). As in *The Wizard of Oz*, Joan recognizes that he is not a bad man, he is just not a good wizard. She therefore begins to empathize with her mother, and to realize how embittered and miserable her life was. Before the end of the novel, she realizes that her mother's legacy is the death-in-life of the woman who gives up her life for a man who is neither a rescuer nor a god. Her bitterness at having sacrificed herself makes her into the potential murderer of her daughter. The references to Tennyson's "The Lady of Shalott" and to other women who give up their lives suggest that her mother's curse is a recurring one in the lives of women. Foster/Delacourt examines her own responsibility for her mother's captivity: "She couldn't stand the view from the window, life was her curse. How could I renounce her? She needed her freedom also; she had been my reflection too long. What was the charm, what would set her free . . . my mother . . . I would never be able to make her happy. Or anyone else. Maybe it was time for me to stop trying" (p. 329).

To become free of the terrible man and woman in her head, Joan must learn to think nondualistically. Her mother is not her daughter's possessor, nor is she a victim whom the daughter is responsible for freeing. Her father and her husband are neither rescuers nor particularly villainous. However, it is important for Joan to recognize that her relationship with her husband and the myths surrounding that relationship are killing her as they did her mother. Both dragon-defined situations have made it impossible for the women to explore and to develop their heroic possibilities because the patriarchal situation treats female strength as something monstrous: something to be hidden, repressed, and ultimately destroyed.

Joan's last version of the gothic romance reflects her changed consciousness. Charlotte, the hero of the novel, goes into the maze and finds several versions of its author in the center: Lady Redmond, two other redheads like her, a grotesque fat woman, and a middle-aged woman who looks like Aunt Lou. They explain to her that "every man has more than one wife." As the protagonist tries to escape, she sees Redmond, with "an odd expression in his eyes. Then she knew. Redmond was the killer. He was a killer in disguise, he wanted to murder her as he had murdered his other wives. . . . He wanted to replace her with the other one, the next one, thin and flawless . . . " (p. 342). She steps back, refusing to be doomed. As she does so, he turns into Arthur and then "the flesh fell away from his face, revealing the skull behind it" (p. 343).

In writing this final gothic romance, Joan realizes that the secret horror behind the myth of romantic love is the murder of women's heroic selves. Thinking that Arthur is at the door, she opens the door and hurls a Cinzano bottle at him—only to discover that she has hit a reporter instead. In venting her rage, Joan exorcises her fascination with the killer image and prepares the way for the novel's comic ending. She has reconciled with the mother, demystified the patriarch, and overcome her self-hatred. She has healed the split, been reborn as herself, and gained the treasure of self-regard. And when she discovers her true self and has the courage to express it, she can have the first honest relationship of her life. We leave her attracted to the reporter because, she says, "he's the only person who knows anything about me" (p. 345).

In discussing works of various genres, this chapter has defined and explored the key elements of the female hero's journey. The following three chapters explore the stages of the journey in more detail. In Joseph Campbell's terms, they examine the departure, the meeting with the god and tempter of the opposite sex, and the reconciliation with the god of the same sex, respectively.

This sequential approach has its limitations. Although it portrays a full, heroic journey leading to an "ultimate boon," in some literary works a more accurate approach would be to view each stage as a journey in itself. The three stages can be seen as different metaphorical vehicles, which in varying degrees of depth and complexity act out the same myth.

Any effort to define and illustrate these stages is complicated by the fact that they do not necessarily occur in the same order, nor are they always clearly separate: The same moment or situation in the hero's life may include several of these events simultaneously, or the event may occur over a long period of time. Unlike the literal dragon-slaying in myth, epic, and romance, which usually occurs as a single episode, the struggle with the dragon in realistic literature may be depicted as an instant of epiphany or as a gradual process that lasts through several scenes. Furthermore, it may be an isolated experience in the hero's journey or it may occur simultaneously with one of the other stages.

One example in which the exit and the slaying occur at the same time is found in Brecht's *Mother Courage and Her Children*. The protagonist is determined that her daughter Katrin remain chaste so that a nice man will marry her when the war is over. Katrin, who is mute, behaves passively throughout the play until the end, when she rushes out and climbs the roof to bang on a kettle, warning the villagers that the enemy is coming. In one gesture, she defies her captor mother, rejects the myths of virginity and romantic love that have imprisoned her, exits from the garden, slays both inner and outer dragons, and transforms herself from a damsel in distress into a hero. Those few moments are in fact her entire journey, because the enemy soldiers shoot and kill her as she is sabotaging their plan of attack.

Marie, the central character in Agnes Smedley's *Daughter of Earth*, on the other hand, conducts a battle against capitalism that lasts many years, and it is during this ongoing external conflict that she begins to conquer her distaste for her own body and for sexuality. Del in Alice Munro's *Lives of Girls and Women* slays the dragon myths of female inferiority and vulnerability, of virginity and romantic love, through a series of typical adolescent experiences that culminate in her physical struggle with and subsequent rejection of her first lover, Garnet French.

The hero seldom proceeds directly to the treasure. Her journey is more often a circuitous, labyrinthine one, in which she moves back and forth between dualities, and through an incongruous series of true and false guides and trials. She repeatedly confuses appearance and reality. Furthermore, self-doubt may follow each positive action and turn her good feelings and sense of personal growth to ashes. The hero is constantly searching, losing her way, and discovering unexpected truths about herself and about the world. Positive and negative agents are often difficult to distinguish, and even the most destructive situations are not necessarily fatal. Each seducer, false dragon, wrong road, or seemingly unproductive endeavor or conflict brings her closer to a full understanding of herself.

The journey is complicated further by the human tendency not to understand completely all the ramifications of a single experience. In some ways, the metaphors of the departure, the meeting with the god and tempter, and the reconciliation with the mother repeat in varying degrees of complexity the same general pattern, while simultaneously building complexity and depth. In each, the female hero identifies and slays a dragon and wins a related treasure. Thus, the journey is more adequately described by spiral or circular metaphors than as a linear path. The protagonist of Margaret Atwood's *Lady Oracle* humorously comments on the contrast between her own complicated journey and the simpler route her husband appears to travel: "That was the difference between us: for Arthur there were true paths, several of them perhaps, but only one at a time. For me there were no paths at all. Thickets, ditches, ponds, labyrinths, morasses, but no paths."[9]

Chapter 4
The Exit from the Garden

*How annoying for God (not to mention Adam), after all, if Eve
had just walked out of Eden without waiting to be evicted, and
left behind her pangs of guilt, as it were, with her leaf apron?*
Constance Beresford-Howe, *The Book of Eve*

The woman who departs from the role prescribed for her by patriarchal society is
one of the most popular figures in Western literature. However much women may
be encouraged to remain in the garden, even the patriarchal God could not create a
woman who would stay. According to Hebrew legends, the first woman was not
Eve, but Lilith. Lilith ran off into the woods just as God was about to marry her to
Adam, and thereby refused the whole idea of subservience. Then God created Eve,
who, out of her desire for knowledge, ate the forbidden apple and precipitated
humankind's fortunate fall out of innocence into moral responsibility. In classical
myth, the archetype is also prevalent. Pandora opens the box; Psyche looks at
Cupid. Virtually every female hero in British and American literature disobeys
patriarchal injunctions concerning virtuous female behavior and thereby reenacts
the primordial "fall."

In British and American stories, the hero typically departs from a confining
house rather than a garden. Samuel Richardson's Clarissa runs away from home.
Catherine Earnshaw Linton in Emily Brontë's *Wuthering Heights* dies as a result of
her frustration with the limitations of the Lintons' house and the manners and
mores associated with it; and after her death, she roams the heath. Edna Pontellier,
in Kate Chopin's *The Awakening*, moves out of her husband's house into a smaller
one nearby. Virginia Woolf argues that each woman needs to separate herself from
the family unit and find a space of her own, even if it is only a separate room.

The physical exit is also a psychological refusal, and it is the psychological
more than the physical separation that is the crucial first step in the hero's journey.
In the simplest sense, the hero recognizes, sometimes in a blinding flash and other
times as the result of a gradual process, that things-as-they-are are not inevitable.
Her exit affirms her sense that there must be a better way. For the most conservative character—for example, Samuel Richardson's Pamela—the refusal may include
a rejection of only part of the destructive message. Pamela continues to believe in
many patriarchal myths. Caught in the contradiction between the myths—between
the injunctions to obey her master, who pursues her sexually, and to maintain her

chastity—she first attempts to reconcile the two. Finally, however, she chooses chastity, but refuses obedience, and the choice is a self-affirming act that is applauded by Richardson's readers.

The moment of heroic exit is potentially present in every woman's life at every moment. Paul Roche, in his contemporary poem "What Makes Her Special," pays tribute to the plain-looking woman, observed at the automat, whose unobtrusive facade he imagines to disguise a great power to initiate daring action—even murder—as her own personal vision dictates. Her heroic act of self-affirmation is manifested even in the uneventful and repetitive details of her daily life, in which, the poet comprehends, "She walks with what she's chosen to some shore."[1] A protagonist may exit under any circumstances, no matter how hopeless. Ibsen's Nora leaves home after years of playing the dependent doll-wife. Maria in *Play It As It Lays* experiences a whole gauntlet of destructive situations and people in plastic Hollywood, including commitment to a mental institution, before she suddenly affirms herself and life in spite of all of them.

In many cases, women begin new lives in old age. The statement of Vita Sackville-West's Lady Slone, in *All Passion Spent*, suggests that advancing age may encourage rather than prohibit the heroic exit. She shocks her children by announcing at the dinner table that she will not live with one of them but will live by herself. When they suggest that the world might disapprove of such a decision, she responds by saying, "I have considered the eyes of the world for so long that I think it is time I had a little holiday from them. If one is not to please oneself in old age, when is one to please oneself? There is so little time left!"[2] Dorothy Bryant's Anna Giardino in *Miss Giardino* exits at age sixty-eight. Eva in Constance Beresford-Howe's *The Book of Eve* is sixty-five when she leaves her suburban home and ailing husband. She closes the front door and immediately finds a taxi. When the driver asks her destination, she finds herself shaking with laughter; in fact, she has no idea where to go. Even in her confusion, however, she is already freer and less lonely after escaping because she is being herself.

The hero's departure, no matter how shocking it seems at the time, helps to liberate those she "abandons" as well. When Eva stops serving her invalid husband and leaves him alone in their suburban home, he gets well and begins the additions to the house he had talked about for years. Eva talks on the phone with her son Neil from her new home in Toronto, and he tells her, "The fact is, Mum, I've admired you more since you up and left than I ever did before. Once I got over my moral outrage, that is. You shook me up plenty. Ever since then I've felt different about quite a lot of things."[3]

There are, of course, circumstances in which a hero does not have the option of beginning a new life; her only option is to die nobly—as Joan of Arc and Antigone do. In such cases, her death sends a shock wave of liberation that may last through the ages. Such a hero is the protagonist of May Sarton's *As We Are Now*, a woman too old and too ill to walk out the door of the dehumanizing rest home in which she is incarcerated. Aware that people are social beings, and that we are constantly altered and resocialized by our surroundings, Caro Spenser recognizes that she cannot long remain herself when she is treated as if she were senile or invisible. She is dying "from a lack of love," for the method of the nursing home staff is to act as though the patients have no feelings and are only confused and senile if they act hurt or upset.[4] In her words, "The most cruel response to a *cri de coeur* is not to believe it, or to pretend that it is a lie" (p. 80). When she stands up for an old man whose screams of pain and requests for a doctor are being ignored, she is punished by being left alone in the dark, heavily sedated, for three days. After that, she learns not to rebel outwardly—although she does find a way to arrange an inspection of the home (which, although in violation of virtually every code, is not closed because there is nowhere else for the patients to stay).

She holds out as long as she can against the pressure to become a docile vegetable and then determines to die with dignity while she still has command of herself. "I, Caro, am still here," she says, "I still have to manage to die, and whatever powers I have must be concentrated on doing it soon. I want my death to be something more like me than slow disintegration. 'Do not go gentle into that good night' . . . the words, so hackneyed by now, come back to me like a command from somewhere way down inside, where there is still fire, if only the fire of anger and disgust" (p. 121). The only patient left in full command of her mental faculties, she reasons that it is her responsibility to "open this locked world" before departing from the earth. She develops a plan to destroy the home while dying with dignity. She will hide her notebooks, which tell the story of her imprisonment, in the refrigerator; then she will burn the rest home down. Better "death by fire," she reasons, than "death by bad smells and bedpans and lost minds in sordidly failing bodies" (p. 41).

As she successfully executes this plan, she feels "at peace," emphasizing that the survival of the copybooks is "the important thing" (p. 133). It is so, because only if people read them will her death and her act of cleansing violence promote life. Years before she had been angry when "people refused to admit that the concentration camps existed" and, when the proof was overwhelming, said "Why dwell on it?" To affirm life over death, she reasons, we must stop shutting "ourselves away from what is painful" and truly experience "the truth as far as it could be imagined. . . . Only when we emphatically experience the pain others suffer, and own it, can we be fully human, and can we stop such cruelty" (p. 49). By leaving her notebooks behind, Caro acts to transform the kingdom, for by encouraging others to face the grim and repressive reality of the nursing home, she strives to change such institutions.

As Sarton implies, the woman who affirms her self-worth by rejecting the forces that stabilize and limit growth also affirms life. In Erica Jong's *How to Save Your Own Life*, the famous old American writer (patterned after Henry Miller) tells Isadora Wing: "The trick is not how much pain you feel—but how much joy you feel. Any idiot can feel pain. Life is full of excuses to feel pain, excuses not to live, excuses, excuses, excuses. . . . Watch out for the death-people, . . . the people who want to die and want everyone else to die with them. They're the ones to avoid."[5] When the hero says no to those who tell her to live as everyone else does and be a slave to convention, she affirms her own worth and she promotes life. Competent and independent and innately worthy rather than sinful, she no longer needs institutions, individuals, or gods to protect her, rescue her, or tell her what to do. In Mary Staton's feminist utopian novel, *From the Legend of Biel*, the villagers of Lir collectively reject the parent Thoacdien culture, and in doing so assert their freedom and basic goodness. One villager explains:

> We have come to the meadows as our first genuine rudeness.
> We have said no to all systems good or bad, and to all who run
> systems, good or bad. I came to the meadows when I . . .

embraced the fact of my basic goodness, my basic and first desire to be positive—which is possible—in a universe where most other people want the same. I had almost come to believe that I did need an artificial framework for my life—in my case the technocracy of Thoacdien—in order to survive. . . . We find here that this is not true.[6]

By affirming her independence and responsibility for her own life—in violation of the expectations about women's lifelong dependency—a woman is, in fact, choosing to become an adult. In Vita Sackville-West's *The Edwardians*, Viola Chevron decides to take control of her own life, and moves out of the house where she has lived as a child. Her exit is a shock to the entire family, but particularly to the innocent young Lucy: "Viola had rebelled; on one unforgettable evening at Chevron, after dinner, she had announced that she had taken a flat in London. 'You prevented me from going to Cambridge, Mother, but you can't prevent me from doing this. I'm of age.' That phrase had entered Lucy's soul as a dagger. She had never heard it before as applied to a girl."[7]

Charlotte Perkins Gilman, the nineteenth-century activist and author, describes in her diary her own moment of exit, an experience that she defines as "one of the major events of a lifetime making an indelible impression" and "opening an entire new world of action." When Charlotte is around sixteen years old, her mother tells her that she must apologize for something that she had not done or leave the house. Charlotte recognizes the injustice of her choices and replies, "I am not going to do it—and I am not going to leave you—and what are you going to do about it?" The metaphor for her exit is birth, hence emphasizing the life-giving function of the exit: "I was realizing with immense illumination that neither she, nor anyone, could make me do anything. One could suffer, one could die if it came to that, but one could not be coerced. I was born."[8]

The hero's exit is, then, a solitary act of self-affirmation. Jane Eyre leaves a series of repressive environments—the Reeds' house, the orphanage at Lowood, Rochester's Thornfield, and the home of St. John Rivers. As she leaves Thornfield, she explains, "*I care for myself. The more solitary, the more friendless, the more unsustained I am, the more I will respect myself.*"[9] In Marge Piercy's *Small Changes*, Beth writes her own song, which begins, "Everything says no to me./Everything tells me not./Only I say yes."[10]

However self-confident and life-affirming the hero may be, she often feels alone and confused. She may even feel that she does not know who she is. Lewis Carroll's Alice, for example, responds to the caterpillar's question, "Who are you?" by saying "Well, I knew when I got up this morning, but I have changed several times since then."[11] Having lost faith in the culture's categories, the hero may wander, like Dorothy in *The Wizard of Oz*, in a world she does not recognize. Further, for Alice and Dorothy, the environment is filled with unknown and potentially unrecognized dangers. In fact, disorientation is an inherent part of any transition from the known to the unknown, and the heroic descent into the primal chaos is a necessary prerequisite to the moment of rebirth. Bereft of the conventional truths that have given life meaning and order, the hero descends to the primal chaos of unexplained reality, which is followed by a rebirth in which she sees the world in a new way. Margaret Mead entitled her autobiography *Blackberry Winter*, which she explains is "that time when the hoarfrost lies on the blackberry blossoms; without this frost the berries will not set. It is the forerunner of a rich harvest."[12]

Anaïs Nin, in *House of Incest*, describes the period between the death of the old self and the birth of the new in this way. Her protagonist lies in a strange hotel room, psychologically separating herself from everyone she loves. She severs all connections and confronts the terrifying reality of the world without substance or order and without an identity of her own. Like many heroes who face the possibility of exit, she fears that, in her exploration of the psychological and physical unknown, she will awake "next morning mad or a whore." She also knows that what follows the sundering of all ties could be the birth of something new: "An entirely new life could begin." She recognizes, as she rushes out of the room, that she is prevented from completing the experience because of "the terror of this new life, more than the terror of dying."[13]

Although the exit is seldom easy and the outcome of the quest is unknown, the decision to depart on the quest is always a positive one. Charlotte Perkins Gilman, the author of *The Yellow Wallpaper*, writes in her autobiography, *The Living of Charlotte Perkins Gilman*, of the serious depression with which she had to cope during her marriage and from which she only began to emerge after she had left her husband: "The moment I left home I began to recover. It seemed right to give up a mistaken marriage."[14] Because some damage has usually been done to the ego prior to her separation, the beginning of the hero's journey may have to be devoted to the restoration and strengthening of the self. In Gilman's case, Dr. Mary Putnam Jacobi devised a program to help her to "reestablish the capacity for action" (p. 97).

The outcome of the quest differs according to the hero's circumstances and abilities. The exit does not by itself promise success, happiness, or love. What it does provide is independence, integrity, and self-respect. Adrienne Rich in "Prospective Immigrants Please Note" warns that the exit from the garden carries with it "a risk" that the hero will not remember her true "name": "The door itself/makes no promises./ It is only a door."[15] The poet Hilda Doolittle, in "The Walls Do Not Fall" Part 43, speaks of the female hero as the discoverer of the "not-known," the "unrecorded." She has "no maps" as she strives to reach "haven/heaven."[16]

The Call to the Quest

> How to make you realize the imperative of this moment? How to stretch out a hand and whisper, yes, here, step out over the edge, the drop is only magnetized toward your density's grave center.
>
>   May your insurrection and your resurrection be the same.
>
> Robin Morgan, *Going Too Far*

Because the quest appears to be so terrifying and uncertain, at least one key factor may distinguish the successful hero from the confused victim: a single voice—among the chorus of voices echoing the dragon myths about being a woman—telling her that she is worthwhile, that she has a right to happiness and fulfillment, and that she has the ability to find it. This voice parallels the call to adventure and the intervention of supernatural aid that informs the classical hero's departure on the quest.

Like her classical male counterpart, the hero is inclined to refuse the initial call to adventure until an encounter reinforces her and gives her courage. For example, the title character of Louis Auchincloss's short story "The 'True Story' of Lavinia Todd" is unhappily married to a prominent lawyer. At Ada Tilney's dinner party, Lavinia's unhappiness and her sense that she is being discarded suddenly overwhelm her and she starts to cry at the dinner table. The hostess's daughter, Fran, leads her upstairs, listens to her life story, and then insists that she write it down for publication. This encounter and the subsequent recognition that she receives as an author give her the courage and clarity of vision to agree to her husband's previous request for a divorce and to begin a new life. Often, as in this case, the initial call to the quest appears to be a negative occurrence (emptiness and the end of a marriage). The supportive guide or voice helps the hero to recognize the heroic opportunity obscured by the apparent catastrophe.

The voice that cuts through the paralysis of conformity to conventional life may be another person, a natural force, or a commanding impulse from within the hero. But this force always urges the hero to take risks, to be fully alive, and to avoid those who would tell her to stifle her energy, passion, and individuality. In Erica Jong's *How to Save Your Own Life*, Isadora hears of the death of the poet, Jeannie (patterned after Anne Sexton), and she senses that "some new element entered my chronic, anguishing indecision. 'Live or die,' she seemed to be saying to me from the grave."[17] For Margaret Drabble's Frances Wingate in *The Realms of Gold*, the message comes from the newts that she saw in the backyard when she was a child. The hero initially struggles with an inherited psychological tendency to despair, and it is the newts who teach her about survival and about pleasure:

> They were surely a sign to her, a blessing. They floated there, green-gray, pink-bellied, frill-backed, survivors from a world of prehistory, born before the Romans arrived, before the bits of bronze-age pot sank in the swamp, remembering in their tiny bones the great bones of the stegosaurus, a symbol of God's undying contract with the earth. They floated with an intense pleasure; she felt it herself, in the warm sun. And then, suddenly, silently, with one accord, they sank, swimming downward with their small graceful limbs, leaving bubbles to rise behind them from the depths. She had been left on the bank. But did not forget them.[18]

The protagonist in Annie Dillard's *Pilgrim at Tinker Creek* has a mystical adventure into nature, during which she receives an even more direct sensation of becoming visible and alive for the first time in her life: "It was less like seeing than like being for the first time seen, knocked breathless by a powerful glance. . . . I had been my whole life a bell, and never knew it until at that moment I was lifted and struck."[19]

Beresford-Howe's Eva, in *The Book of Eve*, tries to explain to the reader and to herself why on earth she decided suddenly, as she was carrying yet another tray up to her husband, to stop, gather up her coat and high blood pressure medicine and transistor radio and pension check, and walk out the door of their suburban home for good. In retrospect, she reflects, the exit seemed to be prompted by the arrival of the first pension check, the clocks striking throughout the house, and "the cold white autumn light pouring through the landing window as I climbed with the tray."[20]

Many times the call is a common event, a change in circumstances, which forces the hero to move beyond the familiar and secure life, and to discover new possibilities in the world and in herself. In Charlotte Brontë's *Villette*, Lucy Snowe comments, "I knew not that I was of a self-reliant or active nature; but self-reliance and exertion were forced upon me by circumstances, as they are upon thousands besides."[21] Like the traditional classical hero, Lucy Snowe is an orphan who is forced out of a conventional existence by the death of her parents. She must embark on a quest for survival. The call to the quest comes to Lucy Snowe in the form of a series of storms, which destroy the people who have promised to protect her and to provide her with a normal, conventional, "happy" life. We learn no details about her parents' death, only that "there was a storm, and that not of one hour nor one day. For many days and nights neither sun or stars appeared; we cast with our own hands the tackling out of the ship; a heavy tempest lay on us; all hope that we should be saved was taken away. In fine, the ship was lost, the crew perished" (p. 28). Left in poverty, she at first resists becoming a companion to the ailing Miss Marchmont, because she would be shut up in the house with no chance to experiment or grow; and yet, she agrees to this dull, secure service because of her admiration for the aged woman. Her choice suggests that, to her, goodness and suffering are synonymous. She admires Miss Marchmont for the way she endures her pain, and she evidences her respect by agreeing to be with her continually. Lucy recognizes that she "would have crawled on with her for twenty years, if for twenty years longer her life of endurance had been protracted" (p. 31).

Lucy recognizes, however, that "another decree was written. It seemed I must be stimulated into action. I must be goaded, driven, stung, forced to energy." She must be forced by catastrophe into the insecurity and vitality of life, because she "wants to compromise with Fate: to escape occasional great agonies by submitting to a whole life of privation and small pains." She concludes that "Fate would not be so pacified; nor would Providence sanction this shrinking sloth and cowardly indolence" (p. 31).

Looking back on her life, Lucy recognizes that "three times in the course of my life, events had taught me that these strange accents in the storm—this restless, hopeless cry—denote a coming state of atmosphere unpropitious to life." The second storm occurs while she is staying with Miss Marchmont. Lucy associates the storm, which rages all night, with "disturbed volcanic action, . . . rivers suddenly rushing above their bands" and "strange high tides flowing furiously in on low sea-coasts" (p. 31). By morning, the virtuous Miss Marchmont is dead.

Shaken in nerves and virtually bereft of finances, Lucy crosses the Channel to France in hopes of finding work as a governess. On board, she hears of a Madame Beck who has a school in Villette. Arriving in Villette at night, she has difficulty communicating, for she knows little French. She is befriended by a "true young English gentleman" who helps her with her bags; when she follows his directions to an inn, she finds herself at the door of Madame Beck's establishment. This seemingly supernatural intercession gives Lucy courage. She recognizes, "I planned nothing, and considered nothing: I had not time. Providence said, 'Stop here; this is your inn.' Fate took me in her strong hand" (p. 55).

Fate has to take a strong hand with Lucy, because she is so ambivalent about her freedom. Established at Madame Beck's, she rises from a position as governess of small children to that of English mistress of the school. From total isolation, she becomes part of the more respected society of the town. Within her reach, she recognizes, is the possibility of independence, of saving enough to open her own school. Yet she complains of the selfishness of this goal, and she mourns that there will be "nothing . . . dearer to me than myself. . . . Nothing at whose feet I can willingly lay down the whole burden of human egotism, and gloriously take up the nobler charge of labouring and living for others" (p. 329).

For Lucy, teaching school is not helping others; it is a means toward selfish independence. What she clearly desires is to "lay down the whole burden of human egotism" at the feet of a man. She falls in love with M. Paul, who aids her in setting up her own school and then goes off on a sea voyage. The years of his absence "were the three happiest years" of her life. Her school is a success; she buys the house next door, runs an inn, and prepares the house for his return. She notes, "I thought I loved him when he went away; I love him now in another degree; he is more my own" (p. 450). In spite of her veritable idolatry of this generous man, the reader understands that his return may limit her independence. He is, after all, as jealous as he is kind; in her words, he is "a tyrant." He disapproves of pink dresses and full-blown flowers in her bonnet, finally compromising on virginal buds. It is not likely that this man would facilitate the full blossoming of Lucy's passionate and independent nature. At this point, a third storm intercedes and saves Lucy from herself. It "did not cease till the Atlantic was strewn with wrecks: it did not lull till the deeps gorged their full of sustenance" (p. 451). Paul, who is returning to her from "an Indian Isle," is drowned.

These storms do not simply kill off people for whom Lucy would gladly martyr herself; they also come to her aid, and miraculously provide her with friendship when she is isolated and lonely to the point of despair. Left alone at Madame Beck's during vacation, Lucy is desperately lonely. She sees no end to the emotional void that characterizes her life. She is in such pain that her feelings become deadened, and she writes, "Oh, my childhood! I have feelings; passive as I lived, little as I spoke, cold as I looked, when I thought of past days, I *could* feel. About the present, it was better to be stoical; about the future—such a future as mine—to be dead. And in catalepsy and a dead trance, I studiously held the quick of my nature" (p. 140). Her stoicism, however, cannot contain her despair, and she visits a priest in a confessional just to have someone to talk to. Leaving, she realizes that she must not talk to him again, for then he "would have shown me all that was tender, and comforting, and gentle, in the honest Popish superstition. Then he would have tried to kindle, blow and stir up in me the zeal of good works." She realizes that the probable outcome would be that "instead of writing this heretic narrative," she would "be counting my beads in the cell of a certain Carmelite convent on the Boulevard of Crecy, in Villette" (p. 146).

She resolves to keep her independence of mind at all costs, and faints in the storm on the way home from confession. Recreating her experience, she hypothesizes that her soul went to heaven and was turned away and guided down "weeping" to reenter "her prison with pain, with reluctance, and with a mean and a long shiver" (p. 148). The storm corresponds to her inward emotions that rebel against the static, limited life she is living; this inward storm affirms her need for love, for friendship, and for a chance to grow and develop. Further, the storm again brings the change she needs. She is found, having fainted, by Dr. John, and taken home to his mother. It turns out that his mother is her godmother and their home, Bretton, the scene of her happiest childhood memories. Madame Bretton and her son, Dr. John, nurse her back to health and provide her with friendship and an introduction into society without threatening her independence. This is sometimes painful for Lucy, who loves Dr. John, and finds he sees her as only a rather casual friend. In the end, she gets not what she wants, but what she needs to facilitate her heroic life—a community that supports her but does not take away the burden of responsibility for her own life.

Like Richardson's Pamela, Lucy is not a complete rebel. She lives by the Protestant work ethic, and she remains as long-suffering and humble as her Protestant faith prescribes. The end of the novel is characterized by Lucy's enraged and stoical despair because she must live without the wealth, grace, and privilege that Dr. John and his bride Pauline take for granted. It is as though the outer storms conform with some inner instinct for survival that forces her to grow and to be adventurous in spite of her conventional opinions. At one point, discoursing on the injustice of her lot, she asserts, "Religious reader, you will preach to me a long sermon about what I have just written, and so will you, moralist; and you, stern sage: you stoic, will frown; you cynic, sneer; you, epicure, laugh . . . perhaps you are all right: and perhaps, circumstanced like me, you would have been like me, wrong" (p. 141). Like Huck Finn, she remains a reluctant hero and an ambivalent heretic. The years of M. Paul's absence were the happiest of her life—as she tested her powers by running a school and later a hotel as well. Yet her grief, when she learns of his death, reflects a yearning for the conventional female life that she has been taught to want. As we see in this case, the forces that aid the hero in the heroic departure may or may not be recognized by her or by her creator as fortunate.

As Lucy's story suggests, the physical difficulties associated with the exit may be very real. There is, for example, the problem of poverty in a society in which women are designated as lifetime dependents of fathers and husbands. Rita Mae Brown's Molly Bolt, in *Rubyfruit Jungle,* after she has run away from home, does not have enough clothes to keep her warm in New York in the winter: "My toes were ice cubes. I didn't have any socks. Who wears socks in Florida? . . . Now what the flying hell am I going to do?" Still she refuses to be kept by a rich woman in New York, saying, "Chryssa Hart, I'm not taking your enticing money. . . . I'm going to sit in that rathole and stay proud but poor."[22]

Poverty is limiting to the hero because it restricts opportunity for adventure and experimentation. However, affluence has its own dangers, as most religions have warned. Some heroes embarking on a quest therefore choose to leave possessions behind. The protagonist of Anne Tyler's *Earthly Possessions* notes that "my life has been a history of casting off encumbrances, paring down to the bare essentials, stripping for the journey." Possessions and relationships make her nervous because they delay her journey. "My only important belonging since I have grown up is a pair of excellent walking shoes."[23] She is determined to leave her husband, children, and all belongings, but as she goes to the bank to collect the needed funds for her getaway, she is kidnapped by a bank robber, and begins her journey without funds and also without the freedom to go where she pleases.

The important fact in both Brontë's and Tyler's stories is that it is not the physical difficulties that ultimately keep a protagonist unhappy in her new life beyond the garden or drive her back to her conventional environment. In both cases it is the inability to extricate herself psychologically from convention that makes her physical departure finally unsuccessful. Neither protagonist can see what Isadora Wing in Jong's *Fear of Flying* acknowledges: "I was a hostage . . . of my false definitions."[24] It is symbolically significant that the kidnapper of the protagonist in Tyler's novel is her double: She is metaphorically the hostage of her own attitudes, which may either free her or commit her to further entrapment.

Without the necessary confidence and determination, the hero may exit for a time and then return prematurely to the garden. Sasha Davis, in Alix Kates Shulman's *Memoirs of an Ex-Prom Queen*, gives up her quest for fulfillment and settles for having her hairstyle changed instead. The potential hero may doubt her ability to succeed on her own; she may be convinced that a woman can be happy only in the conventional role; or, like Huck Finn, who decides to free Jim from slavery and risk going to hell, she may act heroically but still believe that she is villainous. Lucy Snowe continues to be disappointed in her life even after she is financially secure with a school of her own, because she cannot extricate herself psychologically from society's message that a woman finds happiness only in marriage. For her the Cinderella myth never dies.

The hero who exits fully is the one who extricates herself psychologically from the messages of convention that may follow her out of the physical garden. For the hero who is able to free herself psychologically, even an involuntary expulsion becomes a blessed event in her life—although it often takes her a while to appreciate the "call" in the rejection. Specifically, when the initial separation from convention is involuntary, as in the case of the orphan, the "ruined woman," and the divorcée or widow, the hero may lose her prescribed place and subsequently have the freedom of action and of attitude to discover other possibilities, which her previous assigned position obscured from her. When society or the family rejects the hero it is usually because according to their rules she has sinned or has failed to fulfill her role as woman. In Rita Mae Brown's *Rubyfruit Jungle*, Molly's mother sees her daughter as completely disreputable:

> "I don't want to hear nothing you say. . . . You never obeyed nobody's rules—mine, the school's, and now you go defying God's rules. Go on, get outa here. I don't want you. . . . I can see conceit writ all over you face."
> "Then you'd better live to see me dead." I picked up my suitcase and walked into the cool night air.[25]

At the moment of rejection, Molly discovers her own strength of self-determination. As the novel progresses, she becomes increasingly in tune with what she knows and what she wants and increasingly careful not to capitulate that valuable self to any outside pressure. Hester Prynne in Nathaniel Hawthorne's *The Scarlet Letter*, Ruth in Elizabeth Gaskell's *Ruth*, and Rosamund in Margaret Drabble's *Thank You All Very Much* are all "fallen women." Each becomes wiser and more heroic as a result of her deviant experience and subsequent social exile. Picaresque heroes like Moll Flanders are freer to experiment with life than their more middle-class counterparts, who internalize the myths of virginity and self-sacrifice.

Heroes in literature exit when their actual experience conflicts painfully with the images of women that they have tried to live up to. Because women must wear masks to live up to unrealistic feminine ideals, they must hide their real personalities and are therefore extremely lonely. No one really knows the hero prior to her exit, for she plays out the projections of the culture, and perhaps also those of husband, lover, mother, and father. Until the moment of exit, she cannot truly love, for, as Anais Nin argues in *House of Incest*, to love one another we must "all escape from this house of incest, where we only love ourselves in the other."[26] This isolation and the unreality of the projections can ultimately drive women to madness. Nin suggests that the fear of insanity forces women to heal the split between self and world to depart on the quest: "Fear of madness, only the fear of madness will drive us out of the precincts of our solitude, out of the sacredness of our solitude. The fear of madness will burn down the walls of our secret house and send us out into the world seeking warm contact" (p. 47).

Whether she is thrown out of the garden or forced by events to acknowledge the extent of her solitude and victimization, the hero's dominant emotion may be murderous rage. Medea, for example, endures the role of selfless supporting character in the life of the insensitive and self-seeking Jason until he deserts her to marry a younger woman. Unable to accept this ultimately humiliating and deprived state, she is inflamed by anger sufficient to kill their two sons and Jason's new bride. In Sylvia Plath's "Stings," the speaker in the poem realizes that other women "thought death was worth it, but I / Have a self to recover, a queen." Plath pictures this queen as "flying / More terrible than she ever was."[27] In Plath's "Lady Lazarus," the protagonist after several suicide attempts is reborn like a phoenix and will "eat men like air."[28]

In response to the initial rage, the female hero, formerly passive and supportive by nature, may change abruptly into a dominating, destructive fury, as in the case of Medea or the speaker in Plath's poems. This rage may destroy the hero—or it may be a liberating call to the quest.

Indeed, consciously acknowledged rage turned toward the external source of one's oppression can be a sign that the heroic exit has occurred. Such rage, paradoxically, promotes life. In Joseph Heller's *Catch-22*, a woman in a brothel—so objectified that she is known only as "Nately's whore"—steps out of her role as a passive, sexual object because of her outrage at the news of Nately's death. She repeatedly tries to kill Yossarian (who gives her the news of her lover's death), although Nately was killed—like many others—senselessly in the war. Yossarian sees her violence against him as justified, however, because the cowardice that has kept him from challenging the military (and the macho assumptions behind it) contributed to Nately's death. Both Yossarian and Nately's whore are victims of this system, and both perpetuate it until they refuse to be exploited further. Yossarian recognizes that

> it was a man's world, and she and everyone younger had every right to blame him and everyone older for every unnatural tragedy that befell them; just as she, even in her grief, was to blame for every man-made misery that landed on her kid sister and on all other children behind her. Someone had to do something sometime. Every victim was a culprit, every culprit a victim, and somebody had to stand up sometime to try to break the lousy chain of inherited habit that was imperiling them all.[29]

Because Nately's whore rejects the passive, exploited role and reacts with anger, Yossarian finds the courage to reject the macho role and stop flying bombing missions. Both "break the lousy chain of inherited habit" by refusing to be victims and by asserting their responsibility to stop the creeping death that defines the culture. The humor of the novel suggests that beyond the rage is liberating laughter and hence hope.

Dorothy Bryant's *Miss Giardino* dramatizes the idea that rage can entrap or liberate, depending on whether it is acknowledged and accurately directed. Anna Giardino grows up in a poor Italian immigrant family. Her father, who "sang and was happy" in Italy, comes to America in search of a better life, and instead faces poverty and long years of labor in the coal mines. He begins to drink, to go into murderous rages, and to terrorize his family. Anna first exits on her quest during one of his drunken tirades. Having thrown a knife at one of his daughters, he comes at Anna, while his wife and all the other children cry in terror. She is described as standing still, "saying over and over in my head, I hate you, I hate you. I know if I stop saying it I will flinch, fall, even cry like Mama. I won't let him make me cry. I will die first."[30] Instead, she asserts, in English, that she is not afraid, knowing that "the words in English" would "hit his eyes like a whip," because it is "the language of the people who own the mines" (p. 8).

Her rage against her father makes it possible for her to defy him and a traditional life. She goes to college even though he disowns her when she does so, kicking her out and throwing her clothes out the window. Yet, to the end, they are like one another. For instance, in the large family, she is the only child who looks like him. As he lies dying of black lung disease, he is secretly pleased that his daughter has a college degree. And before his death, he tells her, "I . . . like you." When he says this, she recognizes that "he loves me. He has envied me and hated me, abused me, resented me. He has projected upon me all his bitterness and disappointment. And yet he does love me. He has always loved me" (p. 18). The tragedy of his life is that his rage, his hatred for his oppression, is directed not toward the world that oppresses him, but toward other victims like himself. He admires his daughter's accuracy and courage when she directs her anger toward him and then affirms herself in opposition to him and to the unsympathetic world.

Anna Giardino becomes a school teacher because of her commitment to the joys of intellectual growth—and also because it is one of the few occupations open to a woman in her time. Miss Giardino's role as a teacher is to call others to the quest. She wishes them to begin the process of intellectual and ethical growth, and comes to understand that what appears to be stupidity is more often a triumph of convention, of a decision not to grow. She once looks at a student, and sees

> that he has decided not to grow, but instead to use whatever intelligence he has to defeat my efforts to teach him. . . . Always after Willis, I see that look behind the eyes of any student who says, "I can't," the look that says "I won't," I hold them all responsible for that decision. I work with them patiently, persistently, but I never accept their refusal, never agree that, yes, they must be too stupid to learn. Maybe that is why, in later years, it is the ones who most disliked me who come back to see me. Those who had decided not to learn still knew that I respected their minds as they had not, that I saw their incapacity as a decision, that I never have given up trying to make them reverse that decision. (p. 72)

For most of the years Miss Giardino teaches, she courts her students' rage by pushing them beyond what they have come to expect. For them, as for her, the rage leads to growth and independence.

In later years, however, the philosophy of teaching changes. The other teachers, because they want to be liked by their students, in many ways abrogate their responsibility as teachers. Miss Giardino stands alone. When the students threaten to "break up and charge" teachers who presume to come through the front door of the school, all the other teachers go through the side door; Miss

Giardino, however, runs "that gauntlet" every day. At the same time, she is ridiculed by students and teachers alike for being a "hatchet-faced old maid." Instead of supporting her efforts to push every student to learn to his or her highest potential, the other teachers tell the students that she is repressive and conservative. Finally, the students stop letting her teach them.

Booker T. Henderson, a black student who refuses to do any assignments at all, becomes a test case. All the other teachers just pass him on. When she gives him an *F*, the other teachers and the student's union are outraged—ironically, charging racism. But finally, Booker writes a paper expressing his hatred for her, and she is thrilled. "Full of hate" and "full of errors," the paper nevertheless shows he is intelligent and teachable. Returning the paper full of corrections and encouragement, she recognizes that "he was on that edge, that edge whole classes used to be on, hating me because I threatened to change them, demanded work of them, demanded growth. That edge, where they would have to let go. Oh, they could pretend to hate me, outside of class, make fun of me, call me the old maid battleaxe, but in class they'd have to let go, secretly, one by one, they would give in, surrender, and let me teach them" (p. 133). Because he receives reinforcement from others only in his contempt for her and perhaps also because she requires too much surrender, he leaves school, blaming her.

Only years later, in retirement, does she vent her anger about the loss of human potential—hers as well as the students'—and then, like her father, she does so at the wrong target. She is angry at Booker, who at that moment symbolizes "everything I hated, everything that had gone wrong, everything about the school, about my life" (p. 143). Only when she acts on the rage that is paralyzing her does she come to understand it: "Madness piles up, fills you up, and must be let out. Was it as simple as that? Released madness makes others mad, and they too, must let it break out. Simple. An exchange of fury, endlessly repeated, the history of human life, the trading of destruction. What was there to be learned from this? That no one was exempt? That there was no way of stopping the future and destructive exchange?" (p. 145). Recognizing her own violence, she thinks of her father and understands him: "She had learned to understand him by becoming him. He had a vision of a better life and had strained himself to the utmost to go after it. So had she. He had been used and abused by the forces in which he had put all his hope. So had she. He had become filled with hatred and bitterness and despair, and had vented his hatred on the nearest targets. So, finally, had she" (p. 145). However, she recognizes a difference between them—her self-knowledge makes it possible for her to break this chain in a way that her father could not. If she fails to learn from her experience—if she stops growing and changing—she will "die in the same despair as her father, without even his hope of a new generation to benefit from his sacrifice" (p. 146).

Miss Giardino has placed all her hopes in education, just as her father had on emigrating to America. Disillusioned with her dream, she is on her way to burn down the school when Booker grabs at her purse. The very irrationality of being enraged with Booker—himself a victim—forces her to reexamine her motivations and enables her to become free of her obsession with educational institutions. She need not burn down the school because it did not fulfill her dream.

She sells her house, leaves all her possessions, and determines to "let go of it all. . . . Be free. No belongings. . . . Cut loose from responsibility" (p. 160). She is both alone and consciously part of a family tradition. She refuses to marry her old friend David and live with him in Europe, because to do so would be to imply that her "parents' struggle was for nothing" (p. 167).

At age sixty-eight, Miss Giardino begins a new life, freed finally from paralysis of despair and repressed anger. Having turned down David's proposal, she goes for a walk: "Just to her right, the fog had broken into a streak of blue, as if the sky were about to split wide open and unveil . . . 'angel wings!' said Anna, then laughed" (p. 168). Like many other female heroes, Anna Giardino learns that when she lets out her rage and learns from it, she feels exhilarated, as if she were flying, and her rage turns to laughter.

The call to the quest, then, may occur as catastrophe, alienation, disillusionment, or anger. It is the darkness before the dawn and the winter before the renewal of spring. Works about the heroic departure typically end with images of spring or dawn, suggesting faith in human worth and the efficacy of human endeavor. No matter how dismal the situation may be—and, as we have seen with the examples from the novels of Sarton, Heller, and Bryant, the situation is often very grim—these works suggest the capacity of heroic women to learn from their experience and to change their world. It is perhaps this optimism that makes the novel of the departure more often comic than tragic; yet even when tragic, works about the departure affirm our sense of human value and give us courage.

Another Universe

> There is always an enormous temptation in all of life to diddle around making itsy-bitsy friends and meals and journeys for itsy-bitsy years on end. It is so self-conscious, so apparently moral, simply to step aside from the gaps where the creeks and winds pour down, saying, I never merited this grace, quite rightly, and then to sulk along the rest of your days on the edge of rage. I won't have it. The world is wilder than that in all directions, more dangerous and bitter, more extravagant and bright. We are making hay when we should be making whoopee; we are raising tomatoes when we should be raising Cain, or Lazarus.
>
> Annie Dillard, *Pilgrim at Tinker Creek*

The departure anticipates the wholeness and community experienced in the heroic return. The "treasure" that is the hero's reward, therefore, exists potentially throughout the journey. At the moment of departure, the hero metaphorically moves into a new universe, a new way of seeing. Three contemporary fantasies—Tom Robbins's *Even Cowgirls Get the Blues*, Lisa Alther's *Kinflicks*, and May Sarton's *Joanna and Ulysses*—make explicit the change in consciousness that is implicit in more realistic works. Each novel portrays a woman living in a context that seems hopeless. From her own point of view or that of others, she is a victim who would do well merely to endure. She learns of an optimistic, heroic alternative, however, that changes her life by changing the way she interprets that life. In Robbins's words, "One can change things by the manner in which one looks at them."[31] Or, as Robbins's Bonanza Jellybean explains to the hero, Sissy Hankshaw, "Heaven and Hell are right here on Earth. Heaven is living in your hopes and Hell is living in your fears. It's up to each individual which he [she] chooses" (p. 129). In each work, this optimistic view is communicated by the comic tone of the novel. No matter how terrible the circumstances faced by the protagonist, the rather absurd humor of the novel continually undercuts a tragic view of human life.

Robbins's fantasy is absurdist and apocalyptic: He portrays American culture busy destroying itself. At the end of the work, his main characters are hidden away to await the inevitable apocalypse. The hero of Robbins's work, Sissy, is born with oversized thumbs. She receives her call to the quest when she is a young child, asleep under some newspapers. She overhears her father making fun of her thumbs to her uncle. In passing she hears her uncle say, " 'One thing. . . . That youngun would make one hell of a hitchhiker. . . .' Hitchhiker? The word startled Sissy. The word tinkled in her head with a supernatural echo, frozen in mystery, causing her to stir and rustle the funny papers so that she failed to hear the conclusion of her uncle's sentence: '. . . if she were a boy, I mean' "(p. 12).

The message that she has an unusual destiny is reinforced by the palm reader, Madame Zoe. Sissy's mother wants Sissy's palm read to see if she will marry. Although Madame Zoe assures her that Sissy will marry and have children, the palm reader's main emphasis affirms Sissy's heroic potential. Madame Zoe notes that "large thumbs denote strength of character and belong to persons who act with great determination and self-reliance," and she warns Sissy that she has "the qualities to become a really powerful force in society—God, if you were only a male!" (p. 27). She is disturbed by the quality and magnitude of these qualities, for Sissy's heroic potential is in a trickster mode: Sissy has "a capacity for foolish or clownish behavior, a refusal to accept responsibility or to take things seriously and a bent to be disrespectful of those who do . . . watch out for signs of irrationality" (p. 26).

The trickster tradition in Robbins's work defines an alternative to the static, death-oriented consciousness he identifies with American society. The trickster figure classically pokes fun at whatever society believes to be sacred, and represents the qualities society represses. In Robbins's novel, the society's repressiveness is linked to an overemphasis on order, conformity, seriousness, and rationality, and to the devaluation of sexuality and of women. The trickster philosophy values individuality, irrationality, spontaneity, natural sexuality, and femaleness. The novel opens with a comic dedication to the novel's mascot: the amoeba. The amoeba lives in water; water is "always in motion, ever-flowing (whether at steam rate or glacier speed), rhythmic, dynamic, ubiquitous, changing and working its changes, a mathematics turned wrong side out, a philosophy in reverse, the ongoing odyssey of water is virtually irresistible. And wherever water goes, amoebae go along for the ride" (p. 2). Like the amoeba, Sissy, the hitchhiker, is always in motion and leaves no traces. Rather than attempting to dominate and control her fate, she enjoys riding the flux of life.

The novel's guru, comically called "the Chink" (he is of Japanese, not Chinese, origin), has built a "clock works" that ticks (or gongs) chaotically. In the individualistic trickster tradition he refuses to talk with the many pilgrims who journey to him, seeking the "meaning of life." He is a helpful mentor to Sissy partly because he embodies this comic, trickster ideal, but also because he—unlike her husband Julian—does not try to control, define, or rescue her.

Although Sissy learns to understand her situation through interaction with mentors such as the Chink and Bonanza Jellybean, she says no to the culture's view of her and affirms her own potential long before she meets them and long before she comes in contact with political and philosophical ideas that give a context to her actions. Taken as a teenager by a social worker to a dance for handicapped students, she "screamed, 'I'M NOT HANDICAPPED, GODDAMN IT!' The cry turned Guy Lombardo's sugar to lumps. The dancers stopped, some taking longer to wind down than others. They stared at her. A few of them giggled and cackled. Then, one by one, they began to applaud (some of them clapping with one hand, in flailing and unintentional illustration of Zen Buddhism's most famous koan)."[32] In Robbins's view, the students are not "handicapped"; they are unique.

Sissy's moment of enlightenment is reinforced when she stands before her mirror and realizes that she is beautiful. She could work, save her money, and have plastic surgery, and then she could lead a "normal human female life." But every time she thinks "normal life,"

> Her thumbs talked back to her in thumbtalk: tingles, throbs and itches. Until at last she knew. Accepted what she had always sensed.
>
> She had been correct when she had howled at the dance. They were not a handicap. Rather, they were an invitation, a privilege audaciously and impolitely granted, perfumed with danger and surprise, offering her greater freedom of movement, *inviting her to live life at some "other" level*. If she dared. (p. 43)

Sissy accepts the challenge. Not only does she become the best hitchhiker in the world; she also transforms hitchhiking into a Zen experience.

Sissy succumbs to convention twice. The first time, she does so out of loneliness, marrying Julian and settling down to be a housewife. When she cannot adjust to a static life and begins to feel the urge to hitchhike again, Julian takes her to a psychiatrist. He wants her "to overcome her affliction instead of reveling in it" (p. 171). However, Dr. Goldman admits that he can only help "crazy people" who "can be made to confront the source of their damage, to compensate for it, to reduce their disadvantageous substitutions and to adjust to the degree that they can meet most social requirements without painful difficulty." In other words, he can only help people who accept the societal verdict that they are damaged. He has no luck with people like Sissy, "because the only way you can get them to give up their craziness is to convince them that the world is actually sane" (p. 172).

Goldman assigns Dr. Robbins to Sissy's case, and he—not she—is profoundly changed by the encounter. Initially, Dr. Robbins confronts Sissy with her crime—which was the act of setting Julian's birds free. He tells her it was an inhumane gesture because they "had been in a cage their whole lives with somebody to provide for them. Now they're having to fend for themselves in a huge alien city where they don't know the rules and where they're probably frightened and confused! They won't be happy being free." Sissy demonstrates the wisdom she has acquired in her attempt to be a normal housewife: "There's just one thing in this life that's better than happiness and that's freedom. It's more important to be free than to be happy" (p. 174). After talking with Sissy, Dr. Robbins "calls in well" and quits his job.

Sissy's first rejection of conventional living and affirmation of the magic potential of her thumbs was done in innocence. The second time she exits—from the confines of a marriage—she does so with knowledge, gained from her negative experience in the marriage and from the positive example of Chink and the cowgirls of the Rubber Rose Ranch. In both cases, she learns a prolife, pronature, feminist ethic. The Chink explicitly teaches Sissy about a female tradition in Western culture more viable and more in keeping with her nature than the patriarchal one: "Yes, if you scratch back past the Christian conquest into your true heritage, you will find women doing wondrous things. . . . Women controlled the Old Religion. It had few priests, many priestesses. There was no dogma; each priestess interpreted the religion in her own fashion. The Great Mother—creator and destroyer—instructed the Old God," and was "his equal and ecstatic partner" (p. 233).

Patriarchy and Christianity in Robbins's novels are aligned with death-in-life, and pagan matriarchal religions (like the trickster tradition) with joy, fertility, and life. Robbins explains that the word "carnival" is derived from *carrus navalis* ("cart of the sea"), which comes down to us from matriarchal times through the later rites of Dionysus. He notes that we have carnivals because "pagan festivals were deeply entrenched in the hearts and minds of the people, and they weren't inclined to give them up. Substitute the cross of guilt and suffering for the sea cart of joy and fecundity? Somehow that didn't seem like an A-1 good deal" (p. 272).

The villain of the novel is the Countess, a millionaire who has made his fortune selling feminine deodorant spray. This spray (Yoni Yum) is a symbol of the antilife, antifemale bias of the death-aligned culture. The Countess ran the Rubber Rose as a health spa where women lost weight, learned how to be attractive to men, and most of all learned not to smell. The cowgirls, who were workers on the ranch, rebel and take it over, teaching women to have pride in themselves and their womanhood. Appropriately, the whooping cranes, the symbol of nature's survival in the modern world, change their migratory patterns to stay on the cowgirls' land.

Sissy has learned from the Chink and the cowgirls, but it takes a crisis to move her out of her captivity. And the crisis comes. When the Countess insults the cowgirls as "smelly" and "sluts," and says he is going to inform the authorities that they have the whooping cranes, Sissy's formerly peaceful thumbs move into action and she beats the Countess until he is virtually a vegetable. Sissy escapes and hitches a ride with a man who tries to rape her, all the time telling her how much women like to be humiliated and hurt. Once again her thumbs strike out in fury.

Horrified, Sissy retreats. She decides to amputate her thumbs, for she is afraid of her own anger and her power to destroy. After one thumb is amputated, however, she is "jostled awake, alive" by the news that the whooping cranes have been located at the Rubber Rose Ranch. Her love for the cowgirls and her need to affirm female power enable her to keep her one magic thumb and join the cowgirls in their struggle with the antihuman, antifemale, anti-whooping crane G-Men.

Although Robbins shows that it is crucial that Sissy not turn her anger on herself and amputate her specialness, violence is dangerous and to be avoided. Bonanza Jellybean, whose role models are macho cowboys, dies in the conflict, acting out her childhood fantasy of being shot in the stomach with a silver bullet. It is clear to the reader that the cowgirls are no match for the violent overkill planned by the G-Men.

They are saved from destruction by the intervention of a vision. Just as the battle is about to begin, "Niwatukame, the Great Mother," appears to Delores in a vision and provides a female tradition of rescue. In this case, the message is first to value the self enough to save it: that is, the cowgirls should run away rather than be killed in a fruitless battle with the patriarchy. Second, it reminds them of a female tradition and a way of seeing that frees the cowgirls from the "us or them" mentality characteristic of patriarchy. The real villain, the Great Mother reveals, is not men, but limited patriarchal ways of seeing: "the tyranny of the dull mind." (Note that Anna Giardino in Bryant's novel experiences a similar realization when she recognizes that burning down the high school will not stop the forces that stifle growth. To work against the status quo, she must first free her imagination from the despair and rage that paralyze her and keep her in the grasp of old ways of seeing.)

The violent, confrontational mode, Robbins suggests, shows a failure of imagination. The Chink explains that picking "fights with authority" is stupid. "They're waiting for that; they invite it; it helps keep them powerful. Authority is to be ridiculed, outwitted and avoided." He suggests ignoring the death-aligned culture while it destroys itself. In the meantime, "If you believe in peace, act peacefully; if you believe in love, act lovingly; if you believe in every which way, then act every which way, that's perfectly valid—but don't go out trying to sell your beliefs to the System. . . . If you want to change the world, change yourself" (p. 352). Sissy, Delores, and Dr. Robbins move into the Chink's cave, creating a new society on the fringes of the old. The whooping cranes learn to survive by altering their once predictable migratory pattern to an unpredictable one: "The birds moved on—and are still moving. Nobody knows where they'll turn up next" (p. 360).

In this way, the matriarchal-pagan and trickster traditions come together in Robbins's novel to suggest a viable, anarchistic, comic alternative to the patriarchal status quo. The antidotes to violence and rage are imagination and laughter; hence the outlandish humor that informs much of Robbins's novel. The absurdist comic mode, furthermore, serves to communicate the consciousness associated with the heroic departure and espoused by Robbins in this work. As Dr. Robbins explains to Dr. Goldman, patriarchal culture encourages people to try to control their lives, to dominate others, and to seek security rather than adventure—or else, in a more mystic mode, it teaches them to transcend experience. Setting up Sissy as a model, Robbins argues that the transcendent model smacks of hierarchy and the class system: People always want to leave where they are and move to a higher social status or a higher state of consciousness.

> The trick is not to transcend things but to *transform* them. Not to degrade them or deny them—and that's what transcendence amounts to—but to reveal them more fully, to heighten their reality, to search for their latent significance. I fail to detect a single healthy impulse in the cowardly attempt to transcend the physical world. On the other hand, to transform a physical entity by changing the climate around it through the manner in which one regards it is a marvelous undertaking, creative and courageous.
>
> And that's what Sissy has done since childhood. By erasing accepted standards of perception, she transformed her thumbs while affirming them. (p. 239)

It is this affirmation of life, and the imaginative altering of one's relationship to life, that in Robbins's novel signifies the consciousness that liberates the hero from captivity.

Affirmation and transformation are accompanied by related beliefs in the importance of growth and personal autonomy and in the world of endless possibility. When Dr. Goldman condemns Sissy for being "immature," Dr. Robbins suggests that the hero should not be mature (i.e., "predictable and unchanging") but always growing, changing, learning: ". . . she's still growing, it means she's still alive. Alive in a dying culture" (p. 240).

The terms that Robbins uses to describe Sissy's successful exit from the garden of convention are those that define the archetypal heroic departure—action, change, rescue, knowledge, freedom, vision, transformation, growth, and life. *Even Cowgirls Get the Blues* may be considered an example of the heroic journey that follows the initial exit; or it may be viewed, as it has been here, as one long exit, which is executed gradually, in stages, as the hero gains strength from each partial success at independence. Because the moment of exit takes the hero from the world of stasis and convention into the world of potential, the qualities inherent in the moment of departure are the same as those discovered at the end of the journey. Thus the moment of departure may be considered to contain, in potential form, all the qualities of the return. In fact, the experience of the exit itself—to borrow Robbins's phrase, "a marvelous undertaking, creative and courageous"—is the first treasure that the hero receives; but the treasure, implicit in the exit, is not fully realized until the return. Sissy has "transformed her thumbs while affirming them" since childhood. Her antagonists undermine her vision and also, by their obstructiveness, enable her to identify the forces that threaten to limit and stifle her and her kingdom. Her mentors aid her in intellectually understanding and fully affirming the heroic mode she embodies. By the end of the novel, therefore, she fully understands and owns the qualities she has intuitively valued since infancy.

While not every work encourages an anarchistic solution, works describing the heroic departure all affirm life and emphasize the importance to the hero of growth and autonomy. The rejected environment, which values authority and orthodoxy and represses the process of experience and feeling, may receive several labels. For Robbins, as for many feminist authors, the hero's consciousness is associated with a matriarchal-pagan tradition. Nineteenth-century works, of course, are not likely to use these terms. Lucy Snowe, in Charlotte Brontë's *Villette*, contrasts her Protestantism with the "slavishness" of the Catholics who surround her. Whatever the labels—patriarchy versus matriarchy, classicalism versus romanticism, Catholicism versus Protestantism, Christianity versus pagan religions, conservative philosophy versus radical idealism—the shift in consciousness involves similar elements. In each case, the hero renounces the values of the old world because these values, which may have rejuvenated the culture in times past, have become the new orthodoxy that strangles new growth. The attributes she embodies must be a countertradition in her culture—that is, there must be some sympathy in the culture for these ideas—or she will be portrayed as deviant or mad, rather than heroic. If her values are shared only by the reader and not by the fictionalized culture the hero inhabits, she is likely to die, go mad, or give up and conform.

Although the ideas the hero embodies may well be an important strain in the culture, she does not ordinarily accept a new orthodoxy—except as one stage in her growth process. Doris Lessing's Martha Quest, in *The Four-Gated City*, initially rejects the conservatism that dominates the culture and becomes a Marxist. She leaves the Communist party, however, when she recognizes that Marxism is another cage that limits her intellectual growth. The progress that Martha Quest and other female heroes make is an interesting feminist variation on the dialectical process. Disillusioned with the conventional values of her society, the hero adopts their apparent opposite, only to recognize in the end that the antithesis is very like the thesis. Martha Quest moves beyond her culture's way of perceiving the world when it becomes clear to her that both capitalists and Marxists see the world in similar ways. The new, undefined alternative she creates challenges the assumptions that were axiomatic to both capitalists and Marxists. For example, Martha does not accept the economic determinism or the male dominance that characterize both capitalism and socialism in England. The discovery of an additional alternative beyond those the culture provides (for Martha Quest, this discovery involves psychic phenomena) seems to move the protagonist into a different universe from that she previously inhabited.

This progression from thesis to antithesis to an entirely new way of seeing is typical of the beginning stages of the hero's journey. In Lisa Alther's comic novel *Kinflicks*, for example, Ginny Babcock begins in a conservative, death-aligned household. The first sentence of the novel sums up her conditioning: "My family has always been into death."[33] Paralyzed by an awareness of death, the family is afraid to live. Ginny remembers spending her childhood in cemeteries or listening to her mother writing her epitaph and rewriting her funeral ceremony. Her mother has also accepted a deathlike life in that she martyrs herself for her children. The mother had "smothered" her children "with her martyrdom" (p. 261). Ginny escapes this gloomy and limiting atmosphere as well as her masochistic relationship with a high school boy when she is forced to go to college. Fleeing the traditional role for women, she initially becomes enamored with its opposite. Since women conventionally have had the choice of being mothers or unmarried, virginal career women (usually teachers), the first role model Ginny finds is Miss Head, her college professor. With the beginnings of the radicalism of the 1960s, however, Ginny goes beyond the ivory-tower example of Miss Head. Recognizing the need for sexuality and for political action, she becomes a lesbian and a radical, lives in a commune, and eats health food; but she is still defined externally. She chooses this life-style not because she particularly believes in it but because she wants to please her female lover, Eddie.

Her life is less a viable alternative than a simple antithesis of the conventional life she has rejected. Thus the portrait of Eddie—like that of Miss Head—is a caricature: Eddie is as domineering and violent as the redneck men she hates. Overcome by hatred of macho men riding their snowmobiles across the commune land, Eddie strings a single strand of barbed wire at neck level to stop them. Going on a "kamikaze mission, in which she would mow down as many of the congregated snow machines and drivers as possible," she runs into the barbed wire herself, and almost literally "loses her head" because of her suicidal anger.

In another act of simplistic revolt, Ginny responds to her disillusionment with radical lesbianism by marrying Ira, one of the snowmobile drivers, and by having a child. When he catches her rather ineptly trying to have an affair, she goes home to mother, only to find that her mother is in the hospital with leukemia, and is bleeding to death internally.

In many ways Mrs. Babcock is Ginny's mirror—the self Ginny is to become if she goes back to Ira and her child. Mrs. Babcock's death is congruent with the way she has led her life: "The pattern had always been Mrs. Babcock's bleeding herself dry, as it were, for the children. . . . 'I live but to serve,' she had quipped gaily. . . . But there had been truth in this quip, she now knew. Ceasing to serve, she had collapsed, mentally and physically" (p. 261). Mrs. Babcock is filled with rage as she realizes the irony of her life. She notes that she raised three children as an amateur and "now that she was a professional, having turned out three finished products, her skills were no longer in demand, and it was too late to rectify mistakes committed during her apprenticeship" (p. 261). Her rage and sense of having been cheated, however, do not lead her to find a new life. Instead, her blood cells turn on her and eat her up. It becomes clear in this case that sacrifice does not bring life or salvation, but merely more death and sacrifice.

Ginny stays with her mother, hoping that she will learn from her some great human truth that will help her make some sense out of her life. She feels unparented, because she has been taught by her parents—and by Eddie and Miss Head—a great deal about death, but little that is useful about how to live. Finding some fledglings that have fallen out of their nest and been deserted by their parents, she sees in their plight an analogy to her own. She consults a bird book, only to learn that the experts say that since birds in the swift family "feed on partially digested regurgitated food from the parent bird," they cannot be kept alive in captivity. The expert, Wilbur J. Birdsall, suggests "it is best to kill such birds should they be found, to avoid prolonging their suffering" (p. 24).

Women are frequently associated with birds. In Richardson's novel *Clarissa*, Lovelace likens Clarissa to a caged bird who should learn to love her captivity and her captor; Hardy's Tess is likened to a hunted bird; Chopin's Edna Pontellier is symbolically associated with a caged parrot and later with a bird with a broken wing, trying to fly; Robbins's Sissy lets Julian's birds escape. Ginny's determination to save the birds is linked in her mind with her desire to live a free, liberated life, not merely to live out a prescribed maternal, intellectual, or radical role. Should the birds live, she believes, the experts would be proved wrong, and she also might be able really to live—not merely to fill a stereotyped role. "She wouldn't buckle under to the verdict of Wilbur J. Birdsall, world renowned authority or not" (p. 263). And as her mother reexamines her life, she is able to reinforce Ginny's skepticism about "expert advice," particularly since the doctor's expert opinion is always useless, if not entirely wrong.

One of the birds Ginny rescues lives to learn to fly. Ginny interprets this as a good omen. But the bird kills itself—needlessly. It begins to fly indoors and instinctively flies toward the light, hitting a closed window. Retreating, it sees itself in the mirror and panics, believing the mirror-image to be an enemy. The bird flies back and forth between mirror and closed window. As Ginny tells her dying mother, "the bird beat itself to death on a closed window, but the door next to it was *wide open*" (p. 261).

This parable, of course, exposes, in Robbins's term, "the tyranny of the dull mind." Like the self-destructive bird, Ginny has flown from the traditional female role to various versions perceived as its opposite or mirror image. She wants "meaning," and defines that meaning as a prescribed role of some sort. Without an adequate role model for her behavior, she finds life meaningless. Confused and feeling unable to choose between a number of inadequate alternatives, she attempts in turn unsuccessfully to drown and then to shoot herself. Finally, she succeeds in making "a small experimental cut on her left wrist" with a hunting knife. Watching the blood, she begins to wonder whether she, like each blood cell, might be

> a cell in some infinitely larger organism, an organism that
> couldn't be bothered with her activities any more than she
> could be with those of the 60 trillion cells in her own body, as

long as they performed their assigned functions? And were there, say, white blood cells that—not being able to see themselves as Ginny could, as a group, under magnification, stained to highlight determining characteristics—had not been able to figure out what their "assigned function" was, whether they were supposed to perform as macrophages or neutrophils or eosinophils and lymphocytes? And did those perplexed blood cells then take it upon themselves to self-destruct in a huff at not receiving enough individual attention and guidance from her personally? Autophagy, it was called, when cells unleashed on their own cytoplasm their suicide bags of digestive enzymes. Autophagy, which literally meant "self-eating." (p. 518)

Ginny's mother's cells kill her when they do just that. Alther's conceit here suggests that contemporary humankind, hurling the culture toward suicide because of its own alienation, despair, and rootlessness, is guilty of egotistical—albeit potentially fatal—posturing in demanding "meaning" and a clear sense of its own role. In short, each "cell" is taking itself too seriously.

Ginny's final understanding is comic. Considering "autophagy" or "self-eating," she thinks of a former boyfriend's description of an "incident during his adolescence in which he and his hoodlum friends had hunched over their own laps, vainly trying to eat themselves" (p. 518). This association makes Ginny laugh, and she notes that "her proposed suicide had degenerated into burlesque. Apparently she was condemned to survival." A comic recognition of the interdependence of all things enables her to walk through the door, "to go where she had no idea" (p. 518). The hero departs with a humble yet confident stance. She recognizes that she can live without road maps, without sure knowledge of where she is going or what she will do. She sees, sometimes only faintly in the beginning of the journey, that the culture's dualistic definitions are false and inappropriate and that there is something inherently comic about the inexplicable mystery of existence.

This is the recognition that frees both Alther's Ginny and the protagonist in May Sarton's *Joanna and Ulysses*. Joanna at first assumes that she can be either a conventional woman, living for others (her father in this case), or a professional painter "with all that implies of competition and status."[34] She chooses the former until at age thirty she takes her first holiday—a painting holiday on the Greek island of Santorini. She recognizes that had she been a professional painter, she "might never have found the joy that was with me this morning when I *saw* the essence of a few stones and was able to communicate it, at least to myself" (p. 52). In the holiday, she adopts neither the persona of the helpmate nor that of the status-conscious professional. Instead, she devotes herself "to the impossible," and recognizes that "there lies joy" (p. 51). The impossible, moreover, is to see clearly, without limited cultural preconceptions, the world outside the self.

Like Ginny, Joanna learns of the open door beyond the mirror and the closed window, apparently by accident. She expects her holiday to provide a temporary relief from the prison of her despair but not to free her altogether. She greets her holiday thankfully, for it comes after "years and years of waiting for this moment, years of war, years of near starvation, years of such stress and horror that she put them behind her" (p. 11). She has been mother to her father and two brothers since she was fifteen and her mother was killed by the Nazis. Her mother worked with the Resistance, helping prisoners escape, and finally was captured. Her torturers put burning cigarettes in her son's ears to make her talk, but he screamed, "Don't tell, mother, don't tell!—And she didn't tell." They tortured her and "when she was no use to them or to anyone else, they shot her." Joanna goes on to explain how her father never recovered, but sat in a dark room and "tried to die himself" (p. 63).

Joanna spends the next fifteen years of her life serving her family, but "deep down inside there was a being who was not the dutiful daughter she had forced herself to become." That self is an artist. Sarton's account of her encounter with the inner, secret self is fantasy—in tone, almost a fairy tale. She chooses the island Santorini for her holiday "because it is inaccessible and remote as a dream" (p. 13).

The first thing she encounters on reaching the island is the very suffering and cruelty that she has tried to escape. Two impoverished men are beating an ailing donkey to force it to carry a heavy load up a hill. Joanna challenges them, warning them that the donkey is dying. They reply that they are poor and cannot afford to feed a sick animal; they only hope it will carry the load to the top before it dies. Enraged, Joanna loses all rationality and does the only thing she can think of to free the suffering animal. She buys it—at a ridiculously inflated cost. Thus, she begins her holiday with funds depleted, walking along with a half-dead donkey behind her.

It is this unlikely animal that calls her to the quest. She immediately christens the donkey Ulysses, and thereby Sarton suggests a link between her quest and that of great Greek heroes. As in Robbins's and Alther's novels, the heroic awareness is comic. Joanna's hidden heroic self is symbolized not by an impressive animal, but by a comic, awkward one. As she nurses Ulysses' wounds and strokes his ears, "she . . . felt life come back into her fingers" (p. 65). Like Heller's Nately's whore, she brings life by saying no to, in her own words, "the endless chain of suffering" (p. 65). After her holiday, she cannot bear to part with Ulysses and takes him home to Athens, where she hides him in the cellar. She recognizes that "this was more than just hiding a donkey from her father, that in fact what she was doing was trying to bring together two parts of herself" (p. 105). Furthermore, she sees that part of herself—the artist and the hero—which is personified in Ulysses as foolish. Both her father and the Santorini villagers think her a fool, and she laughs with recognition that

> the real Joanna whom she had kept secret for so long had now assumed a visible shape—she had to laugh, for it seemed appropriate that this shape should be that of a donkey! Yet perhaps for the very reason that Ulysses had become the symbol of her other self, she found it impossible to tell her father and be done with it, once and for all. She was frightened not only of his anger, and impatience with what would seem to him the purest folly of course, but she was also afraid that if she had to render Ulysses up, she would, so to speak, be giving up the living part of herself which had begun to paint again. (p. 110)

She gains the liberating comic or foolish vision on Santorini not only from a donkey, but also from a young boy who often comes to talk with her. Although she, her father, and her brothers have never spoken of the tragic death of her mother, she tells the young Nicholas about it when he asks her why she has never married.

When she allows herself to remember her mother, Joanna remembers not so much the pain as her mother's passionate, vital nature. She sees her "coming up the path, waving a great bunch of wild red anemones and crying out . . . anemones—the blood of Adonis . . . aren't they a splendor? Look at their dark hearts" (p. 62).

When she tells Nicholas about the torture of her mother and brother, he reacts, not with shock and horror, but with exultation. He explains, "I am so proud of your mother. I am so proud of your brother" (p. 63). His exultation opens the door of new possibilities for Joanna. In a moment of time, she focuses not on the ugliness and cruelty, but on the beautiful, heroic courage of her mother and brother. At this moment of the shift in consciousness, Ulysses begins braying at another donkey "like . . . some demon in agony. It was very funny—such unholy sounds emerging from such a meek creature, and especially as they were the sounds of love" (p. 64). Joanna and Nicholas dissolve in laughter. When the young boy leaves, she muses that "Nicholas had not even tasted the bitterness; he had swallowed the hard exhilarating liquor of freedom instead. . . . And it was as if she were being brought out at last from a dank, dark cell where all she could think of was suffering, the endless chain of suffering" (p. 65).

Back in Athens, when she shows her father her paintings, Ulysses emerges from the cellar (having chewed through the rope). The donkey's emergence from the cellar is a literal enactment of the emergence of Joanna's heroism and art from their imprisonment in the cellar of her despair. Her father is astounded by the quality of her paintings, and equally astounded by learning that he is sharing his home with a donkey. Joanna's heroic departure from convention has a ripple effect. Her saying no to suffering and bringing her artistic self out of hiding enable her father to live once again. He recognizes her "fire" and says, "Don't just stand there looking like your mother!" For the first time, they can talk about her. Joanna tells him how "if you shut out pain, you shut out everything, Papa! . . . Don't you see, how everything stopped—my painting became trivial, my life too. I could not remember Mother as she was. We shut her out . . . like shutting out life itself!" (p. 124).

Their refusal to live was a way of sparing themselves the agony of loss, but it had the effect of denying everything Joanna and her father valued in her mother. Joanna says, "Even her death was an act for life. That is what I learned on Santorini . . . a little boy, Nicholas he was called . . . he shone like a star when I told him the story. . . . Nicholas made me remember what it is to be a Greek, to rejoice and be proud! Do we mourn the dead at Thermopylae? No, we rejoice in them. They give us courage" (p. 124).

Her father understands; he encourages her to quit her clerical job and paint. Recognizing that she is afraid to take the chance, he enjoins her to "remember your mother and her power to dare! Oh that woman and her daring power! For her, nothing was impossible. Even to die was not impossible" (p. 125). The affirmation of life that characterizes the hero includes all of life. R. D. Laing explains the psychological principle: "It has always been recognized that if you split Being down the middle, if you insist on grabbing *this* without *that*, if you cling to the good without the bad, denying one for the other, what happens is that the dissociated evil impulse, now avails in a double sense, returns to permeate and possess the good and turn it into itself."[35] Because they were trying to escape death, Joanna and her father could not live; because they were trying to escape pain, they felt neither love nor joy. Through absurdly affirming life and death, pain and joy—apparent contradictions—they can live fully and heroically. It is only with this heroic consciousness that Joanna can transform her life. Her apparent options—the martyr role and its apparent opposite, the professional role, "with all that implies of status and competition"—stultify full creativity and the ability to see the essence of things. Joanna affirms all of life and makes a decision to continue to grow in pain as well as joy. Thus she creates a third option: She can be an artist.

Sarton ends the parable with a saying very close to Robbins's "Great Secret." Because Joanna has claimed her absurd, artistic self, Ulysses is no longer her double. She no longer projects onto him. Instead he is merely a needy donkey and friend who she recognizes would never be happy living in a cellar in Athens. She gives him to Flavis, who sells weavings on the beautiful island of Mikonos, and who closes the novel with the assertion that "sometimes fantasy and fact become indistinguishable, or, if you will, the hard facts may be turned into miracles when love, imagination, and sheer necessity all work together."[36]

The comedy of Robbins, Alther, and Sarton does not suggest that the hero will always overcome adversity; she may, in fact, like Joanna's heroic mother, even be tortured or die. Although killed, she is not broken, and her death testifies to human courage and to the life force. Further, in these comic works, the death of the hero is not motivated by "hubris"—for the heroes are proud, but humble in that they understand their essential vulnerability. Like Robbins's amoeba or whooping crane, they cannot totally control their social or natural environment; but they can learn to live in that environment in a heroic and imaginative way and to learn ways to affirm life against an environment that is violent, repressive, and conformist.

As we have seen, the most negative occurrences often force the heroine to a heroic and noble life. As Math says in Evangeline Walton's contemporary fantasy *The Children of Llyr*, "Even energy that has been turned to pure evil has its part in the pattern. . . . But I think that only gods could bear to look at the pattern."[37] The hero is not "above," looking down on human endeavor; she is often confused, living in the flux. Therefore, she does not try to eliminate all suffering and pain, but to affirm life in all its manifestations, and through this affirmation to transform it.

Shattering the Mirror

> *The female, in the terrifying, exhilarating experience of becoming rather than reflecting, would discover that they too have been infected by the dynamics of the Mirror World. . . . Looking inside for something there, they would be confused by what at first would appear to be an endless Hall of Mirrors. What to copy? What model to imitate? Where to look? What is a mere mirror to do? But wait—How could a mere mirror even frame such a question? The question itself is the beginning of an answer that keeps unfolding itself.*
>
> Mary Daly, *Beyond God the Father*

The exit, or liberating moment, becomes possible for the female protagonist when she identifies the particular figures in conventional society who have restricted her and who have, more importantly, taught her that she must repress and doubt herself. These representatives of the status quo endeavor to pass on to her the conventional myths about women, which degrade her, limit her freedom, and cause her to distrust her own perceptions. In keeping with classical heroic terminology, we will call these representatives of conventional society the captors. Those who discourage the hero's journey may be friends, teachers, employers, children, or any others with political, social, economic, or psychological power over the hero. The final two sections of this chapter will focus on the hero's relationship with her most common captors: parents, and husbands or lovers.

In fairy tales, the maternal and paternal captors are the Wicked Witch and the Ogre Tyrant. In realistic fiction, they are the parent figures who first socialize the young girl to be ladylike. In this way, the parents hold up the mirror that keeps her, like the Lady of Shalott, enthralled by an image. In this mirror, she measures herself against the ideal of feminine beauty, selflessness, and chastity. She is trained to believe that she will die if she stops being a reflection of the culture's ideas about women and acts out of her own understanding and her own desires.

The parental captors—whether actual parents, guardians, or symbols of the culture's maternal and paternal ideals—have the power to arrest the hero's development only to the degree that she is, or perceives herself to be, a dependent child in need of their protection and approval. Anaïs Nin points out in her diaries that the world appears monstrous, and the captors enormous, only from a child's point of view. The imposing figure of the "Enormous Parent . . . does not need to be permanent."[38]

The heroic exit occurs, moreover, only when the hero stops believing that she must convert her captor in order to begin her quest. Nin notes that in order to be liberated it is not necessary to destroy the "Enormous Parent" nor to impose "our own truths" on our captors. The hero classically departs alone, recognizing both her freedom and her ability to determine her own life. The women of the Boston Women's Health Collective write in *Our Bodies, Ourselves*, "We began to see our passive helpless ways of handing power over to others as crippling to us. What became clear to us was that we had to change our expectations for ourselves. There was no factual reason why we could not assert and affirm our own experience and do and act for ourselves."[39]

Such direct and creative action is possible only when the hero is no longer bound by dependence on the love and approval of her captors. Molly Haskell in her study of women in the movies, *From Reverence to Rape*, asserts that women become heroes instead of victims when they stop seeing themselves through the mirror of others' opinions. Haskell cites a scene from *Beyond the Forest*, starring Bette Davis. " 'I don't want people to love me,' Rosa says—one of the most difficult things for a woman to bring herself to say, ever, and one of the most important. . . . The superfemale becomes the superwoman by taking life into her own hands, her own way."[40]

The hero shatters the mirror when she values herself enough not to be imprisoned by her need for love or social approval. The heroic departure may be the only possible resolution to the conflict between her need to grow up and her desire to please her parents. The tension the hero faces is not different in kind from that experienced by the male hero; it differs only in degree. The female hero's departure from childhood dependence on the parents is complicated by two factors. First, the culture does not encourage women to be fully independent and adult; therefore, a girl's decision to march to the beat of her own drummer seems a more unusual and unnecessary act than a similar decision on the part of her brother. Boys are expected to grow up at some point. Girls, on the other hand, are expected to be dependent on, and protected by, first parents and then husbands. Their independence—because unexpected—is more likely to be interpreted as a rejection of the parents than is a boy's more expected rebellion. Second, the potential female hero has internalized the myth of female inferiority; therefore, she has a greater need for approval and validation than does her brother. It is thus harder for her to risk her parents' displeasure.

The mother and the father often initially appear as captors to the girl child. In some instances, the daughter remains a captive; in others she escapes to freedom. But rarely does she depart easily or without regret, for however negative the parents' influence has become, she typically both loves and needs her parents. The initial exit from parental captors, then, often feels more like a dismemberment than like a liberation. The symbolic "slaying" of the mother and the father feels like the destruction of part of the self.

Two circumstances make her departure easier, however. In some cases, the parents themselves may recognize the inadequacy of the traditional images of women and thus encourage their daughter to shatter the mirror and undertake the heroic life. In others, the parent figures are unbending, but the hero in studying her parents recognizes that they are themselves victims. Ella Price in Dorothy Bryant's *Ella Price's Journal* questions why her parents had "to keep rushing me and trying to cram me into the same molds that have made them so unhappy."[41]

The departure in such cases may focus on the need to escape the fate of the parents. Christie, in Louisa May Alcott's *Work: A Story of Experience*, explains to her Aunt Betsey that she is leaving her home before she becomes as "sharp and bitter and distrustful" as her uncle; but it is also clear that she wishes to be independent. Christie tries all the respectable (and some not so respectable) occupations for young women: She becomes a servant, an actress, a governess, a companion, and a seamstress. Many years later, after marrying, having a child, and being widowed, she becomes a feminist activist. In the end, she finds she is much happier living such a varied and adventurous life than her more security-minded aunt and uncle: "Nearly twenty years since I set out to seek my fortune. It has been a long search, but I think I have found it at last." A feminist organizer and mother, who feels both independent and useful, she asserts, "I *know* I am happy."[42]

In traditional myth and literature, the captor is more likely to be female than male; in fairy tales, she is the wicked witch or stepmother. In *Snow White*, for example, the wicked queen sees herself as a competitor to the young Snow White. Her most characteristic act is looking in the "magic mirror" to discover "who is the fairest one of all." When the aging queen discovers it is Snow White and not she who is the fairest, she dedicates her life to destroying the young girl. The reader is to assume that women are by nature competitors. The wicked stepmother's main function is to be cruel to her children. In fact, Cinderella's stepmother is gratuitously cruel, forcing her stepdaughter to slave away while her other daughters go to the ball. In *Hansel and Gretel*, the stepmother talks the apparently powerless father into abandoning his children in the forest, presumably to starve to death. Once the children are in the forest, the witch takes over and attempts to eat Hansel. When Gretel kills the witch, the stepmother magically disappears, and the father retrieves his children.

The fairy-tale explanation for the hero's dependence on the stepmother or witch is that her good, biological mother is dead. The dual image of good, dead mother and wicked stepmother represents conflicting cultural myths: the belief that mothers are all-sacrificing, quasi-divine martyrs and the equally strong belief that women are inherently evil and use their power destructively. They also provide the hero with two role models that are mirror images of each other: the good, dead mother and the evil stepmother.

Contemporary literature tends to fuse the two images. In twentieth-century fiction, the chaste, selfless martyr is seen as destroyed or as destructive. In Ira Levin's *The Stepford Wives*, suburban wives are systematically killed and replaced with Disney-style robots who make superior housewives and lovers because they have no ambitions or desires of their own. In Philip Roth's *Portnoy's Complaint*, the martyr-mother destroys the son. Twentieth-century literature about the female hero focuses on the discovery by the hero that the conventional role will both destroy her and make her a destroyer.

The unhappy mother turns her rage on her potentially heroic daughter because the mother believes that only the daughter can justify her original sacrifice—by duplicating it. Ella Price, the hero of Dorothy Bryant's novel *Ella Price's Journal*, writes, "I remember my mother always saying, 'Well, raising a baby is the hardest job in the world,' and that sentence was full of meanings. It meant 'I worked so hard raising you.' It meant, 'Nobody could ever be as good a mother as I was.' It meant, 'Now you must sacrifice yourself as I did.' "[43]

The hero may break the chain of hereditary feminine martyrdom, however, by determining to choose a life different from that of her mother. Ella Price does so, as does Marie in Agnes Smedley's *Daughter of Earth*. Marie's family is very poor, and her father becomes a drunkard because of his own broken dreams and thwarted aspirations. Her malnourished mother, who works long hours taking in other people's laundry, is beaten and deserted by her husband. She sacrifices all she can for children who most likely will live the same life she did. Marie notes that "her tears they embittered my life."[44] Marie determines not to have children, because to do so would doom her to a life of powerless dependence like that of her mother. Instead of turning her anger on children or other women, she becomes a Wicked Witch in a new, revolutionary sense, turning her fury on the economic system that oppresses her father and mother.

For the traditional woman, however, women's conventional roles seem unalterable, so that the mother may feel that it is an evidence of love to repress her daughter enough that she is not likely to deviate from the expected role. If the daughter automatically polices herself, the logic goes, she will not be punished for deviation. If she is so repressed that she does not know her life is limited, she will not suffer from unfulfilled yearnings for a more adventurous life. Charlotte Perkins Gilman's mother, according to her daughter's autobiography, discouraged anything other than traditional female behavior. She believed that a daughter should "remain in her mother's sphere until she entered her husband's." At sixteen, Charlotte eagerly shares her first poetry with her mother, who listens with little interest and then tells Charlotte to "go and put the kettle on." Her mother's message is a complex one. She does not want to encourage her daughter's ambitions, since they will only be thwarted. Nor does she want to encourage sensibility. Charlotte's mother felt she had suffered because of her romanticism and her susceptibility to love. As a result, she denied her daughter all expressions of affection. Later she explains, "I did not want you to suffer as I had suffered."[45]

Mothers who feel victimized often blame their martyrdom on sexuality and emotions. They discourage their daughters from trusting their own feelings. Like Del Jordan's mother in *Lives of Girls and Women*, they warn their daughters that men are beasts out to ruin them. They counsel, not revolution, but chastity or frigidity, because sexuality for women leads to ruin or domination. Mrs. Quest in Doris Lessing's *The Four-Gated City* tells Martha that men are "filthy creatures. . . . Sex. That's all they think of."[46] Because Martha is having an affair with her employer and friend, her mother accuses her of being evil and perverted. Mrs. Quest is "possessed" by her own feelings of betrayal and anger because she has not been rewarded for her acceptance of the traditional female role. Rather than admit she has been deceived, she hates both men and the sexuality that made her vulnerable to them, and projects her own conflicts onto Martha.

Martha yearns for her mother's love and approval and therefore is ambivalent about living a more liberated life than her mother did. When she finally realizes that her mother is imprisoned by her own anger, Martha is freed from paralysis. She sends her mother to a psychiatrist and thereby asserts her own judgment that her mother (and not she) is sick. Mrs. Quest interprets this judgment as a rejection and leaves Martha's house and her life. Having asserted that it is her mother, not herself, that needs help, Martha is free to confront the inner voices that have always echoed her mother's charges of depravity and selfishness.

The fairy tale of Rapunzel allegorically presents the dilemma discussed here. The witch entraps the beautiful maiden because she loves her. Chastity protects the mother-daughter bond from romantic love, for if the daughter (or the mother for that matter) falls in love, it is expected that her love for the prince will take precedence over her love for mother or child. Chastity, however, is its own confining tower; hence, Rapunzel, in choosing to remain cloistered, to deny her sexuality, also rejects the witch—whom it is clear she loves.

In this matriarchal variation on the Adam and Eve story, Rapunzel and the Prince's sexual assignation precipitates "the fall." Both literally "fall" from the tower. His punishment is blindness; hers is childbirth. It is her suffering, moreover, that eventually cures his blindness, and allows him to see. In feminist literature, the young girl's rejection of the Wicked Witch is usually followed by a similar rejection of her role as suffering redeemer of her male sexual partner. Hence, her suffering at the loss of both mother and lover leads not so much to a man's renewed ability to see or understand, as to her own.

Clara Maugham of Margaret Drabble's *Jerusalem the Golden* embarks on a quest because she is terrified that she will become as imprisoned and devoid of feeling as her mother. She also fears she will eventually become enslaved by her mother's helplessness. If she returns home to care for her mother, she will live a life as drab and bare of feeling, sensation, and beauty as her mother's. The mother's internalized rage has made her numb. When her husband dies, she tells Clara, "Well, he's gone and I can't say I'm sorry."[47] Clara's tears at the cemetery are "not for her father, but for the meanness and lack of love." Her mother's initial response to Clara's birth is negative: She chose the name Clara after a Wesleyan great-aunt, "not as an unusual and charming conceit, but as a preconceived penance for her daughter whose only offenses at that tender age were her existence and her sex." Mrs. Maugham did not like the name; she "chose it through a characteristic mixture of duty and malice" (p. 5).

Clara's mother disapproves of her intelligence and accomplishments, "yet her mother herself was no fool, she had never herself possessed the lovely blessing of stupidity; she had merely crushed and deformed and dissembled what rights she had once had, in deference to what? To a way of life, perhaps to a town, to a suburb in a town in the north of England?" (p. 6). The recognition of her mother's deformity gives Clara the courage to seek a freer, more beautiful, and more varied mode of existence. She begins a quest to avoid becoming her mother and meets the handsome and fascinating Gabriel. Unlike Rapunzel, however, she refuses to remain with the Prince, for "it was not one man that she needed, but through one man a view of other things, a sensation of other ways of being, she wished to feel herself attached to the world" (p. 207).

Clara fears that she will live her life for her mother because she does, after all, love her. Her situation is doubly complicated because she needs and loves her mother and because the mother seldom acknowledges to herself (much less to her daughter) that she is, in part, an unhappy, frustrated oppressor. The daughter longs for love from her mother. She longs for encouragement to grow, to experiment, and to live a freer life than women have had before. Kate Millett, in her autobiography writes of the conflict she feels about maintaining a bisexual life-style in the face of her mother's disapproval. Millett wants a freer life than her mother had, but she also wants her mother's love and approval. As she works on her next book, Millett decides, "I will dedicate this book to Mother. . . . It will heal. The perfect pipe-dream, ultimate pie in the sky. She will read me and know who I am and accept. Always she says, 'Write a book I can show to my friends.' This will hardly satisfy the requirement. Mother living in St. Paul—with my queer notoriety, her first pride in my success turned to gall. And how much worse this time? But what if she accepted my dedication? I'll try it!"[48]

In Anne Sexton's case, the impossibility of gaining her mother's approval leads to a debilitating obsession with the relationship. In "The Division of Parts," she writes of trying "to shed my daughterhood," yet she recognizes she is a "fool" to try. She writes, "I fumble my lost childhood / for a mother" and while she tries "to exorcise the memory of each event," she remains "still a mixed child," the prisoner of the "Sweet witch" whose love she craves."[49] Many of Anne Sexton's poems speak of the pain she feels because her mother takes the daughter's unhappiness as a rejection. In "The Double Image" Sexton writes of returning to her mother's house "to catch at her" and finding that she has "lost her." "I cannot forgive your suicide, my mother said. / And she never could. She had my portrait / done instead."[50]

The attempt to win the approval of an angry mother may lead to great achievement, as it does in Sexton's or in Millett's case. On the other hand, it may motivate the daughter to attempt to live a life very much like the mother's. When the mother appears to be happy in the traditional role, the daughter has more difficulty escaping. She not only feels that she will lose her mother's love and approval if she lives a nontraditional life, but she is also likely to believe that since her mother insists that she is happy in the traditional role, there is something wrong with her (the daughter) if she wants something more. Sasha Davis's mother, for example, in Alix Kates Shulman's Memoirs of an Ex-Prom Queen, teaches her that she cannot function in the world without a man. In her view, beauty, passivity, and a degree of helpless suffering will get a rich man and, with him, automatic security and happiness.

Sasha's mother is so anxious for the Cinderella myth to be fulfilled in her daughter's life that she simply insists that it will be. She refuses to admit her daughter's human imperfections, and therefore fails to help her daughter understand and deal with her actual fears and self-doubts. Even the braces on her teeth, which are meant to ensure Sasha's beauty, undercut her confidence. Sasha contrasts her attitude with her mother's. "While to her, busily imagining the future, the advent of my braces only made the eventual triumph of my beauty more certain—indeed, it was for the sake of my looks that they had been mounted at all—to me they discredited my mother's optimism."[51]

Sasha is susceptible to belief in the Cinderella myth and its rewards. She passively waits and wishes for a miracle, because her mother appears to have fulfilled it. When it became apparent to the world that her father would have a "brilliant career" as a lawyer, Sasha reports, "My mother, as clever and ambitious as he, heeded the predictions and married him. Already loved by my father at a distance, my mother, the youngest and fairest of the family of lovely sisters on my father's ghetto block, had no trouble at all—so went the story. In America beautiful clever girls do not long remain schoolteachers" (p. 51). The result of Sasha's belief in the myth is that she feels inadequate and guilty for failing to be happy as a wife and mother.

When the hero is unhappy in the traditional role, the mother who seeks validation through her daughter may withdraw her love. Miriam, in Marge Piercy's *Small Changes*, gives up a thriving career and has a baby in a futile attempt to become a "good girl" and propitiate her long-dead mother. Her mother had died accusing Miriam of not loving her and of being a whore. Eventually, trying to be "good," Miriam shrinks into a nagging, insecure, dependent heroine, afraid to leave the husband who rants at her, belittles her, and will soon, we are led to believe, leave her. Thus, the conflicting desires for a strong mother-daughter bond and for a heroic life paralyze the daughter when the mother is committed to traditional sex roles. The woman who gave the hero life and who gave her own life to nurture and protect her growing children may nevertheless bind her daughter's mind as Chinese mothers bound their daughters' feet. She tells the hero that she must not only stop growing and give herself to the service of husband and children, but that she must do so joyfully and without question. To choose the self is often, then, to deny the mother; to choose the mother is to deny the self. Either option appears unthinkable.

Given this double bind, one might assume that it would be best if mothers gave their daughters no advice at all. Yet literature also recounts the destructiveness of a total absence of maternal guidance. Daisy Miller's mother, in Henry James's short novel *Daisy Miller*, is so innocent and weak that she cannot help Daisy learn the rules of European society, which they enter. Daisy is snubbed by her hostess at a party for her indiscreet flirtatiousness. The hostess, Mrs. Walker, turns her back on Daisy, and her mother does not even notice what has happened: "Daisy turned very pale, and looked at her mother; but Mrs. Miller was humbly unconscious of any violation of the usual social forms."[52] In fact, Daisy takes care of her mother. It is symbolically significant that Daisy at one point gives her mother her shawl to wear and later takes ill from the damp Italian night air and dies.

Mrs. Miller consistently expresses dislike for all Daisy's suitors, yet offers her daughter no constructive advice on how to be wise or self-sufficient in relationship to men. Daisy then turns to men to guide her—to men who assume the roles of judges or seducers. Daisy is, as Winterbourne says, a "flirt." Because she turns to men for approval and protection, she is snubbed by the conventional European women (her wicked stepmother). Against society's conventions, she goes with Giovanelli to the Colosseum at midnight, and as a result dies of Roman fever. It is clear, however, that her death could have been prevented if she had received affection and guidance from any source. Winterbourne, the conventional narrator, recognizes too late, "She would have appreciated one's esteem. . . . She would have reciprocated one's affections" (p. 132).

James's story is conventionally (and rightly) interpreted as a study in the deleterious effects of American innocence. But it is also an indictment of specifically *female* innocence—in Daisy and in her mother. Daisy Miller does not want the protected life of the conventional woman, but she has been given neither the knowledge nor the strength to deal with the world on her own. Like Madame Bovary, she makes the initial leap to happiness and self-fulfillment but is ultimately destroyed. Yet her capacity to think for herself, her courage to undertake unconventional behavior, seem preferable to the uneventful life of the more socially acceptable, conventional young woman. James's novel might discourage unconventional behavior in women, as it reinforces the idea that women who deviate from cultural norms die. At the same time, the story clearly implies that it is the society, the repressed mother, and the would-be lover, Winterbourne, who are responsible for Daisy's destruction.

The naive, ineffectual mother is a stock figure of comedy. Jane Austen, for example, often satirizes such women as Mrs. Bennet in *Pride and Prejudice*, described as "a woman of mean understanding, little information, and uncertain temper. When she was discontented she fancied herself nervous. The business of her life was to get her daughters married."[53] Mrs. Jennings in *Sense and Sensibility* is similarly parodied: "a widow, with an ample jointure. She had only two daughters, both of whom she had lived to see respectably married, and she had now therefore nothing to do but marry all the rest of the world."[54]

The obsession with marriage is a natural extension of the woman's sense that women as women are insignificant. She understands the importance of men's loving women, but not of women's loving each other or themselves. Jacqueline Lapidus, in the contemporary poem "Coming Out," speaks of the pain of loving a mother who does not return her passion. Instead of loving her daughter, the mother advises her to find a man to love her "for herself." The poetic persona mourns that "She couldn't tell me / ways to love myself / she didn't know."[55]

Connie, the protagonist of Marge Piercy's utopian novel *Woman on the Edge of Time*, does not feel loved by her own mother and consequently cannot love herself. In turn, she is ambivalent about her child. Connie has wanted her mother's comfort. She has wanted her mother to share her pursuit of knowledge and some better way to life. "She had never been mothered enough and had grown up with a hunger for mothering. To be loved as [her brother] Luis had been loved."[56] In turn, she realizes that she has failed her daughter: "She should have loved her better; but to love you must love yourself, she knew that now, especially to love a daughter you see as yourself reborn" (p. 56).

The central characters of Lisa Alther's *Kinflicks*, Margaret Atwood's *Surfacing*, and Anne Tyler's *Earthly Possessions* all have similarly ambivalent relationships with their mothers. Each attends her dying mother, hoping finally for truth that will give meaning to her life; when the mother fails to provide this legacy, the daugher feels bereft, deserted, unmothered. Tyler's Charlotte Emory sums up the hope, saying, "I couldn't let loose of her yet. She was like some unsolvable math problem you keep straining at, worrying the edges of, chafing and cursing. She had used me up, worn me out, and now was dying without answering any really important questions or telling me a single truth that mattered. I was furious."[57]

Charlotte's mother, who has internalized the message of her own inadequacy and hence assumed her daughter to be inadequate, has always complained that Charlotte was the wrong daughter, that the nurses switched babies in the hospital. Somewhere her real, beautiful, blonde baby was living with the wrong parents. On her deathbed, the mother gives Charlotte a picture of a little blonde girl, and Charlotte assumes it to be her mother's "real" daughter. In a sense it is: It is a picture of the mother as a child. Charlotte finally recognizes that the hostility the mother feels toward her has nothing to do with her; it concerns only her mother's lost self. Further, Charlotte's mother cannot provide her with the wisdom she needs, because her mother has not lived in any full sense. Instead she got fat, "sat home and ate chocolate caramels, and made things—pincushions, Kleenex-box covers, Modess-pad lady-dolls to stand on bureau tops. . . . she lived her life alone behind her gauze curtains" (p. 13). Charlotte can engage fully in life only when she recognizes that she is not responsible for her mother's victimization and conversely that the mother is not responsible for the daughter's entrapment. Charlotte remains in an unfulfilling marriage, but not for her mother's sake. She chooses to remain in the town she hates and in the marriage she finds so dull and inadequate even after her mother's death, but she is forced to confront the fact that she is responsible for her own life.

Ginny Babcock, in Lisa Alther's *Kinflicks*, has a similar moment of realization after her mother's death. When Ginny's estranged husband suggests a reconciliation, she at first sees his proposal in the light of her guilt-ridden relationship with her mother:

> Ginny froze, thinking of her bruised mother, who had been a real wife, a real mother—for as long as she was needed. How would her mother advise her? To profit from her example and behave differently, or to copy her martyrdom and thus validate it? Ginny studied the question. Then she remembered that what her *mother* wanted or didn't want of her was no longer to be the determining factor in her life. The leading lady had magnanimously removed herself from Ginny's script. Ginny was on her own.[58]

Ginny departs on her heroic journey for the first time when she makes this choice for herself: "No," she says, because "there was too little time left to condemn herself to a living death at age twenty-seven" (p. 511). She makes this decision for herself, not for her mother. However, her choice validates her mother's potential, if not her example. Protagonists such as Ella Price in *Ella Price's Journal*, Martha Quest in the Children of Violence series, and Isadora Wing in *Fear of Flying* all reject their mother's example. They all, however, are able to do so only when they see their mothers, not as ideal women role models, but as victims of patriarchal roles.

Because of the absence, the complexity, or (as will be made evident in a later chapter) the invisibility and potential subversiveness of the mother-daughter relationship in patriarchal society, many authors choose to avoid it. Most women in literature have mothers who are either dead or absent. Daniel Defoe's Moll Flanders, Jane Austen's Emma Woodhouse, George Eliot's Dorothea Brooke, Charlotte Brontë's Lucy Snowe and Jane Eyre, and Henry James's Isabella Archer are only a few of the well-known protagonists without mothers. But whether the mother is dead, absent, or merely an inadequate role model and mentor, the fictional protagonist feels a void in her life and yearns for a positive, heroic, and nurturing tie with a maternal model. Adrienne Rich in "Re-Forming the Crystal" mourns that "The Woman / I needed to call my mother / Was silenced before I was Born."[59] In *Of Woman Born*, Rich argues that it is not only the victimization of individual mothers that binds the minds of their daughters, but also the cultural myth of female inferiority, which teaches the protagonist that she is inadequate—that she is not important in herself, but only in relationship to men and children. Each daughter covertly expects her mother to be wise and loving enough to counter this antifemale message. Rich concludes, "Whatever our rational forgiveness, whatever the individual mother's love and strength, the child in us, the small female who grew up in a male-controlled world, still feels at moments, wildly unmothered."[60]

The resulting frustration can either cause women to be hostile to all other women or motivate a quest in search of a mother-daughter bond positive enough to counter the patriarchy's undermining message about femaleness. In this instance, the sense of being "wildly unmothered" serves as a call to the quest. The contemporary author Margaret Drabble, during an interview, noted that

> For many years my mother was very depressed. . . . One had to find some images of liveliness or color or love that were different from what one had been brought up on. I don't know how I would have developed if I'd known my mother as she is now. She is so much more cheerful and active. I might have had a completely different view of needing to leave the family or having to find other mother figures. But I certainly do—did, I think—look for other mother figures. I think everyone does. What one is looking for is just patterns of living in other people.[61]

The narrator of Muriel Rukeyser's poem "More Clues" says that her mother's silence has forced her to go "searching in women's faces" for "the lost word."[62]

The search, however, may produce only further disillusionment and unfulfilled yearning if the women encountered have repressed their own desire to find "the lost word." Kate Millett in her autobiographical novel, *Flying*, speaks of the dilemma of being both a feminist and a lesbian. As she observes the faces of the traditional women in the Time-Life Plaza, to whom she looks for sympathy and support, she feels instead shame for having shocked "the tourist ladies in the little hats with veils over their sparkle glasses, my mother's hats from my own Middle West. . . . For a moment embarrassed at having assaulted their reality, its values neatly arranged like Mother's. In order. Is it not some species of cruelty even to exist when your existence so affronts others? Was it out of this consideration that we have hidden for centuries? We who are your children."[63] This female complicity in oppression between women of different generations leads Millett to say, "Mirrors are endless reflections, lively like water and light. In another woman you see yourself. . . . But for me my mirrored self has always been a stigma, accusing me" (p. 297). In an essay called "The Woman-Identified Woman," the Radicalesbian Collective also uses the mirror metaphor in arguing that because of the myth of female inferiority and because of women's powerlessness in society, traditional women identify, not with other women, but with the powerful, "superior" male:

> They try to escape by identifying with the oppressor, living through him, gaining status and identity from his ego, his power, his accomplishments. And by not identifying with other "empty vessels" like themselves, women resist relating on all levels to other women who will reflect their own oppression, their own secondary status, their own self-hate. For

to confront another woman is finally to confront one's self—the self we have gone to such lengths to avoid. And in that mirror we know we cannot really respect and love that which we have been made to be.[64]

Without support from other women, the hero is likely to flounder and, in some cases, even to give up the quest.

In Kate Chopin's nineteenth-century American novel *The Awakening*, Edna Pontellier's mother is not discussed. The women she sees around her, who are potential role models and substitute mothers, give her no indication of how one combines selfhood and motherhood. As Edna begins to awaken to her own powers, she observes with horror the egotistical selflessness of these women, whom she calls the "mother-women": "It was easy to know them, fluttering about with extended protecting wings when any harm, real or imaginary, threatened their precious brood. They were women who idolized their children, worshipped their husbands, and esteemed it as a holy privilege to efface themselves as individuals and grow wings as ministering angels."[65] Edna kills herself because she has no model for any way to be true to herself without destroying her children.

Ella Price in Dorothy Bryant's *Ella Price's Journal* complains that such women refuse to tell the truth about motherhood and punish or silence women who do so. Ironically, the act of giving birth—the most obvious capacity that differentiates women from men—is defined by male attitudes. Ella notes,

> I remember that when I had Lulu a lot of women were having "natural childbirth" (as if there's any other kind) and I read some articles that said women only felt pain in childbirth if they were tense and neurotic. It seemed as if, if you couldn't hypnotize yourself into believing it didn't hurt, you were a nut. Such a profound experience for so many women—and you can't even be honest with yourself about it much less talk about it. Right after Lulu was born, when I looked at her I felt afraid. I felt a part of me has been cut away from me. It can get into danger, it can drift off from me into the world, and what happens to it happens to me, but I can't control what will happen. I felt helpless and vulnerable in a way I never had felt before. And I knew I always would feel that way. I didn't like the feeling.[66]

The protagonist of Jane Lazarre's *The Mother Knot* wonders if she will be able to share honestly the wonder, terror, and horror of her experience as a mother even with a women's consciousness-raising group. When she finally confesses to a friend on the telephone that motherhood is "quite miserable and exhausting," the friend "maturely" advises her not to say that. As a result, she stops going to the group, because she is convinced that "I was the only mother in the world who had such hateful feelings for the child I loved so intensely." She determines to hide her "real feelings in order to avoid the terrible looks which say, I am not like you nor have I ever been."[67] She recognizes that the conspiracy of silence about motherhood denies her own experience and, in a more general sense, denies her.

Central to the departure is the act of naming—of perceiving the realities obscured by myths about motherhood and about women and relabeling them. One recurring plot situation, as suggested in this chapter, is the young woman's confrontation with an older, maternal figure who lives a traditional life and who personifies the values the culture associates with femininity or womanliness. This figure serves as a living embodiment of what the heroine is expected to become. When the hero realizes that the role is destructive to the maternal figure and to those around her, she is free to reject the role without rejecting the women who embody it.

Literature frequently deals with the experience of the preheroic woman as she observes in another woman the destruction and falsity of the traditional role. Iris Murdoch's contemporary novel *The Unicorn* is an allegorical study of the woman who becomes a slave to conventional myths. The potentially heroic character who learns from the imprisoned woman is Marian Taylor. Marian answers an ad in the paper for a governess at a remote estate in the English countryside and finds she is in fact expected to be a companion to a grown woman.

The woman, Hannah Crean-Smith, turns out to be a damsel in distress who is caught in a spell, not before but after Prince Charming has taken her away from her family and set her up in a castle. Murdoch explains that Hannah is trapped in Gaze Castle because she is under "a psychological spell, half believing by now that she's somehow *got* to stay here."[68] The fascination for Marian, as for many female heroes, is what keeps the other woman, the traditional one, voluntarily living the confined life, submitting to her own oppression.

The story of Hannah Crean-Smith, as Marian Taylor learns it, is that she is very rich; her family owns Gaze Castle and all the land around it. She has married her cousin, Peter Crean-Smith, who has turned out to be both brutal and perverse. Marian is told that he was "a drinker and a runner after women and violent to his wife and other things more. It was not a good marriage. She was unhappy" (p. 62). Hannah and Philip Lejoin, who lives in the adjoining estate, "fell in love with each other, and they made love to each other" (p. 63). One day, seven years before Marian's arrival, Peter finds them in bed together. A scene follows in which Peter rushes after Hannah to the cliffs; somehow, he falls over the edge and is rescued from death only by a ledge jutting out below. It is not clear whether Hannah vented her rage against her husband by pushing him over the edge, but the public is convinced, and they justify her husband's decision to confine her by believing that "she deceived him and tried to kill him" (p. 62).

Ironically, the very forbidden emotions—sexuality and rage—that lead some women to exit from the cage motivate the traditional woman's complicity in her confinement. Hannah Crean-Smith is her own jailor out of guilt for her own sexuality, expressed as a result of a need for love, and for her feelings of hatred toward her husband. The only emotion less socially acceptable than free sexuality for the traditional woman is rage against men. The more rage she feels the more guilty she becomes, and the more she colludes with her captors in her punishment. She is imprisoned by guilt and self-hatred.

Hannah also exhibits the kind of inertia that everyone in the novel shares. Even her former lover, Philip Lejoin, "watches and waits" (p. 65). Each character seems to be a damsel in distress of one kind or another, waiting in the garden without personal will for someone else to act and break the spell. This passive state associated with traditional women has become characteristic of everyone in Murdoch's world. Hannah, for example, "was, in some mysterious way, it seemed, totally resigned, almost as if she were condemned to death or already dead" (pp. 77–78). Her resignation precludes any consideration of happiness or freedom, which seem frightening, evil, distasteful, and threatening to the spell that protects her from feeling and choosing for herself.

Free of responsibility for herself, she has become the powerful mythic center of her immediate world. She controls and entraps those around her because of her suffering, and they find themselves unable to leave as well. Murdoch suggests that she is the ultimate traditional woman—obedient, repressed, entrapped, mythologized, "a great placid golden idol," who also appears as a figure of "odd spiritual, tormented yet resigned beauty" (p. 75). Murdoch also exposes the enormous egotism of this traditional role. Hannah's guilt justifies her imprisonment, but she also sees herself and is seen as a selfless Christ-figure, suffering for the sins—especially sexual sins—of the world. She is the unicorn, which is "the image of Christ," and also what one of her observers calls "an ordinary guilty person" (p. 101). Marian eventually recognizes the presumption and egotism behind the claim to suffer for or redeem others. "Hannah," she comments, "you are the most sublime egoist that I have ever met" (p. 231). Many have written of the destructive powers of the martyr "Mom" in the twentieth century; Murdoch has one of the male characters sum up the victim-victimizer essence of the traditional role: "She may be just a sort of enchantress, a Circe, a spiritual Penelope keeping her suitors spellbound and enslaved" (p. 102).

Murdoch's novel, then, illustrates "the violence that lay behind the legend of the sleeping beauty" (p. 185). The enchanted princess victimizes the prince, the dwarfs, and the other princesses, and she is also victimized by them. Murdoch suggests that they feed on each other in a closed system that excludes life and that is typified by ennui and a vague sense of dread. Effingham tells Marian that the function of Hannah is that of a ritual communion: "We're all eating her up somehow, all of us" (p. 146). Her suffering is envisioned as "eating" evil and sorrow and thereby ridding the world of it. When word comes that Peter is returning, Effingham remarks, "Hannah would make it all well. She would swallow it all up, she would assimilate the evil news and make it not be, she would suffer Peter internally as she had always done, and there would no more be heard" (p. 185).

Hannah sees no alternative to her role. A spiritual orphan, she has no mother. When she once attempted an escape from her husband to her father's house, he refused to see her and sent her back. Marian comes to recognize that Hannah's wholehearted adoption of the role of scapegoat and martyr is her way of surviving her total dependence on an oppressive husband.

> She began, this is how I see it anyway, by being simply afraid of that beastly man, just paralyzed with fear. Then she became rather apathetic and miserable. Then she began to find her situation sort of interesting, spiritually interesting. People have got to survive, and they'll always invent some way of surviving, of seeing their situation as tolerable. At the time when Hannah might have survived by just hating them all, or might have survived by just bursting out and kicking it all to bits, she decided to become religious instead. . . . Hannah took to religion, or the spiritual life or whatever the hell it is, like someone taking to drugs. She had to." (p. 222)

The traditional woman, represented by Hannah, is the scapegoat for the culture. She suffers for Peter's crimes as well as her own. As Max, one of her observers, comments, "She is our image of the significance of suffering" (p. 101). She adopts this role because everyone tells her she cannot be free. "She is a legend in this part of the country. They believe that if she comes outside the garden she will die" (p. 66). To become a suffering martyr is her only way to make her inevitable captivity dignified and significant. Marian observes: "All the time she was being more and more hypnotized by the situation itself and by all those people surrounding her and murmuring into her ear in different tones, but all murmuring it: you're imprisoned. And now she's simply spellbound. She's psychologically paralyzed. She's lost her sense of freedom" (p. 122).

The final horror of Hannah's confined life is that, in fact, she knows how illusory it is. In a confessional moment, Hannah tells Marian, "And do you know what I have been really? Nothing, a legend. A hand stretched out from the real world went through me as through paper. . . . I have lived on my audience, on my worshipers, I have lived by their thoughts, by your thoughts—just as you have lived by what you thought were mine. And we have deceived each other. . . . It was your belief in the significance of my suffering that kept me going. . . . I lived in your gaze like a false God. But it is the punishment of a false God to become unreal" (pp. 229–230).

Murdoch's novel, however, is as much about freedom as it is about captivity. The author refers repeatedly to the need "to break the mirror, to go out through the gate" (p. 261). Marian, both fascinated and horrified by Hannah, yearns to rescue her, "to let the fresh air in at last" (p. 131). She, Effingham, Pip, and others imagine ways to break the spell and free the princess. In particular, Marian proposes to "give her a shock. Pull her out of it just far enough to make her realize that she *is* free and that she's got to make her own decisions" (p. 123). Marian resolves to "convince her that she won't die if she goes outside the walls" (p. 123). In an attempt to free her, Marian and Effingham kidnap Hannah; but Hannah is unprepared for such an abrupt physical escape. In her subsequent state of despair, because she does not believe that she can exist without worship or protection, Hannah rushes out on her own and throws herself over a cliff.

The spell is broken when Hannah dies, and Marian feels free to leave. However, she feels guilty for her inability to free Hannah. That guilt threatens to limit her psychological freedom. To reassure her, Effingham tells Marian that there is nothing any of them could have done "since she—gave herself—away" (p. 211). People can aid and support each other in their journeys, but neither princes nor princesses can rescue a sleeping beauty and make her a hero.

In the end, Marian recovers the self-affirmation and capacity for spontaneous action associated with a heroic departure. Murdoch suggests that the new recovery of selfhood and freedom that all who surrounded Hannah feel will lead to healthier and more innocent relationships between them. Of Marian's sexual encounter with Denis, another of the castle's residents, Murdoch says, "This encounter was the unclassifiable encounter that liberates. But she did not know what Denis was, and this ignorance cast a darkness back upon herself which made her quiver with reality. They were two unique beings meeting each other" (p. 213). She feels for the first time "totally innocent" (p. 214). Understanding the perniciously destructive nature of the old sex roles, she can discard them. She can see the world and relationships anew—not in the mirror of old attitudes, but freshly and directly. At the end of the novel, Marian feels "as one who is leaving a theatre after some tragic play, worn, torn, yet rejoiced and set free with a new appetite for the difficult world" (p. 215).

The hero's exit, represented in gothic form in Murdoch's novel, is a departure from the conventional role. The protagonist observes the lives of conventional women around her. She understands, consciously or, at first, unconsciously, that the traditional female ideal of assuming responsibility for the lives of those around her is not only egotistical but doomed to failure. She realizes that the myth that women are spiritually superior—responsible for saving men and children through remaining spiritually pure and selfless—oppresses both women and those around them. The female hero ceases to be the still center of power, inactive herself, who seeks to control the actions of those around her. By electing to live her own life, she automatically frees those around her to live theirs. By refusing to play the selfless, dependent, other-directed role, the female hero becomes less selfish, less egotistical rather than more so. By emerging from behind the false facade of the ideal female image to be admired, she frees those around her of the guilt that her saintly countenance and selfless sacrifice impose on them, binding them to her and impeding their own psychological development.

After living with Hannah in her castle prison, Marian Taylor symbolically understands the damage inherent in women's prescribed role in patriarchal society. Other protagonists realize the need to free themselves from convention after becoming captors for a time themselves. Such is the case of Emma Woodhouse in Jane Austen's early nineteenth-century novel *Emma*. The protagonist, Emma Woodhouse, believes society's widely held Cinderella myth that happiness ever after comes as a result of marrying above one's social station. However, the more damaging conventional role from which she must extricate herself in order to find happiness is that of the other-directed woman who sets aside her own development for the sake of manipulating other people's lives. In the beginning of the novel, Emma cares for her demanding and petty father and rapidly becomes a social snob and a matchmaker. She assumes that her friend Harriet Smith, because she is attractive and intelligent, does not belong in the social station to which she was born. Further, Emma believes, in accordance with the Cinderella myth, that the best fate for such an exceptional woman is to raise her social station by marrying well. Emma therefore ignores the fact that Harriet genuinely cares for Robert Martin, and begins selecting a series of men who are appropriately charming and wealthy. Emma believes that her attempt to rescue Harriet from her "unfortunate" circumstances is good, innocent, selfless, and absolutely appropriate to a woman. At the very least, the attempt casts Emma in the favorable light of savior: "*She* would notice her; she would improve her; she would detach her from her bad acquaintances, and introduce her into good society, she would form her opinions and her manners. It would be interesting, and certainly a very kind undertaking; highly becoming her own situation in life, her leisure, and power."[69] But Emma Woodhouse's parenting project consists of encouraging cold-blooded ambition rather than friendship and good sense. She tells Harriet: "I want to see you permanently well connected, and to that end it will be advisable to have as few odd acquaintances as may be" (p. 18).

Mr. Knightley, Emma's conscience and eventual partner, understands that Emma's machinations arrest her own development. He comments that her relationship precludes Emma's own growth because "how can Emma imagine she had anything to learn herself, while Harriet is presently such a delightful inferiority" (p. 29). Because Emma is so convinced of her own superiority, she is at first utterly blind to the destructiveness of her plot to herself and to Harriet. Austen notes that the woman who indulges in the other-directed life is often rendered more blindly ignorant of the destruction she is wreaking by the belief that she can read others' thoughts and know them better than they know themselves—a belief that justifies the traditional woman's living others' lives for them. Emma finally realizes: "With insufferable vanity had she believed herself in the secret of everybody's feelings! with unpardonable arrogance proposed to arrange everybody's destiny" (p. 273).

Like Eve and most subsequent female protagonists, Emma's intelligence and vitality exceed the restricted, protected, and uneventful place that convention has assigned her. In literature, these women, unless they depart from convention and find a life that allows for the development of their potential, often become domesticated Lady Macbeths, wreaking havoc in the lives of those they are forced to live for and through. In comic literature such as Pope's *The Rape of the Lock* and Austen's novels of manners, the woman's heroic qualities of intelligence, energy, and wit must be expressed within a ludicrously limited and trivial drama. Frequently, power over trivial issues is decided in a conventionally applauded scene of sexual and social gamesmanship. For example, at the dance that Emma has been active in organizing, it becomes important to her that she "must submit to stand second to Mrs. Elton though she had always considered the ball as peculiarly for her. It was almost enough to make her think of marrying" (p. 215). The emphasis on the trivial and the indirect approach to human interaction in Austen's society is symbolized by the riddles that Emma has Harriet Smith collect and transcribe, and with which the age in general was fascinated. Like her society, Emma cares more for the game than for those involved. She is insensitive to the pain Robert Martin suffers when he is rejected by Harriet, and equally insensitive to Frank Churchill's feelings when she is in the process of matching him up with Harriet.

The captor role is frequently the product of a conventional woman's loneliness and boredom. Emma's relationship with Harriet Smith begins when Emma's governess, Miss Temple, marries and moves away, and Emma is left alone with her father. However, Emma finds that the traditional woman's role of living through others is not the vehicle of the true companionship she hungers for. In fact, her conventional thinking and behavior tend to produce three types of negative relationships between women, which Austen portrays in Emma's interactions with Harriet Smith, Miss Bates, and Jane Fairfax respectively.

First of all, in her relationship with Harriet Smith, Emma substitutes social manipulation for true friendship. Second, with Miss Bates, she is contemptuous of the courageous, impoverished woman on her own, who is neither clever nor beautiful but who is able to survive and to remain generous in spirit in the shabbiness of genteel poverty. It is only after Emma insults Miss Bates at the Box Hill picnic for her lack of wit that she sees the vulnerable woman's pain and realizes how insensitive she has been.

Third, encouraged to be trivial and diffuse (for Emma, "it was easier to chat than to study"), Emma is jealous of any praise given to the woman who has, with discipline and a sense of her own self-worth, developed her own talents. When she finds herself resenting others' comments about Jane Fairfax's fine piano playing, she remembers that her friend Mr. Knightley "had once told her it was because she saw in her [Jane] the really accomplished young woman which she wanted to be thought herself" (p. 123). In general, her relationship with other women is an unsympathetic, competitive one.

Austen's protagonist exits—that is, she ceases to follow blindly the persuasion and prejudice of conventional society—when she realizes the self-deception, destructiveness, and loneliness of this manipulative role. She learns what Hannah

Crean-Smith in Murdoch's *The Unicorn* manifests so graphically: that the role entraps the entrapper most of all, and that the seemingly selfless behavior is paradoxically the product of hubris. Emma finds herself deceived by her own plans, "myself creating what I saw" (p. 278). She sees that she causes pain and unhappiness because she does not allow others to pursue their own desires or develop their own potential. She is cut off from life because, as the detached creator-manipulator, she lives a vicarious existence. Finally, Emma realizes what parents and others seemingly in control of other human beings discover: that the power to live others' lives is severely limited. Harriet and Robert Martin get together in spite of her meddling.

Furthermore, Emma departs from her blind devotion to conventional behavior because she discovers that convention is not to be trusted. Society lies. It has taught her the social prejudices that determine her behavior. Emma rejects Robert Martin as a suitable suitor for Harriet because he is plain, without gentility, and according to Emma, "a completely gross, vulgar farmer, totally inattentive to appearances." She seeks to match up Harriet and Mr. Elton, who has more manners but less character. In reality, Robert Martin has an integrated and, Austen suggests, androgynous character: "strong and concise, [and] diffuse" (p. 37). In his letter to Harriet, "the language though plain, was strong and unaffected. . . . It was short, but expressed good sense, warm attachment, liberality, propriety, even delicacy of feeling" (p. 37). Emma assumes that men of the middle class lack sensibility and postulates that perhaps his sister helped him to write the letter. Through her irony, Austen makes the point that the same positive human qualities are found in men and women and in all classes.

Society has encouraged Emma to exercise gamesmanship instead of honesty, to control rather than to share, to live through others rather than find her own fulfillment. The final discovery that prompts Emma's exit is the paradoxical truth that no matter how hard people may try to maintain convention, conventions themselves change with the passing of time; thus, those rigidly committed to certain forms and manners eventually find that even convention has moved beyond them. When Emma hears of the union of Jane Fairfax and Frank Churchill and of the possible union of Mr. Knightley and Harriet Smith, she acknowledges the instability of her world: "Was it a new circumstance for a man of first-rate abilities to be captivated by very inferior powers? Was it new for one, perhaps too busy to seek, to be the prize of a girl who would seek him? Was it new for anything in this world to be unequal, inconsistent, incongruous—or for chance and circumstances (as second causes) to direct human fate?" (p. 274). When Emma admits to herself that she cannot control others' lives or force the world to conform to her orderly image of it, she is able to care for others. Thus, she is able to share genuine affection with Harriet, with Miss Bates, and with Jane Fairfax. After Emma repents her attack on Miss Bates at the Box Hill picnic, Austen says, "In the warmth of true contrition she would call upon her the very next morning, and it should be the beginning, on her side, of a regular, equal, kindly intercourse" (p. 250). When she hears that Harriet Smith and Robert Martin are engaged, she says, "I . . . most sincerely wish them happy" (p. 314) and Austen makes it clear that she means it.

Most important, Emma resolves to free herself from triviality, prejudice, hypocrisy, and manipulation. Near the end of the novel, Emma exclaims in response to Jane Fairfax's revelation that she and Frank Churchill plan to be married shortly: "Oh! if you knew how much I love everything that is decided and open!" (p. 304). No longer manipulating or living through others, enjoying her own happiness, Emma feels "joy . . . gratitude, . . . exquisite delight. . . . The disguise, equivocation, mystery, so hateful to her to practice, might soon be over" (p. 314).

As part of this process, Emma awakens from her romantic infatuation with Frank Churchill and discovers the attractions of the appropriately named Mr. Knightley. In fact, her engagement to the man who is the novel's ideal in morals, manners, kindness, and good sense symbolizes her attainment of these qualities. Although the ending is unambiguously portrayed as a happy one (Miss Woodhouse and Mr. Knightley move from despair to "total happiness"), it is clear that Mr. Knightley, many years Emma's senior, is as much a father figure as he is a lover. Emma rejects the egotistical maternal captor role, but she clearly identifies her fiancé as her mentor and superior in wisdom. Thus, it is not clear at the end of the novel whether she has found that ideal of personal responsibility which precludes the inclination to run others' lives or to turn over one's life to another.

In Iris Murdoch's novel, Hannah Crean-Smith's death precedes and in some sense makes possible Marian's escape. Similarly, Emma Woodhouse's psychological liberation occurs when she slays, symbolically, the captor within herself. Both narratives, then, are reminiscent of the fairy tale in which the young hero escapes from or kills the wicked stepmother. Because the culture encourages heroes—whether male or female—to see mothers as captors, fictional characters are likely to reject or destroy the maternal rather than the paternal captor. Mira, in Marilyn French's *The Women's Room*, muses that although "there are lots of wicked stepmothers and old witches and crones," there are "no bad kings in fairyland, although there are a few giants of unsavory reputation."[70] When a father blithely gives his daughter's hand in marriage as a prize (along with half the kingdom) to a particularly brave knight or great athlete, his action is rarely viewed critically. Only in the story of Atalanta is the issue of the daughter's feeling in the matter even raised. In this Greek myth, Atalanta is to be given in marriage to the man who is the fastest runner in the kingdom. She demands a chance to run in the race herself. If she wins, she does not have to marry. The race ends happily in a tie with the man she loves, which allows the father figure once again to escape being criticized and rejected.

In fairy tales, the woman typically escapes by rejecting or slaying an actual woman. In realistic fiction, similarly, the hero may begin her journey by rejecting her mother, all conventional women, even all women. The important discovery that she eventually makes in the process of her quest is that the Wicked Witch is *not* an actual woman. She and her idealized opposite, the Chaste Martyr, are patriarchal projections. When the hero realizes that her view of herself and of other women is male-defined, she then rejects and destroys not the woman but the image that society has pressured her and other women into assuming. By destroying that image, she frees not only herself but the oppressive conventional woman as well.

In many works about the departure, the hero also extricates herself from the male captor who defines and thereby controls her. The conventional, preheroic woman lives in the mirror of male opinion. As Marilyn French points out in her discussion of fairyland in *The Women's Room*, although other women embody images of appropriate or ideal womanhood, those images are all male-defined. French's protagonist, Mira, as her name implies, "lived by her mirror as much as the Queen in Snow White. A lot of us did: we absorbed and believed the things people said about us. I always took the psychological quizzes in the magazines: are you a good wife? a good mother? Are you keeping the romance in your marriage? I believed Philip Wylie when he said mothers were a generation of vipers, and I swore never, never to act that way. I believed Sigmund's 'anatomy is destiny' and tried to develop a sympathetic, responsive nature'' (p. 17).

Doris Lessing's Kate Brown in *The Summer before the Dark* comes to realize that the one choice she thought she had made—choosing a husband—was her mirror's choice not her own.

> Oh it was all so wearying, so humiliating. . . .Had she really spent so many years of her life—it would almost certainly add up to years!—in front of a looking glass? Just like all women. Years spent asleep, or tranced. Did a woman choose *him*, or allow herself to be chosen by *him*, because he admired that face she had so much attended to, and touched, and turned this way and that—she wouldn't be surprised, she wouldn't be surprised at all! For the whole of her life, or since she was sixteen—yes, the girl making love to her own face had been that age—she had looked into mirrors and seen what other people would judge her by.[71]

The patriarch—whether the heavenly or the earthly father—has been given the power to judge and define: to name all of creation, and, hence, to name women. Kate Brown's best friend helps prepare her for her exit years before her actual departure by beginning the ritual of "cow sessions." During these sessions, they "spat on, insulted, belittled" all the patriarchal terms that normally define their lives: "They could not stop themselves. They began improvising, telling anecdotes or describing situations, in which certain words were bound to come up: wife, husband, man, woman . . . they laughed and laughed. 'The father of my children,' one woman would say; 'the breadwinner,' said the other, and they shrieked like harpies" (p. 166). When she shatters the mirror, the hero reclaims the power of naming. She thereby asserts that she exists separate from patriarchal myths about her identity. Lewis Carroll in *Alice's Adventures in Wonderland* parodies the belief that those with political power can define the identities of the powerless. One aspect of this belief is the notion that women do not exist except in the mirror of male attention. Tweedledum and Tweedledee tell Alice that she is only the creation of the Red King's imagination:

> "He's dreaming now," said Tweedledee: "and what do you think he's dreaming about?"
> Alice said, "Nobody can guess that."
> "Why about you!" Tweedledee exclaimed, clapping his hands triumphantly. "And if he left off dreaming about you, where do you suppose you'd be?"
> "Where I am now, of course," said Alice.
> "You'd be nowhere. Why, you're only a sort of thing in his dream!"
> "If that there King was to wake," added Tweedledum, "you'd go out—bang!—just like a candle!" (p. 165)

It is, typically, the hero's father who first indicates to her what her identity in the patriarchal world will be. His power to define her is intensified by the fact that society gives him the authority, as the patriarch of the household, to judge the young girl. His role conventionally differs from that of the mother, moreover, because he is around the children—and especially girl children—very little. While modern psychology has stressed the responsibility of mothers for every trauma, it largely ignores the effect on children of the absence of fathers. The father's absence, coupled with society's definition of the male as the strong, wise authority in the world, renders him somewhat mythic. Furthermore, the more successful the father is considered in the public world, the less likely he is to spend time with his children. While the opinion of this distant, mythic patriarch becomes increasingly crucial to the self-esteem of the daughter as she begins to be concerned about male approval, his absence and neglect suggest to her his disapproval and disappointment.

Although both male and female children labor to please the father, the male child gets approval by independent action and by accomplishments; the daughter typically pleases by being attractive and agreeable. Anaïs Nin remembers her father's rare moments of attention, when he would take her picture, and her own longing to present a pleasing image: "Did he bring out the woman's coquettishness in the little girl? Eyes of the father behind a camera. But always a critical eye. That eye had to be exorcised, or else like that of a demanding god, pleased. I had to labor at presenting a pleasing image." Nin also wonders, "Can a child's confidence, once shaken and destroyed, have such repercussions on a whole life? Why should my father's insufficient love remain indelible; why was it not effaced by all the loves I received since he left me?"[72]

Marguerite Johnson, In Maya Angelou's *I Know Why the Caged Bird Sings*, worships her father even though he left when she was a little girl. This worship leads her to reflect on her own inadequacy. She describes herself as, like Eve, an afterthought to keep her superior brother company: "I was so proud of him [her father] it was hard to wait for the gossip to get around that he was in town. Wouldn't the kids be surprised at how handsome our daddy was? And that he loved us enough to come down to Stamps and visit? . . . Then the possibility of being compared with him occurred to me, and I didn't want anyone to see him. Maybe he wasn't my real father. Bailey was his son, true enough, but I was an orphan that they picked up to provide Bailey with company."[73] Marguerite believes she is not pretty enough to be his child. Her self-hatred, and her belief in the myth of male superiority, lead her to worship her brother, Bailey, as well. "My pretty Black brother was my Kingdom Come" (p. 19). "Where I was big, elbowy and grating, he was small, graceful and smooth. When I was described by our playmates as being shit color, he was lauded for his velvet-black skin. His hair fell down in black curls, and my head was covered with black steel wool" (p. 17). The major reinforcement for any sense of self-worth comes from her realization that Bailey loves her.

The conventional patriarchal father may also convey negative messages to his daughter about her sexuality. He does this because it is a frightening taboo element in their relationship and because it may eventually take her away from him. (He may also fear sexuality, especially female sexuality.) In Eugene O'Neill's play *Mourning Becomes Electra*, and in Katherine Anne Porter's "Daughters of the Late Colonel," the daughter is so much the psychological captive of her father as to elect never to leave the family home even after he is dead. In a similar case, Emily's father in William Faulkner's "A Rose for Emily" has cut her off from the world by driving away her suitors. When she is older and her father is dead, Emily emulates him in a more literal mode by killing her lover so that he can never leave her.

Like the captor mother, the captor father may hinder his daughter's development from the best of intentions—to prevent her from becoming dependent on someone else as a result of sex and marriage. Beatrice, in Nathaniel

Hawthorne's "Rappacini's Daughter," is literally a captive in her father's garden. He has given her a poisonous breath that kills any living thing with which it comes into contact. Even at her death, he insists on the benefits of her invulnerability as compared to the alternatives: "Dost thou deem it misery to be endowed with marvelous gifts against which no power or strength could avail an enemy—misery, to be able to quell the mightiest with a breath—misery, to be as terrible as thou art beautiful? Wouldst thou, then, have preferred the condition of a weak woman, exposed to all evil and capable of none?"[74] Rappacini wants his daughter to be powerful and respected, and he assumes that to achieve this, she must be chaste. The poisonous breath renders her sexually unapproachable. In this story, Beatrice exudes sexuality, but it is potential sexuality. The implication is that when a woman's sexuality is realized, even symbolically, real or figurative death results.

The narrator, and would-be lover, feels some ambivalence about his attraction to Beatrice because he is literally frightened of her breath, and symbolically frightened that he will be destroyed by sexual involvement. Overcome by love for her, he concocts an antidote to the poison to free her so that she can marry him. Knowing it will kill her, Beatrice drinks and dies, saying to her father, "I would fain have been loved, not feared." To the lover who was willing to risk her death to rid her of the poison, her last words are "O, was there not, from the first, more poison in thy nature than in mine?" (p. 350). The father, like the mother, keeps the daughter captive (and hence metaphorically kills her) because he assumes that this is the only way he can protect her from the indignity of subjugation in marriage or the "debasement" of sexual involvement. The lover may collude in her destruction because of his conviction that a woman must be perfectly chaste to be worthy of his love.

Because his opinion is highly valued as that of an authority figure representing the patriarchal world, a father's indifference can be as paralyzing to the hero as his explicit negative judgments or his overprotectiveness. In her diary, the Canadian artist Emily Carr describes her real father as being physically present but emotionally indifferent. She imagines his lack of interest in her birth or in the woman who was giving birth:

> Sixty-six years ago tonight I was hardly me. . . . I wonder what Father felt. I can't imagine him being half as interested as Mother. More to Father's taste was a nice juicy steak served piping on the great pewter hotwater dish. That made his eyes twinkle. I wonder if he ever succored Mother up with a tender word or two after she'd been through a birth or whether he was as rigid as ever, waiting for her to buck up and wait on him. He ignored new babies until they were old enough to admire him, old enough to have wills to break.[75]

When the father is indifferent, the hero may delay the departure because she needs his attention in order to reject him. A major theme in the poems of Sylvia Plath is the poet's obsession with her father, who was largely absent during her childhood and is now dead. Plath struggles not only to be recognized by the indifferent god, her father, but to understand him. She must do this in order to free herself from the captivity of her obsession with him. In her poem "The Colossus," she imagines him as an enormous statue that like the Colossus of Rhodes guards the waterway to the sea. For her he is too large to comprehend. She finds that at thirty she has become arrested, totally cut off from life, by the obsession to do so:

"Thirty years now I have labored / To dredge the silt from your throat. / I am none the wiser."[76] In the poem "Daddy," Plath speaks of being inwardly torn because she loves him and needs his validation, but at the same time she knows that he was a Nazi. Thus, she is debilitated as much by her guilt at needing him as she is by her fear that he did not love or value her. Consequently, she embarks on a series of guilt-ridden relationships with macho, Nazi-style men, whom she leaves in symbolic attempts to kill her father: "If I've killed one man, I've killed two— / The vampire who said he was you / And drank my blood."[77]

Potential heroes may waste their lives embroiled in relationships with men in which they continually reenact the painful relationship with the father, without ever finding a way to exit from the male-defined garden. Mary Shelley's fiction reveals a deep longing for her father's approval. Her famous, feminist-radical, free-thinking mother, Mary Wollstonecraft, died giving birth to Mary. Her equally radical father, William Godwin, made certain that she felt she must make up for the great loss to the world and to Godwin by being her mother's equal and, in some sense, by taking her place. When Mary ran off with the poet Percy Shelley and practiced the free love her parents preached, her father disowned her and publicly discussed her "immorality."

At this time (1818), Mary Shelley wrote *Frankenstein*, a gothic novel about a scientist who creates a monster and then is overcome with hatred and revulsion for his creation. The monster, portrayed sympathetically, is filled with "bitter anguish" at the rejection. He reproves his creator in words that clearly speak Mary Shelley's anger, guilt, and yearning: "All men hate the wretched; how, then, must I be hated, who are miserable beyond all living things! Yet you, my creator, detest and spurn me, thy creature, to whom thou art bound by ties only dissoluble by the annihilation of one of us." He continues: "Oh, Frankenstein, be not equitable to every other, and trample upon me alone, to whom thy justice, and even thy clemency and affection, is most due. Remember, that I am thy creature; I ought to be thy Adam; but I am rather the fallen angel, whom thou drivest from joy for no misdeed. Everywhere I see bliss, from which I alone am irrevocably excluded."[78]

The captor parents may cause the daughter to remain paralyzed or spellbound by her own hateful reflection in their eyes. They may keep her devoted to self-repression and self-destruction until the end of her life. However, always potentially present within these two oppressive gatekeeper figures in the hero's life are their opposites—the parents who encourage their daughter to be her fullest heroic self. Such positive, affirming parental figures appear in literature about women, though less prominently or frequently than their repressive counterparts. In Madeleine L'Engle's children's science fiction classic *A Wrinkle in Time*, for example, both father and mother are great scientists and both encourage all of their children to be responsible, heroic, and loving—and to be themselves. Their only daughter, Meg, however, is not immune to cultural myths about women. She believes that she is unattractive, both in her appearance and in her behavior. She is astounded when the popular Calvin O'Keefe likes her. Meg claims she is a "biological mistake" and wishes she were "a different person."[79] She believes that her younger brother, Charles Wallace, who is brilliant and telepathic, takes care of her, when in fact the opposite is the case.

The basic plot motivation is the father's absence. He has developed a theory of the tesseract, or wrinkle in time, which makes instantaneous interplanetary travel possible. He attempts it, but ends up on the wrong planet. No one knows where he is; the government merely explains that he is on a top-secret mission—like the more realistically drawn conventional father, he is mysteriously working. Meg and Charles miss their father, but they set out to find him only when called to the quest by Mrs. Whatsit, Mrs. Which, and Mrs. Who.

Whatsit, Which, and Who accompany the Murray children and their friend Calvin on a search for their father, which involves visits to a number of planets and finally to the giggly "Happy Medium," who looks into her crystal ball and locates him. They discover that there is a negative force in the universe, a "dark thing" that hovers over Earth and controls the "dark planet" Camazotz (where Mr. Murray is imprisoned). The dark thing is the power of death, of nothingness, and of mindless conformity, and it is this dark thing that is responsible for absent fathers, and for alienation generally.

On Camazotz, people are defined by their social roles; within that definition they are interchangeable. All the women are housewives, and all come to the door to call their children at precisely the same moment, like a "string of paper dolls." All the boys are outside bouncing balls in precisely the same rhythm. The one boy who bounces the ball irregularly is reconditioned so that he will never consider deviating again. All the men are working and rushing. The rationale for such mindless conformity is that on Camazotz "everybody is the same as everybody else." Theoretically, this ensures that there are no inequities. But Meg notes that "like and equal are two entirely different things" (p. 158). On a symbolic level, her beloved father is entrapped in his patriarchal role. She discovers him imprisoned in a transparent column, wearing an expression of stoic suffering. He is the prisoner of IT, a huge disembodied brain that despotically rules the planet. IT is all brain and no heart: Its solution to disease is to kill everyone who suffers (from as mild a symptom as a head cold) and thereby to create a society free from disease as well as from disorder and rebellion.

Who, Whatsit, and Which cannot go to Camazotz, so the children set out to free their father on their own. Meg assumes that her brother Charles Wallace will do the freeing; but he falls prey to IT because of his egotistical assumption that he is strong enough to communicate with IT without becoming controlled by it. Both Charles and Mr. Murray fall because of hubris, as the traditional male hero traditionally does—Mr. Murray landed on Camazotz because of his assumption that he could control the tesseract process.

Meg, on the other hand, almost fails because of her sense of inferiority and her emotional dependence on male protection. It is Meg who frees her father, but as she throws herself in his arms, she thinks with relief: "This was the moment for which she had been waiting, not only since Mrs. Which whisked them off on their journeys, but during the long months and years before, when the letters stopped coming, when people made remarks about Charles Wallace, when Mrs. Murray showed a rare flash of loneliness or grief. This was the moment that meant that now and forever everything would be all right" (p. 149). Moments later, summoned to appear before IT, Meg is disillusioned. She muses, "Charles Wallace was no longer Charles Wallace. Her father had been found but he had not made everything all right. Instead everything was worse than ever, and her adored father was bearded and thin and white and not omnipotent after all. No matter what happened next, things could be no more terrible or frightening than they already were" (p. 158).

To save themselves, Mr. Murray, Calvin, and Meg tesseract away from the planet, leaving Charles Wallace behind. Because of her father's inexperience, Meg almost dies in the process. When she recovers, she is overcome with rage at her father because "everything kept getting worse and worse . . . and her omnipotent father was doing nothing." She is immobilized—"frozen"—by her rage and disappointment until her father explains to her that he never claimed to be omnipotent:

"My daughter, I am not a Mrs. Whatsit, a Mrs. Who, or a Mrs. Which. . . . I am a human being, and a very fallible one" (p. 172). Meg comes to recognize that in part her rage is motivated by her own wish to avoid responsibility. She is frightened of being a hero; she profoundly wishes that her father can do it for her. But finally she understands that he cannot; she must return to Camazotz to rescue Charles Wallace: "It has to be me. It can't be anyone else. I'm the one who's closest to him. Father's been away for so long, since Charles Wallace was a baby. They don't know each other. And Calvin's only known Charles for such a little time" (p. 19).

Meg returns to Camazotz, frees her brother, and then successfully takes on IT. Advised to use the power she has that IT does not have, she realizes that the power is love. When she asserts her love for Charles Wallace, IT backs off and Charles Wallace comes back to himself.

L'Engle's story ends with a loving reunion of the whole family, a "tremendous happy jumble of arms and legs and laughing" (p. 208). Symbolically, the author affirms the fact that the female hero can save father and brother along with herself: Having acted independently, she is no longer defined by her helpless, dependent role. This enables her to free the two males from the impossible role of all-powerful, all-knowing protector. The collective result is that people are no longer alienated or "absent" from themselves and from genuine relationships. Women's and men's simple (and courageous) humanity is affirmed.

"She Just Up and Left Him"

Liberty is terrifying but it is also exhilarating. Life is not easier or more pleasant for the Noras who have set off on their journey to awareness, but it is more interesting, nobler even. Such counsel will be called encouragement of irresponsibility, but the woman who accepts a way of life which she has not knowingly chosen, acting out a series of contingencies falsely presented as destiny, is truly irresponsible. To abdicate one's own moral understanding, to tolerate crimes against humanity, to leave everything to someone else, the father-ruler-king-computer, is the only irresponsibility. To deny that a mistake has been made when its results are chaos visible and tangible on all sides, that is irresponsibility. What oppression lays upon us is not responsibility but guilt.

Germaine Greer, *The Female Eunuch*

The exit may occur when the hero leaves her parents, to begin defining and discovering herself and the world on her own. However, because of the power of conventional myths to influence her during her younger years, she may proceed docilely from conventional daughterhood to wife-and-motherhood before realizing that she is alienated, confined, and in need of fresher air in which to grow. Often, it is not until this second family situation is found to be repressive that the hero decides to exit.

The story of a woman walking out on her husband or lover, leaving behind the traditional helpmate role, dominates the more popular feminist fiction. In Erica Jong's *How to Save Your Own Life*, as Isadora Wing is attempting to leave her husband, she begins to notice how pervasive the theme is in literature and in popular mythology: " 'And then she just up and left him.' That classic line is inevitably pronounced with a mixture of contempt and envy—but vicarious elation underlines them both. Another prisoner has escaped! Another bird has flown her gilded cage! The line stirs us, no matter how many times we have heard it repeated. Freedom, freedom is the theme."[80] This particular recurrent theme excites Isadora as she struggles to take the crucial first step. Full of self-knowledge, yet unable to act, she muses, "I was obsessed with leaving, yet I could not leave. In the manner of psychotics who project their own delusions on the environment, I began to convince myself that the entire world was obsessed with leaving its husband, that leaving one's husband was the *only*, the cosmic, theme" (p. 56). Only when she has made her exit from the garden will other themes become relevant for her.

It is very difficult indeed to depart from a relationship that, according to conventional wisdom, provides the meaning of a woman's life, giving her status and security. By and large, heroes leave their mates when they begin to feel caged, diminished, or actually swallowed up by their husbands. For example, in Marge Piercy's *Small Changes*, Beth's call to the quest comes when her body protests the limitations of her role as Jim's wife by refusing to eat. Beth is sitting in the kitchen, eating meatloaf and considering her fate, when all of a sudden she cannot finish it. She identifies with meat because she feels eaten up by her relationship with her husband.

She then compares her life with that of a turtle that she had as a childhood pet. She remembers that "all day the turtle went round and round the chicken wire, butting his head against the fence and standing up awkwardly on edge and flopping over backward trying to get out."[81] She identifies with the turtle's determination, acknowledging with wry humor her own turtlelike slowness in progressing toward freedom. However, as she let her turtle go as a child, she now allows herself to escape. Beth sympathizes with her husband, but she also sees that he is her captor: "He was willing to trap her. That made him the enemy. Who then was the ally? Only herself. Only the records and books that gave her energy. Only the Turtle Flag she was flying secretly" (p. 41). However much she sympathizes, she cannot respect someone who would willingly take over another person's life. His throwing away her birth control pills is the last straw. "He had meant well, he said he loved her, though she had grown so mistrustful of that word she did not think she would ever again be able to use it except as she might say, I love to swim, or I love strawberries, I love to eat up Bethie. Bethie is mine. No, she would steal his property from him and belong to no one but herself" (p. 42). Later in the novel, Jim demonstrates that he does indeed regard Beth as his property: He attempts to rape her and claims rape as his right.

Because Beth recognizes how much of a captive she is, she is able to escape. She does not, however, know that she has a right to leave. So she prepares elaborate plans to sneak away and then to hide her whereabouts. (She believes, as Jack does, that he has the legal right to force her—his property—to return to him.) Even so, as the plane takes off, she is filled with exhilaration: She "clasped her hands and joy pierced her. She was wiry with joy and tingling. How beautiful to be up here! How beautiful was flight and how free (even though it cost money). She was the only flying turtle under the sun" (p. 46).

Marian MacAlpin in Margaret Atwood's *The Edible Woman* also experiences her call to the quest as a sudden loss of appetite. Engaged to be married, she notices that people begin treating her differently, as if she were an adjunct or a part of her fiancé, Peter. At first she, like Beth, cannot eat meat, but little by little she stops being able to eat anything. It finally becomes clear to her that she cannot eat because she feels she is being eaten up. Like Beth, Marian recognizes that on some level Peter knows that he is consuming her separate identity and assumes it is his right to do so: She must exit or starve. Rather than sneak out, she conceives a ritual in which a substitute sacrifice will be made.

She bakes a cake, decorated like a woman, "an elegant antique china figurine."[82] When Peter arrives, she goes into the kitchen and returns "bearing the platter in front of her, carefully and with reverence, as though she was carrying something sacred in a procession, an icon or the crown on a cushion in a play." She kneels down and sets the cake on the coffee table, immediately in front of Peter: " 'You've been trying to destroy me, haven't you,' she said. 'You've been trying to assimilate me. But I've made you a substitute, something you'll like much better. This is what you really wanted all along, isn't it? I'll get you a fork' " (p. 278). Peter flees with alarm, and Marian regains her appetite. The novel ends with the characteristic good humor associated with the departure. Marian sits eating the cake when her roommate Ainsley comes in to accuse her: "You're rejecting your femininity!" Marian replies, "Nonsense. . . . It's only a cake" (p. 280).

For some protagonists, the departure comes only when they have lived out the helpmate role. Often, the hero does not understand that female fulfillment in marriage is a myth until she has tried it for many years. Isadora Wing, in *How to Save Your Own Life*, writes, "We think we are buying security with our slavery—and then, a decade later, we leave and let them keep the furniture, realizing that it is a blessing to be rid of their tyranny at any material cost and that there is no such thing as security anyway."[83] The pressure on women to marry is so great that some women marry in full awareness that they are entering a cage. They even know at some level that they will not remain there. Martha, in Doris Lessing's *Martha Quest*, before her wedding, "said to herself that now she could free herself, she need not marry him; at the same time, she knew quite well she would marry him; she could not help it, whether she liked it or not. She also heard a voice remarking calmly within her that she would not stay married to him; but this voice had no time to make itself heard."[84]

For Dorothy Bryant's Ella Price, in *Ella Price's Journal*, the exit begins when her child is in high school. On her thirty-fifth birthday, she muses that the first half of her life has been lived conventionally: She has been a good traditional wife and mother, determining her actions by what would be useful to others. She recognizes that the culture has no myths to define women's existence past the time their children grow up:

> That first lifetime was decided for me by other people, or outside forces. But I have to make a second one—make it up as I go along.
>
> Six months ago I believed this second half of life would be like a prison sentence, locked up in life with nothing to do. But now I know that just because no one has any "use" for me, no one has any plan for me, no one has taken account of my presence because I'm invisible,—well, that's not such a tragedy. Maybe it's a form of freedom. Maybe I have to decide what to make of the rest of this life. I can make it up day by day, not like a cake by the recipe but like making a statue come out of a rock by chipping at it.[85]

She returns to school and begins chipping away to discover the identity of her potential self.

In the process, however, she finds her relationship with her husband changing. He is threatened by her return to college, and with good reason. He believes she should be satisfied with her life at home as he is satisfied with his life. She has always believed that something was wrong with her, and that her husband, Joe, is the ideal because everyone likes him. As she begins to think for herself, however, she becomes critical of him. When he refuses to make any effort to grow, she is surprised when she finds herself comparing him to a contented pig.

Later in the work, however, she becomes more tolerant, commenting, "Joe is happy in the world, he fits, and people love him because he's that way, so why should he change" (p. 186). She cannot stay with him, however, because the price he demands is for her to forgo growth, too. To keep her, he pressures her to have a baby. Her psychiatrist agrees that a baby will "cure" her. She becomes pregnant, but ultimately decides to have an abortion and to move out. Her friend, Laura, to comfort her, suggests that perhaps her leaving will shake Joe up enough to change him. But Ella sadly notes, "I don't think they'll let him. . . . Everybody will tell him what a poor abused fellow he is, such a nice guy to be treated this way. They'll invite him to dinner, introduce him to eligible women . . . he'll be uncomfortable for awhile. Then he'll find someone else" (p. 186).

As Joe's case indicates, a man's social advantage may in some ways be a disadvantage, for he may never be forced to challenge his own assumptions. He may never have to grow beyond childish selfishness, the desire to have his own way. Such a case is Torvald in Henrik Ibsen's *A Doll's House*. His wife, Nora, is a captive primarily because she believes conventional myths about the different, but supposedly equal, responsibilities of husbands and wives. To fulfill her part of the bargain, she becomes a skillful actress. Her husband, Torvald, delights in his belief that she is an inept and innocent child. To please him, she disguises and represses her capacity for wisdom and independent action. She believes that it is his function to take care of her, so that when she borrows money to save his life, she never tells him. She uses the image of the childish, scatterbrained spendthrift to mask the fact that she has been working for years to repay the money. Ironically, because she is defined as helpless, she feels the need to hide her strength. In the process, she also hides the great sacrifices she daily makes for him.

Nora elects to leave this marriage, not, however, because it demands constant deceit and thankless sacrifice, but because at a moment of crisis, when she needs her husband to protect her, he thinks only of his own reputation. She has been willing to protect him, because she believed that if necessary he would fulfill his part of the traditional bargain; he would, in a pinch, defend her against the world. He not only refuses to do so, but seeks to punish her for the risks that she has taken to secure his restored health and financial survival. Instead of being grateful, he reacts by depriving her of his love and the charge of her own children. When she says that she expected him to defend her in the face of the threatening world, he states, "One doesn't sacrifice one's honor for love's sake," to which she replies, "Millions of women have done so."[86]

This confrontation strips the blinders from Nora's eyes. She recognizes the inequity inherent in their relationship: She has acted the part of an idiot in exchange for protection that is not even forthcoming. Most painful to her, however, is the awareness that she has forsaken her own human journey to serve him. Before slamming the door on her dollhouse existence for good, she explains to the uncomprehending Torvald, "I believe that before all else I am a human being, just as you are—or at least that I should try and become one. I know that most people would agree with you, Torvald—and that's what they say in books. But I can no longer be satisfied with what most people say—or what they write in books. I must think things out for myself—get clear about them" (p. 77). Because the whole culture agrees with him, he has no motivation to move beyond convention. He cannot truly see or love his wife, nor can he begin his own journey.

The husband or lover, then, is often the hero's initial captor and antagonist because in him "the tyranny of the dull mind" has triumphed. Given this fact, it is no surprise that the patriarchal culture, in myths such as that of Cupid and Psyche, warns women against holding up a taper to examine the true identity of their supposedly godlike mates. A number of novels suggest, as Psyche's sisters do, that to see the husband or lover correctly is to demythologize him. Two famous nineteenth-century novels, George Eliot's *Middlemarch* and George Meredith's *The Egoist*, hold the taper up to the apparently godlike man and show him to be what he really is, a very fallible mortal. Further, the pretense of being godlike makes the man obtuse. Consequently, each is greatly inferior to the heroic woman who loves him.

George Eliot's *Middlemarch* explores the fate of an exceptional woman who accepts the culture's dictum that it is a woman's destiny to marry. "With some endowment of stupidity and conceit," Eliot hypothesizes, Dorothea Brooke could have been happy leading the conventional life of a young lady. Unfortunately, "from such contentment poor Dorothea was shut out. The intensity of her religious disposition, the coercion it exercised over her life, was but one aspect of a nature altogether ardent, theoretic, and intellectually consequent."[87]

Dorothea assumes she will marry, but identifies two problems that affect her choice. First, if she is to give her life to the service of a man, he must truly be her superior or such a dependency would be demeaning. Second, she wishes to grow and learn, so that in choosing a husband—and hence a life—she wishes to find someone to facilitate her growth: "The union which attracted her was one that would deliver her from the girlish submission to her own ignorance, and give her the freedom of voluntary submission to a guide who would take her along the greenest path" (p. 83).

When Dorothea meets the learned Mr. Casaubon, she feels her dilemma has been solved. Because her education has consisted only of "that toy-box history of the world adapted to young ladies," Mr. Casaubon's discourse about his work in progress, "The Key to All Mythologies," sounds eminently scholarly and exciting. She is thrilled when she discovers that he has asked her uncle and guardian for permission to marry her, because she concludes, "I should learn everything then." She thrills that "it would be like marrying Pascal. I should learn to see the truth by the same light as great men have seen it" (p. 21). Eliot is clearly demonstrating the deleterious effect of denying young girls a full chance for an adequate education; she is also poking fun at the wisdom of "great men." Often Dorothea's "failure" to appreciate the work of so-called geniuses shows more sense than is to be found in the scholarly wisdom of the ages.

The great man who is most disappointing, however, is Dorothea's new husband. On their honeymoon in Rome, she becomes depressed, for "in the weeks since her marriage, Dorothea . . . felt with a stifling depression, that the large vistas and wide fresh air which she had dreamed of finding in her husband's mind were replaced by anterooms and winding passages which seemed to lead no-where" (p. 146). Mr. Casaubon is merely a pedant, and one not oblivious to his incapacities. He fears he will never be capable of completing his great work, and he "was in painful doubt as to what was really thought" even of his pamphlets. Eliot identifies his twin problems as egotism and presumption. He is obsessed with himself precisely because he has pretended to be more than he is. Having assumed the role of the patriarch, he has pretended to be God—to understand every-thing—and does not succeed even in being a good man. His self-doubt "brought that melancholy embitterment which is the consequence of all excessive claim: even his religious faith wavered with his wavering trust in his own authorship and the consolations of the Christian hope in immortality seemed to lean on the immortality of the still unwritten Key to All Mythologies." Eliot editorializes, "For my part I am very sorry for him. It is an uneasy lot at best, to be what we call highly taught and yet not to enjoy: to be present at this great spectacle of life and never to be liberated from a small hungry shivering self" (p. 207).

Mr. Casaubon's insecurity makes him suspicious of Dorothea, imagining that her worship of him "might be replaced by presumption," by criticism (p. 49). As a result of his fears—especially that she might prefer his nephew Will Ladislaw to himself—he becomes cold, suspicious, and dictatorial. After one particularly pain-ful rebuff, Dorothea withdraws to her room to consider her plight. If he were loving, she thinks, she would never ask herself, "Is he worth living for?" Yet she does judge him, and her conclusions are devastating: "And what, exactly, was he?—she was able enough to estimate him—she who waited on his glances with trembling, and shut her best soul in prison, paying it only hidden visits, that she might be pretty enough to please him." "In such a crisis as this," Eliot comments, "some women begin to hate" (p. 313).

Soon after Dorothea's spiritual exit, Casaubon conveniently dies. After much soul-searching and denial, she gives up Casaubon's fortune to marry Will Ladislaw. She has always enjoyed her discussions with Will, and she comments with pleasure on their "young equality." Will does not think he is a god; he and Dorothea see each other as equals. In fact, she has a slight edge, being recognizably more determined and disciplined as well as richer. The marriage promises, then, to be as egalitarian as an individual solution can make it in nineteenth-century England. Still, as Eliot points out, Will becomes "an ardent public man" and a member of Parliament; she becomes a wife and mother. "Many who knew her, thought it a pity that so substantive and rare a creature should have been absorbed into the life of another, and be only known in a certain circle as a wife and mother. But no one stated exactly what else that was in her power she ought rather to have done" (p. 611).

George Meredith's *The Egoist*, as the title implies, also exposes the reality behind the myth of male superiority. Clara Middleton initially falls in love with Willoughby Patterne because, in the world's eye, he is "the great match of the county."[88] When she gets to know the man to whom she is betrothed, however, she discovers that he is "a gentleman nurtured in idolatry" (p. 418), a man "utterly unconscious of giving vent to the grossest selfishness" (p. 81). After a typical exchange between them, Clara goes away "feeling the contempt of the brain feverish quickened and fine-pointed, for the brain chewing the cud in the happy pasture of unawakenedness" (p. 84).

Willoughby is not so comfortable in his self-worship as he appears, however. He needs Clara to worship him. In fact, he wants her to be a "mirror of himself" (p. 38), to be totally his in "every thought, every feeling" (p. 49). His chivalrous facade is a disguise for his insecurity, because of which he needs to possess Clara entirely. When she seeks freedom from him, the urge to repress her becomes potentially violent. He considers "that he could love her better after punishing her" (p. 160). Later, the "desire to do her intolerable hurt became an ecstasy in his veins" (p. 310).

Clara begins to feel trapped. She wishes to break the engagement, but like other female protagonists, she is at a disadvantage in making her case because "the world was favorable to him" (p. 164). The social pressure on her is compounded by her belief in male superiority and in female duty. Meredith explains that she is one of those women who live with "a shadow of the male Egoist . . . in the chamber of their brains overawing them" (p. 93). She loved Willoughby because he seemed to be the knight and savior promised by the myth of romantic love. Little by little, Clara realizes that "in a dream somehow she had committed herself to a life-long imprisonment; and, oh terror! not in a quiet dungeon; the barren walls closed around her, talked, called for ardour, expected admiration" (p. 78). She and her friend Laetitia Dale discuss how Willoughby's dominance increases their timidity, passivity, and self-doubt. From these discussions, Clara comes to recognize that her own cowardice imprisons her more than any outside force: "My crying for help confesses that," she tells herself (p. 84).

Only the extremity of Willoughby's self-involvement, stupidity, and emotional cruelty makes her angry enough to reject the internal and external myths that compel her obedience. Eventually, "she was full of revolt and anger, she was burning with her situation; if sensible of shame now at anything that she did, it turned to wrath and threw the burden on the author of her desperate distress" (p. 175). Clara is fully freed from guilt for wishing to break her engagement by her discovery that Willoughby has secretly proposed to Laetitia Dale while Clara and he are still publicly engaged. Meredith reports, "Something like 'heaven forgives me!' was in Clara's mind" (p. 358). While the realization of his unfaithfulness eases her path, she ultimately leaves because she understands that the essence of her conflict is "a dispute between the conventional idea of obligation and an injury to her nature" (p. 250).

Willoughby and his pastoral world represent unconscious convention, the dull mind from which the hero must extricate herself to become fully conscious. However, like most female heroes, Clara Middleton is captive in a labyrinth of dragon myths and captor figures, which gain strength from each other in their denial of her every impulse to freedom. These forces obscure the true nature of themselves, of herself, and of the actual conflict. Indeed, like the child heroes of "The Emperor's New Clothes" and Alice's Adventures in Wonderland, Clara must exist in a totally inverted world. In this world, her feelings and perceptions are labeled either evil, weak, or crazy, and her potential captors are defined as her superior and loving protectors. Her father, for example, who is motivated by a selfish desire for the luxurious life of Patterne Hall, accuses Clara, when she makes a genuine plea for freedom and honesty, of being "mad as Cassandra" (p. 359), and the "epitome . . . of all the contradictions and mutabilities ascribed to women from the beginning!" (p. 360).

All heroes depart alone. But because the female hero's departure is met with special opposition, she often takes much of her spiritual journey in secret before she ever publicly leaves the garden. Clara finds herself in that "horrible isolation of secrecy in a world amiable in unsuspectingness." Furthermore, such secrecy gives all her heroic decisions the appearance of being impulsive and irresponsible. She finally realizes, "I cannot do right, whatever I do" (p. 224).

In order to overturn the myths of the inverted patriarchal world, Clara must conquer her own need for approval from others, particularly her father. She must slay two dragon myths as well—the ideal of virginity and the dream of romantic love. Although Clara Middleton remains sexually inexperienced to the end of the novel, Meredith makes it clear that she is not the passive, static, unquestioning, pure heroine idealized by the myth of romantic love, but a strong-willed hero, and that, moreover, such a woman, "capaciously strong in soul . . . will ultimately detect an infinite grossness in the demand for purity infinite, spotless bloom" (pp. 91–92). In order to conquer the myth of romantic love, Clara and her friend Laetitia Dale must awaken, not *to* the kiss of Prince Charming, but *from* the myth of Prince Charming itself. When both have managed to demythologize Willoughby Patterne as romantic rescuer, Laetitia refers to herself as "an exceedingly foolish, romantic girl" (p. 329) who is "thankful to have broken a spell" (p. 332).

Willoughby functions in Clara's heroic exit, as most male captors do, by becoming overconfident. He thus unwittingly reveals his demythologized self. Meredith writes, "Miss Middleton owed it to Sir Willoughby Patterne that she ceased to think like a girl" (p. 78). Furthermore, Meredith recognizes that Clara is not an exception but is rather representative of the whole female sex, which has disguised its heroic character in order to fulfill the male sex's sentimentalized image of women. Meredith argues that a woman must escape the gilded cage or the oppressive garden; she must take the responsibility for embarking on her own quest. Whereas Willoughby fears and despises the world beyond the garden because he wants constant adoration, Clara longs for that world. She ultimately succeeds in breaking off her engagement. She departs physically for the Alps and emotionally for a freer, more honest, more equal relationship—eventually, we are led to believe, a marital relationship—with Vernon Whitford. Their love, like that of Dorothea Brooke and Will Ladislaw, holds out the possibility of an honest, egalitarian relationship, which begins as a friendship. When Clara, Mr. Middleton, and Vernon have gone, the wise Mrs. Mountstuart remarks at the end of the novel, "She was, I am certain, in love with Vernon Whitford all along" (p. 422).

Often, works that concentrate on the character of the captor show him to be not only pitiable and presumptuous, as Casaubon is, but also, like Willoughby, potentially violent toward women—especially toward women who are not completely controlled by the individual man or by cultural images of ideal feminine behavior. In Joyce Carol Oates's *Wonderland*, for example, the protagonist's daughter, Shelley, runs off with Noel to travel around the country. On the surface, her escape from her father seems liberating. She leaves a conventional family, where she is most unhappy, to join the 1960s counterculture. However, Noel believes that to liberate Shelley, he must destroy her individuality. His tactic for encouraging selflessness is humiliation. He notes, "I made her nothing at all, I ground her down to nothing and freed her! She didn't even know her name when I was through." Shelley has learned from her immediate family, as well as from the culture at large, a distrust of femaleness and especially of female sexuality. She therefore agrees with Noel about the benefits of female self-annihilation. Half-dead from hunger and illness, strung out on drugs, and totally dependent, she feels restored to virgin purity: "Noel made me pure like a madonna, like an angel. . . . He brought so many men to me to make me pure again, to make me into nothing."[89]

Shelley cannot depart on the journey because she believes she deserves to be destroyed. For most female protagonists, however, the knowledge that their lover does, in fact, wish to destroy them makes it possible to exit. In Doris Lessing's *The Four-Gated City*, Martha Quest's lover Jack illustrates the psychological basis for the captor's motivation to strip the women around him of power, of their sense of identity and worth. Martha has a relationship with Jack twice in her life. The first time he is a supportive friend, and their sexual relationship puts her in touch with psychic realities beyond herself. She leaves him because she has a sense that the relationship might limit her growth.

The latent threat he poses becomes explicit the next time they encounter each other. She finds him much changed, and discovers that he now specializes in "breaking in" prostitutes. He employs a process of degradation, ridding women of self-esteem so that they will do whatever the pimp wants. Martha muses, "It was an absolutely clear process, without ambiguity. He needed that his mind, his will, using the clumsiest of techniques for interesting, then arousing women, should bring her physically into a position where she had to submit to bullying. But the point was not the physical bullying at all—she [Martha] could swear that was not what interested him. It was the breakdown that got her there which he needed."[90] He makes women acquiesce to their own dehumanization, and then exploits their guilt to make them agree to more and more dehumanization, more sadomasochistic encounters.

Martha is paralyzed by her fascination with Jack and his game, until she is finally able to understand him. His domination of women is an extension of his own denial of his humanity and love. He was socialized to repress vulnerability by a father who regularly beat him, and by his experiences with death in the war. Martha at one point speculates that Jack may have died in the war and someone else assumed his body. Then she recognizes that, although he had tried to overcome his conditioning, to move beyond his hatred of his father, he has become "stuck" in the "place" of hate: "He had become cruel, hard, driving; all domination and hurt" (p. 406). Finally, because she understands the man he has become, Martha is able to leave him for good.

Joe Christmas, in William Faulkner's *Light in August*, is a similar male character. Joe cannot deal with his sexuality or vulnerability, which he associates with the possibilities that he is illegitimate and has black blood. Blackness and female sexuality are connected in his mind: visiting the black section of a southern town, he describes it as the "hot wet primogenitive Female."[91] The sordid sadomasochism that characterizes his relationship with Joanna Burden is a product, for both, of their Puritanism and racial phobia: Both fear female sexuality and blackness. Joe Christmas is both fascinated and repelled by the emergence of her long-repressed sexuality. When she becomes chaste and hence independent of the relationship, he murders her. (Faulkner implies that she withdraws sexually because she reaches menopause.) To add insult to injury, she does not see herself as "his" because of their previous sexual relationship. Instead, she wants to reform him; she wants him to help her in her work—the liberation of the black race.

Literature is full of portraits of the temptress, which reveal men's obsessive fear of the sexuality that they project onto women. The male characters find themselves "possessed" by the sexual energy that they have sought to repress because they have identified it as female. Such fear of female power explains the violence of poems like Dylan Thomas's "Ballad of the Long-Legged Bait," in which "Sin who had a woman's shape," otherwise defined as "all the wanting flesh his enemy / Thrown to sea in the shell of a girl." The female projection of the male's sexuality and mortality is thrown overboard and is raped and killed by the surrounding whales.[92]

The importance of the temptress in patriarchal literature, moreover, is accentuated by the understandable fear of all oppressors that the people they oppress will turn the tables on them. The merciless woman in a poem such as Keats's "La Belle Dame sans Merci" keeps a man in "thrall" by his love for her, and then abandons him. The male captor has been taught, moreover, that if he is truly a man he will be in control of himself, his environment, and "his women." His murderous impulses emerge when a woman is clearly out of control, because she undermines his position as patriarch. An exaggerated example of such a man is the Duke in Robert Browning's poem "My Last Duchess," who has his wife killed because she smiles at everyone equally and hence is not entirely his. Because she is grateful for lesser gifts from others, he concludes that she does not value sufficiently his 900-year-old name. Dead, she is finally the ideal wife, a beautiful portrait that smiles at the Duke alone. In Browning's "Porphyria's Lover," the central character murders his lover because, although she worships him at the moment, he fears that his total control over her is inevitably temporary. He takes her in his arms, knowing that at this "moment she was mine, mine, fair, / Perfectly pure and good!" To guard against any change from this attitude, he strangles her with her hair.[93]

A rather comic story, told from the would-be captor's point of view, is Norman Mailer's "The Time of Her Time." O'Shaughnessy initially believes that as a man he is a woman's only hope of salvation. He prides himself on his prowess as a conquerer of women. He meets a young woman whom, although he does not like her, he sees as a challenge: "There had been all sorts of Lesbian hysterics in her shrieking laugh and they warred with that excess of strength, complacency and deprecation which I found in many Jewish women."[94] His anti-Semitism and misogyny combine in his desire to aid her in entering "the Time of her Time" (p. 374). Although she is sexually experienced, she has never achieved a sexual climax. He wishes to be responsible for her first total sexual response so that "she would be forced to remember him"—so that, in some way, she will be "his." Sex for O'Shaughnessy is domination. When she does not reach orgasm during their lovemaking, he feels, "There was one little part of me remaining cold and murderous because she had deprived me, she had fled the domination which was liberty for her" (p. 367). He likens their sexual encounter to a bullfight. When she finally does have an orgasm, he feels triumphant: "Finally, I had won" (p. 382). The next morning, however, she gets up and leaves. With the admiration that results from seeing one's own heroic ideal fulfilled, he reports: "From thirty feet away I could see the look in her eyes, that unmistakable point for the kill that you find in the eyes of very few bullfighters, and then having created her pause, she came on for her moment of truth by saying, 'He told me your whole life is a lie, and you do nothing but run away from the homosexual that is you.' " Mailer ends his story with this appreciative sentence: "And like a real killer, she did not look back" (p. 383).

Mira, the protagonist of Marilyn French's The Women's Room, knowingly chooses the conventional role of wife because she fears such male predators. As a teenager, she recognizes that marriage is "a woman's first, last and only choice": "To choose a husband is to choose a life."[95] At the same time, she has the revolutionary desire to retain choices, "to pick her own life" (p. 41). In college, her boyfriend, Lanny, leaves her in a bar because he is furious with her for refusing to have intercourse with him. Innocently (not aware that a woman alone in a bar appears to be looking for sex), she remains to drink and dance with the men there; to her surprise, she escapes being gang-raped later only by the intercession of her friend Biff: "She thought about what had happened had Biff not been there and her mind went black with the horror, the blood, the desecration. It was not her virginity she treasured, but her right to herself, to her own mind and body" (p. 53). She also realizes that had she been raped, her "beloved Lanny would no doubt have called her slut and . . . erased her from the list of women one is required to treat with respect" (p. 53).

"Defeated," she marries. She believes that "no matter how much the history books pretended that women's suffrage had ended in equality, or that women's feet had been bound only in ancient and outmoded and foreign places like China, she was constitutionally unfree. She could not go out alone at night" (p. 53). So she settles for the nicest, most respectful man she can find. She is determined to "devote herself to Norm," to creep "into his arms as into a fortress" (p. 55). She puts him through law school, takes his inadequate advice on birth control, and finds herself pregnant. When she tells him, he first accuses her of ruining *his* life and then implies that the child is not his. Mira, in despair, thinks that although she thought her marriage was an escape, "all she had done was to let the enemy into her house . . . he, like them, believed in things they called virginity and purity, or corruption and whoredom, in women." Since she believes he is "among the best of men . . . there was no hope. It was not worthwhile living in such a world." In despair, determined to put an end to her life, she "went into a quiet darkened place in her mind. . . . She would never again have to feel what she was feeling now, which was just like what she had been feeling for years, except stronger" (p. 62). But instead of killing herself, she gets up and makes Norm dinner. She has the child, and then another; inevitably, she becomes a housewife in suburbia.

Mira has no illusions about Norm. He is, as his name implies, the norm. He is, like the husbands of her friends and neighbors, a "Tin God." She notes that the culture defines a man as he who "screws," "kills," and makes money, but the men she knows "haven't much indulged in killing and are no great shakes at screwing and have made money (for the most part) in only moderate amounts." Worse, "they haven't been anything else either. They're just dull. Maybe that is the price of being on the winning side" (p. 288). She believes she has made the best of a bad bargain, however: She is a model housekeeper and mother, who lives with respect and comfort. One evening, however, Norm announces that he wants a divorce. Her resulting exit "did not feel like good freedom to her, it felt more like being thrown out of the igloo in the middle of a snowstorm" (p. 308).

Her life, however, picks up when she gets a scholarship to Cambridge, meets some supportive feminists, and begins a relationship with a man that seems, finally, to be ideal. They are companions; their sexual relationship is fulfilling; they easily find ways to balance time together with time alone or with other friends. Mira is extremely happy until Ben is offered a once-in-a-lifetime chance to go to Africa. He automatically assumes that she will leave her work to accompany him. Ignoring the fact of her Ph.D., he suggests blithely that she might find a "secretarial job or learn the language and do translating." Horrified, she notes that he never asked her to go with him, but merely assumed she would because he wanted her to. She charges, "You never, never once . . . never thought about me! About my needs, my life, my desires! You eradicated me, me as a person apart from you, as successfully as Norm did!" (p. 664). Ben not only cannot understand when she explains that she wants to pursue the work she loves so much; he also assumes that in her forties she will have another child. Finding that all his "assumptions" are nonnegotiable, Mira exits—this time by her own volition. She concludes from her two experiences that it is not only some individual men who oppress women in this society, but all men.

The society, set up for men, gives them "money and a certain ease in the world, a sense of legitimacy, that, in turn, creates in them a vacancy, a mindlessness" (p. 287). Understanding this, she cannot remain in captivity to such creatures. But hers is not the happiest of departures—it lacks the exuberance found in most works about the heroic exit. Mira has not fully exorcised her combined fear of and dependency on men. She still has nightmares about a man with "a set of mindless eyes, a vacant, unthinking threat" (p. 686). Nevertheless, she does stop being a mirror, reflecting others' realities; she "can no longer speak anything but truth" (p. 287).

Kate Brown, the central character in Doris Lessing's *The Summer before the Dark*, also finds support for her exit from other women. Her neighbor, Mary Finchley, has miraculously remained untouched by the cultural myths of virginity, romantic love, and maternal self-sacrifice. She does what she wants without guilt. Not only that, she does so with impunity: Everyone says that is just the way she is. The only limits to Mary's support of Kate are Kate's unwillingness to admit to herself the realities of her life. After their ritualized "cow sessions," Kate feels guilty and avoids Mary for a while. Kate's second support comes from a young girl, Maureen, whom she meets in the course of her journey. Kate discovers that this young girl is confronting the same choices that Kate did at the same age. A supportive camaraderie develops, based on a mutual sense of the undesirability of all the choices available to women.

At the beginning of the work, Kate Brown is reexamining her entire life. Her husband, a neurologist "of some standing," is visiting America and presumably continuing his habit of having brief affairs with young women. Her "tact" prevents her from accompanying him, for she does not want to "cramp his style." For the first time, none of her children are home. Faced with an empty house, she decides to take a position with Global Foods as a translator—for the summer only. Although she is so successful in her work that she is offered a position as a conference organizer, she does not remain in this job for long, for she recognizes that her role is "to be the supplier of some kind of invisible fluid, or emanation, like a queen termite, whose spirit (some such word—electricity) filled the nest, making a whole of individuals who could have no other connection."[96] She does not want to continue in business the same role she had in her family—a role in which she feels cheated and abused. "She and her contemporaries were machines set for one function, to manage and arrange and adjust and foresee and order and bother and worry and organize. To fuss" (p. 105).

She has gained the requisite qualities—"Patience. Self-discipline. Self-control. Self-abnegation. Chastity. Adaptability to others—this above all" (p. 102)—at tremendous personal cost. Always putting her family's needs before her own, she has felt "starved" for years. She often sits alone "raging under the knowledge of intolerable unfairness" (p. 59). The ultimate injustice is that now that the children have grown up, she is not honored for her sacrifices: Children, husband, and casual friends treat her as an embarrassment, "as something that had to be put up with. . . . She was like an old nurse who had given her years to the family and must now be put up with" (p. 105).

She has nightmares about being first chosen and then abandoned by a prince. In her dream she begins running away, followed by the villagers who run after her, shouting: "She had become an enemy, because she had been discarded" (p. 159). She learns that this denigration and the resulting erosion of confidence is normal for women of her generation. She notices the faces and gaits of middle-aged women, compared with the "swinging grace" and freedom of young women. "The faces and movements of most middle-aged women are those of prisoners or slaves" (p. 103).

Like her husband, she tries to reclaim her youth by having an affair with a younger man—she even travels with him for some time. However, she finds that her feelings for him are primarily maternal. Moreover, he is experiencing a sex-role crisis of his own, because he does not want to take on the responsibilities of adult manhood as defined by the culture. Leaving him, ill, she returns to London where she spends weeks alone, ill herself, in a hotel room. There she faces her painful dilemma squarely. She understands that "what matters most is what we learn through living. . . . We are what we learn" (p. 7).

Simultaneously, she goes through both conscious and unconscious growing. On the conscious level, she examines her life and comes to understand the destructiveness of the role of wife and mother. Unlike most of the protagonists discussed in this section, she does not believe that her husband is responsible for her captivity—although he has certainly benefited from her services. But she does demythologize him. She notes, "The truth was, she had lost respect for her husband" because he avoids deep feeling. Furthermore, he arranges every-thing—even his love affairs—for his own convenience: "That made him seem trivial to her" (p. 71). However, it is not the husband, but the wifely role itself, and the myth of romantic love, that Kate finds have entrapped her. She is freed from her slavery to romantic love when she attends a play in which the leading lady (at the advanced age of twenty-nine) is in despair because she is growing older and losing her power over men. While the rest of the audience vibrates with emotion, Kate "hoots" aloud.

With some disgust, she admits to herself that she accepted the myth as a young girl. After marriage, everything she did and said—especially her appearance—was calculatingly designed to be "appropriate for this middle-class suburb and her position in it as her husband's wife. And, of course, as the mother of her children" (p. 10). She experiments with altering her appearance; depending on how she looks, she is alternately whistled at, treated with respect, or ignored. All her life, she has played roles so that she would be "held upright by an invisible fluid, the notice of other people" (p. 198). The cost of her artistry, however, is devastating. While she has been playing her assigned role, "all the time she had been holding in her hands something else, the something precious, to everyone she knew—but it had never been taken, had not been noticed. But this thing she had offered, without knowing she was doing it, which had been ignored by herself and by everyone else, was what was real in her" (p. 140). The symbol of her decision to refuse the roles, to be herself, is her refusal to continue to dye her greying hair: "Now she was saying no: no, no, no, NO: a statement which would be concentrated into her hair" (p. 270).

Along with her quest for understanding, Kate experiences a dream journey. The first inkling she has of repressed, starved personal identity is a dream about a "strange thing" that she first thinks is a "giant slug." The grotesqueness of the image suggests the internalized message about women that she has received—that is, if she has a self, with needs of its own, it must be ugly. It is not a slug, however, but a "seal, lying stranded and helpless among dry rocks high on a cold hillside" (p. 34). Women in a patriarchy, the dream implies, are like seals on dry land —perishing, suffering, thirsting for life-giving water. Throughout the summer, Kate dreams of carrying this heavy seal self across rough terrain, looking for the sea, without much hope that the sea exists. Near the end she is cold, her feet are bleeding, and she fears the seal is dead; but after experiencing a vision of a "silvery-pink cherry tree in full bloom" growing out of the snow (p. 253), she finds the sea. Only then, when she sees the seal "swimming. . . swerving and diving, playing," does she know that "her journey was over" (p. 266). Seeing a "large, light, brilliant, buoyant, tumultuous sun that seemed to sing" (p. 267), she knows that she is ready to go home. She can now begin a new life—not as a wife and mother, but as herself. She is able, finally, to live if necessary without the good opinion of other people.

Initially, Kate and her husband know that the role of wife and mother is damaging to women, but they believe that by understanding the process they can make themselves immune to it. What Kate learns ultimately is that no one is immune: Experience changes people; the roles they play and the institutions they live in continually resocialize them. Kate can retain her new vision, her recaptured sense of identity, in her home environment only if she changes her relationship to that environment. She must create a new role for herself. Otherwise, it is inevitable that she will slip back into her former victimized, unconscious state.

The novels of awakening discussed in this chapter, then, describe a journey from innocence and unconsciousness to consciousness—a journey that, as we have seen, often begins with an escape from entrapment by a captor. While most literary works emphasize the mother, father, or lover as the hero's captor, some protagonists must deal with all three. Del Jordan, in Alice Munro's *Lives of Girls and Women*, rejects all three when she is quite young. She is bombarded with captor messages from popular magazines, F. Scott Fitzgerald novels, and songs on the radio; but somehow she can never summon any sustained interest in her appearance. She refuses to wash, curl, pluck, and shade in order to make herself "as soft and as pink as the nursery."[97] The demand that she demonstrate virginal perfection is satisfied through scholarly achievement. In retrospect, she realizes that although she made straight *A*'s, "I never had enough of them. No sooner had I hauled one lot of them home with me than I had to start thinking of the next. They did seem to be tangible and heavy as iron. I had them stacked around me like barricades, and if I missed one I could feel a dangerous gap" (p. 162). The resulting habit of avid reading provides her with the support system that she needs, for in novels written by women she finds the understanding of her plight that is absent in her family and friends.

For the most part, her friends struggle to live out the myths about "being a woman" because they know no alternative. Del speaks of the ways that a clique of working girls and those who have just left jobs to marry continually hide what they really think and feel. She feels both failure and relief on the morning after a disastrous evening of drinking, laughing, and pretending to enjoy the company of the "wild" boys at the Gay-la Dance Hall; to recover from the subsequent hangover, she spends the day in bed reading *The Life of Charlotte Brontë*. Naomi, her friend, has also spent the evening pretending to be entertained by Bert and Clive. On going home, she is beaten by her father. Naomi continues to go out with Bert Matthews even though she will be beaten again because, she tells Del, she has to have "a normal life." A normal life is that "paradoxical combination of abuse and boredom in the company of the young men among whom one hopes to grab a husband," as well as what Del refers to as "the complicated feminine order" of "showers, linen and pots and pans and silverware" (p. 161).

Even though Del's inability to play the role with any serious attention—her preference for Charlotte Brontë ultimately saves her from Naomi's fate, she still finds it difficult to escape the jurisdiction of her male captors. Her father, who has little actual relationship with his daughter, is fond of misogynistic insults, such as "no good ever comes of any girl that drunk beer" (p. 191). At the same time, he chivalrously praises her housecleaning, will not let her brothers fight with her, and never jokes with her as he does with the working girls in town. Wherever she goes, Del finds male authorities explaining female limitations. She reads an article in a magazine in which a Freudian psychiatrist declares that girls naturally prefer washing their hair to exploring the universe: "For a woman, everything is personal" (p. 150).

Del wants to believe differently. Her mother seems to support her by telling her that it is all "male nonsense." But Del is arrested by the myths of male and intellectual authority: "Surely a New York psychiatrist must *know*. And women like mother were in the minority, I could see that. Moreover, I did not want to be like mother, with her virginal brusqueness, her innocence. I wanted me to love me, *and* I wanted to think of the universe when I looked at the moon. I felt trapped, stranded; it seemed there had to be a choice" (p. 150). Like other female heroes, Del begins by looking into the mirror of her mother's image and that of other women to get some idea of what she is and can be. She learns from her mother and her female contemporaries the reality that underlies the romantic myths of womanhood. By doing so, she manages simultaneously to demythologize her parents and to prepare realistically for her own future. Although she initially worships her mother both for her contentment and for her apparent power, she comes to see her eventually as a frizzy-haired, discontented, aging woman with a growling stomach and a handful of unfulfilled dreams.

The actual support Del receives from her mother is minimal. Mrs. Jordan warns her daughter that male domination is an imminent danger, that sex leads automatically to pregnancy, and that women must marry and have children or suffer serious social and psychological retribution. Del also realizes that her mother has unfulfilled academic and professional ambitions, which she intends for Del to realize at any sacrifice of personal relationships.

Thus, when her mother warns her of the dangers of her romantic attraction to Garnet French—of the fact that she will end up "the wife of a lumberyard worker" and a member of "the Baptist Ladies Aid"—Del is unable to trust her mother's advice. Like all heroes, she must learn through her own experience. In a final scene, at the Third Bridge where she and Garnet French go to make love and take a swim, Garnet tells her that, in accordance with his Baptist religion, she must be baptized before they can be married. When he insists, "You have to get saved sometime," she replies, "Why do I have to?" and their playful argument leads to a serious ritualistic struggle. Garnet teasingly grabs her and tries to baptize her in the water and she suddenly realizes, "though it would have been so easy, just a joke, to give in, I was not able to do it." As she continues to refuse, his efforts become more serious. Then it becomes clear to Del, as it did to Clara Middleton, that the impulse to save her is actually an impulse to destroy her. Del is increasingly prepared, as Garnet pushes her down each time, to hold her breath and fight him, because she comprehends "that it was not a game at all, or if it was, it was a game that required you to be buried alive" (pp. 197–198). Shocked to discover the murderous captor behind the romantic image, Del discovers that her infatuation is not with Garnet but with the myth of romantic love. She and Garnet are merely playing out roles defined by the myth: "I had never really wanted his secret or his violence or himself taken out of the context of that peculiar and magical and, it seemed now, possibly fatal game" (p. 198). As she comprehends that he becomes violent when he realizes that he cannot control her, she moves beyond her fear and anger to amazement that she could have imagined him to have any "real power" over her: "It seemed to me impossible that he should not understand that all the powers I granted him were in play" (p. 197).

Del walks away, through a cemetery, back to town, accomplishing for herself, without violence, another kind of symbolic death and rebirth than that planned by Garnet. She returns home to a scene of psychological separation from her mother as well. Del realizes, "When I had failed to win the scholarship, something she had never questioned—her hopes for the future, through her children—had collapsed" (p. 199). Her mother, who is in bed when Del gets home, says to her in bitterness what Del has just discovered for herself: "You will have to do what you want" (p. 200). On Monday morning, Del sits with a cup of coffee, a pencil, and the want ads. As she studies the newspaper, the sense of loss that she has been experiencing is gradually replaced by "a mild sensible gratitude for these printed words, these strange possibilities. Cities existed: telephone operators were wanted; the future could be furnished without love or scholarships. Now at last without fantasies or confusion of the past, grave and simple, carrying a small suitcase, getting on a bus, like girls in movies leaving home, convents, lovers, I supposed I would get started on my real life" (p. 201).

Chapter 5
The Emperor's New Clothes

> All of the greatest fiction of the modern age showed women
> falling for vile seducers and dying as a result. They died under
> breaking waves, under the wheels of trains, in childbirth.
> Someone had to break the curse, someone had to wake Sleep-
> ing Beauty without ultimately sending her to her destruction,
> someone had to shout once and for all: Fly and live to tell the
> tale!
>
> Erica Jong, How to Save Your Own Life

For both female and male heroes the heroic quest involves a fall from innocence
into experience. The hero begins the journey by emerging from a static spiritual
purity into a state of energy and chaos. The hero's involvement in each new
situation along the road also represents some version of the change from a state of
timelessness to participation in time, from immortality to mortality, from ignorance
to knowledge.

The "fall" into life ultimately leads to death. In John Keats's "The Eve of St.
Agnes," entry into the world of experience is symbolized by the exit of Madeline
and her lover from her family's ancient castle into a violent storm. In spite of the
inherent dangers, this entrance into the life process is referred to as "a fortunate
fall." The fall occasions growth and the acquisition of wisdom for both individuals
and cultures; it also offers love and community, which the condition of stasis and
purity does not. In William Blake's poem "Thel," the refusal of the fall symbolizes
the avoidance of life. The protagonist in Blake's poem is invited to enter the vale of
tears because only there can she find love. Thel is afraid to immerse herself in the
pain of life and elects not to exit from her pastoral world. Thus, she remains in
spiritual limbo forever.

The Seducer

The hero often hesitates to leave the garden and confront the life-denying forces.
When this happens, an outside agent may cause the fall that precipitates the heroic

quest. It is the myth of romantic love, for example, that leads Sasha Davis, in Alix Kates Shulman's *Memoirs of an Ex-Prom Queen*, to develop herself—to refuse "to let that habit system take hold." Sasha sees becoming "somebody" as a means of attracting a man: "Being somebody had to come first, because, of course, some-body could get a much better husband than nobody."[1]

Any idea or person may entice the female hero into a new situation that teaches her an important lesson. It may be a parent, a lover, a husband, the past, a new job, a return to academia, the role of virgin or mother or feminist, a political ideology, or a new psychological theory. Such an encounter, however, often restricts the hero so that she cannot act independently to slay the dragon by her own hand, in her own way. In such cases, the agent of the fall is a seducer—that is, a mentor who serves initially to rescue the hero, but eventually threatens her with another form of entrapment.

The hero may long for foolproof maps and easier roads. That longing for security and ease becomes itself a powerful dragon. Lucy Snowe says in Charlotte Brontë's *Villette*: "I had wanted to compromise with Fate—to escape occasional great agonies by submitting to a whole life of privation and small pains."[2] She longs for something or someone "at whose feet I can willingly lay down the whole burden of human egotism" (p. 380) in order to escape from what she calls her "single-handed conflict with Life, with Death, with Grief, with Fate" (p. 186). Even when the hero's initial purpose is to leave her parents for a life of self-reliance and exploration, the exit itself may be so frightening that she immediately becomes seduced into another trap remarkably like the one she just escaped. Some never learn. Gustave Flaubert's Madame Bovary continues to her death to rest her hopes for a freer, more satisfying life, first, on a husband who only succeeds in boring her, and then, on a series of romantic lovers, all of whom desert her.

The hero usually meets with a series of seducers of various types— individuals, groups, philosophies—that ultimately leave her disappointed. Each time, she is inevitably thrown back on her own resources. The first seducers are the parents, who, after promising to provide her with a place in the world, betray their inability to do so by changing, aging, and dying. They present themselves to the child as all-knowing spiritual guides, but they turn out to be only mortal human beings, as confused and lost as the hero is. Furthermore, they appear to live only for the hero, but ultimately reveal separate selves and lives for which she may be totally unprepared. In Margaret Atwood's novel *Surfacing*, the protagonist is en-ticed away from her present life in the city in part by the idealized images of her parents and of her own childhood home. She feels betrayed at every step, as she finds that the ideal picture of the past has been illusory. From the first moment she enters the rural world of the Canadian woods, she realizes that the world has not stayed as she wanted and needed it to: "Madame makes tea on a new electric stove. . . . I felt betrayed. She should have remained loyal to her wood range."[3]

Because women are expected to find their primary fulfillment through love and marriage, the major seducers in a woman's journey are often men. By promis-ing to complete and protect her, they perpetuate the belief that she need not undertake a heroic journey: They will slay the dragons for her. The "seducer" may literally seduce and abandon her. He may marry her, placing her in a new captive situation so unbearable that she chooses to return to the freedom of the road. Sometimes, as in the case of the fallen woman, she is exiled from the society. In any of these cases, the seducer aids in her quest by placing her between two views of the world. The conflict between two systems frees the hero to see the fallacy of certain myths, which enables her to realize that her own life is incompatible with them. Hester Prynne, in Nathaniel Hawthorne's *The Scarlet Letter*, is caught between the Puritanism of the New England village and the romanticism of the forest; out of this conflict, she discovers another way of seeing the world, which includes both, but is not limited to either.

In all these cases, the seducer's "betrayal" results from destructive myths governing male behavior. He may "seduce and abandon" the hero in accordance with the myth that men are predators who demonstrate their virility by "ruining" virtuous and attractive women. He may limit her freedom because he believes his masculinity depends on controlling a submissive and loving woman. Or, as in the case of Dimmesdale in *The Scarlet Letter*, he may lack the courage to face the implications of his own "fortunate fall." He may also be reluctant to lose male patriarchal status and power (in Dimmesdale's case, the privilege associated with being a Puritan minister). Finally, the hero may leave the seducer because he does not (and cannot) live up to myths about the larger-than-life, all-powerful romantic hero.

Wise men or women may refuse to "rescue" the hero, knowing that no one can undertake another's quest. In Tom Robbins's *Even Cowgirls Get the Blues*, people undertake pilgrimages to the hermit known as the "Chink" because they see him as a guru. When Sissy Hankshaw reproves him for failing to help them, he explains the folly of the master-disciple relationship: "If your master really loved you, he would not demand your devotion. He would set you free—from himself, first of all." He continues, "Even the wisest guides are blind in *your* section of the burrow. No, all a person can do in this life is to gather about him his integrity, his imagination and his individuality—and with these ever with him, out front and in sharp focus, leap into the dance of experience."[4]

In any case, the failure of persons, groups, and myths to define and fulfill her propels the hero on down the road, less encumbered each time. She is strengthened by a clearer sense of the necessarily independent nature of the life journey. Whether she leaves the seducer or is left, she often feels a sense of loss, frustration, or anxiety as she moves out of the illusion that promised to be paradise. However, in the act of spiritual separation, she realizes that no one else can rescue her. Thus she discovers her own independence and self-reliance. The protagonist in Doris Lessing's *The Golden Notebook* first explores redemption through romantic love and Marxist politics. Then, when Michael leaves her and she leaves the party, she feels herself propelled ahead into life: "It's a stage of my life finished. And what next? I'm going out willing it, into something new, and I've got to."[5]

When the hero is liberated from the belief that her fulfillment will come from a man who will take care of her, she takes responsibility for her own life. One aspect of this newfound responsibility is a new attitude toward work. For some women, this may mean entering the "male" workplace for the first time; for others, it means a new seriousness about a profession; still others redefine the culture's view of work and transform what they do from drudgery to vocation.

Ellen Glasgow's *Barren Ground*, Willa Cather's *O Pioneers*, and George Gissing's *The Odd Women* all illustrate aspects of this pattern. From the first page of *Barren Ground*, Glasgow emphasizes the vitality of the protagonist, Dorinda Oakley, who even as a young girl is "running toward life."[6] She has an instinct that says, "I will not be broken" (p. 367). "There's something deep down in me," she notes, "that I value more than love or happiness or anything outside myself. It may be only pride, but it comes first of all" (p. 251). Her antagonist is the impoverished farm community in rural Virginia where the "barren ground" drains away the vitality and hope of those who work it and where the culture is as depleted and sterile as the soil.

This society is committed to the Puritan ethic that denies pleasure and adventure, associating them with sexuality, laziness, and deception. Dorinda herself never entirely escapes this value system. She describes Nathan Pedler's daughter, Lena, in words that suggest the association of forbidden qualities: Lena, she notes, is "scheming, capricious, dangerously oversexed and underworked" (p. 304). As a young girl, Dorinda consistently denies herself in order to help her family: "A deep-rooted instinct persuaded her, in spite of secret recoils, that dullness, not pleasure, was the fundamental law of morality" (p. 63). A commitment to dullness, duty, and conformity leads to society's admiration—and to a totally unemotional personality. Dorinda comments later on her sense of power over her husband, Nathan Pedler, because he cares and she does not: "It seemed to her one of the inconsistencies of human nature that strength should be measured by indifference rather than by love" (p. 298).

Dorinda's mother, Rose Emily Oakley, is a victim of the "trap of life" (p. 44) characteristic of this community; more specifically, she is victimized by the ideal of wifely and maternal self-sacrifice. Dorinda is saddened and frustrated by her mother's "slow martyrdom" (p. 46) and "morbid unselfishness" (p. 36); she laments that marriage "had conquered her" (p. 79). When Mrs. Oakley unselfishly lies in court to protect her son, Rufus, from a murder charge, she violates her religious beliefs. After this ethical collapse, she takes to her bed and dies. Dorinda sees her martyrdom not as "unselfish" but as "sentimental." It is typical of the maternal softness that contributed to her brother Rufus's "moral failure." Ironically, we learn that her mother was once energetic and optimistic. Her dream of becoming a missionary came to an end when the man who was to take her to Africa was killed. After a period of madness from which she never fully recovers, Rose Emily marries Dorinda's staid father and devotes herself to repressing the "wild streak in me" that continues to yearn for the adventure of the missionary life. With satisfaction, she confesses that "with the Lord's help, I've managed to stamp it out" (p. 94).

Yet the dream that troubles her mother provides the daughter with a counterforce to her self-denial. Mrs. Oakley tells her that the importance of romantic love is that it provides a means for women to partake of adventure. Through her mother's tragic life, Dorinda learns that vitality can never be fully destroyed: Her mother's "visionary eyes looked out of the ravaged face through a film of despair" (p. 204). Dorinda also has a model for the integration of autonomy, nurturance, wisdom, and power in Aunt Mehitabel Green, the black matriarch, midwife, and "conjour woman" (p. 104) who in time of crisis comforts and sympathizes with her.

The vital, indestructible heroic spirit embodied in Dorinda is symbolized by the broom sedge, "the one growth in the landscape that thrived on barrenness, the solitary life that possessed an inexhaustible vitality. To fight it was like fighting the wild, free principle of nature. Yet they had always fought it. They had spent their force for generations in the futile endeavors to uproot it from the soil, as they had striven to uproot all that was wild and free in the spirit of man" (p. 98).

When Dorinda falls in love with Jason Greylock, romantic love seems to offer escape from "the endless captivity of things as they are" (p. 81). She loses her virginity without trauma, recognizing that sexuality is a natural expression of her love for Jason and of her own passionate nature. When her mother convinces her one evening not to meet Jason because she should not let a man interfere with her life, Dorinda learns that the power women have traditionally gained over men from such sexual and emotional self-denial is "one of those victories . . . which are defeats" (p. 82).

Jason Greylock does not, however, deserve her love; his nature is suggested by his surname. Entrapped by his dull, conformist conditioning, he is neither as strong nor as liberated as Dorinda. He denies his love for her by bowing to pressure to marry the vacuous, passive Geneva Ellgood, to whom he was previously engaged. The effect of his betrayal is devastating to Dorinda. In a nightmarish scene in the midst of a storm, old Doctor Greylock tells her of Jason's decision. She suddenly understands that Jason is incapable of rescuing her, of transforming her life, or of giving her a home. She realizes to her horror that she has always known him to be "false, vain, contemptible, a coward" (p. 13), and yet "she had given him power over her. She had placed her life in his hands, and he had ruined it" (p. 130).

Glasgow manages to give an exceptionally realistic and thorough account of the emotions and actions that typically accompany the heroic exit. Following her discovery of Jason's marriage, Dorinda has a tragic vision of life stripped of illusion. At that moment, she realizes her own isolation. Her sensations are of emptiness, chaos, and death. As a result of her worldly experience, Dorinda becomes keenly aware of being spiritually alienated from her parents—a stranger even to her mother. She also feels "caught under" life; to free herself from the victim role, she must "do something." Initially, she goes out with a gun to kill Jason. But the gun goes off in her hand before he appears. Her love for him has turned to hate. Nathan Pedler says she looks as if she's gone "dirt crazy," a local expression that connects madness to its root in the sterility of the soil that surrounds her.

Glasgow suggests periodically throughout the novel that nature and the analogous primitive depths of human nature act as a rescuer. At this stage, "a deep instinct, like the instinct that drives a wounded animal to flight, was urging her to go somewhere—anywhere—as long as it was to a different place" (p. 138). She understands that she must now care about herself. She must not be deterred by her pity for her father, who "would have to manage without her" (p. 143). Just as the miracle of religion does not save her mother, the miracle of romantic love has not saved her. In fact, she realizes the inadequacies and the destructive powers of all external forces and guiding figures. She knows "there was no help outside herself" (p. 143). As the train leaves, Dorinda feels "alone on the earth" (p. 148). She is aware of nothing but the broom sedge, nothing, that is, but the indestructible, vital desire for life at the core of her being. She is not guilt-ridden, paralyzed, or inclined to self-destruction like the traditional betrayed woman, however. Instead, she interprets her experience in terms of the Presbyterian concept of predestination (p. 156). Her state is one of spiritual indifference: "her capacity for emotion was dead" (p. 172); she feels "dried up to the core" (p. 174).

When she awakens in a hospital in New York, having had a miscarriage, she appears to herself to be "all eyes" (p. 174), seeing but not feeling. The passion that Jason's love inspired is aborted as well. She also understands, "I've finished with love, and until I find something else to fill my life, I shall be only an empty shell" (p. 176). At the same time, she enjoys the spiritual numbness that follows the experience of intense emotion: "In the security of her disenchantment, there was the quiet that follows the storm" (p. 179). Even after she returns to the farm, she has periods when "her senses remained benumbed by toil" (p. 241).

Her indifference expresses itself in a "diabolic sense of humour" (p. 172), a sardonic sense that everything, including her own tragedy, is humorous; yet she knows that she, like the broom sedge, remains "too much alive. She felt that she hated the broom sedge because it would wake her suffering again" (p. 180). At a concert that she attends, the powerful music causes her to experience again "the pure essence of sensation," and to feel alive for the first time since her discovery of Jason's weakness.

Dorinda's feelings at this point in her life are erratic. She repeatedly and unexpectedly experiences the painful memories of Jason. Each time, she must return to the struggle to free herself. She devotes herself persistently to the cause of rebuilding her ruined life, but at times of weariness, everything seems a mistake; she is overcome by a sense of futility. She realizes, however, "I've got to go straight, no matter how I feel" (p. 216). Initially, she associates the part of her that is hungry for life with Jason. She identifies this hunger as "a secret enemy who could spring out of the wilderness and strike when she was defenseless" (p. 194). Later she recognizes that "the strong impulses which had once wrecked her happiness were the forces that had enabled her to rebuild her life out of the ruins" (p. 368). Along with this hunger, her natural optimism, her "superior intelligence," and her "worldly knowledge and disillusioned experience" give her the courage to take risks, redefine the world, and act according to her own definitions. She tells herself, "I was able to take risks because I was too unhappy to be afraid. . . . The courage of desperation . . . had saved her from failure" (p. 269). Finally, the "keynote of her character" is the impulse "to protect, to lift up, rebuild and restore" (p. 271).

Like Marie in Agnes Smedley's *Daughter of Earth,* Dorinda rejects romantic love and sexuality because she has no role model for a positive sexual relationship. Geneva Greylock insists to Dorinda that she and Jason are "blissfully happy" (p. 273), but other characters describe Geneva as having "the face of a dead woman" (p.278). Before she finally drowns, Geneva has periods of insanity when she goes about telling people that she had a child and Jason killed it. On the metaphoric level, her charge (connected thematically with Dorinda's miscarriage) suggests that Jason always snuffs out any life he may engender. In opposition to life as symbolized by nature, Jason approaches farming as his neighbors do, attempting to fight and conquer the barren land with little success.

Although Dorinda never again trusts her sexuality—she marries Nathan Pedler on the condition that he not touch her—she does trust herself to redefine her view of herself, of sex roles, and of the relationship of humankind to nature. She understands that it is neither nature nor herself that is evil or destructive, but the social and religious attitudes toward it. The poverty of the soil, like the restricted roles for women in patriarchal society, is considered "immutable and everlasting" (p. 10). But Dorinda refuses to accept either as unredeemable. The secret in both instances is choice: In the words of Old Matthew, "It wa'nt the land that was wrong, but the way you treated it" (p. 5). In the case of the land, she learns modern farming techniques while in New York and brings the soil back to life by rotating the crops. In the case of her own life, she finds herself through work and her relationship with the land. To find self-actualization where others find only drudgery, duty, and self-denial, however, she has not only to rotate crops, but to feel differently toward the land than her neighbors do. Combining intelligence with love, she is the land's mate rather than its antagonist. When she buys the land that Jason has let go to ruin, and brings it, as well as her own vital, creative self, to life, Dorinda experiences "something more ancient than sex" (p. 310).

Glasgow's description of Dorinda's approach to farming evokes terms more often used to recount sexual experiences: "For the next few years she gave herself completely to Five Oaks. Only by giving herself completely, only by enriching the land with her abundant vitality, could she hope to restore the farm. Reclaiming the abandoned fields had become less a reasonable purpose than a devouring passion in her mind and heart" (p. 137). Throughout the novel, Glasgow describes Dorinda with imagery from the natural world: At one point her nature is "a hidden field" that is burning (p. 10). The land is her rescuer and her sympathetic counterpart in the world; she is its product, its conquerer, and finally its mate: "To the land she had given her mind and heart [and her body and passionate nature as well] with the abandonment that she had found disastrous in human relations" (p. 407). Nature, the spiritualized physical world, is immortal, and is therefore superior to the society that would entrap and repress her vital spirit. With the land she has a primitive affinity; in it she finds not only her truest self but a fulfilling community, "that sympathy which was deeper than all other emotions of her heart . . . the living communion with the earth under her feet" (p. 408). From the very beginning of her quest, she knew "the spirit was flowing into her, and her own spirit, strengthened and refreshed, was flowing out again toward life. This was the permanent self, she knew" (p. 14).

The final section of Glasgow's novel, called "Life-everlasting," yokes Dorinda's life with spiritual rebirth and the creation of a new plant. Like the fisher-king of classic myth, Dorinda Oakley is identified with the natural world; her heroic quest and return revitalize the kingdom. In her case, she restores the fertility—in her own life and in the land—that the patriarchal sterility, alienation, and violence has destroyed. To avoid a patriarchal society, and because of her own betrayal by Greylock's cowardice and shallowness, she establishes, at first, an all-female community, farming land that belongs to her mother. Dorinda and her mother initially do all the milking, make the butter, care for the chickens, and gather the eggs. Later, when both men and women work on the farm, she hires only women to milk the cows. Fluvanna, the black woman who comes to live with Dorinda, becomes not only an able co-worker, but an affectionate friend and companion. Further, Dorinda notes that in her successful revitalization of the land, "her mother's frustrated passion to redeem the world was finding concrete expression" (p. 268).

By healing the patriarchal dichotomy between spirit and matter, self and world, Dorinda also redefines and redeems work. The daily joyless, unrewarding toil that slowly destroys her parents is also the means by which her mother avoids facing the passionate core of her nature. Although Dorinda at times uses ceaseless toil to bury her emotions, she also uses it to establish a creative relationship with something outside herself. As Dorinda redefines it, work is symbolic of a woman's freedom to exist in direct relationship to the world and to unleash her full vitality. It replaces the passive, dependent female role defined by the myths of virginity, romantic love, and maternal self-sacrifice. It also renders unnecessary the traditional male role, according to which the man slaves in an inhuman natural or economic world, sacrificing himself *for her*.

Dorinda's reward is financial security, as well as a respected place in the community that no other person, and certainly no other woman, in Pedler's Mill is granted. She enjoys the admiring looks as she enters church in her new dress. She has loving female comrades and a good, sustained, affectionate friendship with her stepson, John Abner, who lives with her and admires her adventurous and energetic spirit. She is also freed from her anger as well as from her love for Jason, because she understands that he is more a victim of his weakness than she is. He, in contrast to patriarchal stereotypes, is not as well equipped to survive his betrayal as the woman he betrayed. After feeling for him first love and trust, then hatred when he fails to save her, she eventually pities him, for he is only a mortal, and a less powerful mortal than herself. She is finally charitable toward the pitiful, degenerate, and impoverished Jason, whom she allows to spend his last days in her home so that he will not have to be taken to the poorhouse.

Dorinda never reclaims her sexuality directly, noting that "I'm thankful to have finished with all that" (p. 409). As the narrator explains, "You couldn't have everything" (p. 365). In realistic literature, the transformation of the kingdom is rarely total; but some evolution beyond the restrictive status quo always occurs. It is because of this movement forward that the hero symbolizes the life force. Glasgow, like many other authors writing about female heroes, confesses that writing the novel transformed her life: "I had won my way to the other side of the wilderness, and had discovered, with astonishment, that I was another and a very different person" (p. v).

Alexandra Bergson of Willa Cather's *O Pioneers* (1913) is very like Dorinda Oakley. From the beginning of the novel, her strength is contrasted with the defeat of the men around her. "A shabby little traveling man" exclaims with awe when he sees her "shining mass of hair," and when she gives him "a glance of Amazonian fierceness," Cather writes, he "suddenly wished himself more of a man."[7] Her father, John Bergson, who is dying, is convinced he is a failure, for in "eleven long years," he has made "but little impression upon the wild land he had come to tame. It was still a wild thing that had its ugly moods; and no one knew when they were likely to come, or why" (p. 20). He "had the Old-World belief that land, in itself, is desirable. But his land was an enigma. It was like a horse that no one knows how to break to harness, that runs wild and kicks things to pieces" (p. 22). Yet he recognizes in his daughter the intelligence and strength of his own father: "He had come up from the sea himself, had built up a proud little business with no capital but his own skill and foresight, and proved himself a man. In his daughter, John Bergson recognizes the strength of will, and the simple direct way of thinking things out, that characterized his father in his better days" (p. 24). He therefore leaves her in charge of the farm, wishing that one of his sons had her leadership qualities but recognizing that he has no choice.

From the very beginning, Alexandra knows that she is wiser and stronger than the men around her, so she has no illusions that she will find a man to "take care" of her or protect her. She does, however, want comradeship and understanding, which little by little those she loves deny her. Carl Linstrom, the only person in the area in whom Alexandra can really confide, leaves to seek his fortune in the city. He wishes to avoid the inevitable defeat by "the land . . . which seemed to overwhelm the little beginnings of human society that struggled in its sombre wastes. It was from facing this vast hardness that the boy's mouth had become so bitter; because he felt that men were too weak to make any mark here, that the land wanted to be let alone, to preserve its own fierce strength, its peculiar, savage kind of beauty, its uninterrupted mournfulness" (p. 15). When he leaves, he is concerned about "running off and leaving" Alexandra "to face the worst of it, "but he also fears he would be "only one more drag, one more thing you look out for and feel responsible for" (p. 50). She encourages him to go but says, "It's by understanding me . . . that you've helped me. . . . I think you are about the only one that ever helped me. Somehow it will take more courage to bear you going than everything that has happened before" (p. 51).

Like Dorinda, however, she rises to the occasion. She takes a scientific approach to farming, traveling around, talking to farmers and learning what crops might flourish on the "high land." Like Dorinda, moreover, she combines intelligence with a new relationship to nature. In contrast with the men who have seen the land as a horse to be tamed, she works it with love. The narrator exclaims, "For the first time, perhaps, since that land emerged from the waters of geologic ages, a human face was set toward it with love and yearning. It seemed beautiful to her, rich and strong and glorious. Her eyes drank in the breadth of it, until her tears blinded her. Then the Genius of the Divide, the great, free spirit which breathes across it, must have bent lower than it ever bent to a human will before" (p. 65). She makes herself and her brothers wealthy, becoming one of the most respected people in the community: "Any one thereabouts would have told you that this was one of the richest farms on the Divide, and that the farmer was a woman, Alexandra Bergson" (p. 83). Her brothers Oscar and Lou then betray her by their ungrateful claim that her share of the farm, along with what she has given them, "belongs to the men of the family, no matter about the title" (p. 169). She stands firm, advising them to consult a lawyer because "the authority you can exert by law is the only influence you will ever have over me again" (p. 172).

Oscar and Lou are concerned because Carl Linstrom has returned; they fear Alexandra will marry him so that their own children will not inherit her farm. They admonish her, "Everybody knows he's nearly five years younger than you, and is after your money. Why, Alexandra, you are forty years old!" (p. 172). Alexandra's favorite brother, Emil, who is almost a surrogate son to her, does not understand either, but he is at least supportive. She explains, "I've had a pretty lonely life, Emil. Besides Marie, Carl is the only friend I have ever had" (p. 177).

Carl, however, betrays her again by his weakness. He leaves because "he feels he must make some money to marry her." He explains, "I must have something to show for myself. To take what you would give me, I should have to be either a very large man or a very small one, and I am only in the middle class" (p. 182). She feels further betrayed when Emil and her best female friend, Marie Tovesky die as a result of their passion for one another. (They are discovered and killed by Marie's husband, Frank.) Alexandra has difficulty understanding their action because she has kept such a tight reign on her own emotions in order to take care of the family. Totally alone, abandoned by everyone she loves, she learns to make more allowances for emotional needs, even her own. It is at this point that Carl returns, having made a start on a new enterprise. It is not his increased prosperity that allows him to marry Alexandra, however, but his recognition that "the moment I knew you were in trouble, the moment I thought you might need me, it all looked different" (p. 302).

Talking with him, she becomes reconciled to the deaths of Emil and Marie. When she bitterly tells Carl that "I would have been cut to pieces, little by little, before I would have betrayed Marie's trust in me!" he explains that "she [Marie] was cut to pieces by her love for Emil. Alexandra's father comforts her by pointing out that it was their very vitality, repressed by their surroundings, that caused their tragedy: "They were both the best you had here" (p. 305).

Alexandra never experiences sexual passion equivalent to that of her brother and Marie. In fact, she contrasts her affection for Carl positively with their destructive love, saying, "When friends marry, they are safe. We don't suffer like—those young ones." Hers is a love that signals a release from isolation. She no longer has to be strong all the time for everyone else. As Carl kisses her "softly, on her lips and on her eyes," Alexandra leans on his shoulder, murmuring "I am tired . . . I have been very lonely" (p. 309).

Alexandra and Dorinda both deny passionate sexual love when they reject the myth of fulfillment through romantic love with a superior, powerful male. Their passion is expressed, instead, in a relationship with the earth that brings fertility back to the land. In this way Cather's novel supports the theory, explored in Denis de Rougemont's *Love in the Western World*, that romantic love is a modern adaptation of a fertility myth that connects sexuality and death. Alexandra partakes of this drama through her relationship with the land, dreaming of a romantic lover "yellow like the sunlight" with "the smell of ripe cornfields about him." He is "a man like no man she knew; he was much larger and stronger and swifter, and he carried her as easily as if she were a sheaf of wheat" (p. 206). Only after Emil's death does she recognize that the man she dreams of when she is exhausted is "the mightiest of all lovers" who will eventually carry her to death (p. 283). The novel closes with a transcendental, pantheistic image of Alexandra's death as sexual union that will give birth to new life: "Fortunate country, that is one day to receive hearts like Alexandra's into its bosom, to give them out again in the yellow wheat, in the rustling corn, in the shining eyes of youth!" (p. 309).

George Gissing's *The Odd Women* focuses on a very different sort of "barren ground"—the lives of the "half a million" women in turn-of-the-century England who are bred to be wives, and wives only, but who will not marry because there are so many more women then men. Rhoda Nunn, hero of the work, laughingly calls them "*odd* women—no making a pair with them. The pessimists call them useless, lost, futile lives. I, naturally—being one of them myself—take another view."[8] The novel dramatizes the plight of poor, lonely women who lead futile lives, juxtaposing them against the equally desperate lives of married women. For example, Monica, who escapes poverty and loneliness by marrying Widdowson, soon learns that marriage is captivity. He loves her passionately, "yet in his view of their relations he was unconsciously the most complete despot, a monument of male autocracy. Never had it occurred to Widdowson that a wife remains an individual, with rights and obligations independent of her wifely condition. Everything he said presupposed his own supremacy; he took for granted that it was his to direct, hers to be guided" (p. 152). Desperate, she embarks on an affair, but her lover betrays her. He is afraid to run the risk of losing his family's good opinion and his livelihood by running away with her as they have planned. The despairing Monica dies after giving birth to a baby girl.

Rhoda Nunn escapes either fate through her commitment to her vocation: She trains women in the skills necessary to enter the then male sphere of well-paid clerical work. In the process, she also teaches them self-regard. This commitment leads to a joyous, independent, meaningful life. Rhoda's elder colleague, Miss Barfoot, tells her that she is "proud of your magnificent independence, proud of your pride, dear, and of your stainless heart." Conscious that it is their grand cause that makes their lives so full and joyous, she exclaims, "It's better to be a woman, in our day. . . . Men have only material progress to think about. But we—we are winning souls, propagating a new religion, purifying the earth!" (p. 86). She concludes her "rhapsody" by saying, "Thank Heaven we are women!" (p. 87).

Miss Barfoot's goals are revolutionary. As she shares a platform with a man who decries the invasion of women into the male economic sphere, calling for them to remain in the home, or at least in womanly occupations, Miss Barfoot notes that "a womanly occupation means, practically, an occupation that a man disdains." For women to be free, they must be self-supporting: Miss Barfoot explains that she does not care

> whether we crowd out the men or not. I don't care *what* results, if only women are made strong and self-reliant and nobly independent! The world must look to its concerns. Most likely we shall have a revolution in the social order greater than any that yet seems possible. Let it come, and let *us* help its coming. When I think of the contemptible wretchedness of women enslaved by custom, by their weakness, by their desire, I am ready to cry, Let the world perish in tumult rather than things go on this way! (p. 136)

Barfoot, the ethical ideal of the novel, does not envision a world in which women act like men. As women move into the male sphere, they must develop the positive qualities society has reserved for men (strength, self-reliance, independence, a commitment to theory), but without losing the nurturance and compassion that have been characteristic of women. On this point, the two young revolutionaries are at odds. Rhoda, described as "masculine," is deficient in "womanly compassion." When a young student, Bella Royston, returns in disgrace after running off with a man, requesting that Miss Barfoot take her back, Rhoda, outraged, talks her mentor out of it. When the disheartened Bella kills herself, Rhoda persists in showing no sympathy. Miss Barfoot reproves her severely, saying, "You have hardened your heart with theory. Guard yourself, Rhoda! To work for women one must keep one's womanhood" (p. 134).

Indeed, Rhoda has so little sympathy for Bella Royston because she is still busy repressing "the fires of her nature." Though hidden, they are "not yet smothered." When Miss Barfoot's cousin, Everard, begins courting Rhoda, she is tempted: "If only she had once been loved, like other women," she muses, "if she had listened to an offer of devotion, and rejected it—her heart would be more securely at peace. So she thought. . . . And moreover, it took away from the merit of her position as a leader and encourager of women living independently. There might be some who said or thought, that she made a virtue of necessity" (p. 147). She finds that although she knows Everard to be a rake, "her moral disapprobation wavered" in response to his charm. To "compensate for this" she severely condemns Bella's behavior (p. 147).

The novel implies that the awakening of romantic love and the integration of repressed sexuality are preconditions for heroic compassion, yet the women are provided with no men who are their equals. Miss Barfoot, who once loved her cousin Everard, admits that he "is a fine specimen of a man . . . in body and mind," but he is a "poor ineffectual creature compared with" Rhoda (p. 86). Indeed, events prove her evaluation correct. Although Everard falls in love with Rhoda, his primary interest is conquest. When he considers marrying her, he concludes that "to obtain her consent to marriage would mean nothing at all; it would afford him no satisfaction. But so to play upon her emotions that the proud, intellectual, earnest woman was willing to defy society for his sake—ah! that would be an end worth achieving" (p. 177). She does fall in love with him, passionately. After they spend a "perfect day" together, he proposes a liberated union, free of formal bonds. She rejects his plan, and they part. She distrusts him because she has heard he unethically abandoned a woman he had "ruined." His defense reveals the patriarchal bias of his thinking. First, he says it was all right for him to leave the woman because she was not a "nice" woman. Second, he refuses to give more information because he wants—at this critical juncture in their relationship—for Rhoda to be so in his power that she has total faith in him despite rather damning evidence. When she suspends judgment until she knows more, he is furious.

Everard's betrayal, however, does not end with his oppressive egotism. Ultimately, his shallowness and weakness make any reconciliation impossible. Feeling spurned, he seeks solace with Agnes Brissenden, who does not threaten him. Soon, he begins to share the world's opinion that the wealthy, charming, and pretty Agnes is Rhoda's superior—despite her intellectual and ethical weakness. Rhoda, while at first overwhelmed by suffering, learns from her experience. She learns to empathize with other women's weakness and pain, and she also conceptually rejects marriage because it oppresses women. Both her compassion and her theory are strengthened by her experience.

Before proposing marriage to Agnes, Everard visits Rhoda, and seeing her, again feels admiration and love for her. In particular, he is aware again of her superiority of intellect and character. He proposes, but she refuses, saying, "I won't marry you with the forms of marriage" (p. 326). When he professes a newfound commitment to social forms, she charges that he would "never love any woman—even as well as you love me" (p. 327). Thus, Rhoda Nunn, like her comrade Miss Barfoot, remains single because there is no man in her world who is her equal in passion, intellect, character, or courage.

The implication of Gissing's work is that Rhoda, like Miss Barfoot before her, is able to work for a revolutionary cause without losing her "womanly" compassion because she has allowed herself to feel genuine passion. Furthermore, having turned down marriage with the most desirable of men, she can sympathize with other women's yearning for love without envy, for she knows that her political commitment is more gratifying to her than romantic passion. The union of compassion with rigor enables her to counsel the "disgraced" Monica Widdowson in a very different spirit from that in which she condemned Bella Royston. She reminds Monica that she is only twenty-two. "At your age one talks so readily of 'wrecked life' and 'hopeless future,' and all that kind of thing. My dear girl, you may live to be one of the most contented and most useful women in England. Your life isn't wrecked at all—nonsense! You have gone through a storm, that's true; but more likely than not you will be all the better for it" (p. 316). Rhoda cannot save Monica's life, but she does take responsibility for her baby, and determines to "make a brave woman of her." When we last see Rhoda, she is living a full, happy life. Feeding the baby, she speaks of the paper they are soon to publish, and notes, "Miss Barfoot was never in such health and spirits—nor I myself. The world is moving!" (p. 336).

Glasgow, Cather, and Gissing all demonstrate the ways that the seducer's failure to save the protagonist allows her to develop within herself the "masculine" qualities of autonomy, intelligence, courage, and achievement. Further, her recognition of the defects of the male example allows her to redefine these qualities so that they are shorn of their negative element: She is independent but not alienated, courageous but not contemptuous of the weak, powerful without dominating others, and rational but not unfeeling. Finally, the primary joy of her life is her work, because that work expresses rather than denies her full humanity.

The Fortunate Fall

Dorinda, Alexandra, and Rhoda to a greater or lesser extent sublimate their sexuality, reject the seducer, and ultimately choose relationships with comrades, not lovers. More often in traditional literature, however, the meeting with a seducer results in an awakening of sexuality and Dionysian energy. The seducer rescues the Princess from the myth of virginity, which denies her sexuality and will. When she meets him, she experiences her sexuality for the first time, and she evidences her will by defying parents and convention to be with him. A modern version of this plot is found in Joyce Carol Oates's *Do with Me What You Will*. In this novel Elena, initially portrayed as a lifeless "doll," comes to life because of the love of a "dark man." Rather than love's first kiss, traditional in fairy tales, it is her first orgasm with her lover Jack that propels her into life. When she begins to develop a will of her own, she is capable for the first time of independent action; she chooses to leave her husband to live with Jack. The ending of this modern version of the Pygmalion–Sleeping Beauty–Snow White–Rapunzel myth is ambiguous. Its narrator makes clear that Elena's lover and rescuer is fast becoming a threat to her newly found independence. She will have to fight him or he will become her new captor.

In some works, sexual experience initiates the hero into a new, positive relationship with her body, which enables her to defy the society's captor messages and trust her own perceptions. If the predicted ruin does not follow the fall, the hero may be freed of the debilitating fear that prevents her from challenging myths about womanhood. Alice Munro, in *Lives of Girls and Women*, describes the protagonist's first exploration of her own sexuality. Del Jordan undresses and lies across the bed of her high school boyfriend, Jerry Storey, so that he may educate himself by observing her anatomy. Meanwhile she is busy examining the feelings she has in this new, strangely powerful role. She discovers that the humiliation her mother has implied she would feel does not occur; she feels, rather, "absurd and dazzling." Jerry also helps to make this meeting a positive experience: During the unromantic examination, he quips in Pogo dialect, "Yo' is shore a handsome figger of a woman," and the next day at school he returns her left-behind garter belt in a brown paper bag with more quips in Pogoese to make light of their awkward encounter. Del recounts, "So we left it, and oddly enough got on after this fiasco much better than before. We treated each other's bodies now with a mixture of wariness and familiarity, and no longer made demands."[9] In a later, more passionate scene of sexual initiation, Del and Garnet French begin by leaning against the side of the house fully clothed and end up fallen across the flower bed. Del is so delighted with "the glory of the whole episode" that, without telling her mother what has happened, she asks her the next day to come out and see the spot of blood on the flower. Her mother provides negative commentary throughout the novel about how sex leads inevitably to pregnancy, social disgrace, and male domination. In this case she reveals her attitude toward sexuality by assuming that the spot of blood is from a bird torn apart by a striped tomcat she had seen the day before: "Vicious beasts," she remarks (p. 189). As a result of her own sexual experience,

Del can ignore her mother's negative messages and feel pride and delight in her body and in herself.

In some cases, a sexual encounter with the seducer is also the vehicle that allows the hero to make contact with the many realms of experience outside that of ordinary everyday reality—for example, Dionysian ecstasy, poetic inspiration, spirituality, the unconscious, or even extrasensory perception. Martha Quest, in Doris Lessing's *The Four-Gated City,* experiences sexuality with Jack as "the slow building up, over hour after hour, from the moment of meeting the woman he was to make love with, a power, a force that, when held and controlled, took her both up and over and away from ordinary consciousness into—an area where no words could be of use."[10] In this realm of passion, beyond reason or individuality, Martha experiences flashes of extrasensory perception in which she accurately envisions events in her later life. In Muriel Rukeyser's poem "Mortal Girl," the moment of Dionysian ecstasy is one in which the speaker is visited—"invaded" and spoken to—and she waits again for the power of the vision "To seal my mouth with fire, make me mad / With song and pain and waiting, leaving me free / . . . / To sing again the entrance of the god."[11]

The fall into experience—into the uncertainty and danger of life itself—involves a willingness to lose control of the self. Del Jordan, in *Lives of Girls and Women,* describes sex as "all surrender—not the woman's to the man but the person's to the body, an act of pure faith, freedom in humility."[12] Whether experienced in mystical or sexual ecstasy or both, the fall carries with it the danger of the loss of the conscious self. It is partially for this reason that sexual experience traditionally has been associated not only with visionary experience, but with death and insanity. In his most negative form, the sexual god who awakens the hero is a male vampire who combines grotesque eroticism with the threat of annihilation. He is analogous to the female erotic destroyer found in John Keats's romantic poem "La Belle Dame sans Merci," and in Nathaniel Hawthorne's *Rappacini's Daughter.* In some works, such as Willa Cather's *O Pioneers,* the link between death and sexuality is explicitly made, and a symbolic seducer is viewed positively because he brings, through death or transcendent love, relief from alienation and solitude. He is therefore both a destroyer who robs the hero of her mortal existence and a rescuer who takes her home to spiritual oneness in the transcendent life. The allegorical gentleman of Emily Dickinson's "Because I Could Not Stop for Death" acts like a lover as he accompanies the poetic persona to death; ambiguously, he represents both the terror and the comfort associated with the end of life.

Frequently, the lover in literary works is a shadow figure, who ambiguously beckons and threatens the hero to confront the repressed qualities she must integrate into her psyche in order to be whole. Many works focus on the dilemma of a hero in a world that splits reality into two separate realms—one Dionysian (chaotic, dynamic, sensual) and one Apollonian (ordered, static, cerebral)—and then denies and represses the passionate, chaotic realm, and associates the forbidden qualities with evil. Two such novels are Thomas Pynchon's *The Crying of Lot 49* (1966) and Emily Brontë's *Wuthering Heights* (1847).

Oedipa Maas, the protagonist of Thomas Pynchon's *The Crying of Lot 49,* is a universal figure whose sense of alienation is typical of contemporary Southern California. In her husband Mucho's used car lot, the sign over the Lot (N.A.D.A.) seems to say to her and to the others who share her world "nada, nada, against the blue sky" (p. 107) while each alienated, robotlike person files "in only to exchange a dented, malfunctioning version of himself for another, just a futureless automotive projection of somebody else's life."[13]

The echo of *Oedipus the King* in Oedipa's name suggests that the sin at the heart of her kingdom, responsible for the sterility and waste, is incest. If so, Oedipa is deluded in looking for the cause of her alienation outside herself: She herself shares the spiritual condition at the root of the culture's decay. Repeated references to incest (especially in a performance of the Jacobean play *The Courtier's Tragedy*, during which Oedipa first hears the name Tristero), narcissism (Oedipa travels to San Narciso and stays at Echo Courts), homosexuality (she visits a "gay" bar during a surrealistic nocturnal search for Tristero), and love as neurotic addiction (she learns of an organization called Inamorato Anonymous, devoted to helping people overcome their need for love) are used to symbolize Oedipa's and her culture's avoidance of union with the Other, both within and without. No one can see anyone else because everyone is busy projecting his or her repressed qualities in perverted form on the world. Instead of confronting others, people interact continually with projections, mirror images of themselves; all place their faith in an outside force that will rescue them, if only by destroying the menacing projections they take to be reality.

Oedipa at first places her hopes of fulfillment in the myth of romantic love. She "conned herself into the curious, Rapunzel-like role of a pensive girl somehow, magically, prisoner among the pines and salt fogs of Kinneret, looking for somebody to say hey, let down your hair" (p. 10). The "rescuer" appears in the person of Pierce Inverarity, a wealthy American capitalist, who ironically is one of the creators of the wasteland she inhabits. She goes with him to Mexico, but "all that had gone between them had really never escaped the confinement of that tower": "Pierce had taken her away from nothing, there'd been no escape" (p. 11). Pynchon outlines the alternatives of such a captive maiden: "She may fall back on superstition, or take up a useful hobby like embroidery, or go mad, or marry a diskjocky" (p. 11). Oedipa does the last; she thus begins to live a "normal" life, attending Tupperware parties.

Pynchon suggests that the American Puritan capitalist ethic fails Pierce late in his life, as it does all the characters in the novel; Oedipa wonders whether the statue of Jay Gould, "the only icon" in Pierce's house, kept on a narrow shelf over the bed, finally fell and hit him in the head. For whatever reason, Pierce goes slightly mad just before his death. One night Oedipa and Mucho are awakened by a phone call from her old lover, speaking in various voices and dialects and threatening a visit from an enigmatic "Shadow." When the Shadow eventually comes, it visits each character in a unique way. The narrator informs us that "the Shadow waited a year before visiting" (p. 3). Mucho is overwhelmed by the visitation, which in his case takes the form of numerous LSD experiences. In Oedipa's case, it begins with a letter naming her executor of the late Pierce's estate. This letter leads her to a discovery of the W.A.S.T.E. (We Await Silent Tristero's Empire) system, or Tristero, and the remainder of the novel recounts her attempts to prove its existence. This alternative system includes the very values and even the people that were sacrificed in the building of Pierce's estate. Oedipa realizes that Pierce's "legacy" was America (p. 134), an America that may have created a shadow state as a by-product of Puritanical repression and capitalism.

Tristero, a repressed version of Oedipa's and the culture's Dionysian qualities, is envisioned by Oedipa as a black, diabolical, menacing figure that threatens destruction. Pierce's legacy, then, disrupts Oedipa's entire sense of herself. When she stays at Echo Courts and first begins to learn of Tristero, she breaks a mirror. She persists in looking for Tristero outside the self, but wakes from a dream staring at herself in a mirror; near the end of the novel, she has nightmares about "the soft dusk of mirrors out of which something was about to walk out of the empty room that waited for her" (p. 131). The possibility that Tristero actually exists shatters her entire world view as well as her self-image. It opens the possibility of allowing previously repressed qualities to enter consciousness. To achieve this integration, however, Oedipa must come to recognize that Tristero is a projection of herself.

Pynchon complicates her task—and the reader's—by hints that the W.A.S.T.E. system is not only a projection. Elaborate conceits based on the "waste" produced from a heat engine suggest that the W.A.S.T.E. system is composed of the waste products of the American capitalist system—not only repressed qualities, but oppressed, wasted people. These alienated individuals, the author suggests, may have formed a shadow state and may communicate through an alternative post office.

Oedipa has some recognition that however threatening Tristero might be to her, it is the key to psychological unity, love, and transcendent meaning. Through her memories of the words of Jesus Arrabal (an anarchist she had met briefly), she notes that it might also be the key to an "anarchist miracle" of a healing revolution where the two partial, and therefore perverse worlds of the overly rational and achievement-oriented America and the chaotic, irrational, and seemingly magic and purposeless Tristero come together. The collision of the two political systems, Pynchon suggests, is analogous to the individual's integration of the shadow; it results in an integrated society that avoids the perversity characteristic of either partial, and therefore repressive, system. Arrabal says, "You know what a miracle is . . . another world's intrusion in this one. Most of the time we co-exist peacefully, but when we do touch, there's cataclysm. Like the church we hate, anarchists believe in another world. Where revolutions break out spontaneous and leaderless, and the soul's talent for consensus allows the masses to work together without effort, automatic as the body itself" (p. 88).

Oedipa fears, however, that she is only imagining Tristero; if so, the daylight Apollonian America is all there is. If there is an alternative realm, it is totally hidden. Describing Oedipa's fear and yearning for a psychological, metaphysical, and political shadow world, Pynchon playfully makes fun of the cultural dualism that creates her dilemma, by likening it to the computer that is the ultimate achievement of Pierce's America.

> For it was now like walking among matrices of a great digital computer, the zeroes and ones turned above. . . . The hieroglyphic streets there would either be a transcendent meaning, or only the earth. . . . Another mode of meaning behind the obvious, or none. Either Oedipa in the orbiting ecstasy of a true paranoid, or a real Tristero. For there either was some Tristero beyond the appearance of the legacy America or there was just America and if there was just America then it seemed the only way she could continue, and manage to be at all relevant to it, was as an alien, unfurrowed, assumed full circle into some paranoia. (p. 137)

Pynchon strongly suggests that the integration of Apollonian and Dionysian qualities within Oedipa and within her culture, as well as the dialectical synthesis of

America (thesis) and the W.A.S.T.E. system (antithesis), promises psychological, metaphysical, and political "Incarnation," which will bring community and meaning back into people's lives. The reference to Incarnation as the transcendent force puts both the psychological and the political dimensions of the novel into a larger, more cosmic context in which chance leads to enlightenment.

> Oedipa remembered drifters she had listened to, Americans speaking their language carefully, scholarly, as if they were in exile from somewhere else invisible yet congruent with the cheered land she lived in; and walkers along the roads at night, zooming in and out of your headlights without looking up, too far from any town to have a real destination. And the voices before and after the dead man's that had phoned at random during the darkest, slowest hours, searching ceaseless among the dial's ten million possibilities for that magical Other who would reveal herself out of the roar of relays, monotone litanies of insult, filth, fantasy, love whose brute repetition must someday call into being the trigger for the unnamable act, the recognition, the Word. (p. 136)

Pynchon suggests, through a series of puns, that a psychological process, analogous to the Incarnation of Christ as Logos, attends her outer search, without her conscious awareness. Similarly, as Jesus Arrabal explains to Oedipa, the anarchist miracle happens "without effort, automatic as the body itself" (p. 88). Near the end of the novel, a doctor tells Oedipa she is pregnant, but she concludes that the "gynecologist has no test for what she is pregnant with" (p. 121). The birth of a unified consciousness caused by the integration of the shadow began when Pierce's chance phone call "pierced" Oedipa with seminal truth. Her sexual encounter with Pierce's emissary, Metzger, begins when his eyes "pierced her" (p. 26). We know this event has significant repercussions because their orgasms "coincide with every light in the place, including the TV tube, suddenly going out, dead, black" (p. 27). Shortly thereafter, Oedipa visits Mike *Fallopian*, *Bloody Chiclets*, and Stanley *Koteks*—allusions to menstruation that are more suggestive of miscarriage than of pregnancy. Pynchon underlines this tension—will Oedipa give birth to the new Logos or abort—when Oedipa talks with the graduate student E. Bortz. His discussion of the Tristero system gives her useful information about its history in Europe, but his words also threaten to abort the deeper psychological process going on within her because his rationality tends to explain everything away. His wife's name, however, is Grace, suggesting again incarnation. It is suggestive that Oedipa gives her name when she goes to the doctor for the pregnancy test.

The novel ends with Oedipa attending a stamp auction, where some W.A.S.T.E. system stamps are to be sold. She hopes to spot the agent of Tristero, who undoubtedly will bid for the stamps. The auctioneer's name is Passerine, combining references to "passover" and "uterine," and he spreads "his arms in a gesture that seemed to belong to the priesthood of some remote culture; perhaps to a descending angel" (p. 138). This menacing gesture threatens death or Incarnation, but the novel ends ambiguously. The reader is left not knowing whether Oedipa's fall into Dionysian knowledge culminates in the birth of a new, integrated consciousness. What is clear by the book's close is alienation and sterility that result from a refusal of this fall.

Although the myth of romantic love and the familiar seduction plot underlie the novel, Pynchon uses these myths primarily to explore the implications of American culture's refusal of the fall; he is only secondarily concerned with the female experience. Pynchon's theme—the deleterious effects of American innocence—is also one of the major American themes, treated by such great writers as Nathaniel Hawthorne, Herman Melville, Henry James, F. Scott Fitzgerald, and William Faulkner. Emily Brontë's *Wuthering Heights,* however, is distinctive in its concern for the effect of this cultural dichotomy on women. In this novel, Brontë focuses on the journeys of women who integrate Apollonian and Dionysian elements in themselves and in the society.

In exposing the dualism that splits human capacities into two parts and denies one of them, *Wuthering Heights* also defies the Christian categories of good and evil to explore the destructive effect on men and women of the repression of passion. The frame of the novel illustrates the repression characteristic of the conventional, civilized, Christian society of the period. Mrs. Dean, a shallow woman, tells the story to the repressed, rational, frightened Lockwood, whose name suggests his psychological limitations. At the end of the story, he flees rather than fall into the experience of primal passion, which, according to Christian convention, is evil.

The story he hears involves the young Catherine. The division of experience into civilized "goodness" and vital "evil" is represented respectively by two men: the kind, refined, aristocratic Edgar Linton and the cruel, passionate foundling, Heathcliff. Declaring her love for Heathcliff, Catherine tells Nelly Dean, "If all else perished, and *he* remained, I should still continue to be; and if all else remained, and he were annihilated, the universe would turn to a might stranger . . . my love for Heathcliff resembles the eternal rocks beneath—a source of little visible delight, but necessary. Nell, I *am* Heathcliff—he's always, always, in my mind—not as a pleasure, any more than I am always a pleasure to myself—but, as my own being—so, don't talk of our separation again."[14] Heathcliff does not, however, by himself satisfy her. He is debased and uncouth. She wants not only passion but civilization, knowledge, refinement as well. Ashamed of Heathcliff, she marries Linton; but it never occurs to her that her marriage may require the sacrifice of herself. She is astounded when her weak, kind husband denies her the right to be with Heathcliff. Unable to reconcile the split in life, she wastes away and dies. Her ghost and Heathcliff's eventually haunt the moors at night.

Before she dies, however, Catherine has a daughter. The seemingly irreconcilable conflict between the Dionysian and Apollonian values are reconciled in the second generation, when the younger Catherine falls in love with Heathcliff's son, Hareton. It is resolved according to the classical prescription illustrated in the fairy tale "Beauty and the Beast." According to this myth, a woman finds a worthy mate by transforming beast into prince through her love for him; her reward is wholeness, love, wealth, and social prestige. Accordingly, Catherine, in love with the passionate but degraded and uncouth Hareton, transforms him from beast into prince through her love and through education. Lockwood notes, "His honest, warm, and intelligent nature shook off rapidly the clouds of ignorance and degradation in which it had been bred; and Catherine's sincere commendations acted as a spur to his industry. His brightening mind brightened her features and added spirit and nobility to their aspect—I could hardly fancy it the same individual" (p. 273). Brontë's novel here is more optimistic than Pynchon's because it suggests that with a loving education, one could become both civilized and passionate at the same time. Brontë also envisions a world in which certain people are seen as evil, but do have a "place." Heathcliff, after all, owns a mansion.

The myth of Beauty and the Beast, which is the basis of Brontë's happy ending, can be viewed as an allegory for the psychological growth of the hero. The second Catherine's relationship with herself is analogous to her relationship with Hareton. When she learns to love the Dionysian qualities within herself, they are transformed from a threatening beast into a comforting internal lover who makes her whole. Her painful relationships with Linton and Heathcliff force her to recognize even the most negative passionate responses, which her early life with her overly refined father encouraged her to repress. Her love for Hareton aids her in combining passion with considerate, refined behavior. Her transformation makes his possible as well. Further, their relationship promises to be an egalitarian one. Although the culture expects the male to be her "master," we last see Catherine as his teacher, not his pupil.

Perhaps Brontë's novel can allow passion because it is a curiously asexual passion. In fact, Pynchon and Brontë write works in which sexual passion is clearly present, but is somehow not important or convincing. The major focus is elsewhere. Many works with female heroes, especially gothic novels, do not deal with sexuality directly. Sex in such works may be a disturbing undertone, with perverse and threatening reverberations. In Ann Radcliffe's eighteenth-century gothic novel *The Mysteries of Udolpho,* the hero's task is to reconcile "sensibility" and "self-command," so that she can safely marry Valentine. He is seen flitting through the woods, more of a shadow than a man, as if he were a disturbing element on the edge of her consciousness. Her adventures include entrapment by cruel, sadistic men, where rape vaguely threatens but never occurs, and the discovery of women who went mad or became murderers because of intemperate passion. However, the hero's own passion is never explicitly sexual.

When the dichotomy between head and heart is defined in literature in such a way that sexuality is left out, then it is easier for women characters to reconcile these opposites. But when the hero's initiation is explicitly sexual, the experience is often profoundly unsettling, because it is usually complicated by the societal prohibitions regarding female sexuality, will, and independence. After sexual initiation, the hero is expected to die or to marry. Her sexuality is viewed as the property of her rapist, lover, or husband; it is not her own. Ingenuity, courage, and will are called forth when the experience places the hero in a hazardous position. If the hero's sexual initiation is not marked by the double standard, the experience is an unqualified source of pleasure and growth. In Alice Munro's *Lives of Girls and Women* Del and her friend Jerry initiate one another, and the experience is the same for both girl and boy. Del comments, "Each of us was the only avenue to discovery that the other had found."[15]

The section that follows explores works in which the hero's task of reconciling Dionysian and Apollonian elements in her psyche is complicated by the myth of virginity, which makes her fall more cataclysmic than that of her male counterpart. In these works, the choice between two culturally irreconcilable sets of qualities is symbolized by two men, one dark and one light.

The Light Man and the Dark Man

In traditional mythology, the only alternative to the seducer is the male rescuer. The seducer usually is portrayed as the dark man (Heathcliff, for example) and is associated with Dionysian qualities of sexuality and evil. He is juxtaposed against the light man (Edgar Linton), who is associated with Apollonian values of spiritual order and who is the agent for conventional morality. According to traditional literature and myth, the dark man is considered to be a secular Satan, who corrupts and then betrays the hero. She can be saved only by the godlike light man who redeems her by marrying her. Nineteenth-century melodramas and gothic novels portray the dualistic concept of the light and dark men with simplistic clarity. In the melodrama, the villain demands the rent and ties the female protagonist to the railroad tracks; the male rescuer arrives just in time to pay the rent, cut the ropes, and propose marriage. In the gothic novel, the male parental-lover figure is similarly divided into the evil tyrant who imprisons the female in the castle and threatens her with physical—symbolically sexual—tortures and the persevering boyfriend who finds and frees her just in the nick of time and then proposes and says he will protect her from evil forever.

Serious literature often shows the reader that the situation is not as simple as the preceding paradigm suggests. The villainous seducer and the would-be husband turn out not to be opposites, because both threaten the hero's autonomy. In the course of the narrative, she discovers that the dark man sees her as prey and seeks to prove his masculinity by conquering and ruining her, while the light man wants to marry her and make her a valuable possession. When she demythologizes both men, she sees that they are neither villains nor saviors, but simple, fallible, and somewhat misguided human individuals who can neither save nor damn her.

The personalities of the villain and the rescuer also reflect the culture's dualistic assumptions. The dark and light men in many instances are symbols of the hero's own sense of being divided into two irreconcilable selves—one sexual and one spiritual. The choice between two men suggests that the hero must choose to be either sexual or virtuous. Through the course of the narrative, the hero or the reader, or both, learn to reject that duality. Just as villain and rescuer are not opposites, Apollonian and Dionysian qualities are not irreconcilable. In fact, as we see by the characters of the light and dark men respectively, they represent perverse and destructive manifestations of the qualities they embody precisely because they are partial and limited; each is debilitated by his repression of the complementary set of traits. The dark men in many works in this mode are not healthily sexual, but sadistic, yearning to destroy the very women they are attracted to. The light men are more conformist than genuinely spiritual or moral.

When the hero sees the destructive repressiveness underlying both partial beings, she recognizes that any choice between Dionysian and Apollonian qualities precludes the full experience of either. Slave neither to her passions nor to her morality, she gains control of her own life. By achieving a state of integration superior to that of any other character in the work, she wins a victory over the stultifying forces in the society that perpetuate dualistic myths and limit the full expression of human potential.

Samuel Richardson's *Clarissa* (1748), Thomas Hardy's *Tess of the D'Urbervilles* (1891), Charlotte Brontë's *Jane Eyre* (1847), Kate Chopin's *The Awakening* (1899), John Barth's *The End of the Road* (1958), and Erica Jong's *Fear of Flying* (1973) all describe a woman's growth from a partial being to a more heroically whole person when her virginal qualities are complemented by the Dionysian ones. Moreover, the hero develops wholeness and independence as a result of encounters with two men, each of whom threatens her autonomy. The degree to which each female hero is allowed to be both autonomous and whole—that is, to reconcile Dionysian and Apollonian qualities—varies according to the historical period and to the sentiments of the particular author. Although the authors range from Christian to naturalist to modern secularist, the basic plight of the protagonists and the plots of the novels are remarkably similar.

The classical problem is outlined in Samuel Richardson's *Clarissa*. The novel begins with the first major crisis of Clarissa's life. Her parents are demanding that she marry the wealthy, conventional man—Mr. Solmes. Clarissa complains to her friend Anne Howe: "He has but a very ordinary share of understanding, is very illiterate, knows nothing but the value of estates and how to improve them, and what belongs to land-jobbing and husbandry."[16] To marry him would be to deny passion completely, because she finds him physically repugnant.

In the eighteenth century, a good woman was expected to obey her parents until she married. Then she was to obey her husband. Such expectations, of course, raised ethical questions that did not escape Richardson. What should a young girl do if her parent or her husband is unreasonable? Clarissa's family literally imprisons her. Her brother, for one, sees her as property to be sold to increase the wealth of the family. Clarissa is shocked when he displays her to Mr. Solmes as if she were a prostitute for hire: "Look at her person! (and he gazed at me, from head to foot). Think of her fine qualities" (p. 157).

Clarissa, who wishes to escape this forced marriage, maintains that she desires nothing more than to remain single, virginal, and relatively autonomous. She accepts the aid of Lovelace, a suitor her parents disapprove of, in her escape, since a proper young lady of her time cannot travel alone, without male protection. She knows, however, that Lovelace is as much of a threat to her autonomy as is Solmes. She writes to Anne Howe:

> Tossed to and fro by the high winds of passionate control (and as I think, unreasonable severity) I behold the desired port, the single state, which I would fain steer into; but am kept off by the foaming billows of a brother's and sister's envy, and by the raging winds of a supposed invalid authority; while I see in Lovelace the rocks on one hand, and in Solmes, the sands on the other; and tremble lest I should split upon the former or strike upon the latter. (p. 139)

By the time Clarissa runs off with Lovelace, everyone but she knows that she loves him. Anne Howe teases her about her obliviousness to her feelings: "To be sure, Lovelace is a charming fellow. And were he only—but I will not make you *glow,* as you read—upon *my word* I will not. Yet, my dear, don't you find . . . your heart . . . going throb, throb, throb, as you read just here!" (Vol. 6, p. 67). Richardson's treatment of Clarissa's sexual desire is a masterful depiction of sublimation. Clarissa's image of herself makes no allowances for her passion. She is as frightened of sexuality as she is drawn to it, partially because her society assumes that women should be punished for sexuality with death, and also because unconsciously she is aware that Lovelace's sexuality is violent, and comes from a desire to destroy her. In her dream "he stabs her in the heart"; then, she reports, he "tumbled me into a deep grave ready dug among two or three half-dissolved carcasses; throwing dirt and earth upon me with his hands; and trampling it down with his feet" (Vol. 8, p. 324).

She fears subjection to masculine domination, and her fear is justified. Lovelace deceives her by taking her to a brothel instead of to a safe and proper

retreat. When his attempts at seduction fail, he rapes her. Lovelace believes he can subdue Clarissa so completely that she will learn to love her captivity and her captor. He imagines that "her exclamations will, in the next place, be turned into blandishment; . . . [she will] like a pretty, playful wanton kitten, with gentle paws and concealed talons, tap your cheek, and with intermingled smiles, and tears, and caresses, implore your consideration for her, and your *constancy*"(Vol. 4, p. 310).

When Lovelace is unable to possess her soul by conquering her body, he is disconsolate. In fact, he seems hardly able to accept his failure, and at her death he grotesquely demands his right to have her heart embalmed: "Surely nobody will dispute my rights to her. Whose was she living—Whose is she dead, but mine?" (Vol. 8, p. 141). Lovelace is determined to prove Clarissa either "an angel or a woman," and the price he asks for her if she is proven a woman is complete subjugation.

Society views her as subjugated already, believing as it does that the dark man who awakens a woman to sexuality then owns and has total control over her. Clarissa, who has been seen as property to be sold, game to be tamed and caged, and an angel to be martyred, is now encouraged by virtually everyone to marry Lovelace to save her honor. According to the morality of the time, marrying Lovelace (and being forever grateful to him for "making an honest woman of her") or dying are the only solutions other than poverty, disgrace, and very likely a life of prostitution.

However, through her encounter with the seducer, Clarissa has de-mythologized her male idol, the agent of romantic love, and sees him as the weak mortal he is. Free of the myth of male superiority, she refuses to marry the man who raped her; in doing so, she asserts her worth over patriarchal society's vision of her. She chooses death, triumphantly affirming, "My will is unviolated" (Vol. 8, p. 198). Saying no both to her parent captors and to her seducer, she declares her own value and autonomy and demonstrates her moral superiority to Lovelace and to every other character in the book. As she lies dying, she exalts her love for Anne Howe and announces that even in death she wants no male hand to touch her (Vol. 8, p. 200). Like many female characters in literature, Clarissa represents sexuality, yet she is not allowed to be sexual.

Leslie Fiedler points out in *Love and Death in the American Novel* that *Clarissa* is a book about Dionysian ecstasy translated into Christian terms. Clarissa's story dramatizes the destruction and repression of the Dionysian principles, which Fiedler sees in this particular novel as archetypally female; he also sees the events' ritual enactment as a sacrifice of the fertility god.[17] Clarissa's death scene contains all the erotic energy that she and her culture are forced to repress. What Fiedler ignores is the degree to which the sexual politics of male dominance underlie Clarissa's tragedy. She can be autonomous, and partake of the Dionysian ecstasy she symbolizes, only in death.

Over a century later, Thomas Hardy, in *Tess of the D'Urbervilles*, sympathetically recounts the story of another "ruined woman" who is superior to the society that condemns and destroys her. Whereas Clarissa is virtuous, Tess is innocent and natural. When we first see her, she is "a mere vessel of emotion untinctured by experience."[18] Even when she is seduced or raped (Hardy leaves it purposely vague) by an aristocratic dark man, Alec D'Urberville, Tess is not mentally conquered. She refuses to remain his mistress, not only because she does not love him, but because she yearns for "sweet independence." Unlike Clarissa, she does not die, for as Hardy emphasizes, fallen women rarely do. In fact, Hardy seems to agree with Tess's mother's comforting words, "Tis nature, after all, and what do please God!" (p. 92).

Tess gives birth to an illegitimate child who dies. Afterward, she slowly recovers her happy spirits and her will to live. She is determined "to taste a new sweet independence at any price" (p. 101), but D'Urberville villainously continues to haunt her. Like Lovelace, he is obsessed by the desire to master her heart and soul: "Remember, my lady, I was your master once! I will be your master again. If you are any man's wife you are mine!" (p. 354). Tess flees her home town, and goes to work at a dairy, which repeatedly is likened to an Edenic garden. There she seems to be succeeding in finding a rich, full life in spite of her fall. As Hardy repeatedly avows, "She had been made to break an accepted social law, but no law known to the environment [nature] in which she fancied herself such an anomaly." At the dairy it seems that "the recuperative power which pervaded organic nature was . . . not denied to maidenhood" (p. 89).

At the dairy, Tess falls in love with Angel Clare, a "light" man, whom Hardy describes as "less Byronic than Shelleyan" (p. 208). He loves Tess "rather ideally and fancifully than with the impassioned thoroughness of her feeling for him" (p. 219). Worse, he is a puritan and a man not large-hearted enough to see past conventional morality. They marry, and on their wedding night he confesses to her that he previously has had an affair. She immediately is cheered by his confession, because she assumes that he must then understand her situation, and she confesses also.

When Clare hears her secret, he immediately sees her not as an individual, but as a stereotype to be spurned. Although he deserts her, she continues to love him and to idealize him as "Apollo" (p. 411). But he has betrayed her more thoroughly than has Alec D'Urberville. Hardy makes certain the reader recognizes that this dehumanizing attitude is symptomatic of the philosophies and institutions characteristic of British culture in the latter half of the nineteenth century. Tess escapes to the northern part of England, where she is in deathlike servitude to the unnatural, mechanistic threshing machines. The work at the dairy was viewed as pleasurable, an experience of fertility and abundance analogous to Tess's love for Angel. This mechanized work fights nature; the alienated laborers are forced into drudgery by oppressive supervisors.

The "instinct for self-preservation," which enabled Tess to leave D'Urberville, at first helps her fight to keep her independence after Clare leaves her. She asks no one for help, and even causes her parents to think she is well cared for. Though her betrayal by Clare represents a moral and emotional fall from innocence rather than a physical one, she learns to blame Clare as well as D'Urberville for her plight. Finally, she is not able to withstand all the pressures of a hostile society. When her family is evicted on the grounds of her "immorality," she becomes D'Urberville's mistress. Deserted by the wealthy Clare, she has no other way to support her family.

Soon afterward Angel Clare returns, but says that as long as Alec D'Urberville lives, he is her real husband. To win the treasure of Clare's love and to free herself from servitude, Tess kills D'Urberville. At this point, Clare finally is able to see Tess in a way that his dualistic puritan notions, which viewed women as either virgins or whores, had not allowed. He promises never again to betray her: "Tenderness was absolutely dominant in Clare at last. He kissed her endlessly with his white lips, and held her hand, and said—'I will not desert you! I will protect you by every means in my power, dearest love, whatever you may have done or not have done!' " (p. 411).

Tess's death, like Clarissa's, educates the reader about the deleterious effects of sex-role definitions on women's lives. Hardy intimates at the end that the cause of Tess's destruction (she is executed for murder) is metaphysical: "Justice was done, and the President of the Immortals, in Aeschylean phase, had ended his sport with Tess" (p. 508). Throughout the novel, however, he undercuts this fatalistic conclusion, suggesting that the problem really is social. He portrays Tess as a complete woman, who is both sexual and spiritual, experienced and virtuous; he makes it clear that she need not have died if societal institutions and myths about female virtue had been more reasonable. The contemporary reader might note that Hardy sees Tess as good in spite of her fall only because she is mentally pure and innocent; however, had she been less naive, she might very well have survived.

Charlotte Brontë's *Jane Eyre* is a more optimistic treatment of the conflict between a woman's empirical reality and the repressive dualistic myths associated with sex-role definitions. Jane Eyre is intelligent and knowledgeable about her situation. She wants "incident, life, [and] feeling," "Liberty, Excitement, Enjoyment"; but she also wants to be realistic, to do her duty, and to live a virtuous, Christian life.[19] From the very beginning of the novel, she strikes out at her captors. The Reeds, her foster parents, continually tell her that she is evil and inadequate. As punishment they lock her in a room, where she confronts her entrapment by the Reeds' concept of her:

> Alas! yes, no jail was ever more secure. Returning, I had to cross before the looking-glass; my fascinated glance involuntarily explored the depth it revealed. All looked colder and darker in that visionary hollow than in reality; and the strange little figure there gazing at me, with a white face and arms specking the gloom, and glittering eyes of fear moving where all else was still, had the effect of a real spirit: I thought it like one of the tiny phantoms, half fairy, half imp. (p. 10)

When she rebels against the Reeds, she escapes from the psychological cage and, asserting her own worth, becomes for the first time truly heroic and human. She confronts Mrs. Reed, calling her "my conqueror" (p. 10).

She is sent to Lowood, a charity school, where those in charge seek to teach her devotion to the myth of virginity. The patron of the school, Brocklehurst, exhorts the kind Miss Temple to cut the girls' hair because "I have a Master to serve whose kingdom is not of this world; to teach them to clothe themselves with shame-facedness and sobriety" (p. 60). Jane is taught that the good Christian woman should repress the self, sublimate her physical desires, and serve others. According to the morality with which she is indoctrinated, there are two kinds of women. The first is embodied in her friend Helen, a spiritually pure but physically weak classmate who dies with Jane beside her. Helen embodies the virginal ideal of pure spiritual goodness, selflessness, and martyrdom. After leaving Lowood, Jane takes a position as a governess at Thornfield, where she falls in love with the handsome master, Rochester. There she encounters the "bad woman," Bertha, the mad woman in the tower, who represents society's worst fears about female sexuality. We learn that Bertha's passion and self-indulgence have resulted in her insanity.

It soon becomes clear that Jane is frightened of her own sexuality. Bertha serves as a Dionysian shadow for the virginal, controlled Jane. As soon as Jane's romance with Rochester (the dark man) begins, she hears Bertha's insane laugh. The night before Jane and Rochester are to wed, the "fiend" appears and rips the bridal veil, a traditional symbol of chastity, "in two parts and flinging both on the floor, tramples . . . on them" (p. 274). At the wedding, Jane learns that Bertha is Rochester's wife. Tempted to stay with the man she loves even though he is married, she likens her mental condition to Bertha's: "It is because I am insane—quite insane with my veins running fire, and my heart beating faster than I can count its throbs" (p. 307).

When Rochester enters the novel, he is presented as a figure similar to Lovelace and D'Urberville, but he is much more sympathetically portrayed. He attempts to trick Jane into an illegal marriage and later tries to convince her to be his mistress. He offers Jane a religion of romantic love, as opposed to Christian doctrine, as he declares, "Since happiness is irrevocably denied me, I have a right to get pleasure out of life: and I *will* get it, cost what it may." He asserts that he will "arrogate" the power of the divine and say, "Let it be right" (p. 132). She recognizes that her love for him is blasphemous: "He stood between me and every thought of religion, as an eclipse intervenes between man and the broad sun. I could not, in those days, see God for his creature of whom I had made an idol" (p. 265).

As with Clarissa, Jane's religious faith is tied to her commitment to independence and self-regard. She will not put her soul in jeopardy even for the man she loves. Indeed, the undercurrent in all her considerations is her fear of losing her autonomy, becoming totally dominated by Rochester. She is quite conscious that he is already her "master" in an economic and social sense. She agrees to marry him immediately after he tells her to call him "Edward"; on this same occasion, she lectures him on their equality. After the interrupted wedding, she refuses to remain with him as his mistress. To remain would be to risk being cast off or derided by her seducer for her fall. She is afraid also of losing self-control. She fears becoming a slave to passion and to Rochester, of losing her very identity to him: "He seemed to devour me with his flaming glance: physically, I felt, at the moment, powerless as stubble exposed to the draught and glow of a furnace—mentally, I still possessed my soul, and with it the certainty of ultimate safety" (p. 307). Rochester, with greater insight than Lovelace, realizes that he cannot get what he wants by force: "Conqueror I might be of the house; but the inmate would escape to heaven before I could call myself possessor of its clay dwelling-place" (p. 208). Looking back later, Jane realizes that had she "listened to passion," she would have been "a slave in a fool's paradise" (p. 348).

When Jane flees Thornfield, she is acutely conscious of the division in her mind between two moralities: Christianity and romantic love. She acts according to the Christian morality, which tells her that she must be a selfless virgin; she heeds the biblical injunction to "pluck out your right eye; yourself cut off your right hand; your heart shall be the victim" (p. 287). She is willing to sacrifice her passion to save her immortal soul as well as her emotional and physical autonomy; but she is torn by guilt at having deserted the man she loves. As she wanders alone on the heath, "birds began singing in brake and copse: she listens as birds were faithful to their mates. . . . What was I? In the midst of my pain of heart, and frantic effort of principle, I abhorred myself" (p. 311). She is rescued from her wandering by a Christian family. In the Rivers household, she literally sits at the feet of Diana and Mary, the two sisters. Brontë's references to classical and Christian virgins suggest Jane's return to the myth of virginity as a mode of life. For a time she feels she has what she always wanted; she is "free and honest" and not a slave to passion. She gains "independence" also in the concrete form of an inheritance.

At this point, Jane meets the light man, St. John Rivers; from him, she learns the horrors of the passionless life. In him she sees traditional virginity as repression that imprisons sexuality, rendering it perverse and destructive. Rivers forthrightly describes his own character: "I am simple, in my original state—stripped of that blood-bleached robe with which Christianity covers human deformity—a cold, hard, ambitious man. . . . Reason, and not Feeling, is my guide" (p. 363). He offers Jane marriage, but not love. He wants only her aid in his missionary work in India. Jane refuses to "abandon half myself; if I go to India, I go to premature death" (p. 392).

The choice between the dark and the light man comes down to a choice of annihilation by fire or by ice. Rochester threatens to destroy Jane's autonomy by passion. He tells her, "a fervent, a solemn passion is conceived in my heart; it leans to you, draws you to my centre and spring of life, wraps my existence about you—and, kindling in pure, powerful flame, fuses you and me in one" (p. 305). Rivers, on the other hand, is symbolically associated with ice. He says, "I am cold: no fervour infects me" (p. 372). Jane cannot accompany him as his wife because she fears she would be destroyed if she repressed her own passionate nature: "Forced to keep the fire of my nature continually low, to compel it to burn inwardly and never utter a cry, though the imprisoned flame consumed vital after vital—this would be unendurable" (p. 408).

Brontë finds a way, however, for Jane to experience the warmth and joy of romantic passion without losing her autonomy or her spiritual salvation. She does so by literally and symbolically lessening Rochester's power over Jane and by making possible a Christian marriage between them. Bertha sets fire to Thornfield and jumps to her death. Rochester loses an eye and a hand, the biblical punishment for lechery. To deal properly with her passionate love for Rochester, Jane has to learn to dissociate her sexuality from lust and insanity, just as she must distinguish her spiritual autonomy from the virginal isolation and lifelessness of her school friend, Helen, and of Diana and Mary Rivers. Bertha is the literal equivalent of Jane's negative inner vision of sexuality; when she understands her own passion as separate from Bertha's, she is free to value her own sexuality and to love Rochester. Rochester's wound and the death of Bertha, therefore, symbolize the resolution of Jane's ambivalence about sexual passion. She learns that she does not have to be dominated by either the dark or the light man. Once she has learned to be her own mistress, she is rewarded with a sense of self-sufficiency and self-worth compatible with marriage to a humanized Rochester.

The happy ending is facilitated by a fortuitous event: Jane inherits money. Her good fortune and Rochester's catastrophe lessen his social and economic advantage over her. She is delighted that she can now be his wife rather than his mistress, and still more delighted that she will not be economically dependent on him. "I am an independent woman now," she informs him. "I am my own mistress." On the literal level, her treasure is both sexual love and psychological and economic independence. She insists, "I love you better now, when I can really be useful to you, than I did in your state of proud independence, when you disdained every part but that of the giver and protector" (p. 433). On the psychological and metaphysical level, Jane finds freedom and happiness by reconciling successfully the dualities of spirit and flesh, reason and emotion, Christian faith and secular love. She achieves the desired state that Rochester intuited to be her ideal early in the novel: "Reason sits firm and holds the reins, and she will not let the feelings burst away and hurry her to wild chasms. The passions may rage furiously, like true heathens, as they are; and the desire may imagine all sorts of vain things; but judgment shall still have the last word in every argument, and the casting vote in every decision" (p. 192).

Kate Chopin's late-nineteenth-century American novel *The Awakening,* written fifty-two years after *Jane Eyre,* is the first of the six works discussed in this section that explicitly sees female sexuality outside of marriage as positive. In this novel, moreover, the role of wife and mother is seen as necessarily inimical to the heroic journey. The hero, Edna Pontellier, finds herself caged in this traditional role. She observes with horror those she calls the "mother-women" around her: "They were women who idolized their children, worshipped their husbands, and esteemed it a holy privilege to efface themselves as individuals and grow wings as ministering angels."[20] She eventually realizes that "the house, the money that provides for it, are not mine" (p. 132). Even she is considered by her husband to be his property: When she returns from the beach with a sunburn, he looks "at his wife as one looks at a valuable piece of personal property which has suffered some damage" (p. 7).

Her moment of awakening comes when she first learns how to swim. She feels like a "little tottering, stumbling, clutching child, who all of a sudden realizes its power, and walks for the first time. . . ." At that moment, "a feeling of exultation overtook her, as if some power of significant import had been given her to control the working of her body and her soul. She grew daring and reckless, overestimating her strength. She wanted to swim far out, where no woman had swum before" (p. 47). Her fall is a fortunate one from innocent childhood into adult experience, from the role of passive heroine to that of active hero. As a result of her awakening, she begins to care for herself in a way that is separate from her traditional role: "A certain light was beginning to dawn dimly within her. . . . In short, Mrs. Pontellier was beginning to realize her position in the universe as a human being, and to recognize her relations as an individual to the world within and about her" (p. 25).

The three seducers who aid in her awakening are the sea, Mademoiselle's music, and Robert Lebrun. To describe the sea, Chopin uses the biblical imagery associated with the tempter: Its "foamy crests . . . coiled back like slow, white serpents" (p. 47). "The voice of the sea is seductive; never ceasing, whispering, clamoring, murmuring, inviting the soul to wander for a spell in abysses of solitude; to lose itself in mazes of inward contemplation" (p. 25). Later, when Edna hears Mademoiselle Reisz's piano rendition of " 'Solitude,' . . . the very passions themselves were aroused within her soul, swaying it, lashing it, as the waves daily beat upon her splendid body" (pp. 44–45). Finally, the man who has been teaching her to swim is Robert Lebrun, one of the group that gathers daily on the beach at Grande Isle, where the Pontelliers are vacationing. The birth of the self is attended by the awakening of sexual passion. This awakening in turn triggers enormously increased creativity and seriousness in her painting.

The myth that governs the novel is the story of Sleeping Beauty, who is awakened by the Prince's kiss. When Lebrun senses the change in her, he runs away to Mexico. Her awakening, which involves sexual passion, completely changes her life. She moves out of her husband's house, uses her mother's legacy to rent a cottage, and works at becoming an accomplished artist. While her husband, the totally conventional, light man, attempts to save appearances by traveling and by having his house redecorated, she begins to keep company with the rakish dark man, Alcée Arobin. Lebrun awakened her to romantic love; Arobin initiates her into sexual passion: His kiss "was the first kiss of her life to which her nature had really responded. It was a flaming torch that kindled desire" (p. 139). This kiss signals the final fall into experience: "She felt as if a mist had been lifted from her eyes, enabling her to look upon and comprehend the significance of life, that monster made up of beauty and brutality." She regrets, however, that "it was not love which had held this cup of life to her lips" (p. 140).

When Robert returns, he admits that he loves her; however, he will not see her unless she is freed by her husband. Robert has seduced Edna into changing her entire life, but his allegiance to conventional patterns of behavior indicates he is incapable of rescuing her. Her response reveals that her liberation has gone way beyond his: "I am no longer one of Mr. Pontellier's possessions to dispose of or not. I give myself where I choose. If he were to say, 'Here Robert, take her and be happy, she is yours,' I should laugh at you both." Robert, turning pale, answers incredulously, "What do you mean?" (p. 178).

Betrayed by Robert's conventionality, Edna fears that she will live her life having a series of sexual relationships with men like Alcée Arobin—men she can enjoy, but cannot love. The requirements of a full, heroic life are clear to her: She feels the need to be independent, to pursue her art, and to be fulfilled sexually. She is willing to live with societal disapproval, for her "feeling of having descended in the social scale" is accompanied by "a corresponding sense of having risen in the spiritual" (p. 156). She has not, however, counted on living without Robert's love. This disappointment is intensified by her anxiety about her children. Called to Adele Ratignolle's bed where Adele gives birth to still another child, Edna witnesses "the scene of torture." Her fear that it is not simply society, but biology, that limits a woman's ability to be a free, whole individual is intensified by Adele's parting injunction: "Think of the children, Edna" (p. 182).

Earlier in the novel, Edna has rejected the myth of selfless motherhood, saying, "I would give up the unessential; I would give my money, I would give my life for my children; but I wouldn't give myself" (p. 80). Edna also recognizes that the inevitable result of free sexuality is illegitimate children and therefore the loss of any last hopes for respectability. She ponders the effect of the resulting social ostracism on her present and likely future children. "The children appeared before her like antagonists who had overcome her, who had overpowered and sought to drag her into the soul's slavery for the rest of her days. But she knew a way to elude them" (p. 189).

In order to save her newborn self from the death-in-life of a conventional existence without condemning her children to social ostracism, she walks into the sea and swims to her death. Like Clarissa's, Edna's death is pictured as a triumph over a society that is antagonistic to the female hero. The imagery associated with the sea suggests the infinite possibilities of the heroic life and the feeling of "going home" that is the hero's ultimate reward. She dies "thinking of the bluegrass meadow that she had traversed when a little child, believing that it had no beginning and no end" (p. 190). As she dies, she sees the sea as the meadow, which enfolds and comforts her, and gives her the sensation of finding a place where a female hero can feel at home.

Echoes of Whitman, moreover, remind us that the ultimate transcendental experience is union with nature through mystic vision or death. Whitman's "Out of the Cradle Endlessly Rocking" is particularly important to Chopin's novel, because the poem so clearly celebrates the ultimate consummation of the passionate yearning of the individual for community in death, because there the hero or the poet no longer feels alienated from nature or other people. The voice that tells about this "delicious" union in death is an "old crone" rocking the cradle of life. Both Whitman and Chopin assume the archetypal association of the sea as the mother of the world.

In this context, both the transcendent basis for Chopin's novel and the function of the sea as surrogate mother become clear. Edna's biological mother is dead. Her female guides—Madame Ratignolle and Mademoiselle Reisz—both have sacrificed human attributes that Edna believes to be necessary to female life. Madame Ratignolle lives the conventional life of wife and mother and is rewarded with the love and approval of husband, children, and friends. Mademoiselle Reisz sacrifices sexuality and community for the joy of pursuing her art. Without an adequate role model to suggest an integrated and full female life and without the nurturant, compassionate understanding for her plight traditionally associated with mother love, Edna goes home to her symbolic mother in death.

The examination of these four novels suggests that a literature recounting women's struggles to achieve sexual fulfillment and autonomy is not a recent phenomenon only. The hero in each of the narratives finds herself in serious and even mortal conflict with the society's assumptions that women are either virgins or whores and that men are either saints or rakes. Society punishes as scapegoats even the innocent and natural women who are involuntarily connected with sexuality. In works such as *Clarissa* and *Tess of the D'Urbervilles,* it is the reader more than the protagonist who understands, from what has happened in the narrative, that sexuality is as natural to women as to men and that the villains are the double standard and the association of sex with domination. The reader who sympathizes with the protagonist to some extent comes to terms with the inner dragon of guilt about her own sexuality.

As in *Jane Eyre,* the traditional love story frequently is about sexuality and autonomy. Many works—especially gothic novels such as *Jane Eyre* and Ann Radcliffe's *The Mysteries of Udolpho*—focus on the development in the hero of self-command. This means, in practice, that the hero becomes psychologically whole: She learns to balance reason and emotion and to develop the ability not to be emotionally dependent on the man she is to marry. Usually, however, the "happy ending" involves something of a compromise. She bargains for as much autonomy as a married woman can have. Chaucer's Wife of Bath explains to the pilgrims how she used trickery to ensure both sexual fulfillment and sovereignty in her marriages. Richardson's Pamela bargains with the "Jewel" of her chastity before marriage and with her moral superiority afterward. The dilemmas and the devices of the hero, and the possible solutions, are all a direct result of the sexual double standard.

Contemporary literature, however, reveals that free love (and available birth control) does not automatically solve the problem. In the autobiography of a British television personality, entitled *Annie: The Female Experience* and written under the pseudonym Anne Zoltan, sexual monomania replaces virginity as a trap for women. Empty, depersonalized sex becomes a substitute for real fulfillment, and the protagonist again finds herself the object rather than the heroic subject of her own life. Annie recognizes that she and others were deceived into

> thinking ourselves actors and authors; but in fact we . . . [were] the prey in the balloon; and while we mated and

> hungered and thought ourselves remarkably interesting, still
> only the prey in the balloon, rolled between the legs of the
> demons and phantoms, rolled frantically across empty shafts
> of Space. Wasted seed, adulterated impulse, and prostituted
> hope; misdirected love making the universe turbulent, rolling
> the demented prey inside the balloon until it pops, and we
> tumble dollwise, to the ground, exhausted, convinced we
> have just had a Great Time in Bed.[21]

According to Carolyn Heilbrun's article "The Woman as Hero," in great modern literature a woman is often a clearer symbol of the modern human condition than a white male because of "the peculiar tension that exists between her apparent freedom and her actual relegation to a constrained destiny."[22] Rennie Morgan (née MacMahon) in John Barth's *The End of the Road* is an example. The modern paradox of apparent freedom and actual restriction is illustrated when she has an affair with her husband's best friend, Jake Horner. Her husband, Joe, admits that he instigated the affair; she becomes pregnant because of a birth control failure, and dies having an illegal abortion.

The Laocoön figure on Jake's mantle is a visual equivalent of Rennie's dilemma. Laocoön traditionally appears being crushed to death with his two sons by two serpents. Jake identifies these serpents as "Knowledge and Imagination, which, grown great in the fullness of time, no longer tempt but annihilate."[23] Joe, the serpent of knowledge, and Jake, the serpent of the imagination, together constrict and destroy both Rennie and her unborn child. In one scene, Rennie sits—bound by the consequences of her involvement with the two men—while they discuss what she should do. Rennie's identity with Laocoön is made explicit when she is strapped to the table, immobile and in pain, while a quack doctor performs the abortion with Jake helping to hold her down.

The End of the Road is a morality play in which Joe and Jake compete for Rennie's soul. The novel demonstrates the inhumanity of the Job story and the everyman dramas in which God allows the devil to test the faith of a follower by causing him to suffer. In Jake's words,

> Joe was The Reason, or Being. . . . I was the Unreason, or
> Not-Being; and the two of us were fighting without quarter for
> possession of Rennie, like God and Satan for the soul of Man.
> This pretty ontological Manicheanism would certainly stand
> no close examination, but it had the triple virtue of excusing
> me from having to assign to Rennie any essence more specific
> than The Human Personality, further of allowing me to forni-
> cate with a Mephistophelean relish, and finally of making it
> possible for me not to question my motive, since what I was
> doing was of the essence of my essence. Does one look for
> introspection from Satan? (p. 123)

The husband and the seducer here are not distinguishable in their effect, for both dehumanize Rennie. Rennie comes to understand their complicity, attacking their assumption that they are contending opposites. She tells Jake, "You're *not* totally different from Joe: you're just like him. . . . You work from the same premises" (p. 59).

Joe engineers his wife's affair with Jake (p. 138) as a test of her faith in him. He says he wants her to learn to be clear-minded, articulate about her ideas, and independent. Rennie, however, understands that in reality he wants her "independently" to choose to think and act just as he does. As with God and mankind, her choice to follow him works to his glory only if she does so out of her own free will. She does not mind recreating herself in his image, however, because as she tells Jake, she'd "rather be a lousy Joe Morgan than a first-rate Rennie MacMahon" (p. 48). To please Joe, "I scrapped every last one of my friends. . . . I had to completely change my mind not only about my parents but about my whole childhood. I'd thought it was a pretty ideal childhood, but now I saw it as just so much cottonwool. I threw out every opinion I owned because I couldn't defend them. I think I completely erased myself, Jake, right down to nothing, so that I could start over" (p. 57). Rennie explains that "I think of Joe as I'd think of God" (p. 58). She daydreams that "Joe had invited the Devil to test me, too. . . . But this Devil scared me, because I wasn't that strong yet and what was a game for Joe was a terrible fight for me" (p. 63).

Like Laocoön, who warned the Trojans not to allow the Trojan horse to enter their walls, Rennie perceives the danger of allowing Jake into the family circle. Jake tempts her to question her husband's divinity. She has opted for safe captivity because she "had peered deeply into herself and had found *nothing*" (p. 62). She does not feel capable of moral and intellectual autonomy. However, Jake makes her acknowledge that Joe is only human. At Jake's suggestion, they watch Joe through the window as he struts around in front of a mirror and then masturbates and simultaneously picks his nose (pp. 65–66).

Joe, Jake, and Rennie choose to play the static, allegorical roles of God, Satan, and Everyperson, respectively, to avoid the chaos and the responsibility of human life. Awareness of this denial of life varies with each character. Jake, for example, realizes how dehumanizing the roles are, whereas Joe plays his part with remarkable innocence. Traditional socialization may explain why none of the three protagonists sees Rennie as the main character in the drama—even though she is the Everyperson figure. The two men see her primarily as a pawn in a male power game. Rennie cannot imagine herself as other than a supporting character in some man's drama. Even when she loses faith in Joe, she cannot act independently because she does not believe she has a self worth saving. Jake notes that "asserting her own opinion by simply refusing to comply with his [Joe's] policy decisions at all—was apparently beyond her strength" (p. 119).

She has the abortion that Joe wants and Jake arranges because she does not think of the unborn child as hers: She sees the child, as she sees herself, as necessarily belonging to one of the men. She begins to sob on the abortionist's table, vomits, and chokes to death. Rennie's example demonstrates that it is possible for the hero to learn the true identity of the light and dark men without learning to see herself as primary or heroic.

Exposés of men's dehumanization of women in their battle with one another are common in contemporary literature, especially in literature by male authors. Ken Kesey's *Sometimes a Great Notion* is an example. As in Barth's story, the plot revolves around a triangle in which two brothers vie for the love of the older brother's wife, Viv. Kesey's characters are more realistically portrayed than Barth's, and Kesey attributes the male contest to an unresolved Oedipal situation. Viv leaves the two men to resolve their own problems, saying "I love them but I cannot give myself for them. Not my whole self. I have no right to do that." She gets on the bus and begins her own journey.[24]

In Erica Jong's *Fear of Flying,* Isadora Wing is sexually emancipated. Like Barth's Rennie, she lives in a mid-twentieth-century world in which a woman is not only allowed to be sexual, but may be denigrated as rigid and castrating if she is not. For Isadora, as for many of her fictional and real-life contemporaries, sexual freedom does not essentially alter the terms of sexual domination and oppression. The dragon to be slain is still that of female dependence, which stems from the woman's continuing conviction that her sexuality is not her own to enjoy and learn from, but the male's and society's to manipulate and restrict. Her life is a continual "manhunt." In fact, Isadora Wing is dominated by men whom she does not even like. As one of the contemporary, liberated, "Free Women," she finds herself repeatedly "waking up in bed with a man I couldn't bear to talk to."[25]

Her exit from the garden occurs when her first husband, Brian Stollerman, goes mad: "It had come down to a choice between me or him, and I chose me." Yet she feels guilty about leaving him. "A good woman would have given over her life to the care and feeding of her husband's madness. I was not a good woman. I had too many other things to do" (p. 210).

The choice of self is complicated by societal pressures, as well as by her internal dragon of guilt and fear. She recognizes that she is trapped by her own "fantasies," "fears," and "false definitions" (p. 47). Her mother's legacy to her is the idea that "being a woman meant being married, frustrated, and always angry. It meant being split into two irreconcilable halves" (p. 48). Later in the novel, she refers to this legacy of the split life. "I was furious with my mother for not teaching me how to be a woman, for not teaching me how to make peace between the raging hunger in my cunt and the hunger in my head" (p. 154).

The irreconcilable split between Isadora as artist and as woman is complicated by her belief that she must choose one man and "belong" to him. She is terrified of being left without a man—even temporarily. As she explains, a single woman in American culture finds herself the object of contempt, ridicule, pity, and even suspicion, while male bachelorhood receives a totally positive press. His status is presumed to be by choice, hers by default. Thus, even the happy single woman is assumed to be waiting to be rescued, "as if she were waiting for Prince Charming to take her away from all this. All what? The solitude of living inside her own soul? The certainty of being her self instead of half of something else?" (pp. 10–11). After five years of marriage to her second husband, Bennett Wing, Isadora finds herself "itchy for men, itchy for solitude" (p. 10). Her conventional life with Bennett deprives her of both sexual passion and autonomy. She relieves her boredom by fantasizing about a sexual encounter with a stranger that would allow her to be both sexual and autonomous because it would be without "power games" or "ulterior motives" (p. 14).

Isadora wants a man who will provide security for her—and to some extent define and complete her—and she also wants a heroic life of adventure. Symbolically, she is torn between two men, who are light and dark in their attributes if not in appearance. Her husband, Bennett, who is an analyst, represents the accepted ideology of the time. This time it is not Puritanism, but Freudianism, that provides life-denying tenets and blind allegiance to the social status quo. Isadora sees the Freudians' liberal stance as covering up a reactionary attitude regarding essential questions of "the family, the position of women, [and] the flow of cash from patient to doctor" (p. 17).

Like many female heroes, Isadora has no model for the truly heroic life. So she turns to the myth of romantic love as a guide to metaphysical and psychological fulfillment. The seducer Adrian offers an alternative, existential ethic of living for the moment: However, like Bennett and his fellow analysts, Adrian hides tyranny under the promise of participatory democracy. His verbal allegiance to a relationship without rules turns out to mean a relationship defined by his whim. As existentialists, "we were forbidden to talk about the future or to act as if the future existed" (p. 177). Full of doubts, she runs off with the rake, only to find that Adrian's existential talk is a mask for a new double standard. Like the traditional "ruined woman," it is she alone who gives up security for adventure by risking the ruin of her marriage. Existential freedom, for him, means that they go by his rules. He ends their adventure just in time to meet his wife and children for a trip, as he had planned all along. She begins to recognize that the husband and seducer labels are inadequate, that Bennett and Adrian are "like Siamese twins. . . . Blood brothers" (p. 144).

When Adrian leaves, Isadora feels as if she is stepping off the edge of the world, into chaos, into the void. Having lived according to the requirements of the two men, she has lost any sense of her own ability to choose for herself. She has the typical sensation of crying to Adrian for help, of falling apart, of cracking up. Her first step is to realize that the assumption that either man is responsible for or able to rescue her is false. She is not "Adrian's child." For the first time she faces the fact of her freedom. She admits, "It was the most terrifying sensation I'd ever known in my life. Like teetering on the edge of the Grand Canyon and hoping you'd learn to fly before you hit bottom" (p. 271). However, she realizes even in her terror that her fall is fortunate. In fact, she claims to have known "all along" that he would betray her; she has deliberately "used him" as a tool in her own psychological progress toward freedom and autonomy (p. 271). At the end of the book, she is in Bennett's hotel room, but the situation is ambiguous: "Perhaps I had only come to take a bath. . . . It was not clear how it would end" (p. 311). What is clear is that her seducer, by placing her beyond the security of definition by a man, has ironically been the agent of a fortunate fall into freedom. For the first time in Isadora's life, she has a sense that she exists alone. "But whatever happened, I knew I would survive it. I knew, above all, that I'd go on working. Surviving meant being born over and over. It wasn't easy, and it was always painful. But there wasn't any other choice except death" (p. 311). Whether she stays with Bennett or leaves him (as she does in the movie version of the novel), she will no longer be dependent on a man for her identity, nor will she feel the fragmentation of herself that such dependence produces.

This moment of freedom and wholeness that she experiences in the hotel room also includes a new sensation of pleasure in her physical and sexual self, which she had imagined to be so emancipated before. In the bathtub, she receives genuine delight from observing and touching her body. She describes its various pleasing parts, and she even makes a comic reference to the heroism reflected there: "I looked down at my body . . . The Tampax string fishing the water like a Hemingway hero. . . . A nice body. Mine. I decided to keep it. I hugged myself. It was my fear that was missing. The cold stone I had worn inside my chest for twenty-nine years was gone" (p. 311). Without this fear, she has a new relationship with herself and her writing, because she no longer has to censor her words, thoughts, actions, or creativity in order to please others.

In this novel Jong moves away from a linear plot. Form tends to follow content in a well-written novel, and although Jong's work is not perfect stylistically, its spiral, associative structure is more similar to work in the "feminist mode" discussed in the next chapter than to the form characteristic of the traditional novel. On the whole, however, the writers discussed in this chapter to one degree or another work from the basic, linear plot structure of the love story. Since the love story is the female version of the male "rags to riches" plot, works such as Cather's *O Pioneers* combine romantic love with a Horatio Alger success story. Often, as is the case with Charlotte Brontë's *Jane Eyre,* there is some disunity of tone because the assumptions behind the plot conflict with themes of the work, which focus on the importance of wholeness and autonomy in a woman's life. While in some cases this disunity causes some problems with the novel form, it also enables authors to camouflage feminist ideas in acceptable, protective wrapping.

Of course, the ultimate problem faced by a writer who uses the romantic love story as a vehicle for exploring a woman's growth toward wholeness and independence is designing an appropriate ending. Most often, the author kills the hero rather than detailing a compromising accommodation to a patriarchal society inimical to female heroism. When accommodation does occur, as in *Barren Ground, O Pioneers,* and *The Odd Women,* the hero usually has some independence from social opinion—as a farmer or revolutionary—and, in addition, sublimates her sexuality. Occasionally, as in *Jane Eyre* or *Wuthering Heights,* the love story ends with an egalitarian relationship between two people, each of whom has stopped repressing the qualities society reserves for the other sex. Whether the hero is married or not, economic independence is primary in order for her to ensure autonomy, but the hero also chooses work—when she can—that expresses her identity. Here again, it is difficult for the hero to find an appropriate social place, for her society defines work as drudgery done only for status and money. Whether through farming, art, teaching (as in *The Odd Women* or Charlotte Brontë's *Villette*), or the managing of a household (as in *Jane Eyre*), the "happy ending" includes autonomy, love, creativity, and achievement.

The female hero who sees her sexuality as inseparable from her spiritual self can become involved in sexual encounters without being dominated. She is the actor and the chooser, in sole possession of her own sexuality. The speaker in Adrienne Rich's poem "Re-forming the Crystal" experiences "Desire" as "the sudden knowledge that the body is sexual." She also knows that the lover she desires and fantasizes going to meet at the airport is "not the source of that energy and joy" that she feels—she is the source. Furthermore, she describes other experiences filled with physical or psychological danger into which the same energy might lead her, and in which she, as one of "the chieftainers," chooses the object on which she will unleash that energy and joy.[26]

Several protagonists in earlier literature are able to enjoy a remarkably similar joy and autonomy in their sexuality. Chaucer's Wife of Bath is perhaps the first well-known female character in English literature not only to achieve sovereignty in a sexual relationship with a man, but also actively and without shame to enjoy her own sexuality in the world: "It tickleth me aboute myn herte roote [root]. / Unto this day it dooth myn herte boote [good] / That I have had my world as in my tyme."[27] G. B. Shaw's Mrs. Warren, in the play *Mrs. Warren's Profession,* is totally without guilt over the fact that she has financed her daughter's stint at Oxford with the income she receives as a successful prostitute. She defends herself against her morally outraged daughter by saying,

> All we had was our appearance and our turn for pleasing men. Do you think we were such fools as to let other people trade on our good looks by employing us as shop girls, or barmaids,

or waitresses when we could trade in them ourselves and get all the profits instead of starvation wages? . . . What is any respectable girl brought up to do, but to catch some rich man's fancy and get the benefit of his money by marrying him?—as if a marriage ceremony could make any difference in the right or wrong of the thing![28]

The fallen woman in Thomas Hardy's poem "The Ruined Maid" is also delighted with the advantages—economic, social, and cultural—of her newly acquired sexual experience. Her responses to her former country acquaintance, whom she meets in town, indicate that every aspect of her life has changed for the better. When the country innocent envys her freedom and "fine sweeping gown," the maid replies " 'My dear—a raw country girl, such as you be, / Cannot quite expect that. You ain't ruined.' said she."[29] Very few heroes of myth and literature are so sanguine about prostitution; at best, it is chosen as the least of several evils. However, when the hero successfully slays the dragons of virginity and romantic love, her body is hers; accordingly, she and only she can decide how and when her sexuality should manifest itself.

Even when sexuality leads to pregnancy, many heroes do not sacrifice their autonomy. Ursula Brangwen, in D. H. Lawrence's *The Rainbow,* refuses to marry her lover, Anton Skrebensky, even though she is pregnant. After a miscarriage she muses, "There would be no child: she was glad. If there had been a child, it would have made little difference, however. She would have kept the child and herself, she would not have gone to Skrebensky."[30]

When the hero demythologizes the male and reconciles sexuality with autonomy, she heals the split between mind and body, spirit and flesh. The state of wholeness and independence that is her treasure is embodied in the ancient concept of the Virgin-Mother goddess. M. Esther Harding writes in *Woman's Mysteries: Ancient and Modern:*

> The term virgin, then, when used of the ancient goddess, clearly has a meaning not of today. It may be used of a woman who has had much sexual experience; it may even be applied to a prostitute. Its real significance is to be found in its use as contrasted with "married" . . . a girl belongs to *herself* while she is virgin—unwed—and may not be compelled either to maintain chastity or to yield to an unwanted embrace. As virgin she belongs to herself alone, she is "one-in-herself."[31]

Further, the state of wholeness she achieves is not static: Her sexuality, her creativity—in fact, all her activities and achievements—emanate from and express her individuality. Accordingly, self-expression replaces self-denial as the informing principle of the female hero's life.

Chapter 6
A Woman Is Her Mother

Before sisterhood, there was the knowledge—transitory, fragmented, perhaps, but original and crucial—of mother and daughterhood.

Adrienne Rich, *Of Woman Born*

According to the traditional view of the hero, both men and women dissociate themselves from the mother at the beginning of the heroic quest. The traditional quest is a search for the father, who will initiate the hero into the world. Through the discovery of the father, the hero finds an appropriate identity and place in society. During the quest, the male hero is to develop his father's positive qualities—autonomy, courage, intelligence, independence, and self-control—so that he can replace his father as "master of the world." (His wife is both a symbol of the world and one of the people he conquers and governs.) The female, however, is not expected to develop the father's qualities. Her task is to learn to sublimate her desire for autonomy and growth and to find identity through her relationship with a man. In Joseph Campbell's words, her task is "to *be* the mastered world."[1]

When women are portrayed as heroes, however, their journeys do not conform to traditional theory. The female hero does initially leave the childhood home,and she often rejects her mother when she begins a search for fulfillment through romantic love. At some point, however, as we have seen, she becomes disillusioned. Rejecting both the man she finds and the idea of being a helpmate, object, or symbol in his heroic journey, she elects instead to develop within herself the heroic qualities society has seen as male. To the degree that the traditional male mode of heroism is assumed by the author to be *the* pattern of human heroism, her journey will end at this point. In a larger number of works, the female hero goes one step further: Having discovered the powerful father within herself, she reconsiders her original repudiation of the mother. Her quest becomes a search for her true, powerful female parent.

The reconciliation with the mother allows the hero to develop within herself human qualities such as nurturance, intuition, and compassion, which the culture denigrates as female. By extension, she is able to develop positive, sympathetic affiliations with other women. The hero comes to understand that neither "male" nor "female" qualities are positive when isolated from their complements. For example, self-interest and compassion are positive only when combined. Thus, she not only develops both her male and female qualities, but redefines their meaning.

A fully integrated human being, she is in a position to understand that the distinction between male and female qualities is created by the inequitable power relationship between men and women. This integrated selfhood, which the hero achieves in the process of her journey, precludes her assuming the role of dominating matriarch, the equivalent of the male conqueror-ruler. Because, to her, all humans are candidates for full heroism, no one is to be mastered or master.

Awareness of the limitations of the traditional patriarchal model of heroism has led many male heroes also to be ambivalent, at best, about being heroic in the traditional sense. The classical Western hero, for example, rides off into the sunset to avoid accepting the position of authority in the community he has served. In the twentieth century, most male protagonists refuse to be heroic according to patriarchal guidelines—that is, to conquer nature or other people—and are thereby identified dualistically as anti-heroes. For men as well as for women, the repudiation of this traditional heroic model increasingly is associated with the reconciliation with the mother. Ken Kesey in *Garage Sale* credits the women's movement with teaching him that men can no longer continue to rape "Mother Earth"; Robert Bly in *Sleepers Joining Hands* calls for men to be reconciled with the archetypal Great Mother, to stop repressing the feminine qualities. Too often such male writers are oblivious to the need for political action to change the status of women, assuming that "woman" equals nature and the unconscious. Nevertheless, it is encouraging to see the emergence of a new pattern in which the male hero also reaches reconciliation with qualities he has previously denigrated as feminine. This reconciliation with the mother, combined with the emergence of the redefined female hero, suggests that a new egalitarian, fully human model of heroism for both men and women is becoming the norm. Kurt Vonnegut, Jr., humorously rejects the classic search-for-the-father theme that pervades Western literature by asserting the greater contemporary importance of the rediscovery of the powerful mother: "It seems to me that really truthful American novels would have the heroes and heroines alike looking for *mothers* instead . . . I wouldn't feel particularly good if I found another father."[2]

Authors who are consciously feminist emphasize the female hero's reconciliation with her mother as crucial to a successful journey. In works that make the patriarchal assumptions of traditional heroic theory, the mother-daughter bond is notable by its absence or by its subordinate position relative to the father-daughter relationship. Before exploring the reconciliation with the mother in more fully feminist works, it is important to note the implications for the potential hero of failure to challenge traditional sex-role assumptions.

Fanny Burney's *Evelina* (1778) is a case in point. Evelina's mother is dead; she is estranged from her father. Her mother, Caroline Evelyn, died in poverty and disgrace after Evelina's wealthy father repudiated her, unjustly charging her with infidelity. Evelina hopes to attain a social place by marrying an appropriately rich, moral, and handsome man who, according to the myth of romantic love, will provide her with a social identity, including a new name. She looks for a man who is like her kind, moral foster father, Rev. Villars—but rich as well.

However, she feels that her own worth is tainted by her mother's alleged crime. She must be reconciled with her real, biological father, Sir John Belmont. Without her father's money and good social name, and without his acknowledgement that the mother was guiltless, Evelina cannot marry the wealthy, moral, and mannerly Lord Orville. Evelina herself emphasizes not these practical considerations, but her own role as a loving, dutiful daughter who yearns to know her real father. After many years, Evelina is presented to her father. He is convinced that she is his daughter because she looks exactly like her mother. He exclaims, "My God! does Caroline Evelyn still live!"[3] Evelina kneels before her father. She tells of her love for him, offering to sacrifice her life if the "sight of me were terrible to you." The reader might well wonder, along with the father, "Wilt thou . . . own thy father, the destroyer of thy mother?" (pp. 366–367). The answer is yes, because in a patriarchal situation women are expected to submit themselves to the male for sanction. Evelina brings with her a letter from her mother asking him "to clear her name, and receive her child." In the letter, Evelina's dead mother speaks of her love and forgiveness for the man who killed her. Sir John implores Evelina, "though representative of my departed wife, speak to me in her name, and say that the remorse which tears my soul tortures me not in vain." But Evelina replies, ". . . it is against nature for child to bless parent." She asks rather, "My dear, my long-lost father, leave me not, I beseech you! Take pity on your child, and rob her not of the parent she so fondly hoped would cherish her' " (p. 355). Evelina, like her mother, is a supplicant of the man who has wronged her. Her reward for such self-deprecation is marriage to Lord Orville, wealth, and social prestige. Evelina's action, therefore, may be interpreted as self-serving.

Moreover, the submissive forgiveness that Evelina and the author so freely grant to the father is not extended to other women in the novel. Evelina's grandmother, who is Evelina's guardian in Paris, is held responsible for being a wicked, immoral, and improper "stepmother." Primarily, Mrs. Duval is condemned because she insists on taking Evelina to "improper" places and making her do "improper" things. To do so will ruin Evelina's reputation, preventing Lord Orville—or another aristocratic and "moral" man—from marrying her. When a number of men are heaping insults on women for their lack of intelligence and morality, Evelina's letter to Rev. Villars criticizes not the men but the one woman, Mrs. Selwyn, who defends her sex. Evelina writes piously, ". . . how many enemies, my dear Sir, does this unbounded severity excite!" (p. 344). Evelina's intolerance toward women and leniency toward her father can be explained as social self-interest. It is also a projection of female self-hatred, a legacy from her self-effacing mother. Evelina, writing her story to her stepfather, Rev. Villars, is clearly trying to demonstrate her own worthiness to him. It is within the expectations of patriarchal tradition that she must prove her worth to a father figure such as Villars, who, in this case, is associated with a patriarchal theology as well. At the same time, she is expected to deny female worth by forgiving, without hesitation, the man who has killed her mother and rejected her. In acting "appropriately," she renounces all allegiance to herself and to other women.

Evelina is the agent of reconciliation between her mother and father. But this reconciliation is satisfactory only in patriarchal terms, because it depends so greatly on self-denial by mother and daughter. Furthermore, it is the mother's chastity and martyrdom—that is, her perfect fulfillment of the traditional myth of virginal purity—that makes her seem worthy in the terms of the novel. Evelina's marriage and reconciliation with her father are presented as a "happy ending." But from any point of view that takes women seriously as primary, autonomous beings, Evelina's denial of the importance of the loss of her mother, along with her acceptance of the myths of virginity, romantic love, and female inferiority, is disastrous. She will remain a secondary figure, living to please her father and her husband.

It is no accident that this work, which fundamentally reinforces female submissiveness, was hailed by such illustrious chauvinists as Dr. Samuel Johnson as a praiseworthy novel. White upper-class male reviewers, publishers, and critics, themselves conditioned by traditional sex roles, assume that literary works that teach women the traditional female role are meritorious.

One destructive effect of the widespread reinforcement of the view of women as adjuncts to men has been the alienation of women from each other and, specifically, of mother and daughter. Adrienne Rich, in *Of Woman Born*, comments: "The loss of daughter to the mother, the mother to the daughter, is the essential female tragedy. We acknowledge Lear (father-daughter split), Hamlet (son and father), and Oedipus (son and mother) as great embodiments of the human tragedy; but there is not presently enduring recognition of mother-daughter passion and rapture."[4] Rich goes on to explain that "there was such a recognition" in the Eleusinian mystery, but "we have lost it." The absence of a female tradition with positive heroic models denies the hero a major source of faith in herself. The following passage from Evangeline Walton's epic fantasy *The Children of Llyr* conveys the intense spiritual loneliness that the female hero experiences without the support of a powerful and sympathetic maternal figure. Brauweven, one of Llyr's daughters, prays to the Mothers, the gods of Welsh mythology, to protect her one surviving brother as she undertakes her own dark and fearsome journey: "But she could not feel the Mothers. She could feel only the great dark about her, the darkness that seemed as vast as the world. Both those she prayed to and those she prayed for seemed as far away as the stars, and she was all alone, shipwrecked and solitary forever."[5]

When the mother is unavailable to the hero as a role model or as a supportive friend, the hero often expresses her deep sense of loss in terms that define through contrast the positive mother-daughter bond. In Joanna Russ's short story "The Autobiography of My Mother," the narrator longs "to be my mother's child," but explicitly attributes her alienation from her mother to her mother's submission to "the Man":

> Something that will never happen: My mother and I, chums, sharing secrets, giggling at the dinner table, writing in each other's slambooks, going to the movies together. Doing up each other's hair. It's not dreadful that she doesn't want me, just embarrassing, considering that I made the proposal first. She would beam, saying sentimental things about her motherhood, anxiously reaching for my hand across the table. She was not wicked, ever, or cruel, or unkind. We'll never go skating together, never make cocoa in the kitchen at midnight, snurfing in our cups and whooping it up behind the stove.[6]

Russ's narrator's description of the longed-for friendship shows that at its best the mother-daughter relationship is a celebration of life that brings joy to both. It may also put the daughter in touch with her own true perceptions about the world, which social myths about womanhood would obscure. Jane Howard's *A Different Woman* is a collection of interviews with contemporary women from various walks of life. The author chose to do the research and to write the book because she had missed the chance to enjoy the same self-revealing conversations with her own mother, who had died when the author was nearly thirty-six. At the end of the book, Howard describes what she imagines as the ideal encounter in which she and her mother and sister could share with honesty and with joy:

You know what I wish the three of us would do, if my mother
came back? We could get into a car and drive off somewhere,
drive up past the undecided pin oaks to the zone where the
trees grow tall and straight, and we would stop and have a
picnic with a bottle of rosé, because she didn't like dry wine.
We would talk about how things really were, how we really
felt, and what we really were afraid of. And while we were at it,
we would laugh.[7]

Jessamyn West, in her autobiographical novel *The Woman Said Yes: Encounters with Life and Death,* shows how the heroic consciousness, which identifies
with life, can emerge as a result of the hero's positive relationship with her mother.
The narrator recounts that there were three women: "The three of us grew up
together: Grace, Jessamyn, and Carmen. But this is chiefly Grace's story—the story
of a woman who said yes to life in her own life, and whose efforts and example
helped her daughters to say yes to the life in her own life, and whose efforts and
example helped her daughters to say yes to the life in their lives, and courageous
enough when one life no longer held life to say yes to death."[8] Jessamyn says she
was "an orphan" when she was a child. She explains that the children of lovers are
always orphans of a special kind (p. 17). The lack of attention that she and other
children in the same situation receive she believes is positive because the children
are freer to lead their own lives. Grace, her mother, loved Jessamyn, but she did not
try to make her daughter into a carbon copy of herself. In fact, she never noticed
what Jessamyn wore or much about what she did.

When she is an adult, Jessamyn discovers that she has tuberculosis. The
doctors have diagnosed it too late, and she is sent home to her mother to die. Grace
will not reconcile herself to her daughter's death. She instills in her a desire to live
and to write. Paradoxically, during her long illness, Jessamyn for the first time feels
able to write, because her sickness absolves her of any conflict between the female
role and the role of a writer. Her mother cheers her up by telling her the story of her
life, and Jessamyn writes novels based on her mother's history. When she finally
recovers enough to become involved in the world again, she finds she is frightened
to do so. Because she thinks of herself as an invalid, she refuses a trip to New York
as potentially dangerous to her health. Her mother insists she change her mind: "I
think you are starting another kind of sickness if you don't [go]. Worse than the
other" (p. 79).

Grace's very name suggests her power to rescue her daughter at the critical
moment, saving her from physical, psychological and spiritual death. Jessamyn, in
a final tribute to her mother, notes, "She had given me birth three times over"
(p. 79). She gave her physical birth; through her stories, she "gave me a life, back in
'the old country,' " as the subject for stories; most important, she rescued her from
despair during her bout with tuberculosis. "One expects a baby to cry, to accept
every defeat as final; but a grown woman's determined despair is more exasperat-
ing. A baby falls, gets up and tries again. The woman-baby fell twice and decided
never to attempt anything as risky as walking again" (p. 80). When Grace herself is
dying, Jessamyn and her mother celebrate their lifelong bond reminiscing over
Grace's role as rescuer: "We had some good times in spite of everything, didn't
we?" Grace remarks. "Still have," Jessamyn replies (p. 80).

Grace's example makes Jessamyn able to nurture her little sister, Carmen,
who has incurable cancer. Carmen asks Jessamyn to help her die before the pain

becomes overwhelming, because she wants to die whole and in control of life. Jessamyn helps her to say yes to death, to die with integrity, when it becomes appropriate. They plot together how to execute the plan. When Carmen takes the pills, Jessamyn stays with her until she becomes unconscious; she then guards her, during the long hours it takes for her to die, to keep doctors or friends from discovering her and attempting to "save" her. In West's autobiographical novel, the mother-daughter and sister bonds are primary even though all three women have husbands whom they love. Furthermore, the female bond is associated with a philosophical outlook that celebrates life to such an extent that even pain and death are accepted and affirmed when they are unavoidable.

Most literary works, however, begin with a different situation. The hero is estranged from her mother and deifies men. She lives in a world that attempts to deny or control experiences and attributes that are judged unpleasant or undesirable. Since the alienation between mother and daughter is caused by the unnatural dependence on men and male approval, the reconciliation with the mother usually occurs only after the hero has demythologized the patriarch. An unexpected result of seeing both men and women as valuable mortals—neither deities nor destroyers—is a major shift in consciousness: All experience and all human attributes are affirmed.

In some works, the reconciliation with the mother and the attendant alteration in ways of perceiving occur as soon as the hero sees that the emperor is naked. Thus the reconciliation may occur at the end of a story that begins with the hero searching for a father figure to validate her. Joanna Russ's "Daddy's Girl," an allegorical gothic tale, is a prototype for this pattern. "Daddy" is associated with patriarchal values, which separate women and men from their true selves; "If mother is Being Daddy is *nada,* the flaw, the crack at the center of the universe, the illusion that implodes as you look at it, the glittery thing you thought was real but it's made out of nothing: seduction, emptiness, cold, the brightness of rooms with air. Terrible energy radiates from this. It's the state of being falsified."[9] The protagonist fantasizes about Motherland: She imagines it as a place where she could be fully and joyously herself, yet she recognizes that "I can never remember the Motherland because my father's country has what's called invalidation" (p. 149). In Fatherland, it is always snowing, but neither the hero nor her imaginary companion, Linda, recognize that they are cold. In place of intimate, loving relationships, Fatherland substitutes sadomasochistic, pornographic sexuality, which reinforces male dominance. Linda is the woman the hero has been taught to be—beautiful, innocent, masochistic, enduring. The hero fantasizes about men: "Every man in the place rams himself into her (it's a treat) with ecstatic ohs! and ahs! (she, not I) bruising her, violating her, hurting her, using her" (p. 153). Meanwhile, Linda "has no sexual thoughts" herself. Enduring all this, she remains innocent (p. 52).

In this parody of a gothic romance, the setting is a castle, and the secret inhabitant is the hero's ultimate love. The hero wishes she were a man. She thinks of the "many paintings in which a woman adores a dead male divinity" (p. 150). All through her fantasy, men see her as "only a means to a sensation" (p. 151). She feels hopeless, incomplete, and humiliated, needing "him so desperately" to fulfill her (p. 153). She searches the corridors night after night, prey to sadomasochistic sexuality, until she finally finds "the Man I'm looking for, the Governor who controls this castle" (p. 155). At the top of the stairs she finds him and he is "Daddy." When she sees him, she recognizes that "in some way that I don't understand," he is "a failure." Like the Wizard of Oz, he is puzzled and frustrated because he cannot live up to the expected godlike role of the patriarch. He takes out his frustration on the women he is close to, assuming that their inability or unwillingness to be weak, submissive subjects undercuts his power. She understands that "he's embittered by the world's refractoriness, by his mother's strength, by the treachery of his daughter" (p. 155). When he begins to heap insults on her and on all women, she likens him to a caged crow: "It would get terribly stirred up and would hop around its cage with a hoarse, loud caw, trying to eat the bars or worry at them with its beak, excited and gratified over things none of us could understand" (p. 156). When she sees that he is a prisoner of Fatherland too, that his power exists "in my head," she forgives her actual father and slays the captor patriarch. Magically—for this is a fairy tale—she and Linda both feel for the first time how cold it is in Fatherland. Saying goodbye, they walk through the door to Motherland. Like the other elements in Russ's fairy tales, the door is an allegorical door. In reality, "the door to the Motherland can be a door in a construction fence that leads nowhere, a door inside a closet that leads to a hidey-hole, a door in the brick front of a house on a street in a town in any part of the world. The trick is to get inside oneself" (p. 157).

The archetype behind this story is the myth of Demeter and Kore. Kore (Persephone), who is imprisoned by Hades in the dark underworld, is rescued by her mother and returns to the daylight world, the world of seasons. Linda and the hero are freed when they discover the strength within themselves. They then go from a world that is always night, always winter, to a daylight world governed by flux and by seasonal change. In Motherland, safe and warm, Linda is transformed from a mindless victim into an active androgynous being: "She pitches a tent, washes her socks, builds a fire, shears a sheep, ploughs a homestead, delivers a baby, sets up a collapsible typewriter, digs a field toilet, and holding a wetted finger up to the wind, accurately predicts the weather for the next twenty-four hours." The final vision of the two women is one of community and of coming home to a symbolic mother. As they settle down in the grass to share stories, they envision themselves "in Her lap this pale, fresh chilly summer dawn" (p. 157).

Doris Lessing's novel *Memoirs of a Survivor* is a mythic variation of this same basic plot. When the female bond is reestablished, the hero's world is suddenly and completely altered. At the beginning of the novel, the society is literally being destroyed by lack of nurturance. Men have been taught to repress their "womanly" nurturing qualities. Everyone expects women to take care of the emotional, integrative aspect of social life, including raising children, while men compete in the "jungle" of the marketplace. Women increasingly reject the traditional feminine role because female attributes and functions are denigrated and trivialized by the society. They become more and more unwilling to take on the society's nurturing function at the expense of careers, independence, and status. The result is a culture dominated by the worst, most primitive aspects of the male mode. Civilization is breaking down; people are moving about in predatory, competitive packs, in which virtually no one takes responsibility for anyone else. By the end of the novel, the newest generation of "sewer" children have grown up without any parenting at all. Amoral, they are totally without empathy or compassion for one another.

The narrator is an anonymous old woman who sits in her apartment observing the breakdown of society. She is surprised one day when a man appears, leaving with her a young girl to care for. About this time, the wall of her apartment begins to open up, showing her events in other times including the young girl's past. She sees that the girl's mother had completely internalized patriarchal values. She observes her charge as a small child watching bereft as her mother pays attention to her younger brother, clearly preferring him because he is male. The same male orientation makes the mother so involved in her career that she resents the demands of caring for her daughter, who internalizes the message that she is inadequate because she is female. As a result, the child learns to please, but never to show her real self.

The narrator is haunted by the continual sound of a baby crying. One day, as she searches in the endless rooms behind the wall, she discovers that the crying child is not the child left in her care, as she had assumed, but the child's mother. The implication of Lessing's allegory is that generation after generation of emotionally crippled women cannot love their girl children adequately because they were not loved. By the end of the novel, however, the protagonist and her charge form a true—if somewhat distant—relationship of love, caring, and mutual protection. Also, the young girl and her boyfriend take responsibility for homeless children. When everyone has left the city except bands of amoral, derelict, and almost inhuman children, suddenly the wall opens; the protagonist's charge, her boyfriend, her dog, and some children they have befriended walk through into another mode of being. Furthermore, because the old woman has learned to be nurturing, she symbolically finds her own positive mother. The visionary woman who leads them to a new consciousness is recognized by the narrator as "the one person I had been looking for all this time . . . : there she was."[10]

Each work that deals with the hero's reconciliation with the mother either implicitly or explicitly refers to the new mode of being that results. It is a state of human wholeness in which the hero now perceives the world without the restrictive context of traditional sex roles. Furthermore, the author typically foresees that the attainment of such a state by a critical mass of women and men would so profoundly change these individuals that it would completely alter society. This transformed state of being incorporates autonomy, achievement, and nurturance, healing the patriarchal split between male and female sex roles. As Lessing's story illustrates, when women are charged with nurturance but not valued for their activities, they tend to begin to reject those values and live by male ones. When the female hero discovers her true mother, she (and her culture) may reclaim the undervalued female attributes. (The new human society that is created when the mother is rediscovered will be discussed in the closing chapter, The Kingdom Transfigured.)

The Rescuer

Reconciliation with the mother, then, is crucial to the female hero. It is both a way of discovering her true identity and heritage and a means of achieving not only a higher mode of consciousness but a new society as well.

Usually, when the hero is at the nadir of despair, a nurturing, strong, and independent woman appears to her. Although the hero associates this figure with her biological mother, often the actual mother is more captor than rescuer. The powerful and heroic woman whom she encounters may be a surrogate mother figure. Unlike the male seducer who claims that he can slay the dragons for her, the female rescue figure tells the hero that she is capable of saving herself. Because her primary problem is the falsification and invalidation that Russ and other writers see as characteristic of patriarchal culture, the hero may not be able to uncover her powerful heroic self unless she is aided by this voice that tells her she can trust her own vision and abilities. An example of this voice in modern American popular culture is Wonder Woman. In the final frame of one of her comic-strip adventures, Wonder Woman explains to the women of England, whom she has inspired by her example to overpower and thereby to free themselves from the Seal men, "You saved yourselves—I only showed you that you could."[11]

When her own mother is more captor than rescuer, the hero typically feels herself a spiritual orphan who must find a positive, powerful, nurturing female mentor. Erica Jong's Isadora Wing, for example, confesses that "I always mutter 'Mother' when I'm scared. The funny thing is I don't even call my mother 'Mother' and I never have."[12] When the hero's biological mother is dead, she may appear to her in a vision. In Charlotte Brontë's *Jane Eyre,* Jane's mother appears to her when Jane is tempted to become Rochester's mistress. She is torn between her love for him and her fear of becoming dependent. At this crucial moment of decision, she looks up at the moon, which changes into a woman before her transfixed gaze:

> I watched her come—watched with the strangest anticipation; as though some word of doom were to be written on her disk. She broke forth as never moon yet burst from cloud; a hand first penetrated the sable folds and waved them away; then, not moon, but a white human form shone in the azure, inclining a glorious brow earthward. It gazed and gazed on me. It spoke to my spirit: immeasurably distant was the tone, yet so near.
> It whispered in my ear—
> "My daughter, flee temptation."
> "Mother, I will."[13]

References to the moon and the sea carry powerful associations—whether cultural or archetypal—with women and with female power. Sylvia Plath writes in her poem "The Moon and the Yew Tree," "The moon is my mother."[14] Doris Lessing in *The Golden Notebook* employs the imagery of the sea to raise Anna's surrogate mother and therapist, "Mother Sugar," to mythic significance. Anna is inspired by this rescue figure to imagine "the kind of life women never lived before," and to perceive her connection with a powerful female tradition: "Behind her voice I could hear the sounds she always evoked at such moments—seas lapping on old beaches, voices of people centuries dead. She had the capacity to evoke a feeling of vast areas of time by a smile or a tone of voice that could delight me, rest me, fill me with joy."[15] These visionary maternal images are reminiscent of Jung's archetype of the Great Mother. They may also evoke suggestions of the anima figure (according to Jung's thought, one aspect of the archetype of the Great Mother). However, they are powerful to the female hero not because they represent half of all human qualities but because they evoke a nonpatriarchal image of women as whole beings; they suggest the reintegration of nurturance, intuition, and compassion into the alienating, competitive, patriarchal world.

Whether the knowledge of heroic possibilities comes to the hero through an actual encounter or in a dream or vision, the rescuer is a projection of the hero's potential. When Isadora Wing is beginning to free herself of her dependency on male approval, she has a dream. The beginning of her dream demonstrates that she has hoped, by her achievements as a writer, to prove that she is not like other women; she should be exempted from traditional female limitations. She is about to be awarded the right to be married to three men simultaneously as a reward for her accomplishments, but is warned that she is expected to reject the "Honor." When she refuses to be a "good woman" who settles for one man only, making a virulent feminist speech, her worst fears are realized. As a result of her frank tirade, she discovers that she has been denied graduation: She has lost a fellowship grant and all three husbands. She moves up the steps to reclaim her diploma, only to find that the judgmental mother figure at the lecturn has turned into a black Colette, whose red hair looks like a halo. "Suddenly I understand that making love to her in public was the real graduation."[16] As the sexually aroused Isadora moves toward the woman, she symbolically rejects her allegiance to men and identifies with women, thus violating and rejecting patriarchal taboos.

In this dream, Isadora confronts the shadow identity she must integrate into the psyche if she is to be whole and autonomous. By making love to a woman like the strong, talented, liberated Colette, Isadora symbolically embraces the qualities that her society despises and would have her deny in herself. Her act also affirms her bond with all other women. The idolatry of men—and the resulting suppression of her own positive qualities—has kept her a dependent heroine, alienated from her mother, from other women, and from herself. Only after she accepts the part of her that is identified as female can she accept all of her qualities as human—as neither exclusively female nor exclusively male. Thus, she heals the split, defying the societal injunction that she cannot both be an artist and have babies (p. 40).

In the novels of Russ, Brontë, and Jong, the traditional message of patriarchal sex-role identification is that women nurture others and men achieve heroic selfhood. Therefore, if a woman is to achieve in the world, she cannot be nurturing. Should a woman move into the male mode, should she be achievement- and self-oriented, it is expected that she will relinquish her female nurturing, unselfish qualities. The positive mother, in contrast, teaches the hero that ego, self-assertiveness, strength, and reason are actually compatible with nurturance and intuition.

The diary of Carolina Maria de Jesus, in which she describes her life as a poor but educated single mother of three in a Brazilian favela, eventually became the most widely sold book in Brazil. In her diary, she pays tribute to her mother, who taught her to be strong, independent, aggressive and intelligent, and also to care about others: "I haven't said anything about my dear mother. She was very good. She wanted me to study to be a teacher. It was the uncertainties of life that made it impossible for her to realize her dream. But she formed my character, taught me to like the humble and the weak."[17]

Elizabeth Gurley Flynn writes in her autobiography, *The Rebel Girl,* of her mother's support for her as a political activist and as a mother. She speaks of the crucial moment in her life, in 1910, when she is nineteen. Her baby is due in a few weeks; her husband, Jack Jones, is unexpectedly absent; she has been arrested and subjected to two trials for her political speaking on behalf of the Industrial Workers of the World (IWW); and Jones has decided that they should move to Butte, Montana, "where he would get a job in the mines. He proposed I should give up speaking and traveling and settle down to live with him in one place." Elizabeth has no desire to "settle down at nineteen"; she realizes how much her mother has contributed to her conviction that her life is naturally, and ought to be, one of risk, change, involvement in the public world in the cause of a more humane and just society:

> A domestic life and possibly a large family had no attractions for me. My mother's aversion to both had undoubtedly affected me profoundly. She was strong for her girls "being somebody" and "having a life of their own." I wanted to speak and write, to travel, to meet people, to see places, to organize for the IWW. I saw no reason why I, as a woman, should give up my work for his [her husband's]. I knew by now I could make more of a contribution to the labor movement than he could. I would not give up. I have had many heartaches and emotional conflicts along the way but always my determination to stick to my self-appointed task has triumphed.[18]

Elizabeth's mother, who gave her the vision and the encouragement to choose the heroic life, also provides her with the emotional and practical support necessary in the life Elizabeth has chosen. She writes of her decision to leave Jones, "I decided to go home to my mother. I knew she would understand and help me solve my problem. . . . She and my sister Kathie helped take care of my child from the day of his birth." Furthermore, her mother and sister come to her defense whenever others criticize her for not renouncing her own nature and goals for her husband or for her child. Her "gentle Mother" explains to her outraged brother, "Elizabeth can't help it. This is her work!" (p. 266).

Often it is only the attentive reader who sees that the hero's strength comes from her mother's example. George Meredith's *The Egoist* focuses on Clara Middleton's escape from a boring, oppressive marriage to the obtuse egoist, Willoughby Patterne. Clara's own wisdom, vitality, and commitment to living, more than anything or anyone outside herself, give her the strength needed to take the unconventional step of leaving a fiancé, affirming her own self-worth. She has a temperament that will not allow her to accept the repression of her self, which the traditional female role of Willoughby Patterne's wife would require. The source of that independent and self-valuing temperament is indicated in only one sentence in the novel, and that sentence is a negative comment by Clara's philosophically myopic father: He remarks, "Her mother had been an amiable woman, of the poetical temperament nevertheless, too enthusiastic, imaginative, impulsive, for the repose of a sober scholar; an admirable woman, still, as you see, a woman, a firework. The girl resembled her."[19]

Like Clara Middleton's mother, the positive mother figure does not rescue her daughter or give her a specific map for her journey; instead, she gives her the skills and the confidence necessary to rescue herself. Moll Flanders's mother gives birth to Moll in Newgate prison. Immediately after, she is transported; but she leaves her daughter with an instinct for survival. Her legacy also includes the example of profitable deviancy: Out of economic necessity, Moll becomes a successful thief, "the richest of her trade in England." Having given her the psychological equipment to make the most of what she potentially is, Moll's mother much later gives her a financial inheritance that frees her to lead her own life, repudiating crime as a means of survival: "My mother had left a sum of money, and had tied her plantation for the payment of it, to be made good to the daughter, if ever she could be heard of, either in England or elsewhere."[20]

Moll Flanders also meets a number of surrogate mothers, who give her practical and spiritual aid in her journey. These women include a wise and sympathetic childhood guardian, a seamstress, a pawnbroker, and a lying-in house mother. Because they have not been protected by or dependent on men, none of these women shares the timidity, self-doubt, or lack of practical survival experience characteristic of the traditional dependent female. Thus, they represent for Moll not only nurturance but strength, self-sufficiency, and knowledge of the world. The women who nurture Moll range from her friends in the brothel to the eminent lady who cares for her when Moll is pregnant and who helps her to find a home for the child.

The female hero who triumphs over the negative messages of the patriarchal world often has more mentors and supporting characters, particularly female ones, than are immediately apparent. The patriarchally defined scene around her is deceptive, because it assumes loyal camaraderie among men and vicious competition among women. Meredith's Clara Middleton is blessed with several women friends who give her the support she needs in her heroic exit, support of which the men in the novel are totally unaware. For example, the men are convinced that Clara is jealous of Laetitia Dale. Laetitia, like Clara, is initially attracted to Willoughby Patterne, who courts her before Clara appears on the scene. In fact, in a series of revealing conversations between the two women, Laetitia adds credibility to Clara's own negative opinion of Willoughby by agreeing with her. Clara's deep friendship with Laetitia gives her the confidence to trust her own inner voices and to act on them. The witty widow, Mrs. Mountstuart, takes delight in complimenting Willoughby on his proposal to Laetitia, which he is trying to keep secret; in doing so, she helps Clara to be justifiably freed of her betrothal to Willoughby. Finally, Clara has the benefit of that invaluable supporting character in the lives of female heroes both fictional and real, the friend—in Clara's case, Lucy Darleton in London—to whom she knows she can go for emotional and practical reinforcement if she decides to make the traumatic exit from an oppressive situation.

As we see here, women friends often serve, individually or collectively, as rescuers, who help the hero to value herself and other women. In contemporary literature, the nurturing figure may be a female lover. In "Like This Together," Adrienne Rich celebrates the safety and nurturance she feels with her lover and friend: "Sometimes at night / you are my mother. . . . I / crawl against you, fighting / for shelter, making you / my cave."[21] In Marge Piercy's *Small Changes*, Beth is rescued by her friend Wanda, who frees her from distrust of her body, first, by teaching her exercises geared toward freeing energy as part of her training to be an actress, and, second, by loving her. The two of them eventually join a women's commune, which is designed to provide an atmosphere in which women can be fully self-actualized and at the same time be nurturing to others. The sisterhood characteristic of the commune enables women to work, to have relationships with women or men, and to raise children without sacrificing either independence or nurturance.

Charlotte Brontë's nineteenth-century novel *Shirley* presents examples of supportive sisterhood. It also describes both visionary and literal encounters with rescuing mother figures. Both Shirley Keeldar and Caroline Helstone are functional orphans. Shirley's parents are dead. Caroline's mother has abandoned her in her infancy: Because Caroline looked like her handsome, aristocratic, and derelict father, her mother feared that Caroline would have his character. Caroline's father, who is a drunkard, leaves her alone all day in a bleak, bare garret, forgets to feed her, and one day threatens to kill her because she is such a burden.

At this point, she is sent to live with her uncle, Mr. Helstone. Mr. Helstone has paid so little attention to his wife that he does not notice when her health begins to fail. He is surprised, but not grief-stricken, when she dies. Caroline confesses to Shirley's former governess and present companion, "Sometimes I wish somebody in the world loved me; but I cannot say that I particularly wish him [Mr. Helstone] to have more affection than he has. . . . It is my uncle's way not to care for women and girls—unless they be ladies that he meets in company."[22]

Both Shirley and Caroline long for a mother figure to nurture and guide them. Both also love men who seem inappropriate. Caroline loves Robert Moore, who appears not to return her love. Shirley loves Robert's brother, Louis, who is poor and a tutor. Shirley, an heiress, is expected to marry a wealthy, perhaps even a titled gentleman. Even though Caroline believes that Robert, the man she loves, loves Shirley, the two women gain immeasurable support from their friendship with each other. Shirley's former governess, Mrs. Pryor, is another supportive figure for both young women.

Shirley, when she was a schoolgirl, provided herself with a model of a positive heroic woman by fantasizing about Eve as an earth-mother goddess. One day, outside a church, when both women are in despair about their loves, this earth-mother appears to Shirley in a vision.

> It was—I now see—a woman-Titan: her robe of blue air spread to the outskirts of the heath, where yonder flock is gazing; a veil white as an avalanche sweeps from her head to her feet, and arabesques of lightning flame on its borders. Under her breath I see her zone, purple like the horizon: through its blush shines the star of evening. Her steady eyes I cannot picture; they are clear—they tremble with the softness of love and the lustre of prayer. Her forehead has the expanse of a cloud, and is paler than the early moon, risen long before dark gathers: she reclines her bosom on the ridge of Stilbro's Moor; her mighty hands are joined beneath it. So kneeling, face to face she speaks with God. (p. 256)

When Caroline suggests they go into the church, Shirley announces, "I will stay out here with my mother Eve. . . . I love her—undying, mighty being!" (p. 257). It is significant that Shirley complements the Christian patriarchal God with the pagan earth mother. The collective image of gods who suggest both male and female attributes is a foundation for a more inclusive pattern of human selfhood than traditional dualistic sex roles allow.

As Shirley needs a mother who embodies female power, Caroline longs for a mother who can provide the love and nurturance she never had. "Shirley had mentioned the word 'mother': that word suggested to Caroline's imagination not the mighty and mystical parent of Shirley's visions, but a gentle human form—the form she ascribed to her own mother; unknown, unloved, but not unlonged for" (p. 257). As Shirley longs for a mother figure to validate and support her own strength and vitality, Caroline yearns for a nurturing figure to let her know that she is worth loving, and help her develop the strength she needs to face the hardships of life:

> The longing of her childhood filled her soul again. The desire which many nights had kept her awake in her crib, and which fear of its fallacy had of late years almost extinguished, relit

> suddenly, and glowed warm in her heart: that her mother
> might come some happy day, and send for her to her
> presence—look upon her fondly with loving eyes, and say to
> her tenderly, in a sweet voice—"Caroline, my child, I have a
> home for you: you shall live with me. All the love you have
> needed, and not tasted, from infancy, I have saved for you
> carefully. Come! it shall cherish you now." (p. 257)

Caroline has cherished the idea that perhaps Robert Moore cares for her. Since he is literally the only love in her life, she throws the whole weight of her emotions into her affection for him. When she becomes convinced that he loves Shirley, she begins a slow "decline" toward dying. While her slow wasting away smacks of melodrama, it is not entirely incredible: While no one loves Caroline, everyone discourages her from seeking a profession and thereby fulfillment through work. There is absolutely no meaning in her life.

Shirley's companion, Mrs. Pryor, who comes to care for Caroline, literally saves Caroline's life by confessing that she is her long-lost mother:

> "But if you are my mother, the world is all changed to me.
> Surely I can live—I should like to recover—"
> "You *must* recover. You drew life and strength from my
> breast when you were a tiny, fair infant, over whose blue eyes I
> used to weep—Daughter! we have been long parted: I return
> now to cherish you again." (p. 340)

Mrs. Pryor cradles her in her arms, rocking her like a baby. In response to love and nurturance, Caroline recovers her health.

The confidence Shirley and Caroline get from the discovery of their symbolic and actual mother is responsible for the "happy ending" of the love plots. Shirley defies convention and marries Louis. Caroline gains the strength to live without Robert because she values herself more and because she has someone else to love. She is rewarded for her newfound independence when Robert proposes. He had been courting Shirley only because he wanted her money. When she spurns him, he begins to understand Caroline's and love's true value. At the novel's end Robert and Caroline marry and plan to live together with Mrs. Pryor.

The implication of this work is that a woman cannot have an egalitarian, positive relationship with a man without discovering her real or symbolic mother, that is, without learning her worth and her heritage as a woman. It is interesting that Brontë assumes—as many other authors do—that the reestablishment of bonds between mother and daughter, and egalitarian bonds between men and women, will create an atmosphere of general felicity that may spread to the community at large. In addition, everyone will be fully human in that they all will combine work and nurturance. Robert exclaims:

> Caroline, the houseless, the starving, the unemployed shall
> come to Hollow's Mill from far and near; and Joe Scott shall
> give them work, and Louis Moore, Esq., shall let them a tene-
> ment, and Mrs. Gill shall mete them a portion till the first
> pay-day. . . . Such a Sunday-school as you will have, Cary!
> such collections as you will get! such a day-school as you and
> Shirley, and Mill Ailley, will have to manage between you!
> (p. 508)

Maya Angelou's contemporary novel *I Know Why the Caged Bird Sings* describes a young black woman's development from dependent child to courageous young adult, her rediscovery of her mother, and her discovery of her own strength and value. Marguerite Johnson feels motherless because she and her brother have been sent to live in Stamps, Arkansas, with their grandmother, Mrs. Henderson, at ages three and four respectively. At the time, Marguerite does not know why her parents sent her away. Later she learns that her parents have divorced and her mother is beginning a new life. She and her brother, Bailey, sneak into town to watch a movie, in which there is a woman who looks like her mother. Later, she recalls nights when the two children cried together because they were "unwanted children."[23]

Marguerite is motherless in two ways. First, she feels rejected by her own mother; she interprets that rejection as a personal failure. When her mother does send for the children, Marguerite takes one look at her and "was struck dumb. I knew immediately why she had sent me away. She was too beautiful to have children" (p. 50). This young girl resigns herself to a life of rejection, assuming that her handsome and charming brother, Bailey, will capture all her mother's love. Marguerite is also motherless in the sense that she is not initially conscious of a role model for black women. Before she is called to her mother, she has internalized white society's ideals. She believes that she is inadequate because she is black and unattractive; she has a recurring fantasy of being miraculously transformed into a beautiful white child: "Wouldn't they be surprised when one day I woke out of my black ugly dream, and my real hair, which was long and blond, would take the place of the kinky mass that Mamma wouldn't let me straighten?" (p. 2).

Marguerite actually has a whole support system of beautiful and courageous black women. Through the action of the book, she learns to value them. Her grandmother is an extremely strong woman who owns and runs the town store. She is the only black woman in Stamps who is called "Mrs.," a title that indicates the respect she inspires. She teaches the children strength; but her lesson is limited in some ways. First, she has learned not to internalize racist messages, but she does not live in a world that provides her with the opportunity to fight racism directly. Marguerite uses fantasy to imagine circumstances in which her grandmother could act directly to assert her own dignity and to end racist practices; but her grandmother does not act out these fantasies because she is responsible for the survival of too many people. In many ways, she shows a model of heroism that involves the repression of the self and of spontaneous emotional reactions, whether anger or love. As a result, she does not show affection to her grandchildren.

From her grandmother, Marguerite learns to control her emotions so that she can be courageous and strong. The lack of affection and nurturance, however, makes her vulnerable to the attentions of her mother's lover, Mr. Freeman. When he is affectionate to her, she is so starved for love that she does not discourage his attentions. When he rapes her, she feels responsible. In court she is pressured to lie, saying that she did not encourage his advances. When relatives kill him, she holds herself responsible for his death.

Her mother sends her back to Stamps, where she is rescued by Bertha Flowers, who is considered "the aristocrat of Black Stamps." Marguerite has refused to talk after her "lie" caused a death, but Mrs. Flowers makes her read aloud. From the books Marguerite learns about the heroic lives of "great" and "common" people. She dislikes herself as a woman and as a black, but Mrs. Flowers teaches her pride. In retrospect Marguerite writes: "She made me proud to be a Negro, just by being herself" (p. 143).

Finally, it is her own mother who teaches her spontaneity, exuberance, and the value of the self. In many ways, her mother's example in not sacrificing her life for her children is crucial to Marguerite's self-actualization. But to develop a truly positive relationship with her mother, Marguerite has to get over her earlier feelings of rejection. She must also conquer her tendency to see her mother as a deity. She needs the mother-daughter bond as validation: She needs the love of the woman who, she felt, rejected her, as well as the approval of a woman who is beautiful. Because of her need, she makes her mother into a goddess. As a child, Marguerite feels a "love at first sight" admiration for her mother's beauty. She recalls, "I could never put my finger on her realness. She was so pretty and quick—I thought she looked like the Virgin Mary" (p. 57). Marguerite's mother refuses the goddess-mother role. She never "mothers" Marguerite in an oppressively attentive way: Her daughter is able, although living in the same house, to hide the fact that she is pregnant until near the time of the birth. Yet the mother-daughter relationship is a positive one. The mother makes it clear that her inattention is not a rejection, but rather a chance for Marguerite to be free, to develop herself without interference.

Marguerite learns from her mother to value herself. She also learns to act constructively to translate her fantasies into reality. Her mother's primary message is "Give it everything you've got. I've told you many times, 'Can't do is like Don't Care.' Neither of them have a home." Translated, that means there is nothing a person cannot do, and there should be nothing a human being does not care about (p. 225). This rescue message of self-worth leads Marguerite eventually to see herself as her mother's equal. Marguerite determines that she will have a job as a "conductorette" on the street car. She challenges the racism of the company —which never hires black women as conductors—by conducting an individual sit-in in the personnel office every day until they agree to give her the job. Her mother not only gives her moral support, but stays up until 4:30 in the morning to drive her to work. When Marguerite finds herself pregnant by a boy she hardly knows, her mother does not advise marriage. "Well, that's that," she counsels. "No use ruining three lives" (p. 244).

The final demythologizing of the mother in Angelou's story occurs when Marguerite learns of the competent mother within herself. After her baby is born, she is terrified that she will not know how to care for it adequately. When she falls asleep in the bed with the baby, her mother awakens her to show that, even in her sleep, she has instinctively done the right thing by cradling the child in her arms. Once again, her mother gives the rescue message to trust herself: "See, you don't have to think about doing the right thing. If you're for the right thing, then you do it without thinking" (p. 246).

Two Mothers

The orphan hero searches to find the positive mother who will give her a sense of self-worth, who will validate her femaleness, and who will serve as a role model. As in the cases of Shirley Keeldar, Caroline Helstone, and Marguerite Johnson, the positive mother may simply be absent until the hero reaches that state in her journey when she is ready to encounter her. However, the hero more often has difficulty in recognizing her "true" mother(s). The hero sorts out the conflicting models and messages to determine for herself which provide guidance and which lead to further captivity. Maxine Hong Kingston's *The Woman Warrior: Memoirs of a Girlhood among Ghosts* describes the confusing maternal advice that the daughter of a Chinese-American family receives. Mother "said I would grow up a wife and a slave, but she taught me the song of the warrior woman, Fa Mu Lan. I would have to grow up a warrior woman." It is not easy to sort out the warrior and slave messages, which imply that the woman's own power is so threatening, so negative, that the society must protect itself by making her a slave: "When we Chinese girls listened to the adults talk-story, we learned that we failed if we grew up to be but wives or slaves. We could be . . . swordswomen. Even if she had to rage across all China, a swordswoman got even with anyone who hurt her family. Perhaps women were once so dangerous that they had to have their feet bound."[24]

The mother may herself try to reconcile strength and servility in her own life. Kingston's mother in *The Woman Warrior* is a doctor, but she also plays the traditional role of passive, subservient Chinese wife. She tells her daughter to be strong and to value herself, but her favorite moral tale concerns an aunt who, against her will, conceived an illegitimate child. Her death and disgrace are meant to be an object lesson for the young hero. She learns that the aunt drowned her baby with herself, and concludes: "It was probably a girl; there is some hope of forgiveness for a boy" (p. 18).

Isadora Wing, in Erica Jong's *Fear of Flying,* concludes after sorting out her mother's conflicting advice that she has two mothers—one good and one bad. The bad mother is the compulsive woman who has been blighted and embittered by her self-sacrifice, and who cannot let Isadora be until she too accepts the martyr role. Her accusation of self-indulgence causes her daughter to feel guilty and defensive. As a result, she feels a need to prove her womanhood through numerous sexual encounters with men. At the same time, the good mother supports her daughter's desire to be a writer—not to sacrifice her talents as she did; this positive maternal message gets through as well. Isadora concludes, "My love for her and my hate for her are so bafflingly intertwined that I can hardly see her."[25] To the extent that the hero perceives her mother as powerful, she may experience that power only in its negative, repressed form. As in Isadora's case, the negative manifestations of female power may be directed toward repressing the potentially heroic daughter.

In order to sort out the "good" and "bad" mothers and be reconciled with the positive, rescuing mother, the hero must teach herself to recognize the affirming maternal self hidden beneath the conventional facade that women have adopted for their own survival in a patriarchal environment. She learns to hear the affirming, nurturing voice, which conventional society tends to drown out. For example, the mother who gives out a negative message, in accordance with the traditional myths of womanhood that she has been afraid to contradict publicly, may also give her daughter a subtler message to value and develop herself. The mother may also be afraid that the daughter will be punished if she does not at least play the traditional role, so she tells her to be strong but to conform. The mother's apparently most negative attributes may actually be a signpost to the female protagonist of potential but repressed strength. Isadora Wing discovers that certain aspects of her mother's bad self are simply an expression of the powerful, creative person she has repressed to be a selfless wife and mother. Isadora laments, "When I think of all the energy, all the misplaced artistic aggression which my mother channeled into her passion for odd clothes and new decorating schemes, I wish she had been a successful artist instead" (p. 149).

Sometimes, as in the story of Isadora Wing, the hero discovers the rescuer mother when she reaches a stage of wisdom and sensitivity sufficient to perceive the positive heroic woman beneath the traditional role. In many works, the daughter is freer than the mother because of increased affluence or the loosening of restrictions on acceptable female behavior. Lennie, in Tillie Olsen's "Tell Me a Riddle," has had much more freedom and opportunity than her mother, a poor immigrant woman, ever had. Although her mother dies, full of bitterness at the waste of her potential, her mother's legacy is the commitment to a full, joyous life even though she was unable to fulfill it in her own life. Sitting at her mother's deathbed, Lennie suffers "not alone for her who was dying, but for that in her which never lived (for that which in him [her father] might never)." She is grateful to her mother for giving her a sense of worth. Watching her mother, now beyond communication with her daughter, she thinks, ". . . goodby mother who taught me to mother myself."[26] Often, as in Olsen's story, the traditional mother may repudiate her own selfless example and advice at the end of her life. In Lisa Alther's novel *Kinflicks*, Ginny is freed when her mother changes from captor to rescuer. Mrs. Babcock rethinks her life before her death, changing her mind about what constitutes healthy, responsible, female behavior. Ginny, who has come home to attend her dying mother in the hospital, confesses that she has left her husband and child. She asks, "What should I *do*, Mother?" Her mother begins to tell her just what Ginny expects:

> "Do your duty, go back to them, make amends, spend the rest of your life in propitiation for the pain you've caused them." Suddenly her mother stops, realizing that her own mother gave her the same advice. "I don't know what you should do, Ginny," she replied finally, with enormous difficulty. "You must do as you think best." Ginny's eyes snapped open, as though she were Sleeping Beauty just kissed by the prince. She stared at her bruised mother. Mrs. Babcock opened her eyes and stared back. Was it possible that the generational spell had actually been broken? They smiled at each other, their delight mixed with distress.[27]

If the mother dies without freeing the protagonist, literature sometimes describes a posthumous reconciliation. Symbolically, the true mother is liberated by the death of the captor mother. In Margaret Drabble's *Jerusalem the Golden*, Clara Maugham returns home as her mother is dying. Her mother dies without a hint of deviance from the captor role. In sorting her mother's photographs, Clara finds one dated 1925, before her marriage, in which she looks "thin and frail and tender . . . lacking the rigid misery that seized her face in the wedding photographs" and that has been characteristic of her for the rest of her life. Clara cries about the tragic waste of her mother's life, but as she falls asleep "she noticed in herself a sense of shocked relief" that she saw a glimpse of her mother as—like her daughter—alive, open, searching, and vulnerable. Clara "was glad to have gone to her place of birth, she was glad that she had, however miserably, preexistence, she felt, for the first time, the satisfaction of her true descent."[28]

In Celia Fremlin's contemporary short story "Don't Be Frightened," the mother's heroic potential has also been obscured by traditional wife-and-motherhood, but the story is an account of the mother's reemergence and the resulting restoration of the mother-daughter bond. Lorna Webster hates her home. Her father always yells at her mother. "And then next day Mummy would scuttle about with red eyes, polishing things, as if a tidy polished house was some sort of protection against quarreling!" She hates her father for his temper, but she hates her mother more because she does not stand up to her father. She resents it that the mother tries "to make this look like a happy home when it isn't!"[29] One evening when her parents are out, the phone rings. She refuses to answer it, suspecting that it is her mother worrying about her. Suddenly she hears someone at the front door; it turns out to be a young girl "no older than herself," who tells her, "Don't be frightened, Lorna—but do please let me in" (p. 63).

The girl, who is forceful, with "a quick temper and a quick wit, and very much a will of her own," says that she used to live there. Lorna immediately feels that they have known each other for a long time. She finds herself confiding in "her new friend," particularly about her mother's desperation. She talks about the cluttered collection of unloved things in the room, which she says were bought on holidays when her mother was pretending to have a good time. When Lorna confesses to hating them, her friend says, "So let's smash them" (p. 63). Lorna at first protests. Then, "something extraordinary began to seep into her soul," which the author describes as joy and a "release of long-pent-up anger," and they both delight in smashing the objects in the room (p. 65).

With the ringing of the phone, both the destruction and the girl disappear. This time Lorna answers immediately, to learn that her mother has been killed in a car wreck. She also realizes the identity of her friend: "For who else could have hated the room as Lorna hated it? Who else would have come back, at the last, to destroy it?" Suddenly, "she was crying; crying with happiness because she and her mother—her real mother, the one hidden beneath the doormat exterior all these years—had understood each other at last" (p. 65).

Whether the true mother appears as the hero's biological mother, the woman her mother could have been, a surrogate mother, or a vision coming after the mother's death, the reconciliation with the mother involves the internalization of this strong and powerful woman. That is, the hero both affirms her spiritual mother and becomes her own true mother. Alice Brown's "The Way of Peace" is a rather scary nineteenth-century variation on this pattern. This gothic story, in which the daughter takes on the identity of the mother, acts out symbolically the process of discovering the true mother. On the literal level, it dramatizes a woman's achievement of autonomy. As a young woman, Lucy Ann Cummings rejects her marriage to care for her mother. Her brother tells, however, that although others pity her, he "knew she had chosen the path she loved."[30] Right before her mother's death, she notices with surprise, "I look just like mother." She then notes with a smile, "I shall be a real comfort to me when mother's gone" (pp. 176–177).

After her mother's death, Lucy wears her mother's clothes. She changes her hairstyle from the usual stern and restricted way she wears it to her mother's free-hanging ringlets. She finds she does not feel lonesome when she looks in the mirror, for "she and the mother she had loved . . . had been fused, by some wonderful alchemy; and instead of being a world apart, they were as one" (p. 180).

As negative as this fusion sounds by twentieth-century standards, Lucy's act actually liberates her. We are led in the story to see the conflict between her opinion and that of the world. She prefers life with her mother to marriage. After her mother's death, she immediately is pressured to live with her married brother, because everyone assumes she will be lonely and frightened living alone; but she refuses to move. She does try to conform to the customs of the time, whereby married people are obliged to share their homes with maiden aunts, and single women are expected to help the married relatives with household tasks. However, after a round of "visiting," Lucy rebels. "Was she always to be subject to the tyranny of those who had set up their heart tones in a more enduring form? Was her home not a home merely because there were no men and children in it?" (p. 190). She gets out of going visiting on Thanksgiving by telling one brother she is going to the other's and vice versa. When she is found out, she asserts her right to stay in her own house. She is not, however, antisocial; she invites the whole family to dinner. Furthermore, she is delighted when her brother's son calls her "grandmother." The gesture indicates that she has replaced her mother in everyone's eyes. No longer a dependent, she is seen as a primary being, with a home of her own.

In many works, the daughter's taking on an independent identity is at first seen as a repudiation of her mother. George Bernard Shaw's play *Mrs. Warren's Profession* shows how a daughter's assertion of her own autonomy may be mistaken even by the most unconventional mother for a rejection. Mrs. Warren becomes a successful prostitute in order to put her daughter through Oxford. In spite of her own unconventional life, she has counted on continuing a conventional mother-daughter relationship, saving her daughter from the hardship that she has experienced. When she tries to give Vivie a secure future in which she can avoid work and struggle, Mrs. Warren discovers that her daughter is more like her than she had bargained for. Vivie explains that she has inherited the joy of working and of being independent. She has no more desire to be a lady of leisure than her mother does: "I am my mother's daughter. I am like you: I must have work, and must make more money than I spend. But my work is not your work, and my way not your way. We must part."[31] In this case, the daughter demonstrates her continuity with the mother's heritage by leaving her mother to live her own life.

In order to be reconciled with the true mother, Vivie must do battle with the captor mother. In fairy tales, this act is often presented metaphorically as the literal killing of the Wicked Witch or Wicked Stepmother. The captor mother is evil partly because she teaches patriarchal society's precepts on how women should behave. Often the daughter has to "kill" or repudiate the aspects of her mother that entrap her. Even the good mother who is a positive role model may be a captor as long as the daughter sees her as a larger-than-life deity against which she must measure herself. When the child's life is determined by the mother's, so that she is not truly autonomous, she may escape from the mother's influence by embarking on a journey to discover her own identity. During this journey, she learns that her mother is merely human—neither a goddess to be worshipped nor a witch to be slain. Coming to terms with the mortality and, in some works, with the actual death of the mother frees the hero to discover and value her own mortal self. It also makes possible egalitarian, noncompetitive relationships with other women.

In the utopian society described in Mary Staton's *From the Legend of Biel*, babies undergo a psychological journey, similar to that described in this book, even before they leave the incubator. Staton's novel focuses on the journey of a young girl, Biel. Biel's heroic exit occurs when she breaks the rules of her society by leaving the incubator. Accompanied by a parent figure, she undertakes a quest during which she learns her name. A man from the patriarchal Earth is fighting to take over Biel's mind so that he can live in the humane world of the Thoacdiens. On a symbolic level, she, like the female hero in patriarchal society, struggles to free herself from the internal patriarchal voice that threatens her. Troubled because she feels like two people, she calls herself "Biel," or "turbulence." At the end of her journey, her name is formally pronounced to the community and she is presented to her mentor, Mikkran. Only at the end of the story is it clear that Biel's journey is a psychological one only.

These psychological adventures during her infancy prepare Biel for a relationship with her parent figure that avoids dependency from the very beginning of their relationship. In the psychological journey, Mikkran finds herself in the role of a maternal martyr. Prevented from revealing her identity to her charge by the Thoacdien society's edict that she should not interfere with a child's quest for identity, she follows Biel during her trek across the desert, leaving food and water for her every night when she is asleep. When provisions become scarce, she stops eating or drinking, to give all to the child. The first step in a healthy relationship between parent figure and child is repudiation of this model of maternal self-sacrifice. Mikkran, near death, calls Biel and asks her help. After Biel brings her water, they travel together as equals, neither sacrificing for the other.

The second event that prepares Biel to have a relationship with her mentor that is not one of dependence occurs when they are captured by a primitive, patriarchal Higgite tribe. Logana, a Higgite who hates herself and other women, murders Mikkran. Logana does this because she is jealous of her husband's admiration for the heroic, liberated Thoacdien woman. When the reader realizes that this drama occurs within the mind of a single individual, it becomes clear that the fight between Mikkran and Logana is an allegorical rendering of the way the repression of the good, powerful mother by the bad captor mother leaves the daughter with no role model.

After escaping from the Higgites, Biel is not only freed from patriarchal ways of seeing, which are vestiges of previous evolutionary stages; she also learns to love her mentor Mikkran without deifying her and without undue dependence. In her dream journey, she confronts the loss of her mentor, is initially overcome with grief, and finally finds she can live, however reluctantly, without her. Later, Biel witnesses with delight a film in which Mikkran joyously makes love to a man. It is only after Biel has developed the capability to love in this free and nonproprietary way that she officially goes through a ritual of "naming" and is presented to her mentor. Mikkran, of course, has also gone through this process; she is able to love Biel without wanting to own her or limit her independence.

Women writers in particular emphasize the female hero's need, following her liberation from male definition, for reconciliation with the mother. They also emphasize how inextricably bound together are the search for the mother and the search for the self. In many works, it is difficult to distinguish attributes of the actual mother from the feelings of the protagonist about herself. Joanna Russ writes in "The Autobiography of My Mother," "Sometimes I'm my mother."[32] Anne Sexton, in "Housewife," concludes that "A Woman *is* her mother. That's the main thing."[33] Isadora Wing, in *Fear of Flying*, comments, "I never know who is who. She is me and I am she and we are all together."[34]

The discovery of the positive mother within and the simultaneous emergence of the nurturing, heroic self are frequently described metaphorically in feminist narratives as the act of giving birth. One famous feminist poster reads, "I am a woman giving birth to myself." In "The Autobiography of My Mother," Joanna Russ writes of becoming her mother's mother. Attempting to escape her captive mother's patriarchal messages, the narrator recognizes that her mother never exited into the world of responsible, autonomous adults. In her imagination, she rocks her mother's baby self, mourning for the woman this child could have been. In doing so, she invokes a matriarchal goddess, who serves as a symbolic representative of the good mother. In "Tiamat's lap" the narrator receives the nurturance she needs to mother herself, and, if need be, her own mother:

> Tiamat broadcasts Herself all over the place and doesn't mind kiddies pulling at Her skirt; call her Nyame and Tanit, call her 'Anat, Atea, Tabits, Tibirra. This is what comes of re-meeting one's mother when she was only two—how willful she was! how charming, and how strong. I wish she had not grown up to be a door-mat, but all the same what a blessing it is not to have been made by somebody's hands like a piece of clay, and then he breathed a spirit in you. . . . What a joy and a pleasure to have been born, just ordinary born, you know, out of dirt and flesh, all of one piece and of the same stuff She is. To be my mother's child. . . . Tiamat is talking. She spoke through me as in the Bible, that is I spoke, knowing the answer: Am I my mother's mother?"[35]

Russ's narrator gives birth to the mother in herself by imaginatively recapturing the woman her mother could have been.

Because the birth of the self is analogous to physical childbirth, the female hero often experiences the birth of a child and the emergence of her heroic nature as complementary events. Often, moreover, the birth of the mother within makes possible a reconciliation with the actual parent. The evolution of the meaning of childbirth and of the mother-daughter relationship is the central metaphor in Joan Didion's novel *Play It As It Lays*. In the beginning of the story, Maria is paralyzed by guilt because she feels she has killed both her mother and her child. She has sacrificed her mother and her own dignity to a sadomasochistic relationship with a man, Ivan Costello, and she feels vaguely responsible for her mother's death:

> Exactly what time had it happened, precisely what had she been doing in New York at the instant her mother lost control of the car outside Tonopah [she assumes that she was with Ivan]. . . . She imagines her mother trying to call her from a pay phone in Tonopah, standing in a booth . . . and then the answering service picking up the call . . . think about the mother dying in the desert light, the daughter unavailable in the Eastern dark. . . . One time Maria had saved enough money to give her mother a trip around the world, but instead she had lent the money to Ivan Costello, and then her mother was dead.[36]

Her first child's autism parallels her own growing isolation and passivity; other characters frequently refer to her as a "thing" or a "vegetable." The aborted fetus, which haunts her, is symbolically associated with the aborted birth of an identity separate from that of her husband, Carter. In both cases, the birth is aborted at her husband's instigation.

As Maria prepares to have an abortion, she longs for the guidance and nurturance of her mother, but her mother is dead. In a desperate effort to recover some bond with her mother, she stares "into a hand mirror, picking out her mother's features" (p. 163). This novel focuses explicitly on the protagonist's growing awareness of the existential void. The void in Maria's life, however, is psychological and social, rather than metaphysical. Implicit in the symbolic association of mother-daughter-grandchild is the recognition of the deprivation and isolation created in the female psyche when society excludes female power. Maria is a victim of the patriarchal myths of female inferiority, virginity, and romantic love; she has never discovered or developed a self. When she stops worshiping her husband and other men, and begins to long for the female tradition that she has been complicit in eradicating, she experiences despair.

She goes back to an area near her hometown of Silver Wells, but she is unable to learn anything else about her mother. Silver Wells is now a nuclear testing site. When her uncle, Benny Austin, comments on how much she looks like her mother—"Jesus if you aren't the picture of Francine" (p. 58)—it becomes apparent that she can escape only by becoming her own mother. Maria's friend BZ, who feels the void in the midst of the patriarchal world, kills himself. Maria responds to that same void by writing a novel to reclaim the events of her life. Symbolically, she has the heroic courage to create her own identity in a world that would discredit that identity by institutionalizing her.

In the process of writing the novel, Maria discovers that metaphysical nothingness is not so terrible when one has reclaimed one's self: "You call it as you see it," Maria concludes, "and stay in the action" (p. 209). Furthermore, when she has addressed the psychological and social void caused by the patriarchal denigration of women, she can assert her own nurturing, life-perpetuating qualities against the existential void. Maria elects to become the mother that her autistic child and her own virtually autistic self require. It is only when she stops destroying herself to atone for her complicity in the murder of her mother and of her child that she can affirm the value of her own selfhood and reestablish the three-generational mother-daughter bond. In affirming the mother within, she restores the connection with her heritage: "Now that I have the answer, my plans for the future are these: (1) get Kate, (2) live with Kate alone, (3) do some canning. . . . There might be a ready market for such canning: you will note that after everything I remain Harry and Francine Wyeth's daughter" (p. 209).

The hero's reconciliation with the mother results in the act of giving birth to the whole self—a reconciliation of self-affirmation with nurturance and self with Other. However, the literal act of having a child is not the only satisfactory metaphor for this experience of rebirth and community. In fact, in many cases, becoming a biological mother is antithetical to female heroism. In order to define the positive union of heroism and motherhood in women, which makes biological motherhood a complement or even an impetus to the mother's self-actualization, it is necessary to define the two factors that render biological motherhood antithetical or at least a major obstacle to heroic self-fulfillment. These factors are the patriarchal concepts of one, motherhood as self-sacrifice, and two, children as property.

First, as discussed earlier, patriarchal society defines ideal motherhood as an all-consuming, totally selfless role, which is a satisfactory substitute for the development of the self and which, when done properly, precludes any consideration for the self. The negative effects of traditional ideas about motherhood are reinforced by practical reality. Patriarchal society delegates to a woman sole responsibility for her children and suggests that any request for help from a male parent or from any other adult or social agency indicates that she is not performing her job well. As a result, the biological mother is denied the time and energy necessary to consider her own needs, or her potential in any area other than parenting. Finally, a woman can use motherhood as a substitute for developing her own potential.

Novelists often juxtapose traditional self-sacrificing motherhood and motherhood that is inseparable from self-actualization, showing the former to be destructive to both mother and child. Connie, in Marge Piercy's *Woman on the Edge of Time,* recognizes that "she should have loved her [daughter] better; but to love you must love yourself, she knew that now, especially to love a daughter you see as yourself reborn."[37] Isadora Wing notes how easy it is to confuse the desire to have a child with the desire to rescue one's own lost childhood self; "Really, I thought, sometimes I *would* like to have a child." She then confesses, "What I really wanted was to give birth to *myself*—the little girl I might have been in a different family, a different world."[38] Ella Price, in Dorothy Bryant's contemporary novel *Ella Price's Journal,* is thirty-five, married, and has one child. Returning to school, she begins to discover those powerful, creative parts of her personality that the traditional life of wife and mother has hidden from her consciousness. When she discovers that she is pregnant, she considers how easy it would be to stop growing and have the baby instead. "The great solution to everything. Get pregnant. Then you don't have to think about anything anymore. You're trapped. Happy trappy. I've seen other women do it so many times. . . . A baby. . . . What better excuse for quitting?"[39] Ella Price refers periodically throughout the novel to a recurring dream in which she is giving birth to a baby girl. In one final nightmare version of the dream, she is surrounded by her lover, her husband, and her psychiatrist, who tell her that there is no baby. It is only a growth, a tumor—which they have thrown away." . . . suddenly I knew. I *had* had a baby girl! I had seen her! They were hiding her from me. They were going kill her" (p. 156). Finally, she understands that the dream does not mean that she wants to have a baby. She tries to explain to her psychiatrist, Dr. Redford: "I have a lot of problems to solve, but wanting a baby isn't one of them, and having a baby only temporarily sidesteps the real problems. I don't think my dream of having a baby has anything to do with wanting a real baby. I think it means I'm trying to make a change in myself. . . . It's me I'm trying to give birth to, a new me" (p. 160). Because she is in the process of giving birth to herself, Ella Price decides to have an abortion.

The second factor causing biological motherhood and heroism to be antithetical to one another is the patriarchal ideal that children are a man's property, often internalized by the mother. In John Barth's *The End of the Road,* Rennie has an illegal abortion, which kills her, because she does not know whether her husband or his friend Jake is the father of the child. It never occurs to her to have the baby because she knows who the mother is, just as it never occurs to her to think of herself as other than Joe's or Jake's possession. When Isadora Wing is considering having a baby, she emphasizes the importance of having the baby for herself and defines the traditional patriarchal context that makes that impossible: "If I have a baby I want it to be all *mine.* A girl like me, but better. A girl who'll also be able to have her own babies. It is not having babies in itself which seems unfair, but having babies for men. Babies who get *their* names. Babies who lock you by means of love to a man you have to please and serve on pain of abandonment."[40]

The heroic woman who is a mother is rarely married. Many times it is the experience of single motherhood itself that forces a woman into heroic consciousness. For Nathaniel Hawthorne's Hester Prynne, for example, the illegitimate birth of Pearl forces her to act heroically in the face of great odds. Because Hester is ostracized from the community—forced to wear a red *A* for "Adulteress" on her chest—she learns to see beyond the rigid, restrictive values of the Puritan settlement, and becomes a freethinker and a feminist. "Standing alone in the world—alone, as to any dependence on society, and with little Pearl to be guided and protected—alone, and hopeless of retrieving her position, even had she not scorned to consider it desirable—she cast away the fragments of a broken chain. The world's law was no law for her mind." Hawthorne comments that revolutionary "thoughts visited her, such as dared to enter no other dwelling in New England."[41]

Although contemporary heroes in general do not risk as severe a social condemnation, it still takes courage to bear an illegitimate child. Rosamund, the hero in Margaret Drabble's *Thank You All Very Much,* elects to give birth to her child and to rear it without acknowledging the father. At the same time, she notes the degree to which societal taboos, such as the one regarding giving birth to a child outside of wedlock, determine our perceptions of the world "before we are aware of it, and . . . what we think we make becomes a rigid prison making us."[42] "At times," she speculates, "I had a vague and complicated sense that this pregnancy had been sent to me in order to reveal to me a scheme of things totally different from the scheme which I inhabited, totally removed from academic enthusiasms, social consciousness, etiolated undefined emotional connections, and exercise of free will" (p. 143). She learns to know her child and, as a result of that knowledge, to experience a reality beyond patriarchal dualities of self and Other: "There was one thing in the world that I knew about, and that one thing was Octavia. I had lost the taste for half-knowledge. George, I could see, knew nothing with such certainty. I neither envied nor pitied his indifference, for he was myself, the self that but for accident, but for fact, but for chance, but for womanhood, I would still have been" (p. 143).

In this and other cases, the act of becoming a mother who is not dependent on a man forces the hero to reconcile nurturance and autonomy. In this way, the child may serve as the rescue figure. Adrienne Rich, in *Of Woman Born,* points out that the experience of pregnancy and giving birth may enable women to reject the dualistic assumptions that self and Other, inner and outer, are realities in opposition. "The child that I carry for nine months can be defined *neither* as me or as not-me."[43] Even after the child is born, the mother is likely to be so attuned to the child's needs that she will not sacrifice the child's needs for her own. In her autobiographical essay *The Mother Knot,* Jane Lazarre writes that after the birth of her child "the ordinary idea of freedom [became] less and less seductive to me. For freedom to do as I pleased meant doing without Benjamin. And that was very simply a tormenting thought."[44] The danger, of course, is that in not seeing any separation between child and self, the mother may sacrifice her own autonomy for the child.

In literature, however, circumstances often force the mother to be courageous, self-actualizing, and heroic for her children. Bertolt Brecht's Mother Courage is courageous and ingenious at least partially to keep her children alive. The child in Brecht's *The Caucasian Chalk Circle* and the child of the black slave, Roxana, in Mark Twain's *The Tragedy of Pudd'nhead Wilson* motivate their respective mothers into extraordinary feats of heroic bravery, strength, power, and intelligence. The first mother manipulates her way through the front lines of war, using physical or mental skills according to necessity; the second travels an equally difficult physical and social road through the racist South in order to secure a position in the white world for her mulatto son. In Marge Piercy's *Small Changes,*

Beth and Wanda demonstrate their heroism most clearly in the kidnapping of Wanda's children. The patriarchy has judged Wanda an unfit mother because she is a lesbian. Clear about her own values, however, she decides she must rescue her children from the antilife messages of her society and of her parents. "I have to get Luis and Johnny with me. I know what it's like for them there. I know my father will punish them daily for being my children, for being alive and vital and earthy and strong. He's going to try to crush us in them. I can't rest while they're captive."[45] Wanda's example teaches Miriam that she has a responsibility to be heroic for the good of her children. Miriam is a vital, powerful woman who finds herself a dependent housewife because of her unresolved self-hatred, her need to prove that she is a "good girl."

> But there was so much life beating in her, she felt as if she too must shine in the dark there in the stairwell to any being with eyes to see the shining she saw in her children. . . . She felt strong in her love, stronger in herself, stronger in the connections she had somehow preserved through attrition. She felt in herself Wanda's strength for her children; maybe not the greater strength it would take to put herself first, but the strength to fight for them, by all means. So she was not alone, but connected to them, and connected still to Beth and Wanda, not only through the money she secreted from household expenses for them but in her daily thoughts, her sense of them as a counterexample to defeat. (p. 538)

By becoming heroic for her children, Wanda is a role model for the reconciliation of autonomy and nurturance in other women. In this novel, women learn to nurture each other and to share child care so that it is no longer an all-consuming role. Between adults, mutual mothering becomes "sisterhood." Thus, the hero discovers not only a positive mother but a whole female support system, and by association, a nurturing, joyous, and powerful female heritage.

Besmilr Brigham, a contemporary poet, stresses that the message of wholeness and self-love that female heroes have learned through the pain of experience must be passed to the next generation of women. She writes in "Tell Our Daughters": "Tell our daughters / they are. . .strong as the rose / deep as a word."[46] Anne Sexton tells her daughter, in "Little Girl, My String Bean, My Lovely Woman," that she can trust herself in the fullest sense: "What I want to say, Linda, / is that there is nothing in your body that lies."[47] Judy Chicago, in *Through the Flower*, writes of how she developed a feminist art collective. In many ways, she is the role model for the students, but she also learns from them. She also wants and needs a

> "mother" who would love me for being independent, something that I wanted as much as any student in the program or woman in the society. That want, which, in my estimation, most women share, is not a function of having had "bad" mothering. Rather it is a result of growing up in a male-dominated society, in which women condition their daughters toward behavior that is "safe" and therefore unchallenging to male domination. To have a mother who loves you for being independent is to have a mother who fosters rebellion in your heart and revolution in your bones. And that can only come to pass in a feminist community.[48]

In *The Mother Knot* Jane Lazarre describes her struggle to reach this positive, heroic mother-daughter relationship, both with her own mother and with her children. What the book makes clear is how difficult achieving that positive state of mutual affirmation and nurturance can be in a society that assumes that mothers will sacrifice themselves for their children. In the beginning, Lazarre has internalized the social myth of motherhood. She assumes that when she gives birth to a child, she will be transformed magically into that all-powerful earth-mother goddess. When this fails to happen, she invokes the being that she has been conditioned to associate with mythic motherhood: "Mother, goddess of love, to whom we all can go for protection and unconditional love, perfect human being we have all been taught to believe in, whom poets compare to the earth itself, who kneels down, arms outstretched, to enclose us and fend off the rains, whom none of us have ever met but who continues to haunt us mercilessly; Mother, I can't find you, let alone be you."[49] Instead of being transformed by childbirth into this ideal thing, the new mother "just wanted her mother" (p. 24).

Lazarre's mother died when she was seven years old, and she explains that she spent most of her childhood searching for her. Later she tries pretending that she is her. As a young adult she feels free of the obsession with her absent mother, until she becomes pregnant. Then her mother begins haunting her dreams. In one dream, she appears as a witch, who warns of some ominous but unclear event. At the same time that she longs for her mother to nurture her as she did as a child, and to show her how to be a mother, she in many ways repudiates her mother's example. Her mother was a successful career woman who was often absent, and the protagonist links her absence in death with her leaving to go to important meetings and conferences. In each case, she felt bereft, rejected, let down. She is therefore determined to stay home with her son, Benjamin, so that he will not have the sense of never having been mothered enough.

The bulk of the book deals with the deleterious effects of the full-time mother role on the author and on all the other mothers she knows. The continual sacrifice of herself for her child leaves her so ambivalent and so obsessive about him that she cannot even fully feel love for him. She is a writer, and she finds that when she does not write, her very self seems diminished and unfulfilled.

It is only when she begins to leave Benjamin in a good cooperative day-care center, so that she can write, that she feels unequivocal love for him and completely enjoys the time she spends with him. She is able to leave him in a day-care center—despite the dire warnings of "experts"—only with the aid of other women who cooperate in demythologizing the mother role. She finds new, supportive friends who tell each other that they can be good mothers without fulfilling the mythic image of the perfect mother-goddess. She also notices that Benjamin loves the day-care center.

Without the interchange of information that belies the stereotypes, all of the mothers would have stayed in the traditional role, suffered the "disease with no name" that Betty Friedan describes in *The Feminine Mystique,* and been secretly convinced of their own private failure to fulfill the expected role. Women friends, Lazarre points out, are crucial to a woman's discovery of the truths obscured by the myths: "It is the process of quiet, loving, insistent identification, the repeated testifying of one to the other that says, I am the same as you—that unlocks the doors and unravels the tangles. That is what women seek in a friend" (p. 148).

Through being mothers these women also find reconciliation with their mothers. Nurturing and caring for Benjamin brings back to Lazarre how good a parent her mother actually was. She remembers taking a bath with her, and her mother gently and ably removing an eyelash from her eye. In fact, when she is successfully mothering Benjamin, she feels she *is* her mother. Exhausted at the end of the day, she feels incapable of caring for her child, but "then my mother's face filled my head, pushing everything else away. And it was with her hand that I patted Benjamin's back until he was asleep and it was with her voice that I sang to him" (p. 115). It is only when she realizes her own need to balance work with nurturance that she forgives her mother for leaving her for a career. In fact, she realizes that she would not have suffered from her mother's absence at work had the other children's mothers not stayed home, thus giving her the culture's message that a working mother did not adequately parent her children.

During this period, she also reaches some reconciliation with her father. He is a loving man who volunteers to care for Benjamin so that she can do some work, yet he resents having to follow through on his promise. At first, he cannot see his daughter clearly; instead, he sees her as her mother. Seeing her crying, he says how much she reminds him of her mother. Furthermore, he expects her to mother *him*. When she goes home to live with him for a short period, they begin to know each other as adults and as equals. He tells her about the difficulties of his life, how it was to not be able to find a job because he was a member of the Communist party, how it was to have the party fall apart, how it was to lose the wife he loved. Initially, he wants only sympathy, but when his daughter is equally honest about the bind she is in, he begins to see her not as he wishes she were, but as she is. She notes then that when he notices her faults, she "felt acknowledged" (p. 153). It is then, she explains, that "I began to forgive him" (p. 153).

It is only when Lazarre is reconciled to her mother that she can combine the traditional male and female worlds, combining motherhood and work. But her father's confessions of bitterness and failure force her to redefine the terms in which she sees work. She is torn between her vocation as an artist and her sense that as a responsible adult she has an obligation to contribute to the support of the household, just as her father was pulled between his commitment to political action and his financial responsibility to the family. Her husband, James, insists that, if she expects him to be a parent to Benjamin, he should not also be expected to be the sole support of the family. She has been preparing herself to take on this traditionally male responsibility by going to graduate school, but recognizes that between motherhood and university teaching, she would never be a writer. Her dilemma is that classically faced by men, one that results from the conflicting definitions of work in the culture: Work, on the one hand, promises self-expression and a sense of achievement; on the other, it is degrading toil that demands the repression of personal desires so that one's family can survive.

After her father's death, she dreams a resolution of her dilemma. In her dream, she searches for her father throughout the house. She finally finds him in the hall closet, which is being held shut with the bookcase that held her school-books. For her to become a professor, she recognizes, would be a failure to learn from her father's confessions to her. That day she leaves graduate school; but she does not go back to an attitude that assumes James's responsibility to support her. She takes a loan from him, which she will pay back as she begins to get income from her writing.

At the end of the work we do not know if she will be successful enough as a writer to support herself and to aid in the support of her child; we do know that she achieves a rather shaky truce in the conflict between her roles as writer and as mother. As the book closes, she thinks about having another child. The personifications of two opposed beings—the mother and the dark lady—preside over her inner debate. Lazarre's imagery of the dark lady suggests that she is still affected by societal myths that oppose the light selfless Virgin Mother and the dark evil woman who wants to live for herself. The dark lady reminds her of the tragic nature of motherhood. "Confidence is destroyed by motherhood. Sooner or later the child disappoints you, perhaps even terrifies you with a small sign of distorted development. . . . And that repeated death and resurrection of confidence which daily besieges you ultimately cripples the proud and brilliant prima donna in you until she can dance no more" (p. 213). The artist must be essentially a child, who can be creative and free. The mother continually betrays the child in herself for the traitorous child she will ultimately lose. The mother figure, on the other hand, speaks of love and of the tragic beauty of motherhood: "The daily grinding friction of motherhood will give you the chance, at least, of relinquishing some of your egotism" and of growing up: "Grownups see a world which, although less colorful, promising and uniformly dazzling than the child's, is also more pitiable and proportioned. The giants of your childhood shrink to normal size. . . . Even your once omnipotently evil parents seem deserving of pity now" (p. 21).

When the dark lady takes off her mask to reveal the mother and simultaneously the mother is revealed as the dark lady, it becomes clear that some accommodation between these mutually conflicting roles is the author's reward. She recognizes that she *is* the mother *and* the dark lady, and she acts out this reconciliation by using her ability as a writer to describe her experience as a mother. Finally, the book she writes attests to the power of literature written by mothers who are also dark ladies.

Reconciliation with the Parents

Unlike the classical, patriarchal hero, the female hero, as Lazarre's narrative illustrates, often seeks reconciliation with both parents. In doing so, she integrates the best qualities associated with each sex role and rejects its life-denying aspects. In allegorical terms, her escape from captivity by the "bad" parents is followed by a discovery of the "true" or "good" parents. In realistic literature, she rejects those attributes of her parents that limit her growth, but she does not reject her parents. The accompanying series of emotional stages is similar to that evoked by the seducer. Her initial love turns to hatred or resentment. She feels they have betrayed her trust because they do not save her. When she accepts their simple human frailty, she often learns that both their positive and negative examples help her learn to live a heroic life. She can love them and learn from them, without living her life in their shadow.

The final three works discussed in this chapter—Margaret Atwood's *Surfacing,* Margaret Drabble's *The Realms of Gold,* and Virginia Woolf's *To the Lighthouse*—explore the lives of women who are alienated from themselves because they have internalized society's contempt for women. In each work, the hero journeys to her ancestral home, where she confronts her disillusionment with sex roles and with patriarchal ways of perceiving reality. The emphasis in each work is on the hero's reconciliation with the mother. But she does not reject positive qualities traditionally assumed to be male. By the end of the work, she is reconciled with both parents. She avoids the trap of simply replacing one stereotypical set of characteristics with another. Instead, she integrates the best of both roles into a mode of action and perception that is life-perpetuating for both self and Other, and thereby reconciles the dark lady and the mother.

The hero of Margaret Atwood's *Surfacing* is a casualty of patriarchal thought processes. She returns to her ancestral home in rural Canada because her father has mysteriously disappeared and is believed to be dead. We soon learn that it is not only out of natural, filial affection that she insists on searching for him, but out of an inability to accept the fact that her seemingly all-knowing, all-powerful father is mortal. She notes, that "if you tell your children God does not exist, they will be forced to believe you are God."[50] She is confronting death in two primary forms in this work—the physical death of her parents (her mother having died earlier), and the death-in-life that she associates with the United States, and that she believes is spreading like a cancer into the Canadian woods.

Atwood's America is similar to Russ's Fatherland. In it, the hero cannot feel, and cannot love. As she travels to her childhood home with her lover, Joe, and with another couple, Anna and David, she questions if she loves Joe, because she is not conscious of feeling anything for him. During the course of the novel, the protagonist learns that Anna and David's seemingly ideal marriage "is built, not on love, but on hatred." David wants to inflict his will on Anna; Anna is dependent on him because she is afraid that she does not exist without him (p. 180). He is a parody of the worst aspects of the macho role. He is violent, cruel, and rational in a way that excludes caring. When he believes his wife is having an affair with Joe, he suggests to the hero of the novel that they "retaliate," for it "would be justice." Appalled, the hero recognizes that "he needed me for an abstract principle; it would be enough for him if our genitals could be detached like two kitchen appliances and copulate in mid-air" (p. 178). Anna is the female object-victim, totally dependent on her husband for her self-esteem. She puts on her makeup before he wakes up, thus performing "the only magic left to her" (p. 194).

Atwood's protagonist, like Russ's in "Daddy's Girl," or like Maria in Didion's *Play It As It Lays,* is emotionally numb because she has given up responsibility for her life to her lover. She associates the loss of self with aborting or giving away her child. On the literal level, it is not clear whether she actually becomes pregnant twice or whether she gives two different accounts of the same experience. The symbolic import of each experience, however, is the same. Her first love, an older married man, convinces her to have the abortion: "He said I should do it, he made me do it; he talked about it as though it was legal, simple, like getting a wart removed." Her acquiescence makes her an "American": "That made me one of them too, a killer. . . . Since then I'd carried that death around inside me, layering it over, a cyst, a tumor, a black pearl" (p. 170). In the second version, she marries and has her husband's child, but, as she says, "I never identified it as mine; I didn't name it before it was born even, the way you're supposed to. It was my husband's, he imposed it on me, all the time it was growing in me I felt like an incubator. . . . He wanted a replica of himself; after it was born I was no more use" (p. 39). When she has the baby in the hospital, she is strapped down, anesthetized, and made to be passive, a thing, "a machine." For her, the sacrifice of the potential child is associated with the sacrifice of herself, because in both cases she renounced volition, simply doing what men said she should.[51] When her present lover, Joe, tries to make love to her, she says, " 'I'll get pregnant,' . . . [and, she muses] it stopped him: flesh making more flesh, miracle, that frightens all of them."[52]

Previously, the protagonist worshiped and sought to identify with her father by emulating what she perceived to be his unemotional, logical approach to life. She has lived by the myths of rationality that her father taught her. As she searches for her father, she gradually confronts the reality of the failure of logic—which presumes that one can control life by making everything explicable. Because logic cannot put her in meaningful human contact with her missing father, she ultimately rejects it and in order to find him acts according to her own deeper sense of mystery and passion.

She learns that her father was collecting pictures of Indian gods before he died. She goes in search of the paintings, hoping to find some sign that his mind did not fail him and that he still lives. Finally, she dives beneath the water, experiencing a symbolic death. She recognizes, moreover, that the overreliance on rationality at the expense of mystery—a kind of emotional death—is within her as well as in the world. Thus, she begins to see her father and other men not as deities to be obeyed or as villains to be opposed, but as mortals like herself. She imagines, also, that near the close of his life her father recognized the inadequacy of his rationality and learned to see in a new way. It is precisely the denial of human mortality and vulnerability that has caused the father, the daughter, and the culture to experience life as a living death. They are possessed by the shadow of the death they attempt to deny. To acknowledge mortality is a prerequisite to an acceptance of the cycle of life.

The demythologizing of the father makes it possible for the protagonist to reclaim the female power to give birth—to the repressed woman within and to a truly human child. She is determined to have a child that is *hers,* that will not take away from the value of her own growing self. A scene in which she has sex with Joe in the moonlight represents her physical and spiritual reunion with the natural, nonrational world. Her description of herself in this scene recalls the picture of a traditional matriarchal deity in her mother's childhood scrapbook: Lying down with "the moon on my left hand and the absent sun on my right" she feels "my lost child surfacing within me, forgiving me, rising from the lake where it has been prisoned for so long" (p. 181).

Having discovered her father's legacy, she acknowledges her need for a maternal heritage. This enables her to identify with other women. Before, she never felt any desire to aid Anna, even when David attempted to force Anna to pose nude in order to humiliate her. The protagonist notes that he is using the camera as something "that could make people vanish . . . like a camera that could steal not only your soul but your body also" (p. 139). A picture is taken as the half-nude Anna attempts to flee. Later the hero throws the film into the lake so that Anna can be "no longer battled and shelved." The intimidated Anna, however, warns, "you better not do that . . . they'll kill you" (p. 195).

Searching for a message from her mother, the hero discovers the legacy in her childhood scrapbook. The pictures in the scrapbook, she realizes, "were my guides, she had saved for me, pictographs." The one that most interests her is one of the traditional matriarchal deity figure: "On the left was a woman with a round moon stomach: the baby was sitting up inside her gazing out. Opposite her was a man with horns on his head like cow horns and a barbed tail" (p. 185). She sees in this picture a rescue message. Her mother, then, is the rescuer, who does not provide her with an answer, but who instead reminds her of the truth she knew on some level even as a child.

To understand these pictures, the hero moves back to a prehuman, nonlinguistic state. After ritually burning or otherwise destroying all the remnants of her personal past, she turns the mirror to the wall. "I must stop being in the mirror. . . . Not to see myself but to see." She becomes perceiver instead of perceived, subject, not object. In doing so, she frees herself from the inner-outer split. "I reverse the mirror so it's toward the wall, it no longer traps me, Anna's soul closed in the gold compact, that and not the camera is what I should have broken" (p. 205). Becoming "a natural woman, in a state of nature" (p. 222), she learns truths about women's nature and potential beyond patriarchal formulations. In a vision, she sees her mother, standing by the house, as she often did when alive, in a life-perpetuating and nurturing pose. Her mother is feeding the birds: "One perches on her wrist, another on her shoulder" (p. 213). Until this moment the protagonist has always faintly pitied her mother: ". . . the only thing that remains [from her mother's past] was a story she once told about how, when she was little, she and her sister had made wings for themselves out of an old umbrella; they'd jumped off the barn roof, attempting to fly, and she broke both her ankles. She would laugh about it but the story seemed to me then chilly and sad, the failure unbearable" (p. 146). In the protagonist's vision, however, the pity for her mother turns to exaltation, as she recognizes nurturing love and freedom as her maternal heritage: "She turns her head quietly and looks at me, past me, as though she knows something is there but she can't quite see it. The jays cry again, they fly up from her, the shadows of their wings ripple over the ground and she's gone. . . . I squint up at them, trying to see her, trying to see which one she is; they hop, twitch their feathers, turn their heads" (pp. 213–214).

She also sees her father in a vision, in which she imagines he has repudiated the rationality he lived by, making him appear even sadder than her mother. As he stands by the house, "his own fence excludes him as logic excludes love. He wants it ended, the borders abolished, he wants the forest to flow back into the places his mind cleared: reparation." In this vision, she learns the awe-inspiring message of natural, amoral, nonhuman power. The vision "gazes at me for a time with its yellow eyes, wolf's eyes, depthless but lambent as the eyes of animals seen at night in the car headlights. Reflectors. It does not approve of me or disapprove of me, it tells me it has nothing to tell me, only the fact itself" (p. 218). She cannot project onto nature; it is both self and other, but not to be understood and ultimately controlled. When she forgives her father for the failure of patriarchal modes of rationality and mastery, she can then accept his death. Indeed, through imagining his own rejection of an inadequate approach to life, she continues to define herself as carrying on his tradition. When she rejects the captor messages implicit in patriarchal sex-role definitions, she accepts her parents' mortality and discovers their valuable legacy to her. Near the end of the novel, she writes, "Our father, Our mother, I pray, Reach down for me, but it won't work: they dwindle, grow, become what they were, human." This realization frees her from the paralysis that comes from envisioning others as larger-than-life gods or villains who determine one's life. She is even free from her fear of her "fake husband," recognizing that he "was only a normal man, middle-aged, second-rate, selfish and kind in the average proportions." No longer seeing through the eyes of a child or a dependent, she understands that her discovery of a new mode of being is not a repudiation of her parents, but a continuation of their heritage. Imperfect, they are neither gods nor villains; they simply made mistakes. Both would want her to reject what in their example promoted death. "They were here though, I trust that, I saw them and they spoke to me, in the other language. . . . To prefer life, I owe them that" (p. 22).

The exorcism of antilife attitudes—including traditional sex-role patterns—leaves the hero free to feel. This freedom enables her to love Joe. She leaves with him to return to the city; but she fears that, as a natural woman, she is in danger of being caged. Traditional society will try to enclose her in "the hospital or the zoo." She sees herself as a revolutionary whose worst enemy is women's traditional passivity and dependence; ". . . above all," she vows, she must "refuse to be a victim. . . . I have to recant, give up the old belief that I am powerless and because of it nothing I can do will ever hurt anyone" (p. 222). The symbolic and literal embodiment of her newborn, natural, free self is the child she carries within her. "It might be the first one, the first true human; it must be born, allowed" (p. 223).

Atwood's novel is a highly symbolic dream-vision in which psychological and physical events merge into one another. Margaret Drabble's novel *The Realms of Gold,* on the surface, is almost the antithesis of *Surfacing.* It reads like an old-fashioned Victorian love story. Yet the force of both novels comes from the same source, for both use the same mythic structure and both are concerned with similar themes. *Surfacing* uses abortion and the inhumanity of the experience of giving birth in a mechanized world as the primary symbol of the death orientation of contemporary society; Drabble's novel uses infanticide as the symbol for the death orientation of all peoples in every known period of human history.

Frances Wingate, the hero of the novel, is an archaeologist. She has come to love the Phoenicians whose city she discovered and excavated, but she cannot reconcile to herself their practice of infant exposure and sacrifice. She associates this phenomenon with the concentration camps in Germany and with the death-in-life existence that has been the fate of most children through the ages: lives marked by "toil and subsistence, cruelty and dullness."[53] The theme of infanticide continues throughout the novel. Frances's cousin Stephen kills his infant child and himself because he believes it is "better to be dead than alive" (p. 344). Frances's mother lectures widely on birth control; Frances reacts against this, not because she actually links birth control with infanticide, but because her mother's interest is clearly related to her antisexual, antihuman feelings. In rebellion against her mother, Frances "pursued sex with determination rather than pleasure" and has had four children. Still, she realizes that "in seeking to avoid her mother's ghost, she had in fact behaved exactly like her mother—she too had turned into a promiscuous and dominating flirt, the only difference being a technical one, in that she slept with the men instead of satisfying herself with verbal homage" (p. 80).

As the novel opens, Wingate is in a fit of depression, wondering whether she is actually programmed for death. She visits a laboratory, where, on seeing a male octopus in a box, she recalls that "the female of the species died, invariably, after giving birth." She wonders what she—who has rejected her lover, Karel—is "programmed" for. She knows that the individual mother octopus never refuses to die, and she questions her own capacity for free will. Her last child now has reached the self-sufficient age of seven. Is she self-destructing out of some biological or conditioned impulse?

As in Atwood's novel, the captor message received from the parents is complicated by the death orientation without. Wingate visits her paternal grandparents' home to find that urban sprawl and pollution have killed off the newts in the backyard pond, which were to her a living symbol of the life force. Survivors from prehistory, they were "a symbol of God's undying contract with the earth. They floated with an intense pleasure" (p. 104). Allusions to Freud's *Beyond the Pleasure Principle* suggest also that the entropic movement toward death may be biologically determined. Frances explains to her brother, Hugh, that Freud "admitted that there was a possibility that all instincts were struggling to restore an earlier state of things, and that earlier state being inanimate, all living things strove for death" (p. 187).

Freud envisions Eros (the life force) as battling against Thanatos (the death force) in the human soul. Frances and her lover, Karel, are associated with Eros. Their joyful and nurturing sexual relationship exemplifies ideal life-perpetuating forces. Both, like the newts, are survivors. Frances Wingate, as her name implies, is a winner. Another character refers to her as a "golden girl." Her own good fortune often amazes her. A famous archaeologist, she has experienced a moment of epiphany, which told her where the Phoenician city she discovers would be. She is almost frightened of her own power: " 'I imagine a city and it exists.' . . . She had imagined herself doing well at school, and had done well. Marrying and had married. Bearing children, and had borne them. Being rich, and had become rich. Being free, and was free. Finding true love, and had found it" (p. 29). She successfully combines her career with caring for her four children—with the help, of course, of babysitters. She feels guilty, however, for having avoided the suffering most people experience. Karel is the sole person in his family. He is the survivor of Nazi concentration camps, because he was his mother's favorite. Faced with a chance to save one child, she chose him.

The reason Frances is so concerned about the self-destructiveness within her is that for no good reason, she has left Karel. In doing so, she has rejected the only joyous, life-oriented sexual relationship she has ever known. She knows that she is acting out an antilife script written by her mother; her destructiveness, she fears, has a hereditary or biological origin. As in Atwood's novel, in order to reaffirm life, she must confront the death within her. She must also redefine her femaleness.

Like her mother (who is, ironically, a feminist), she does not like women. Her reaction to another woman archaeologist at a convention is condescending and competitive; she has no close female friends. In her own life, she is competent, achievement-oriented, selfish, and self-confident. In an interesting sex-role reversal, Karel is nurturing; he is primarily concerned with keeping everyone else happy, even if this means spending endless hours with boring people whom he does not like. Frances begins to value this quality in him. When she mistakenly believes that he has abandoned her, she develops a tumor in her breast, suggesting the death orientation implicit in her rejection of Karel's nurturing ethic.

It is, of course, only when Frances finds a female tradition that seems viable to her that she can stop repudiating her nurturing self. Her captor mother is supplanted by a true rescuing mother when she is called to her father's ancestral home, because her "crazy" Aunt Constance has starved to death. In the course of dealing with the ensuing scandal and arranging for the funeral, she visits Aunt Conn's home. Her visit parallels the ritual passage into nature and the world of pagan deities that Atwood's hero takes. When Frances's cousin, Janet, visited Aunt Conn, she saw her as a "witch," and the bits of bacon fat left for the birds as "sacrifices in some pagan rite of propitiation" (p. 282). When Frances visits Aunt Conn's house, the cottage is "overgrown with thorns and brambles, crumbling and falling but crumbling to nature only, not to man" (p. 296). She recognizes that Aunt

Conn's life was "Pure," that she may not nave been mad; rather, her life was natural, "The Real Thing" (p. 297).

She discovers letters that tell of Aunt Conn's tragedy. She fell in love with a married man, and had a child who died. The man, who never kept his promise to leave his wife, died young. Frances discovers her spiritual mother in Aunt Conn: handsome, with a "touch of style," admirers, and intelligence. Just as she recognizes this kinship with her aunt, the pastor comes in; he is alarmed at her appearance: "You could have been Constance herself, fifty years younger, in this light" (p. 304). Frances acts on this recognition of continuity between herself and her aunt by buying her aunt's cottage to use as a summer home, because, as she explains, it "suits her."

At the same time, Frances is aware that she has avoided Aunt Conn's fate only by the fortunate circumstances of her own birth. Furthermore, while she recognizes the need to take responsibility for the lives of others (Aunt Conn would not have died alone and hungry had anyone looked in on her), she also recognizes a limitation to her ability, or that of any individual, to affect the entropy that governs the world. While to take on all the evils of the world, as Karel does, creates life-denying guilt, it is possible to integrate a commitment to perpetuating life with recognition and acceptance of pain and death. Frances learns to accept suffering, in the same way that she earlier found she could handle her bouts of depression. Rather than trying to fight or deny them, she discovered she could simply accept depression as a cyclical element in her life. She accepts the pain within and without as a necessary part of life. She is also able to take responsibility for others without abdicating the responsibility to the self. In this way, she adopts the best aspects of both sex roles. The symbol of human wholeness is nurturance of the child within and the child without. Near the end of the novel, she mourns the death of Stephen's baby, and expresses the desire to nurture it, while she rocks and comforts herself at the same time: "For days she wept almost without ceasing. If only he had left the baby, she would moan, rocking herself backward and forward. . . . I would have had her" (p. 346).

Her reward for reaching a fully human state, which affirms life for the self and for the Other, is the return of Karel, who has undergone a similar change. He has learned to value himself and to take some responsibility for his own good. That Frances and Karel both have names that are used for both male and female suggests that their androgynous potential was there all along. Their "happy ending" marriage in no way signals a retreat for Frances for her newfound sense of responsibility and love for others. Having found Aunt Constance, she has discovered for the first time her continuity with her father's side of the family. In opposition to her mother's aristocratic descent, her father comes from common stock. In this way, the reconciliation with the surrogate mother is simultaneously a reconciliation with the father. When Frances rediscovers her paternal heritage, she ceases to see herself as better than other people. The treasure of community includes a new sense of identity with women especially, but ultimately with all people.

This sense of community manifests itself in Frances's personal life in newfound friendship with her cousins, David and Janet. Like Anna and David in *Surfacing,* David and Janet exemplify the extremes of the traditional sex roles. David, a geologist who is interested in rocks but not in people, finds a relationship with Karel and Frances to be humanizing. Janet is a repressed, oppressed, passive housewife, who is so bored that she longs for catastrophe. Frances's example helps her come to believe that "instead of confronting a life of boredom, she was merely biding her time" (p. 353).

The marriage at the end of the novel symbolizes fertility. Frances and Karel pass on life and joy to their biological children as well as to the other people they now love. (Both Frances's and Karel's children live with them.) The self-actualizing impulse (which Lazarre in *The Mother Knot* personifies as the dark lady) and the impulse to care for others (which Lazarre's protagonist initially perceives in her mother) are no longer in conflict. In fact, the choosing of one without the other is identified with death.

In Virginia Woolf's *To the Lighthouse*, the female hero finds a prolife, nurturing relationship to both herself and the world without any direct association with biological motherhood. Here, the achievement of human wholeness and the creative and nurturing existence is embodied in the life of the artist Lily Briscoe. Mr. and Mrs. Ramsay are patterned after Virginia Woolf's own parents, so the theme of rebirth through reconciliation would have significance for the author in her own biological relationships. However, Lily Briscoe, who achieves wholeness and the release of her creative power as a result of her experiences with the Ramsays, is not their biological daughter; nor does she have children.

Like the other protagonists discussed in this chapter, Lily Briscoe finds that her creative powers are blocked by an inability to reconcile and thereby to transcend traditional male and female roles. Specifically, she faces a double bind as a woman artist. Not only is she presumed a failure because she is not likely to marry (in fact, she does not wish to marry), but no one believes that she could be a fine artist because she is a woman. Mrs. Ramsay sums up traditional thinking when she discounts Lily by saying, "With her little Chinese eyes and her puckered-up face, she would never marry; one could not take her painting very seriously."[54] As Charles Tansley, the misanthropic graduate student visiting with the Ramsays, puts it, "Women can't paint, can't write" (p. 238). At the dinner table with the Ramsays, Lily continually comforts herself that, like a man, she "has her work." Yet her own confidence is continually shaken by the societal judgment that she is both a failure as a woman and doomed to be a failure as an artist because she is not male.

In order to be a fine artist, Lily gives birth to the mother within herself and forgives the father without. To do so, she must learn to understand the modes of perception of both Mr. and Mrs. Ramsay. Mr. Ramsay's mode of perception is rational, analytic, and detached from any emotional or physical context. He has a "splendid," analytical, categorical mind: "For if thought is like the keyboard of a piano, divided into so many notes, or like the alphabet is ranged in twenty-six letters all in order, then his splendid mind had no sort of difficulty in running over those letters one by one, firmly and accurately, until it had reached, say the letter Q. . . . Very few people in the whole of England ever reach Q" (p. 53). During the course of the novel, Mr. Ramsay is distraught—his ego is in jeopardy—simply because he sees little hope of reaching *R*. The author portrays him as one of the "steady goers . . . plodding and persevering" in opposition to the "inspired who, miraculously, lump all the letters together in one flash—the way of genius" (p. 55). Lily parodies his way of thinking by envisioning his pattern of abstraction as "a scrubbed kitchen table . . . lodged now in the fork of a pear tree" (p. 38). His mental methodology keeps him from noticing context—flowers, the view, his daughter's beauty, what he is eating, or other people's feelings. Consequently, he is alienated: His favorite melodramatic statement is "we perish each alone." It is this parochialism of the mind, combined with acute self-absorption and egotism, that causes Mrs. Ramsay to conclude that men are sterile: "She pitied men always as if they lacked something—women never, as if they had something" (p. 129). This death-oriented sterility breeds violence: Mr. Ramsay's egotistic need for "sympathy" and reassurance is repeatedly envisioned as a beak, a scimitar, or a blade striking out at Mrs. Ramsay or at his children.

Mrs. Ramsay, the nurturer, embodies the way of genius. When we see Mr. Ramsay alone, he is so tortured by his own egotistical need to accomplish that he cannot even see the world around him. Mrs. Ramsay, on the other hand, moves into a meditative, almost transcendent state, a "wedge-shaped core of darkness" (p. 95). In this state she abandons personality; she "came together in this peace, this rest, this eternity" (p. 96) and "leant to inanimate things: trees, streams, flowers; felt they expressed one; felt they became one; felt they knew one, in a sense were one" (p. 97). In this state she also recognizes the tragedy inherent in life—that "there is no reason, order, justice: but suffering, death, the poor" and that "no happiness lasted." Yet, by experiencing her oneness with the world, she experiences "ecstasy" and feels, "It is enough" (p. 100). Mrs. Ramsay's recognition of both the ungarnished facts and the transcendent splendor of life is the artistic ideal Lily later acknowledges: "to be on a level with ordinary experience, to feel simply that's a chair, that's a table, and yet at the same time, 'It's a miracle, it's an ecstasy' " (p. 300).

Mrs. Ramsay translates this unified consciousness into reality through the traditional role of hostess. At a dinner party, she fuses all the separate, alienated, and, in many respects, even hostile guests into a unified whole, and makes "a party together in a hollow, on an island . . . [a] common sense against fluidity out there" (p. 147). Such transcendent moments actually speak to us, Mrs. Ramsay recognizes, "of eternity. . . . there is a coherence in things, a stability; something, she meant, is immune from change, and shines out . . . in the fact of the flowing, the fleeting, the spectral, like a ruby. . . . Of such moments, she thought, the thing is made that endures" (p. 158).

It is this mode of perception, which allows human beings to partake of eternity, that Lily ultimately sees and loves in Mrs. Ramsay. She paints her as a triangular, purple wedge, the triangle being sacred to matriarchal goddesses. Woolf, in order to convey the fertility and power embodied in the truly nurturing self of Mrs. Ramsay, employs the image of a fountain: "Mrs. Ramsay . . . seemed to raise herself with an effort, and at once to pour erect into the air a rain of energy, a column of spray looking at the same time animated and alive as if all her energies were being fused into force, burning and illuminating. . . . And into this delicious fecundity, this fountain and spray of life, the fatal sterility of the male plunged itself, like a beak of brass barren and bare" (p. 58). To achieve reconciliation with the positive essence of Mrs. Ramsay, Lily first needs to dissociate the powers of fertility and nurturance that Mrs. Ramsay represents from the negative manifestations of these qualities within the patriarchally defined roles of wife and mother. Mrs. Ramsay, herself a product of sex-role conditioning, is unable to make the separation. She believes that her creative, nurturing power should be expended completely on men. She gives in to her husband, pressures others into disastrous marriages, and depends for gratification on others' need for her mothering. The negative results are that Mrs. Ramsay not only uses herself up nurturing others, but also urges other women into the same role. Woolf implies that Mrs. Ramsay virtually wears herself out by continually giving to her husband, to eight children, and to assorted visitors.

The novel is divided into three parts. The first, "The Window," focuses on Mr. and Mrs. Ramsay. The second section, "Time Passes," puts both sections in a temporal and natural context. Woolf reports the death of Mrs. Ramsay and of her children Prue and Andrew to childbirth and to war, respectively, in parentheses that punctuate the section and give us a sense of human insignificance in the natural world. The dominant mode of the section is a poetic description of the gradual, entropic assault of nature on the Ramsays' neglected summer home, which gives a heightened sense of the fragility of the order Mrs. Ramsay has created. It also increases the reader's appreciation of Mrs. Ramsay's genius. Understanding the entropy at the heart of nature, Mrs. Ramsay, unlike her husband, does not engage in an attempt to attain immortality through creating literary or other kinds of monuments. Her sense of the eternal has nothing to do with physical artifacts. The "Time Passes" section underlines Mrs. Ramsay's conviction that people are not powerful enough to conquer the flux of nature. Her strength —dramatized in "The Window"—is that she knows she cannot control or change the natural world. Her acceptance of the entropy at the heart of the natural world is contrasted with her husband's singleminded and unimaginative "facing the facts"; at the beginning of the novel, she refuses to disappoint her son James by telling him it will rain tomorrow. When a skull scares her daughter so she cannot go to sleep, Mrs. Ramsay covers it with a shawl.

The third and final part, "The Lighthouse," describes Lily's return to the Ramsays' summer home and her reconciliation with both parent figures. She finds herself angry at Mrs. Ramsay, blaming her for the fact that she cannot finish her painting, understand the world, or live a meaningful life: ". . . it was all Mrs. Ramsay's fault. She was dead" (p. 224). She is also angry at Mr. Ramsay, the patriarch who virtually killed his wife and whom Lily holds responsible for all the misogynistic condescension at the core of her paralysis. She feels fundamentally rejected by both of them. When Mr. Ramsay appears, demanding sympathy, she at first cannot give it to him. Ultimately, however, she sees him not as the bigger-than-life patriarch but as a mortal, quite at a loss without his wife. It is this diminished man for whom she feels a rush of sympathy after she is able quite honestly to compliment him on his boots. Her admiration of his boots reflects her acceptance of him as a simple, flawed human being: She envisions the boots "walking to his room of their own accord, expressive in his absence of pathos, surliness, ill-temper, charm" (p. 229).

As he leaves, able at last to carry out Mrs. Ramsay's injunction to take the children to the lighthouse, Lily begins to discover the Mrs. Ramsay in herself. Not only does she feel sympathy for Mrs. Ramsay, but she moves into a meditative state very like Mrs. Ramsay's "core of darkness." Now Lily is symbolically associated with a fertile fountain. As she paints, ". . . she lost consciousness of outer things, and her name and her personality and her appearance . . . her mind kept throwing up from its depths, scenes, and names, and sayings and memories and ideas, like a fountain spurting over that glaring, hideously difficult white space, while she modelled it with greens and blues" (p. 238).

When she comes out of this state, she yearns for the external mother figure, Mrs. Ramsay herself. Calling out for her, she suddenly sees Mrs. Ramsay at the window as she always was. Her first reaction is to be struck with longing for a mother; ". . . the old horror came back—to want and want and not to have" (p. 300). Then suddenly, having found the positive nurturer in herself, she no longer needs Mrs. Ramsay, for she has become her own mother. Knowing Mrs. Ramsay as both "ordinary experience" and "a miracle," Lily alters the shape of the triangle. Then, as she looks up at Mr. Ramsay in the boat approaching the lighthouse: "She wanted him" (p. 300). Empathetically knowing him as he reaches the lighthouse, she finally makes both Mr. and Mrs. Ramsay a part of her experience. In doing so, Lily, for the first time, is free of the tyranny of the mythological, larger-than-life "mother" and "father." She completes her painting, and observes, "I have had my vision" (p. 310). She realizes that she still lives in a society that will not acknowledge her perception—her paintings will be hung in attics—but this does not ultimately matter. What matters is that for the first time, she can see with her own eyes rather than through the perspective of authority figures.

Implicit in Woolf's novel is an absolute rejection of patriarchal conscious-ness, and, at the same time, a pointed forgiveness of individual men. In fact, Woolf feels the need to forgive Mr. Ramsay three times. Lily forgives him, and his son and daughter, James and Cam, forgive him in turn. Although there is little sense of an actual change in Mr. Ramsay's behavior or consciousness, his arrival at the light-house, by which he completes the journey that Mrs. Ramsay had so encouraged, may signal a transformation analogous to Lily's. He is, after all, on a nurturing mission, delivering the clothes that Mrs. Ramsay altered for the needy family at the lighthouse. He retains the male mode, but acts out a traditionally female function. Woolf's portrait of Mr. Carmichael, a very minor character who is a poet and an opium user, suggests that Lily's integration of the best human qualities associated with both sexes is equally accessible to men. When Mr. Carmichael annoys Mr. Ramsay during the famous dinner scene by asking for a second helping of soup, Mrs. Ramsay "could not help respecting the composure with which he sat there, drinking his soup. If he wanted soup, he asked for soup. Whether people laughed at him or were angry with him, he was the same. . . . He was always content and dignified" (p. 145). Mr. Carmichael initially dislikes Mrs. Ramsay, but during this dinner scene he rather suddenly evidences a realization of their affinity as artists. Poet and hostess, they both create realities that "partake" of "eternity." At the end of the dinner he turns slightly toward her "and bowed to her as if he did her homage" (p. 167), thus signaling his affirmation of the female traits that make his artistic genius possible.

The reconciliation with the parents, then, heals the split created by patriachal sex roles, allowing the hero to become master of two worlds. Nancy Reeves writes in *Womankind:*

> The gap between male and female . . . is not a universal constant. . . . Today the hemisphere of the public has been assigned to the male and the hemisphere of the private to the female. Each sex has become a symbol of its territory. The conflict between them can then be seen as a reflection of the longing of each to be part of the other's sphere, to link the public with the private in our schizoid world, to embrace the whole of life.[55]

Furthermore, to see life whole is not only a new vision, it also implies a radical change in mode of perception. It is a new way of seeing. In contemporary art and literature, in which the patriarchal patterns of thought and behavior are transcended and a new, more whole and humane myth is affirmed, the style and form of the work, as well as the content, reflect the new myth and the new mode. Judy Chicago, in *Through the Flower,* traces the process that leads to the integration of positive aspects of both male and female qualities, and describes the positive effect of such a process on her work in the visual arts. Chicago was trained to be an artist in the male mode, achieving success at the cost of repudiating her womanhood. When she begins working with other women to describe the female experience in art, she works "through the flower" to explore, in her works, "my 'feminine qualities,' . . . as attributes of my humanity. I was able to see that many of the personality traits that are inculcated into women and then disparaged by male culture (heightened intuition, emotional responsiveness, etc.) are actually valuable human abilities, which, if developed by *both* men and women, would greatly improve our society." When she becomes "comfortable about being and expressing myself as a woman in my life and in my art," Chicago makes a breakthrough in her work. Then her art reflects her new, integrated vision in both form and content. This vision requires a change in the form of all art and all social institutions. She concludes that women and men who have developed their repressed female qualities *"can change and mold our environment,* but only if we can be ourselves and express our real points of view."[56]

One of the ways this new vision is expressed in contemporary literary works, such as those of Lessing, Woolf, Nin, and Drabble, is through form, in the absence of linear plot. In these works, nothing happens—that is, dramatic external events that have clear and significant repercussions, and that one has come to expect in the traditional novel, do not occur. Furthermore, what by traditional standards are trivial, irrelevant details exist in equal prominence with the more obviously consequential ones. These stylistic devices symbolize the new way of seeing implicit in a holistic, nonhierarchical world view. As Doris Lessing demonstrates in *The Golden Notebook,* all attempts to put our experience into a narrative with a clearly defined plot falsify human experience by assuming that life occurs according to an obvious cause-and-effect structure. The assumption that life occurs in a logical, linear order is a patriarchal one.

Another patriarchal myth is that certain people, details, and events have more inherent worth than others, often because of their more prestigious position in the patriarchal hierarchy. A vision of life as whole leads to the assumption that life in whatever human or situational form it takes is of value because it is life; to repress or dismiss or define any aspect of life as inferior is to deny life itself. A further implication is that all events, people, and details are manifestations not just of one meaning but of a multitude of contradictory and inseparable interpretations. The author refrains from the tendency typical of patriarchal fiction to submit the concrete particulars to a simplistic or judgmental explication.

Often these stylistically innovative prose works consist of an in-depth look at a small number of phenomena, events, or personalities in order for the reader to see the event as thoroughly as possible in all its complexity and richness. The effect is that the reader sees the subject fresh: The extensive examination from numerous angles makes any attempt to assign it to patriarchal categories impossible. The static dwelling on a single detail or moment conveys the impressionistic aspect of experience, which in traditional narrative form tends to be simplified and distorted by the linear nature of language, the causal assumptions of plot, and the constrictions of the strictly rational viewpoint. In Drabble's *The Realms of Gold,* the narrator interrupts the story to address the reader directly, explaining that Frances's postcard to Karel is in a mailbox and that he will return to her. This takes the reader's attention away from the conventional concern with plot—"what will happen"—and redirects it toward the *process* of how it happens and to the *character* of Frances Wingate. Evelyn Hinz writes in "The Creative Critic," "we could call [Anaïs] Nin's books 'character studies' rather than 'novels' because in a typical novel . . . something happens, whereas in Nin's work we begin with the character and with that point of view."[57]

By avoiding a linear plot, the novelist presents a world that is not fundamentally determined by linear, causal relationships. Plots assume causation. "Jane dies; then Ted dies" is not a plot. "Jane dies, and Ted dies of a broken heart" is a plot. In life, however, acausal events are common; Jane dies, and then Ted dies. Writers who advocate a nurturing, life-affirming ethic often write books in which events occur that are related, but are not causally connected. In Drabble's *The Realms of Gold*, the plot involves one causal incident. Frances Wingate sends a postcard to her lover, and he returns to her. There is no blocking figure, and the events described between the two occurrences—the bulk of the novel—do not affect the outcome. Karel would have returned to Frances immediately, except that he did not receive the postcard. As soon as it is delivered, he gets on a plane to surprise her. The basic structure of the novel is not cause and effect, but coincidence, synchronism. Karel comes back; Frances's great-aunt starves to death; Stephen kills himself and his child; Frances gets acquainted with two cousins. As in life, these events just happen to occur together. Because they do, the coincidences are significant.

The form, therefore, is not linear. The goal is to reveal the essence of the character or event. It is analogous to a process developed in consciousness-raising sessions in which one person begins by describing something she experienced, and other members describe similar experiences in no particular order. The accumulation of all the individual variations on the experience makes the essence of the experience apparent. Similarly, in *The Realms of Gold*, the reader sees Frances Wingate with her children, at a professional conference, being efficient, being depressed, and so on, until he or she *knows* Frances Wingate. In Woolf's *To the Lighthouse*, Lily sees Mr. and Mrs. Ramsay from a variety of angles until she and the reader know them on such a profound level that they become part of her and of the reader. This comprehensive awareness is not achieved as the climax of linear action; rather, it is like the sudden and total perception of a painting that becomes possible when the final brushstroke has been made.

The second characteristic of this innovative mode is a contextual method of development. It follows from the lack of a plot and the de-emphasis on understanding reality in a straightforward, linear way. The essence of the work is revealed by seeing its subject in its many contexts. The central character is not seen as separate from other people and the natural world. To know a character or an event, we must know its context. Mrs. Ramsay thinks of eternity while serving the boeuf en daube.[58] Virginia Woolf never lets us forget the natural and social context: In *Mrs. Dalloway*, she plunges Clarissa Dalloway "into the very heart of the moment" amidst descriptions of her dressing table.[59] Furthermore, Woolf makes us aware not only of the immediate social and physical context, but of increasingly wider contexts. The "Time Passes" section of *To the Lighthouse* puts the Ramsays' experience in the context of natural time, natural process. Thus, Mrs. Ramsay becomes insignificant as a particular person (her death is noted parenthetically), yet we also learn how important and irreplaceable she is to those close to her. Finally, we see her as the epitome of the nurturing mode of perception that the novel celebrates. In *The Realms of Gold,* we consider human experience in the ever-widening contexts of immediate experience; history (Karel is a historian), archaeology (Frances is an archaeologist), and, finally, geology (her cousin David is a geologist).

One result of describing events in their multiple contexts is that conflicting versions of reality are not entirely resolved, but are seen as the elements of a larger reality whose complexity can be acknowledged. By the end of *The Realms of Gold,* Frances realizes that she "had never really understood her Phoenicians [who practiced child sacrifice]: nor had she been able to understand how Stephen could take the child's life as well as his own" (p. 350). In that novel, Frances's joy is seen in the context of most people's misery: Drabble makes no attempt to make Frances's luck and others' misfortunes seem fair to the reader. The divergent experiences are not fair; they just are. Similarly, Lily Briscoe, in *To the Lighthouse,* thinks, "Such was the complexity of things. For what happened to her, especially staying with the Ramsays, was to be made to feel violently two opposite things at the same time; . . . and then they fought together in her mind as now" (p. 154). The form of these novels strives to be complex enough to accommodate conflicting planes of reality that are all true, rather than inflicting a false simplicity on experience.

Finally, the emphasis on complexity and multiple points of view breeds a humble stance and a subjective rather than an objective tone. The tone of this mode lacks the shadow of the huge "I" that Virginia Woolf finds (in *A Room of One's Own*) to be characteristic of twentieth-century writing by males who are self-conscious about their masculinity and who therefore repress their female qualities; yet it incorporates an awareness that any reality presented is only one person's perception. Anaïs Nin writes in her diary: "I do not believe in man's objectivity. All his ideas, systems, philosophies, arts come from a personal source he does not wish to admit."[60] Woolf begins *A Room of One's Own* (originally presented as a lecture to university women) by confessing, with tongue in cheek, that she cannot provide "a nugget of pure truth to wrap up between the pages of your notebooks and keep on the mantlepiece forever." She claims only to be able to "develop in your presence as fully and freely as I can the train of thought which led me to think that women need 500 pounds and rooms of their own to be great writers."[61] In these works, writers acknowledge their humanity and the reader's. Often, they acknowledge the reader directly: Drabble interrupts the narrative with parenthetical comments to the reader, and Woolf invents the "common reader," with whom she sees herself as a team, referred to as "we."

To sum up, the style that grows out of a heroic awareness and that unifies nurturance and self-actualization, self and others, is personal and subjective in tone, contextual in style, and spiral in form. The underlying myth is based on a world view in which reality is immensely complex; all events, objects, and beings are related and valuable; and process and essence rather than action and facts are valued. Although not all the works discussed in this chapter are perfectly consonant in their form and their subject matter, the form of these particular works reflects the new consciousness of the hero.

Having affirmed a commitment to the discovery of the true self in exiting from the garden, and having discovered that she has within her both male and female attributes, the female hero discovers and affirms the full humanity obscured by traditional sex roles. She learns to be autonomous and to achieve without exploiting or dominating others; and she learns nurturance that is not accompanied by a denial of the self. With the achievement of this unified vision, the hero is prepared to return to the kingdom and to enjoy a new relationship with the world.

Part III
The Return

Chapter 7
The New Family

When you open up your life to the living, all things come spilling in on you.
And you're flowing like a river, the Changer and the Changed. . . .
Filling up and spilling over, it's an endless waterfall.

Chris Williamson, "Waterfall"

The treasure the hero claims at the completion of the journey is herself. Discovering herself—her whole and authentic self—she finds that her entire world is transformed. She partakes of the eternal, enjoys a new sense of trust in her perceptions about the world, and thus rejoices over her journey to the underworld. Florida Scott-Maxwell, an actress, short story writer, and dramatist, a political activist on behalf of women's suffrage, a mother, and a practicing Jungian psychologist, writes in praise of the sojourns that she has made into her own unconscious. She considers the experience of the chaos within crucial to the achievement of selfhood.

> The most important thing in my life was the rich experience of the unconscious. This was a gift given to me and I only had the sense to honor and serve it. It taught me that we are fed by great forces, and I know that I am in the hands of what seemed immortal. It hardly matters whether I am mortal or not since I have experienced the immortal. This makes me at rest in much of my being, but not in all. It is almost as if the order in me is barely me, and I still have to deal with the chaos that is mine.[1]

An English psychologist who used the pseudonym Joanna Field also writes in her diary of the unlimited sources of life she discovered by descending beneath what she calls her "personal self":

> On the downs above Ashbury, walking past Wayland Smith's cave. I felt I ought to be thinking about something, getting the most out of the Downs, and yet constantly preoccupied with thoughts. Then I said, "The self in all these things does not know, it just is. I will sink down into my heart and just be." . . .

It struck me as odd that it had taken me so long to reach a feeling of sureness that there was something in me that would get on with the job of living without my continual tampering.[2]

Both women value the self that is discovered in the midst of the dark labyrinth of uncategorized experience. Field found that she could move beyond the conditioned self to a more authentic state of being by automatic writing:

For I had taken the surface ripples for all there was, when actually happenings of vital importance to me had been going on, not somewhere away from me, but just underneath the calm surface of my own mind. . . .

I began to have an idea of my life, not as the slow shaping of achievement to fit my preconceived purposes, but as the gradual discovery and growth of a purpose which I did not know. I wrote: "It will mean walking in a fog for a bit, but it's the only way which is not a presumption, forcing the self into a theory." (pp. 356–357)

Virginia Woolf similarly discovers: "As I write, there rises somewhere in my head that queer and very pleasant sense of something which I want to write; my own point of view."[3] Julie, a patient whom R. D. Laing describes in *The Divided Self*, believes that her mother never wanted her and so feels worthless and dead. In her conversations with Laing, she describes the recovery of belief in herself. Laing comments that from the very beginning of her therapy,

she did value herself if only in a phantom way. There was a belief (however psychotic a belief it was, it was still a form of faith in something of great value in herself) that there was something of great worth deeply lost or buried inside her, as yet undiscovered by herself or by anyone. If one could go deep into the depth of the dark earth one would discover "the bright gold" [a phrase from one of her poems], or if one could get fathoms down one would discover "the pearl at the bottom of the sea."[4]

With all the life-denying characteristics stripped away, the hero ceases to see herself in all the unreal ways. The speaker in Anne Sexton's poem "Kind Sir: These Woods" tells of a childhood game in which she would close her eyes, turn around, and become lost in a world of "strange happenings, untold and unreal." And then she would come back to her self. She opens her eyes in fear only to "search these woods and find nothing worse / than myself, caught between the grapes and the thorns."[5] In Marge Piercy's *Small Changes*, after Beth's husband Jim rapes her, she becomes free of internalized guilt about him. Having determined to belong to no one but herself, she works to learn who that self is. In every little decision, she tries to acquaint herself with herself, to discover what she likes, rather than what she has been taught to like: "In Boston she was lonely, but her loneliness was a positive thing, a free space she thrived in. With everything she tasted and tried, she studied herself suspiciously; do you really like this? She must never again choose by what tasted good to somebody else, even what tasted good to everybody else. 'You can't taste with anybody else's tongue,' she wrote on the wall."[6]

A hero may be committed to the needs and desires of her own nature from the very beginning of her journey; at least some degree of commitment to the self as valuable must exist in order for any initial heroic exit to occur. Nevertheless, it is only at the end of the journey that the hero takes the time to reflect, becoming fully conscious of the self that she has been rescuing and nurturing all along. Having more clearly found herself at the end of the journey, the hero even more firmly refuses to conform to the patriarchal myths of ideal womanhood. She will no longer repress herself for the sake of becoming either an angel in heaven or an angel in the house. Joanna in Russ's *The Female Man* remarks that she would rather be a frogess than a princess any day. Eva, in Constance Beresford-Howe's *The Book of Eve*, leaves her suburban home and invalid husband to live alone in a run-down basement apartment in the heart of Toronto, and delights in watching her hair grow scragglier, her dress more threadbare, and her living quarters more cluttered.

This free expression of the self brings with it a release of power. The hero characteristically validates and celebrates not only her own selfhood but that of all women, and this affirmation releases her fullest creative potential. She may embrace even the most disparaging patriarchal images of female selfhood. In Jean Tepperman's poem "Witch," the speaker rejects the societal message that she should be conventionally feminine and chooses to be powerful and outrageous like a witch.

> Tonight I meet my sisters
> in the graveyard.
> Around midnight
> if you stop at a red light
> in the wet city traffic,
> watch for us against the moon.
> We are screaming,
> we are flying,
> laughing, and won't stop.[7]

Another radical example of the celebration of the whole self is recounted in Box-Car Bertha's autobiographical novel *Sister of the Road*. Bertha looks back on a life that includes a stint as a prostitute, culminating in a case of syphilis, as well as the experiences of looking on helplessly when one lover is hanged and another run over by a train. She declares, "Everything I had ever struggled to learn I found I had already surmised. . . . I had achieved my purpose—everything I had set out in life to do, I had accomplished. I had wanted to know how it felt to be a hobo, a radical, a prostitute, a thief, a reformer, a social worker and a revolutionist. Now I knew. I shuddered. Yes, it was all worthwhile to me. There were no tragedies in my life. Yes, my prayers had been answered."[8]

When she discovers her true, powerful, and heroic self, the female hero, like Alice in Wonderland, realizes that her bizarre experiences are part of *her* dream and not the Red King's as she had been told. She is like the child in "The Emperor's New Clothes," who trusts her own perception that the emperor is naked, when all around her everyone is admiring his new suit. When the hero demythologizes the patriarch, she learns that virtually everything she has been taught falsifies her own experience; for example, distinctions between male and female, mind and body, spirit and flesh, self and Other, are artificial dualities that distort her perceptions of the world.

The treasures that attend the discovery of the true heroic self are wholeness and community. Paradoxically, as a result of her journey inward the hero overcomes alienation and rejoins herself with the world. This hard-won ability to celebrate the self and all experience—without escaping or repressing knowledge, pain, oppression, or evil—enables the hero to love, and to find a community with other people. Box-Car Bertha concludes her narrative by explaining that the fruit of her journey is the newly discovered need "to be responsible for someone, to live for someone else" (p. 228), and she chooses to "settle down" with her daughter. This community of two differs from the captor mother-child bond because it is freely chosen, and because Bertha will not sacrifice herself for her child, nor will she discourage her daughter from embarking on her own quest, from making her own mistakes, or from discovering her own powers. Having learned to love herself, the hero is able to love others without dependence or compulsion. Confident of her own powers of perception and understanding, the returned hero respects the world views of others. Iris Murdoch writes in *Flight from the Enchanter*, "Reality is a cipher with many solutions, all of them right ones."[9]

Heroes in fantasy and myth enjoy a magical, symbiotic relationship with the culture. They slay a dragon and return to the kingdom, which is rejuvenated or transformed as a result of their deed. In realistic literature, the kingdom is not necessarily miraculously transformed but the hero usually is rewarded with love and community on a smaller scale. She may find community with the natural world or with the spiritual world, with women, with men, or with both, and she always feels at home and comfortable with herself. The hero's life contrasts with that of the fairy-tale Damsel in Distress who waits for a Prince to transform her world; unlike the passive damsel, the hero actively affects the outcome of her story and creates or chooses her new family. Ann Spencer writes in the poem "Letter to My Sister" that "it is dangerous for a woman to defy the gods," but it is "worse still if you mince along timidly."[10] Until a woman has the courage to risk everything to achieve her potential, she can never know the joy of independence or of a loving community between heroic equals. It would not, therefore, be an overstatement to say that there are no entirely unhappy endings in stories about female heroes. In the comic mode, the hero returns and becomes part of a rejuvenated human community. In a tragedy, she finds community in the spiritual realm. In both cases, she values herself and therefore is not dependent on social approval or on a male figure to complete and validate her.

How successful the hero is in discovering or creating a community of equals depends on her level of competence and the degree of divergence between her perceptions and those of the culture. In literature, the hero's relationship to the culture is connected to the literary genre in which she appears; the genre in turn often reflects the author's degree of confidence in the power of the individual to affect the world.

In myth, the heroes are gods and goddesses, or occasionally kings, queens, and saints. When the female hero is mortal, her vision is usually so far superior to that of the mass of humanity that she may not find community with other people. Sophocles' Antigone, like Joan of Arc, is executed. Thus, female heroes of myth do not often triumph over their enemies or live to reap rewards in the kingdom, like Ulysses does, for example; perhaps this is because there has been so little acceptance of female power. Contemporary writers and scholars such as Adrienne Rich, Mary Daly, and Elizabeth Gould Davis suggest, however, that the existence of triumphant female mythic heroes has been consistently and methodically hidden from women. The new scholarly interest in recovering myths about strong female heroes and about the goddess in her many guises is beginning to restore female heroes of myth to their rightful place in the culture.

When the protagonist of romance slays the dragon, as does Dorothy in *The Wizard of Oz,* the outer society magically changes, and she finds herself "at home." As we have seen, when Dorothy has become a hero, she returns to a home on the Kansas prairie that is no longer grey. When Jane Eyre learns to be her own mistress, Bertha dies, Thornfield burns down, Rochester is maimed, and Jane inherits money. The situation thus altered, Jane and Rochester can be rewarded with an egalitarian marriage. When Martha Quest defeats the "self-hater" and develops her powers of ESP, an apocalypse creates new mutants with extrasensory powers, thus providing Martha with a community.

In works in which the hero is more capable than those around her, but is similar enough to the general reader to be a positive role model, the idea of magical transformation is shown to have realistic psychological and sociological equivalents. Frances Wingate, in *The Realms of Gold,* achieves everything she wants in life—a fulfilling career, a good love relationship, and the opportunity to use all of her talents—by repeatedly imagining her life as it might be and by acting on her vision. She is also so lucky that it frightens her. An archaeologist, she discovers an ancient civilization because in a moment of intuitive genius she realizes where it must be; she also imagines doing well in school, marrying well, and bearing children, becoming rich, being free and finding (and losing) true love—all with the same positive result. "What next should she imagine? . . . Should she dig again in the desert and uncover gold? Should she plant down her foot and let water spring from the dry land? Should she wave her arm and let the rocks blossom?"[11] Frances is rewarded with a new husband, a new family, love, and deep friendships, but she does not transform the kingdom. Nevertheless, Drabble makes it clear that her journey is a part of the life-perpetuating forces that counter the prevailing entropy, sterility, and despair. Her journey, therefore, resonates with cultural and spiritual implications.

The hero of Grant Allen's *The Woman Who Did* is not so fortunate as Frances Wingate, but her noble, tragic end points toward social and spiritual change. Allen tells of Herminia Barton, a young woman of principle in the nineteenth century, who refuses to marry because she determines that the institution of marriage is at the root of women's oppression. When her wealthy lover dies, leaving her with a daughter, she raises her in poverty, comforted that her daughter may be able to live a liberated and happy life. Herminia has personal esteem and friends among a radical community, and does productive political work. However, when her daughter condemns her as a "ruined woman," and complains that she cannot marry the man she loves because "I couldn't think of burdening an honest man with such a mother-in-law as you are,"[12] Herminia kills herself to facilitate her daughter's happiness. In this case, Herminia's tragedy results from the partial nature of her liberation as much as it does from the divergence between her sense of values and that of her culture. She may have slain the sexual dimension of the virginity myth, but she still believes in being totally selfless. She is found wearing a "pure white dress," with "two crushed white roses just peeping from her bodice." The author notes that her "stainless soul had ceased to exist forever" (p. 223).

To recognize that Herminia's martyrdom is partially motivated by the socialization patterns that define the "good woman" as selfless, however, does not in any way undermine the heroic nature of her rebellion. Martyrs for a cause often help to eliminate the very internal and external forces that defeat them. Herminia's martyrdom, Allen suggests, is tragic in the highest sense, because it will lead to a regenerated, purified kingdom: "Not for nothing does blind fate vouchsafe such martyrs to humanity. From their graves shall spring glorious the church of the future" (p. 223).

The hero who is portrayed as a comic figure (such as a picaro) may have wisdom beyond her peers, but attracts neither social praise nor serious condemnation because she is not seen as a threat to the status quo. Like Ben Franklin's Polly Baker in "The Speech of Polly Baker," or William Faulkner's Lena Grove in *Light in August,* she is associated with nature rather than society. Within limitations, she can be outspoken or violate cultural mores, because no one takes her seriously. As is Moll Flanders, she is often supremely able to have her own way, but has little or no effect on the social order. Like Brecht's Mother Courage, however, her indomitable will makes her able to pick up her carts and carry on, to keep on traveling even in the midst of destruction and chaos. In this way, she symbolizes the indestructible human spirit.

If the hero's superior knowledge is exclusively about meaninglessness and oppression, she is unlikely to move beyond informed despair to affirm her own value in the world or to change it. The masochistic, intensely introspective protagonists of such works as Lois Gould's *Final Analysis* or Erica Jong's *How to Save Your Own Life* are examples of the genre, although both Norma and Isadora find temporary relief from despair through romantic love. Characters such as Maria, in Joan Didion's *Play It As It Lays,* learn to affirm a meaningless world, but do not alter the social order. They may find a separate peace, but they do not find a viable human community.

In most novels, the hero has some power to change her life, but that power is limited by the culture. She may transform her immediate world, as Esther Summerson does in Dickens's *Bleak House,* or she may leave a repressive environment to find a more fulfilling one, as Ella Price does in *Ella Price's Journal.* Like the protagonists of Jane Austen's novels, she may also settle for some accommodation to conventional society. Usually, this accommodation is marked by a marriage to a man who respects the hero and therefore will not exercise the more oppressive aspects of conventional patriarchal power. In such works, the psychological development of the hero includes some dampening of spirit so that she may fit the confines of the conventional role. Austen's Emma, for example, is rewarded with marriage to Mr. Knightley when she acknowledges her limitations and learns to be considerate and not to meddle. Yet her spirit is only dampened, not tamed, and it is clear that she will continue to be autonomous and independent within the limitations of that marriage. Jo March in Louisa May Alcott's *Little Women* is a similar case. Jo's father is proud that she has grown from the girl "who whistles, talks slang" and "lies on the rug" to "a young lady" who pins her collar straight and laces her boots neatly. He notes that "her face is rather thin and pale, . . . but I like to look at it, for it has grown gentler, and her voice is lower; she doesn't bounce, but moves quietly, and takes care of a certain little person [her sister Beth] in a motherly way which delights me." However, his pleasure at her new restraint is somewhat ambiguous, for he notes, "I rather miss my wild girl."[13] Also, although she does not follow through on her determination not to marry, Jo makes a marriage in which she will have significant autonomy and freedom with little or no pressure to be conventionally "feminine"—she marries an older man and runs a school for boys.

George Eliot suggests at the end of *Middlemarch* that although such judicious accommodation does not radically challenge or alter society, the hero's vitality may still aid in the rejuvenation of the culture. Some readers have been disappointed in Dorothea Brooke's acceptance of the helpmate role at the end of the work, and even Eliot clearly sees it as a regrettable though realistic decision. Yet, she notes,

> Her finely touched spirit had still its fine issues, though they were not widely visible. Her full nature like that river of which Cyrus broke the strength, spent itself in channels which had no great name on the earth. But the effect of her being on those around her was incalculably diffusive, for the growing good of the world is partly dependent on unhistoric acts, and that things are not so ill with you and me as they might have been is half owing to the number who lived faithfully a hidden life and rest in unvisited tombs.[14]

The realistic hero compromises when necessary to achieve as much happiness as possible within her cultural context, but she also works when she can for social change. Although she does not magically transform the culture alone, she can change institutions and ideas. Marie, in Agnes Smedley's *Daughter of Earth*, works to educate people to the need for a social revolution. Beth in Marge Piercy's *Small Changes* leaves her husband, believing that she is "the only flying turtle under the sun," but later discovers an entire network of heroic rebels who have left husbands, wives, and jobs, and who are creating a variety of communes; the success of their experiments holds out the possibility of widespread cultural change.

The following two sections of this chapter focus on the communities that the hero gains as a reward for undertaking the solitary journey. The subject of the first is the community of one. Whatever her relationship to society and to other people, the returned hero delights in a sense of wholeness and autonomy and therefore is not lonely when solitary. She finds fulfillment through work and through a sense of communion with the natural and spiritual worlds. In the final section, the orphan hero finds a new family, composed of one or more people. Within this new community, she can express herself without threat of ridicule or condemnation, because her new friends value her liberation and her heroism. These new communities are often formed because the hero has the courage to be herself, and she experiences the joy of being sincerely loved for her true self rather than for her conformity to a role.

Since the discussions of literary works in Part II: The Journey have included a brief description of the return of each individual hero, the following sections will refer only briefly to works previously discussed. References to other stories as well as autobiographies and poems will be used to extend awareness of the nature and implications of the hero's reward. The concluding chapter of the book, "The Kingdom Transfigured," explores women's utopian fiction to describe societies in which a female hero would feel truly at home.

A Community of One

Having slain the dragon alone, the hero becomes her own mother and father, her own child, her own lover, her own friend. She recognizes, as Isadora Wing does, that "people don't complete us. We complete ourselves."[15] Female heroes at the end of the journey frequently refer to the joy of this new community with the self. Released from bondage to myths about themselves and from the need to deny or to accommodate themselves to the expectations of others, they find they are free simply to be. The English psychologist Joanna Field records in her diary, "I used to trouble about what life was for—now being alive seems sufficient."[16] Her freedom from the need for introspection and analysis occurs because "the self in all these things does not know, it just is" (p. 358). Katherine Mansfield speaks of learning to be more relaxed when she stops trying to prove her worth to herself and to others: "When we can begin to take our failures nonseriously, it means we are ceasing to be afraid of them. It is of immense importance to learn to laugh at ourselves . . . [for] 'a touch of easy familiarity and derision' has its value."[17] Anaïs Nin, in her diary, moves past introspection to the easy, peaceful state of community with the self:

> It was in Cadiz that I lay down in a hotel room and fell into a delirious, obsessional reverie, a continuous secret melody of jealousy, fear, doubt, and it was in Cadiz that I stood up and broke the evil curse, as if by a magical act of will, I broke the net, the evil course of obsession. I learned how to break it. It was symbolized by my going into the street. From that day on, suffering became intermittent, subject to interruptions, distractions, not a perpetual condition. I was able to distract myself. I could live for hours without the malady of doubt. There were silences in my head, periods of peace and enjoyment. I would abandon myself completely to the pleasure of multiple relationships, to the beauty of the day, to the joys of the day. It was as if the cancer in me had ceased gnawing me. The cancer of introspection. . . . It seemed to have happened suddenly, like a miracle, but it was the result of years of struggle, of analysis, of passionate living. Introspection is a devouring monster. You have to feed it with much material, much experience, and then it ceases feeding on you. . . . From that moment on, what I experienced were emotional dramas which passed like storms, and left peace behind them.[18]

The self is a community, an easy friend, because the self, body and mind, is whole, but this achieved autonomy is not narcissistic or alienated. Anaïs Nin ends *House of Incest* with an imaginative vision of female completeness, in which a woman dances wildly and alone and yet at one with all things:

> She looked at her hands tightly closed and opened them slowly, opened them completely like Christ; she opened

> them in a gesture of abandon and giving; she relinquished and
> forgave, opening her arms and her hands, permitting all things
> to flow away and beyond her. . . . And she danced; she
> danced with the music and with the rhythm of earth's circles;
> she turned with the earth turning, like a disk, turning all face to
> light and to darkness evenly, dancing towards daylight.[19]

Like this dancer,the hero is often portrayed as a microcosm of the whole world.

In traditional Western literature, the correlation between the inner world of
the heroic self and the outer spiritual or natural world is often envisioned in
Christian terms. Joan of Arc interprets her ''voices'' as coming from God; Emily
Brontë, in ''No Coward Soul Is Mine,'' sees the courageous, heroic life as a
necessary prerequisite to community with the Christian God:

> No trembler in the world's storm-troubled sphere;
> I see Heaven's glories shine,
> And faith shines equal, arming me from fear.[20]

Whether described in Christian terms or not, the hero experiences moments of
mystic and ecstatic union. Loran Hurnscot writes in her diary:

> And suddenly I was swept out of myself—knowing, knowing,
> knowing. Feeling the love of God burning through creation,
> and an ecstasy of bliss pouring through my spirit and down
> into every nerve. I'm ashamed to put it down in these halting
> words. For it was ecstasy—that indissoluble mingling of fire
> and light that the mystics know. There was a scalding sun in my
> breast—the ''kingdom of God within''—that rushed out to
> that All Beauty—its weak rays met those encompassing ones
> and the bliss of heaven filled me.[21]

Because she experiences and thereby internalizes the power of the life
force, the hero becomes a symbol of spiritual vitality and spiritual oneness. Hilary
Stevens, in May Sarton's *Mrs. Stevens Hears the Mermaids Singing,* is an aging poet
and mystic who epitomizes the life energy of the hero. She tells an interviewer
about a violent conflict in her youth with a lover. She is drawn to Dorothea, a
rational, categorizing social scientist, but the relationship is agonizing for her
because Dorothea denies the reality that is the source of Hilary's poetry. Looking
back on the end of the relationship, Hilary remembers feeling ''like a devastated
city after a war.'' This relationship becomes for her a paradigm of the antagonism
between the sterile, rationalistic conventional world and the hero or poet who
experiences self and others fully. ''Under Dorothea's apparent sense of superiority, under her intellectual approach, there was (it now became clear), jealousy.
Sooner or later . . . the creative person, the person who moves from an irrational
source of power, has to face the fact that this power antagonizes. Under all the
superficial praise of the 'creative' is the desire to kill.''[22]

Hilary, unlike many fictional protagonists, sees the unifying creative power
as peculiarly feminine: ''Never to categorize, never to separate one thing from
another—intellect, the senses, the imagination, . . . some total gathering together

where the most realistic and the most mystical can be joined in a celebration of life itself. Woman's work is always toward wholeness" (p. 172). She believes that men often dissociate emotion and intellect, mind and body, self and Other; this leaves them sterile and alienated, and threatened by women's unifying power. When men are alienated in these ways, women fear, and often repress, their power in order to avoid rejection or punishment from men. Hilary complains that we are all haunted by Thurber's cartoon of the "huge, threatening, and devouring emanation over the house . . . and, alas, it comes too close to the American man's fear of women" (p. 173).

According to Hilary's thinking, the male's emphasis on separation, categorization, and delineation limits male sensuality, and thus interferes with his full sexuality and artistry. Women's holistic approach to life and art, she believes, causes a "diffusion of sensuality. Colette could write better than anyone about physical things; they include the feel of a peach in one's hand. A man could only write in this way about a woman's breast" (p. 122).

Virginia Woolf, Anaïs Nin, and May Sarton all attribute to women qualities of diffuse sensuality, mystic oneness, and a unified consciousness. These qualities, which conform to some of the more positive cultural stereotypes about women, also are indicative of the returning female hero. It is important to note, however, that the state of consciousness associated with the female hero's return is shared by many men, and that men achieve this state in the same manner that women do, by developing qualities that society identifies as female. Women's conditioning to be passive and servile and men's conditioning to be aggressive and dominant are both antithetical to this heroic consciousness. The richness, the community, and the joy that male and female heroes find at the end of the journey must be achieved. Most literary works about female heroes assume that men are capable of reaching mystic consciousness, and no one suggests that women innately have it. Sarton and Woolf, in their portraits of Mar, in *Mrs. Stevens Hears the Mermaids Singing,* and Mr. Carmichael, in *To the Lighthouse,* respectively, demonstrate their knowledge of the male potential to find spiritual unity with all things. Sarton suggests, furthermore, through her portrait of Dorothea, that women may be guilty of the kind of egotism, alienation, and sterility that Hilary associates with masculinity. She accuses Dorothea of trying to cut herself off from experience, and of being removed from the subjects of her study: "The trouble with you scientists is that you really begin to imagine you can reach all the answers by a method, some sort of trick, without participating, without being willing to be changed" (p. 164).

Whatever sex differences Sarton's Hilary sees, she asserts that the primary responsibility of each man or woman is to have the courage to be engaged fully in life, to be a "total human being" rather than a "zombie" or machine. She chides Mar, a young man who has determined in despair to seek impersonal lust instead of love, telling him, "It's hard to be growing up in this climate where sex at its most crude and cold is O.K. but feeling is somehow indecent. The monsters are those who go rutting around like monkeys, not those who choose to be human whatever it costs." Thus, she urges him to meet the world and other people with "some real feeling" (p. 26).

Hilary's union of thought and emotion is the basis for communion with the natural world and with other people. Her own response is immediate and intense. Asked to describe the inspiration of her poetry, she says, "Just look at the light on the daffodils! This is the moment. I placed them there to catch the slanting rays, do you see?'' The woman interviewing her immediately understands and when their eyes meet, "the setting sun, falling in one long beam on the mirror and the flowers, made a kind of explosion" (p. 148).

In even the most nihilistic of contemporary novels, the female hero still experiences a sense of unity with the natural world, although she may not feel the magic of Hilary's more mystical connection. The existential hero, however, responds to the world sensuously and passionately without demanding anthropomorphic "meaning" from it. Maria, in Joan Didion's *Play It As It Lays*, for example, learns about "what nothing means" and learns to feel at home with familiar objects that have no spiritual significance: "On the whole I talk to no one, I concentrate on the way light would strike filled Mason jars on the kitchen windowsill. I lie here in the sunlight, watch the hummingbird. This morning I threw the coins in the swimming pool, and they gleamed and turned in the water in such a way that I was almost moved to read them. I refrained."[23]

However, the hero's acceptance and love of nature within and without does not preclude the knowledge of pain, of nothingness, and of her own participation in evil. Annie Dillard, in *Pilgrim at Tinker Creek*, for example, recognizes the cannibalism at the heart of nature. She writes, "An Eskimo shaman said, 'Life's greatest danger lies in the fact that men's food consists entirely of souls.' "[24] Dillard watches while a praying mantis eats her mate, and linking this to the endless pattern of beings eating and being eaten, notes her own spiritual as well as physical participation in this cruel pattern. She writes first, "I am an explorer, and I am also a stalker, or the instrument of the hunt itself" (p. 13), and, later, "I wonder how many bites I have taken, parasite and predator, from family and friends . . . with all the good will in the world . . . we take it out of each other's hides; we chew the bitter skins the rest of our lives" (p. 278). She understands that the dazzling array of the world's wonders is often cruel, but always beautiful, and notes, "The least we can do is try to be there" (p. 8), to see and to affirm. The final acceptance of the cruelty as well as the beauty of nature is, of course, the acceptance of death. She imagines that "the dying pray at the last not 'please,' but 'thank you,' as a guest thanks his host at the door. . . . The universe was not made in jest but in solemn, incomprehensible earnest. By a power that is unfathomably secret, and holy, and fleet. There is nothing to be done about it, but ignore it, or see" (p. 278).

Annie Dillard discovers that when she stops struggling against reality and is open to full sight, then she can feel joyously at one with herself and with the natural world. She ends her work by saying, "Like Billy Bray I go my way, and my left foot says 'Glory,' and my right foot says 'Amen': in and out of Shadow Creek, upstream and down, exultant, in a daze, dancing, to the twin silver trumpets of praise" (p. 279).

It is this readiness to embrace life in all its manifestations that makes possible the relaxed, sensuous, and often ecstatic unity with the worlds within and without that is the hero's reward at the end of the journey.

A Vibrant Twilight

For a number of reasons, including proximity to death, the heroic, aged woman in literature is often credited with this sense of oneness, and with the achievement of autonomy, self-acceptance, honesty, courage, and transcendence. Society

—which defines woman's role as a helpmate to husband and children—prescribes no valued function for the aged woman, especially if she is single, widowed, or divorced. She is forced, therefore, either to seek out her own identity and her own perspective on the world or to retreat from life. Often she develops a healthy disregard for conventional opinion. The hero of Doris Lessing's *The Summer before the Dark* finds herself hooting at a popular play during her rapid transition from middle to old age because she finds it embarrassingly trivial.

Familiar after so many years with her own body and with her own thoughts, the older woman is often able to see even her own physical and mental deterioration with humor. Eudora Welty's Phoenix Jackson in "A Worn Path" is an old, poor, southern black woman. She marches along the rural countryside to obtain medicine for her grandchild. Walking miles, she finds companionship with bushes and scarecrows. She is comfortable with herself and amused by her absent-mindedness and physical awkwardness. As she moves through the field of dead corn that is taller than her head she sees "something tall, black, and skinny there, moving before her":

> She shut her eyes, reached out her hand, and touched a sleeve. She found a coat and inside that an emptiness, cold as ice.
>
> "You scarecrow," she said. Her face lighted. "I ought to be shut up for good," she said with laughter. "My sense is gone. I too old. I the oldest people I ever know. Dance, old scarecrow," she said, "while I dancing with you."[25]

The aged female hero is typically active, even in infirmity. She is also curious and iconoclastic. Eva, in *The Book of Eve,* after she is settled in her basement apartment in the middle of Toronto, enjoys exploring her own past and venturing out every day to see what stray items she might come across in the park or bus station to bring back to her room each day.

Emily Carr, the Canadian artist, enjoys working in the solitude of the mountains. There she communes with her sixty-year-old body, with her own thoughts and recollections of events, and with nature:

> Last night we slept like babies. Each creature has dropped into its own niche. The spirit of freemasonary and intimacy among us all is superb. It's wonderful to watch the delicious joy of the pups playing tag among the cedars. There is a delicious little breeze humming among the leaves without bluster or vulgarity. Today I love life, so do the four dogs, the monkey, and the rat. . . . Last night when the pop shop was shut and everyone was in bed I slipped into a nondescript garment and tumbled into the river. It was wonderful. I lay down on the stones and let the water ripple over me, clear, soft water that made the skin of you feel like something namelessly exquisite, even my sixty-year-old skin. When I had rubbed down and was between the sheets in the Elephant's innards, I felt like a million dollars, only much cleaner and sweeter and nicer. The precious pups were asleep all around, and rat Susie was just outside the window in her hollow cedar, Henry in the tent lean-to. The cedars and pines and river all whispered sooth-

ingly, and there was life, life in the soft blackness of the night.[26]

Because she no longer feels any need to hide her wisdom, the aged woman is often portrayed in literature as the sage. Robert Graves begins his poem "The Great Grandmother" by noting the importance of believing her. "Though to you grandfather, her son, she lied" and to others told half truths, "yet she was honest with herself," and when "disclosure" was "due," told her story.[27] Often, it is the awareness of the proximity of death that motivates the aging woman to forgo illusion and to seek the bare reality. The aging female hero may require some solitude to commune with herself and with truth, which, Graves notes, "the intervening generations" ignore.

She may also choose to be alone intermittently in order to prepare for death. Laia, in Ursula Le Guin's "The Day before the Revolution," has been the primary theorist behind the anarchist revolution she has worked for all her life. The day before the revolution, she wants only to be alone, and she slips "away unnoticed among the people busy with their planning and excitement." Amid discussions of "the funeral strike," she climbs the stairs, recognizing that "above, ahead, in her room, what awaited her? The private stroke."[28] Yet, until that day, she has actively contributed to revolutionary theory, and just that morning had realized she was sexually attracted to a younger man. This need for solitude, accordingly, does not signal in these cases a retreat from life, but the acceptance of death.

Florida Scott-Maxwell discovers that old age gives her time to know herself better: "A notebook might be the very thing for all the old who wave away cross word puzzles, painting, petit point, and knitting. It is more restful than conversation, and for me it has become a companion, more a confessional. It cannot shrive me, but knowing myself better comes near to that."[29] She takes advantage of increasing solitude to learn to meet death as a friend, even as she has learned to accept her infirmities as part of the life she loves: "When a new disability arrives I look about to see if death has come, and I call quietly, 'Death, is that you? Are you there?' So far the disability has answered, 'Don't be silly, it's me' " (p. 36). She speaks whimsically of her relationship with an aging body and with coming death, in a manner reminiscent of Emily Dickinson's poems and of Käthe Kollwitz's prints, in which death comes ambiguously both as an attacker and as a lover or friend. Often, moreover, the hero facing death sees it simultaneously as the end of one journey and the beginning of another. Helen Hunt Jackson writes in "Emigravit": "Oh, write of me, not 'Died in bitter pains,' / But, 'Emigrated to another star!' "[30]

A Separate Peace

The hero's new community with her self requires a place of her own and time to herself. Women speak yearningly of the need for solitude and for a place to work or think without interruption. Virginia Woolf argues that, to be a great writer, a woman needs a room of her own. Louisa May Alcott longs for her own room: "I should want to be there about all the time, and I should go there and sing and think."[31] Later she writes in her diary: "I have at last got the little room I have wanted so long and am very happy about it; it does me good to be alone" (p. 65). Florida Scott-Maxwell writes in her diary, "Only this morning—this mild, sunny morning that charmed me into happiness—I realized my cheer was partly because I was alone."[32] In literature, women characters prize moments of solitude that allow them to experience communion with the sensuous and spiritual worlds inside and out, uninterrupted by society. Miriam Henderson, the protagonist of Dorothy Richardson's *Pilgrimage,* particularly enjoys the moments just after waking, before she rises to meet the day:

> Miriam lay motionless while Emma unfolded and arranged the screens. Then she gazed at the ceiling. . . . She felt strong and languid. She could feel the shape and weight of each limb; sounds came to her with perfect distinctness; the sounds downstairs and a low-voiced conversation across the landing, little faint marks that human beings were making on the great wide stillness, the stillness that brooded along her white ceiling and all around her and right out through the world; the faint scent of her soap-tablet reached her from the distant washstand. She felt that her short sleep must have been perfect, that it carried her down and down into the heart of tranquility where she still lay awake, and drinking as if at a source. Cool streams seemed to be flowing in her brain, through her heart, through every vein; her breath was like a live cool stream flowing through her.[33]

Virginia Woolf's Mrs. Ramsay often stopped when alone, "sitting and looking, with her work in her hands until she became the thing she looked at. . . . It was odd, she thought, how if one was alone, one leant to inanimate things; trees, streams, flowers; felt they expressed one; felt they became one; felt they knew one, in a sense were one; felt an irrational tenderness thus . . . as for oneself." In solitude, Mrs. Ramsay finds there "rose from the lake of one's being, a mist, a bride to meet her lover the object."[34] This time to herself refreshes her and enables her to continue ministering to the needs of her family.

Socialized to be constantly aware of others' desires and feelings, women often speak of the need to be alone in order to discover their own voices. Some women find it helpful to escape the traditional helpmate role entirely. In Mary Wilkins Freeman's "A New England Nun," when the protagonist's fiancé returns from fourteen years of "fortune seeking" in Australia, she sees that his coarseness and clumsiness would destroy the beauty of the private world she has created. She decides to break the engagement in order to maintain the beautiful, ritualized life that she has so carefully designed for herself. Freeman describes her solitary life ahead in terms that evoke both sensuous and religious ecstasy.

> If Louisa Ellis had sold her birthright she did not know it, the taste of the pottage was so delicious, and had been her sole satisfaction for so long. Serenity and placid narrowness had become to her as the birthright itself. She gazed ahead through a long reach of future days strung together like pearls in a rosary, every one like the others, and all smooth and flawless and innocent, and her heart went up in thankfulness.[35]

Mrs. Mallard, the protagonist in Kate Chopin's "The Story of an Hour," hears that her husband is dead. While she is cloistered upstairs with what she expects to be her great grief, she feels the grief gradually replaced by another, unexpected emotion:

> When she abandoned herself a little whispered word escaped her slightly parted lips. She said it over and over under her breath: "free, free, free!" . . .
>
> There would be no one to live for her during those coming years; she would live for herself. There would be no powerful will bending hers in that blind persistence with which men and women believe they have a right to impose a private will upon a fellow-creature. A kind intention or a cruel intention made the act seem no less a crime as she looked upon it in that brief moment of illumination.
>
> And yet she had loved him—sometimes. Often she had not. What did it matter! What could love, the unsolved mystery, count for in face of this possession of self-assertion which she suddenly recognized as the strongest impulse of her being! "Free! body and soul free!" she kept whispering.[36]

Such portraits blatantly contradict the myth that a woman cannot be happy without a man to complete her. In other, more subtle works, the myth is not directly challenged, yet the hero thrives after the death or departure of her lover. In Charlotte Brontë's *Villette,* Lucy Snowe's M. Paul helps her to love herself by valuing her. He sets her up in a school and lodgings of her own, and thereby provides her with a place in society and meaningful work. He also gives her a purpose—someone to live for in gratitude. When he makes a necessary trip just before their wedding and dies at sea, Paul becomes deified in Lucy's mind. In fact, he and God become indistinguishable in her thoughts as her source of love, security, and significance. She grieves, but she also suggests the integration, autonomy, and community with the self that his death makes possible: "I thought I loved him when he went away; I love him now in another degree; he is more my own."[37] One has the sense at the end of the work that she would not have been as happy had he lived. She finds fulfillment through her work and through the joy of self-sufficiency.

Literature that celebrates the woman who has found communion with the self often juxtaposes her peace and her freedom to create with the oppressed and stultifying lives of dependent women. Carolina Maria de Jesus, the Brazilian author, writes in her diary of the pity she feels for the married women who are her neighbors in the *favela*: "While their husbands break the boards of the shack, I and my children sleep peacefully. I don't envy the married women of the favelas who lead lives like Indian slaves. I never got married and I'm not unhappy."[38] As in the case of Emily Dickinson, de Jesus's need to be alone comes from a sense of vocation. She writes: "Señor Gino comes to ask me to go to his shack. That I am neglecting him. I answered: no! I am writing a book to sell. I am hoping that with this money I can buy a place and leave the favela. I don't have time to go to anybody's house. Señor Gino insisted. He told me: 'Just knock and I'll open the door.' But my heart didn't ask me to go to his room" (p. 37).

Whether she lives alone, with friends, with a lover, or with her family, a woman finds that she needs solitude in order to discover her vocation and carry out her work. She may love a few people, many, or no one, but she does not become an appendage to their reality, their vocation. Katherine Mansfield, articulating her priorities, emphasizes the desire to work and to use her full faculties; she does not mention a desire for relationships with other people: "I want to *work*. At what? I want so to live that I work with my hands and my feelings and my brain. I want a garden, a small house, grass, animals, books, pictures, music. And out of this, the expression of this, I want to be writing. . . . But warm, eager living life—to be rooted in life—to learn, to desire to know, to feel, to think, to act. That is what I want. And nothing less."[39] Beyond everything else, the female hero strives for authenticity. "Rooted in life," she discovers, in May Sarton's words, that "there is a difference between solitude and loneliness."[40]

A Subculture of One

The hero's solitude, however, may result from alienation as well as from choice. Carolyn Rodgers in "i have changed so much in this world" defines the dilemma of the hero returning from her quest, who is amazed to find that "the world has changed so little."[41] Too many people fail to understand the female hero. Sissy Hankshaw, the hero of Tom Robbins's apocalyptic fantasy *Even Cowgirls Get the Blues,* appears in the eyes of the world to be "handicapped." From her point of view, her thumbs are a gift that enables her to be the best hitchhiker in the world. Her husband takes her to a Freudian psychologist, and explains "She's lovely and intelligent. She needs only to be taught to overcome her affliction instead of reveling in it."[42] Dr. Goldman, the psychologist, spouts the sociological jargon that is often used to discredit the validity of the hero's vision: "The socially stigmatized individual, by entering a subculture, accepts his alienation from the larger society, and by identifying himself with like souls claims that he is a full-fledged 'normal' or even a superior human being and that it is the others who are lacking." Goldman concludes, "Your wife may have chosen to become a subculture of one, so to speak" (p. 171).

The alienation of the hero from conventional society is part of the male hero's experience as well. However, because of the myths of virginity, romantic love, and maternal self-sacrifice, and because of the tendency of patriarchal society to exclude women from roles of autonomy and leadership, the female faces a greater discrepancy between social myths and her own heroic experience and feelings; and the failure of the social structure to accommodate female power inevitably limits the final community that she is able to establish. Some authors suggest that for a powerful and passionate woman, death is a greater source of fulfillment than conventional living. In *Wuthering Heights,* Catherine's unity in death with Heathcliff and with the heath is clearly preferable to Catherine's conventional life as Mrs. Linton. When Edna Pontellier swims to her death in Kate Chopin's *The Awakening,* the author portrays her suicide as a heroic act of self-affirmation that leads to unity with the natural world.

The protagonist of Margaret Atwood's *Surfacing* recognizes that the heroic woman is in physical and emotional danger from the uncomprehending world. Because she does not conform to the culture's myths about womanhood, she fears that "the real danger" to her is "the hospital or zoo." Having courted insanity to become "a natural woman, [in a] state of nature," she recognizes that society's idea of the natural woman is of a "tanned body on a beach with washed hair waving like scarves." She must be careful so that she is not put away in a hospital for the insane, but "withdrawing is no longer possible, and the alternative to heroism is death."[43]

It is not clear how Atwood's protagonist will handle the discrepancy between her vision and the culture's notion of her. Rejecting death or solitude, some characters simply distance themselves psychologically: Refusing to internalize the dragon myths, they act as if their own values were the accepted ones. Lena Grove, in Faulkner's *Light in August,* for example, is free from self-doubt and is undaunted by the scorn, ridicule, or condescension she evokes in the people she meets. Pregnant and alone, she walks across three states to find the father of her unborn child, only to discover that he is a scoundrel, indifferent to her. When others help her even though she is a "ruined woman," she acts totally oblivious to disgrace. Lena's only response as she moves on down the road into Tennessee, with her baby and her self-appointed protector, Byron Bunch, is, "My, my, a body does get around."[44] Her total lack of self-doubt makes others incapable of condemning her, and in this way, she escapes both conformity and punishment for her deviance.

Faulkner juxtaposes the comic Lena Grove plot with Joe Christmas's tragedy. Although Joe is an outsider, he has internalized—in exaggerated form—the Puritanism and racism of his society. Convinced that he is part black, and full of disgust with his own body and with sexuality, Joe becomes increasingly destructive. He kills a woman with whom he has had a brief affair and ends up publicly castrated and killed, a scapegoat for a town that shares his fear and loathing of sexuality, blacks, and women. It is clear that Joe's violence and destruction of the self and of others typify patriarchal society. Although Faulkner's portrait of Lena is condescending (revealing Faulkner's own bias), he makes it clear that her innocence is associated with the forces that promote life.

The wise fool refuses to succumb to the tyranny of the dull collective mind. However, because the world is corrupt, wisdom and goodness may well be viewed as foolishness. Margaret Pinchwife, in William Wycherley's Restoration comedy *The Country Wife,* triumphs over people who are more experienced in sexual deception by the fact that, being from the country, she is innocent of their games.

Other heroes cling to specific dreams and ideals (what society calls illusions), refusing to surrender them or accept the ordinary life in society. Myra Henshaw, in Willa Cather's *My Mortal Enemy,* elopes with a dashing young man, is disinherited by her father, and becomes the most interesting topic of conversation in the prosaic Kansas town where she grew up. She wishes to live a full, beautiful, courageous life. In spite of her inability to fulfill the romantic ideal to her own satisfaction, she refuses to surrender her idealism, and chooses a place to die that lives up to her vision of the beautiful: She takes a cab and goes to the sea to die alone in the splendor of nature. Her husband, in spite of his limitations, understands her heroic nature. Smiling and straightening his shoulders, proud of his wife even as she rails at him, he tells the narrator: "She's Myra Driscoll, and there was never anybody else like her. She can't endure, but she has enough desperate courage for a regiment."[45] Ibsen's Hedda Gabler is even more unrelentingly committed to her own vision; she kills herself "beautifully" in order to be free of the world that disappointed her romantic expectations and that pressured her to join its mundane ranks.

Such wise fools may live quite effective lives, or they may destroy themselves, but they are not passive, weak Little Nells. However foolish they may seem, they are active, powerful women. So, too, the artist who uses the dichotomy between self and society to advantage may appear trivial and artificial. She is unlike the heroine (discussed in Chapter 2, "The Mirror and the Cage") whose fear causes her to hide her true nature behind an expected role; in contrast, the artist, having returned from the journey, is secure in her identity; if she uses masks she does so not merely to hide, but to alter her environment. Like Orpheus, she translates the truth she knows into appearances that others can handle. As such, she is an example of the highest form of intellect, as John Keats defines it, the one that can sustain opposing truths at once. She is Thomas Carlyle's leader-hero who knows not only the surface reality but "the very fact of things."[46] She has earned the right to live the lie because, like Joseph Conrad's Kurtz (in "The Heart of Darkness"), she knows the reality underneath and in many cases has experienced its horrors alone, but she is not destroyed by the experience. Virginia Woolf's Mrs. Ramsay in *To the Lighthouse*, for example, recognizes that "there is no reason, order, justice: but suffering, death, the poor. There was no treachery too base for the world to commit; she knew that. No happiness lasted; she knew that."[47] Mrs. Ramsay's knowledge provides "the sternness at the heart of her beauty," but it is balanced by her capacity for "exquisite happiness." As she looks at the sun-drenched sea roll "in waves of pure lemon which curved and swelled and broke upon the beach . . . the ecstasy burst in her eyes and waves of pure delight raced over the floor of her mind and she felt, 'It is enough!' " (p. 100).

In the famous dinner party scene, Mrs. Ramsay's ability to "make things happen," and in particular to create a community of isolated, ego-involved people, is seen as an act of heroism equivalent to the active heroism of an Odysseus. Mrs. Ramsay rises to the occasion, exhausted though she might be, to rescue her crew from isolation:

> They all sat separate. And the whole of the effort of merging and flowing and creating rested on her. Again she felt, as a fact without hostility, the sterility of men, for if she did not do it nobody would do it, and so giving herself the little shake that one gives a watch that has stopped, the old familiar pulse began beating . . . she began all this business, as a sailor not without weariness sees the wind fill his sail and yet hardly wants to be off again and thinks how, had the ship sunk, he would have whirled round and round and found rest on the floor of the sea. (p. 126)

Mrs. Ramsay's efforts—made up of social, even trivial conversation—are success-ful. When at her direction the candles are lit, "some change at once went through them all, as if this had really happened, and they were all conscious of making a party together in a hollow, on an island; had their common cause against the fluidity out there" (p. 147).

Virginia Woolf makes it clear to us that what Mrs. Ramsay creates is an incarnation, a unifying of disparate elements into a spiritual community that tran-scends their individual pettiness. Against her accomplishment, the male achieve-ments seem trivial: "Poor fellow! Still, he had his dissertation, the influence of somebody upon something" (p. 156). Like the creator, Mrs. Ramsay rests when her new world is completed:

> Everything seemed right. . . . She hovered like a hawk sus-pended; like a flag floated in an element of joy which filled every nerve of her body fully and sweetly, not noisily, sol-emnly rather, for it arose, she thought, looking at them all eating there, from husband and children and friends; all rising

> in this profound stillness . . . seemed now for no special
> reason to stay there like a smoke, like a fume rising upwards,
> holding them safe together. Nothing need be said; nothing
> could be said. There it was, all round them. It partook, she felt,
> carefully helping Mr. Bankes to a specially tender piece, of
> eternity. . . . Of such moments, she thought, the thing is
> made that endures. (pp. 157–158)

Such artist-heroes are the female equivalents of Shakespeare's Prospero. Although the moments they create take part in whatever in life is enduring, they also speak of transience. As Mrs. Ramsay leaves her dining room, "with her foot on the threshold she waited a moment longer in a scene which was vanishing even as she looked, and then, as she moved and took Minta's arm and left the room, it changed, it shaped itself differently; it had become, she knew, giving one last look at it over her shoulder, already the past" (p. 168). Such transient moments are, of course, the ritual essence of community, and they bind families, friends, and society together.

Both men and women sense the power of such artist-heroes. In Mrs. Ramsay's case, Lily Briscoe, Mr. Ramsay, Mr. Carmichael, and even Charles Tansley acknowledge her power and significance, although—at the same time—they see her as somewhat trivial and childlike, a traditional helpmate who is not to be taken as seriously as her husband, the philosopher. Like the wise fool, the artist promotes life, and thereby counters the forces of death and repression in the culture. Because she wears the traditional mask, however, her heroism does not result in more freedom for women, nor does it provide her with more freedom or a real community. An artist of life, Mrs. Ramsay can create some community for everyone but herself, because she can never show her true self to another.

It is interesting that authors—especially, but not exclusively, male authors—write about female power as something alien and mysterious. Often the very subject of the work is female mystery. When this happens, the woman is portrayed as powerful, but not quite human. Faulkner's women—Caddy in *The Sound and the Fury,* Lena Grove in *Light in August,* and Addie Bundren in *As I Lay Dying*—have a mysterious connection with nature that other characters cannot understand, but they do not quite understand questions of morality or ethics. Their power may be seen as awesome and even divine, but not formed or developed. In *The Return of the Native,* Thomas Hardy begins Chapter 7, "Queen of Night," with the sentence, "Eustacia Vye was the raw material of a divinity."[48] Tennessee Williams writes of Olga, in "The Mattress by the Tomato Patch":

> The perishability of the package she comes in has cast on Olga
> no shadow she can't laugh off. I look at her now, before the
> return of Tiger from Muscle Beach, and if no thought, no
> knowledge has yet taken form in the protean jelly-world of
> brain and nerves, if I am patient enough to wait a few moments
> longer, this landlady of Picasso may spring up from her mat-
> tress and come running into this room with a milky-blue china
> bowl full of reasons and explanations for all that exists.[49]

The mysterious female is always seen from the outside as a static character. She is removed from life and made important to the story by her effect on the characters who strive to understand her secret. Symbolically, she may be seen as a sphinx, as May Bartram is in Henry James's "The Beast in the Jungle." She knows, but will not, or cannot, tell what she knows. The suggestion is that her truth is apocalyptic, and that, if known, it could destroy the listener, the society, and even herself. In some cases, a mysterious female character is clearly a projection of the culture's repressed anima; she seems fearsome because the confrontation between the conscious mind and its repressed elements threatens to destroy the limited consciousness of the main (usually male) character. Edward Albee's Tiny Alice or Thomas Pynchon's enigmatic V are compelling figures that inspire obsession, and yet they threaten the ego with destruction.

More realistically portrayed women may hide their power to protect themselves from a culture that denigrates strength and wisdom in women. Others keep secrets to protect those weaker than themselves. Woolf's Mrs. Ramsay protects Mr. Ramsay from the knowledge of his mortality, and struggles to keep him from seeing through the illusion that he will live on through his "immortal writings." She also perpetuates his illusion that *he* takes care of *her*. Similarly, May Bartram, in Henry James's "The Beast in the Jungle," spends her life understanding and supporting John Marcher. She could teach him to know himself, but chooses to hide from him the knowledge that he has missed life, because that knowledge might destroy him.

There is an inherent revolutionary irony to stories that reveal a woman's secret power and full humanity. Typically, the male hero is somewhat contemptuous of the woman—seeing her as the Other, who does not have the needs or the fully human capacity that he has. John Marcher's tragedy is a result of his sexism, and he is unable to transcend his egotistical blindness and truly see the woman who loves him. She has waited with him her whole life for the great event he believes to be his destiny. When he understands his failing and her heroism, it is too late; she is dead:

> He had been the man of his time, *the* man, to whom nothing on earth was to have happened. That was the rare stroke—that was his visitation. So he saw it, as we say, in pale horror, while the pieces fitted and fitted. So *she* had seen it while he didn't. . . .
>
> The escape would have been to love her; then, *then* he would have lived. She has lived—who could say now with what passion?—since she has loved him for himself; whereas he had never thought of her (ah how it hugely glared at him!) but in the chill of his egotism and the light of her use. . . . The Beast had lurked indeed, and the Beast, at its hour, had sprung.[50]

Somerset Maugham's "The Colonel's Lady" has a similar plot. Colonel Peregrine thinks his wife, Evie, is uninteresting: "A nice woman, of course a good wife, and it wasn't her fault if she was barren, but it was tough on a fellow who wanted an heir of his own loins; she hadn't any vitality, that's what was the matter with her."[51] Evie writes an autobiographical book of poems about a passionate love affair between a woman and a younger man who dies tragically, but the Colonel doesn't read it because he assumes that the poems are harmless, trivial, and sentimental. After the book has become the talk of the town, a critic explains:

> But what makes the book so outstanding is the passion that throbs in every line. So many of these young poets are so

anemic, cold, bloodless, dully intellectual, but here you have real, naked, earthy passion; of course deep, sincere emotion like that is tragic—ah, my dear Colonel, how right Heine was when he said that the poet makes little songs out of his great sorrows. You know, now and then, as I read and reread those heart-rending pages I thought of Sappho. (p. 456)

Unlike John Marcher, Colonel Peregrine never understands the secret life of his wife. When he learns that his wife has had a passionate and tragic love affair, he exclaims: "The truth is, I don't know what I'd do without Evie. But I'll tell you what, there's one thing I shall never understand till my dying day: What in the name of heaven did the fellow ever see in her?" (p. 461). It must be noted, however, that most female heroes have at least some people who understand them. Maugham's Evie, for example, finds sympathy and appreciation from her lover, from the critics, and from her husband's best male friend. The blocking figure who does not see the hero's value is usually a husband, lover, father, or other male figure who epitomizes the blindness of the patriarchy to female wisdom and strength.

Even when the hero is completely misunderstood by the other characters in the work, the hero and the author seem to share a secret smile at the expense of the ignorant world, which believes women to be weak, dependent, and incapable of finding happiness in solitude. In Edwin Arlington Robinson's "The Tree in Pamela's Garden," the neighbors worry about Pamela. Because she is a virgin and lives by herself, they assume she is lonely and unfulfilled: They "Wished Pamela had a cat, or a small bird, / And only would have wondered at her smile / Could they have seen that she had overheard."[52] The same feeling informs Tom Robbins's description of Sissy Hankshaw. At the Rubber Rose Ranch, the self-righteous Miss Adrien delivers a lecture to Sissy on women's first duty, which is to deodorize themselves to please men. "Sissy sat as she usually sat. Supporting her thumbs affectionately upon crossed legs—and smiling. She grinned the invincible soft grin that some people associate with madness, that others attribute to spiritual depth, but that in reality is simply the grin that comes from the secret heart of a very private experience."[53]

No More Masks

The possibilities that exist between two people, or among a group of people, are a kind of alchemy. They are the interesting things in life. The liar is someone who keeps losing sight of those possibilities.

Adrienne Rich, *Women and Honor: Some Notes on Lying*

When she removes the masks and shares her heroic vision through her actions and words, the hero is usually successful at finding or creating a sense of community with other people. Confident in herself, she is able to share her new understanding both of herself and of the world around her. Adrienne Rich, in *Women and Honor: Some Notes on Lying*, argues that the culture discourages women from going "down into the darkness of the core" into the formlessness of the unnamed existence; yet, Rich continues, "if we can risk it, then something born out of that nothing is the beginning of our truth." The continual struggle to uncover that truth is the antidote to ennui and alienation, for "truth is the basis of all true sharing between people." Not only is the hero's discovery recognizable to others who have embarked on their own journeys, but it also helps propel others onto their quest. Rich notes, "Truthfulness anywhere" is a "movement into evolution" because the truth teller creates "the possibility for more truth around her."[54]

Christina, in May Sarton's *Kinds of Love,* finds that at the end of her journey she experiences greater community than she had in middle age, not only with the natural and spiritual worlds, but also with society. Wondering whether her new state of awareness is what young people call "Being Now," she writes, "I feel transparent again. Light flows through me. I am no longer a thick substance composed of lists of things to do, small anxieties, pains."[55] All her life she has dreaded the day that she and her husband, Cornelius, would be old; but then she discovers that "now that we are here, and truly settled in, it is like a whole new era, a new world, and I have moments of pure joy such as I never experienced before" (p. 56). Because she is fully herself and no longer defined by a role, and because her barriers against love, vulnerability, dependence, and the knowledge of mortality have been destroyed, she can love life and other people in a new way. She enjoys a transformed relationship with many people: with Cornelius, who has similarly removed his mask of the successful businessman and is reacting to the world freshly and honestly; with Eben, her would-be lover; with her young, unhappy niece, Cathy; and with her lifelong friend, Ellen, who is embittered by the stresses of a life of poverty. This newfound joy, Christina notes, "has to be set against the pain, fatigue, and exasperation at being caught in a dying body, but when I see the tears shining in Cornelius's eyes when he is moved, I feel as if every day the naked soul comes closer to the surface. He is so beautiful now. I feel that life flows through me in a way it never did before. I can accept Eben's love now. It used to frighten me, and I had to put barriers up against it to protect myself and Cornelius. Now there is no danger, the current is not short-circuited and I feel lit up a bit. I can hug Cathy in a way that perhaps I never did or could hug my own children. Even with Ellen, prickly as we sometimes are and always will be toward each other, some barrier is down since Cornelius's stroke" (p. 56).

Christina understands that the mystery and joy of true friendship is the honest sharing of two souls. Of her relationship with Ellen, she says, "When two people have known each other this long, the past is near the surface. When they meet now, everything is opened up, joy, grief. They knew things about each other that no one else in the world knew" (p. 32). Their communion together obliterates time and language, and thus, like a visionary moment, leads to the infinite: "The wonderful thing when one has known a person as long and intimately as she and I have known each other is that words no longer have the same importance. No explorations are needed of the other. No, it is rather that when we are together the past flows through the present, is, in some strange way, opened up—so often painful, we tend to push it back when alone, but when we are together it is there, alive and precious. So it is being together that matters, not any longer what we may say or not say" (p. 32).

The new world Christina experiences occurs in her immediate relationships and also in her relationship with an entire town. Christina and Cornelius go to their summer home in the town of Willard because it is a quiet place for Cornelius to recuperate from the stroke, and as is often the case in old age, they find themselves in a female-dominated society. Willard is an old town, and a poor one. Because most of the most talented and promising men have left for larger cities, which provide them with opportunities for "success," it is a town "dominated by women . . . a matriarchal society" (p. 157). The town is informed, to some degree, by the heroic consciousness of strong women existing in a patriarchal context. Poverty and conventional ideas limit the lives of both the men and the women who stay; yet, at least, people are not judged by their wealth or status. In Willard, "people can still be judged for themselves, for what they truly are, not what they have been given by chance. . . . Willard is a place where people are still cherished" (p. 157).

The inhabitants of Willard do not exist in a framework bound by hierarchy or ideas of dominance over other people or over the natural world. Their awareness of their interdependence with each other and with the natural world bestows a spiritual sense of transcendence. Eben notes in a speech to the town, "There are no saints in Willard, but we carry, each one of us, some intimation of Mystery, whether we are believers in the usual sense of the word or not, some extra dimension, some holiness, because we live close to a mountain, close to woods and streams and lakes and among trees" (p. 445).

As wealthy "summer people," Christina and Cornelius have been isolated from the poverty that characterizes the town, which "has drawn people who can use adversity well." Thus, only when Cornelius has a stroke and the two begin to confront their mortality, vulnerability, and dependence on others do they become part of the consciousness of Willard. In Christina's words, "We began for the first time to understand the secret of Willard, to get to the heartbeat. It is where we too have been afraid and leaned on a mountain for strength, where we have come to our own" (p. 464). When they do so, Christina and Cornelius are rewarded with a new sense of connection to the self, to each other, to friends, to nature, and to the entire community.

Of course, the hero in literature has always been a part of the family of humanity, but she has not been conscious of the relationship. Before her heroic exit, she was told that she could be part of a family only if she behaved conventionally. Jane, in Alta's poem "#35," for example, has been taught that the price of deviance is isolation, loneliness, and vulnerability to strangers. Although it is true that the hero departs on the quest alone, and that hostile people may surround her, the myths that discourage the departure obscure the truth that the narrator of "#35" understands: To be alone is not necessarily to be lonely; friends tend to appear when they are needed. In this poem, the speaker tells the preheroic Jane of an incident in her life in which a stranger accompanied her to the hospital after an accident and stayed with her while she was being treated. When Jane wonders why the stranger stayed to help, the speaker replies, "i have always found friends when i needed."[56]

Often, even the hero is surprised to find community among strangers. Kate Millett, in *Flying*, writes of attending an underground Gay Liberation meeting to enlist the aid of its members in the care of Winnie, the retarded child of her close friends. She stands up in front of a large crowd to make her appeal: "Then I stop. Wondering. Till I see the slips of paper coming up from addressees. More and then more, a fist full. My treasure spilling out of my hand while they crowd around asking for paper. Here's a pen. The phone number. How do I get there? Can they use people mornings? Am I being a friend? Tears of gratitude for these men open to the troubles of a few strangers."[57] In this brief description Millett conveys the nature of the human community in its best sense—the inclusive attitude, the spirit of equality and sharing, and the understanding of each member's simultaneous need for nurturance and for freedom. She also understands that the existence of community is inseparable from the heroic journey, from the risk, from the exposure of the vulnerable self that occurs when one asks for support from others. Millett describes this experience as the classic journey to the underworld. "Alight with glory bobbing up and down on the leather seat of my cab. I have gone to the underworld, through the labyrinths and waiting, its uncertainties. Asked. And received. From my own people" (p. 212).

Such moments of community occur to the most isolated hero when she is willing honestly to expose her own perceptions. Clara Middleton in George Meredith's *The Egoist* feels hopeless because no one supports her perception that her fiancé, Willoughby Patterne, is being cruel to her. Willoughby secretly proposes to Laetitia Dale after he senses that Clara wishes to be free of him, and enjoys gloating over what he assumes will be the competition and jealousy between two young and attractive women. When Clara confides in Laetitia, however, she finds instead cooperation and sisterly support. The two women share their feelings and agree with each other's perception that Willoughby is something less than "the match of the county," as he is described by conventional society.[58] Experiencing the liberating sense of sanity that comes with receiving support for one's suspicion that the emperor is naked, the two women, at the end of their first intimate conversation, "walked forward, holding hands, deep-hearted to one another" (p. 130).

In Doris Lessing's *The Summer before the Dark,* the exorcism, or unnaming, in which Kate Brown and Mary engage during their "cow sessions" (see Chapter 2) so undercuts Kate's sense of the inevitability of interpreting the world in the prescribed ways that she becomes able to laugh at the most sacred cows of her life: her marriage, the "tragic" role of the aging woman, and her role as a mother. For Ella Price, in Dorothy Bryant's *Ella Price's Journal,* the from-the-heart discussions with her neighbor Laura give her the support and courage to trust her own perceptions over those of her family.

Angela Davis writes in her autobiography, *With My Mind on Freedom,* about the encouragement for her beliefs that she received from other prisoners when she was imprisoned on the charge of murder. When she is put in solitary confinement, women all over the jail carry out a hunger strike. She also writes of her surprise at the discovery that women in the prison had consciously formed new families and thus institutionalized support structures: "A woman a few cells down gave me a fascinating description of a whole system through which the women could adopt their jail friends as relatives. I was bewildered and awed by the way in which the vast majority of the jail population had neatly organized itself into generations of families: mothers/wives, fathers/husbands, sons and daughters, even aunts, uncles, grandmothers and grandfathers."[59]

For Alta, Kate Millett, Kate Brown, Ella Price, and Angela Davis, the community they find when they have the greatest need is as transient as it is unexpected. Yet other heroes discover a whole system of more stable alternative communities that exist outside conventional society. Sissy Hankshaw, for example, discovers the

Rubber Rose Ranch, which, by the end of the novel, becomes "a haven for the twenty-six cowgirls, should any of them need a safe place to retreat from the slings and arrows of outrageous whatever."[60] The cowgirls are free to move back and forth between the road, various new families, and the ranch retreat. In Marge Piercy's *Small Changes*, Beth departs from a repressive marriage without the knowledge of any true alternative, except solitude. She meets Wanda, who is both her mentor and her lover, and they live, in turn, in an all-women's commune, in a mixed commune in which men and women work together as equals, and finally alone together with Wanda's children. In each case, they find community and happiness, marred only by their fear that, because of the society's homophobia, the children may be taken away from them.

The reward of a loving community may occur in the most expectedly traditional places, and yet still be a surprise. Rosamund, in Margaret Drabble's *Thank You All Very Much*, believes she will fall off into darkness and nothingness when she becomes an unwed mother. She is so isolated when she first discovers that she is pregnant that she complains, "There was nobody to tell, nobody to ask, so I was obliged once more to fall back on the dimly reported experiences of friends and . . . cheap fiction."[61] Rejecting the pseudo-community that marriage would provide her, she gives birth and is amazed by the unexpectedly joyous relationship she has with her child:

> She was a very happy child, and once she learned to smile, she never stopped. At first she would smile at anything, at parking meters and dogs and strangers, but as she grew older she began to favor me, and nothing gave me more delight than her evident preference. I suppose I had not really expected her to dislike and resent me from birth, though I was quite prepared for resentment to follow later on, but I certainly had not anticipated such wreathing, dazzling gaiety of affection from her whenever I happened to catch her eye. (p. 96)

Because Rosamund is independent enough not to abort her own quest for that of her child, the community she experiences with the new baby is a liberating and strengthening one.

In each case, the community that is achieved is a reward that the hero has earned by successfully completing some aspect of the journey. In fact, the achievement of community is often an integral part of the task. For example, Lucille Clifton's poem "Sister" celebrates the sense of community between two women who grow up black and poor. They have been friends all their lives, but as they affirm their blackness and their womanhood, their friendship takes on a new dimension, a new depth. Clifton suggests that the ability to "be loving ourselves" is the reward of having together:

> got babies
> got thirty-five
> got black.[62]

In fiction, the unexpected reward of love often seems to be a fortunate coincidence. When Jane, in Charlotte Brontë's *Jane Eyre*, reconciles her desires for independence and for love, she inherits money. When she overcomes her fear of sexuality, Bertha, the mad wife in the tower, burns down Thornfield and herself with it. In this coincidental fire, Rochester loses his sight and a hand, as well as some of his property. Having lessened Rochester's social advantages over Jane, Brontë provides both with the happy ending of an egalitarian relationship.

Jo March of Louisa May Alcott's *Little Women* inherits her aunt's estate when she has reconciled her desire for personal fulfillment with society's demands for unselfishness. Born with a tomboyish, unruly manner, she does not fully absorb the traditional feminine roles of self-sacrifice and coquettishness. Since Jo initially was overly selfish and had a bad temper, her mother's urging of restraint is of help to her. She learns to care about others and to moderate her temper, and some of her rough edges are softened. Unlike more passive women, however, she never gives up her dreams; she never stops wanting personal fulfillment and adventure; and she never learns the maidenly art of modest, courtly role playing. Because she always clearly shows what she is thinking and wanting, she is more likely than any of her more conventional feminine sisters to get what she wants. When Fritz Bhaer, the man she loves, says he is going away, she begins to cry. He asks her what is wrong, and Alcott notes that, had she been more schooled in "this sort of thing she would have said she wasn't crying, had a cold in her head, or told any other feminine fib proper to the occasion; instead of which that undignified creature answered, with an irresistible sob,—'Because you are going away.' "[63] Professor Bhaer immediately proposes.

When her aunt leaves Jo her estate, she refuses to sell it. Instead she determines to open a school for boys. She explains, "Now, my dear people . . . just understand that this isn't a new idea of mine, but a long-cherished plan. Before my Fritz came, I used to think how, when I'd made my fortune, and no one needed me at home, I'd hire a big house, and pick up some poor, forlorn little lads, who hadn't any mothers, and take care of them, and make life jolly for them before it was too late" (p. 514). She is rewarded with the love of her husband, of her "boys," and eventually of children of her own, and by the joy of useful work and dreams fulfilled. Alcott comments, "Yes; Jo was a very happy woman" (p. 518).

To the degree that the hero still internalizes conventional society's messages, she may be unable to recognize the new community when it is offered to her. For example, if Rosamund (in *Thank You All Very Much*) had become convinced that she would have to give up her journey if she had a baby; if Jane Eyre or Jo March had believed they could never reconcile independence and accomplishment with marriage; if Angela Davis had thought prisoners were not her equals and hence not her sisters; if Clara (in *The Egoist*) had not trusted other women; if the persona of Lucille Clifton's poem had been unable to free herself from the myths of black or female inferiority; or if Kate Millett had believed that people were all selfish—each would have been denied the sense of community and loving relationship that was her potential reward.

Mother Sugar, the psychologist in Doris Lessing's *The Golden Notebook*, points out the importance of optimistic openness. She explains to Anna that a sense of isolation is often caused by negative assumptions about the potential receptiveness of other people.

> Look, if I'd said to you . . . yesterday I met a man at a party and I
> recognized in him the wolf, or the knight, or the monk, you'd
> nod and you'd smile. And we'd both feel the joy of recogni-

> tion. But if I'd said: Yesterday I met a man at a party and suddenly he said something, and I thought: *Yes,* there's a hint of something—there's a crack in that man's personality like a gap in a dam, and through that gap the future might pour in a different shape—terrible perhaps, or marvelous, but something new—if I said that, you'd frown.[64]

When the hero is able to recognize someone else whose openness to life and to others opens doors to the future, the encounter is liberating to both. In an autobiography written under the pseudonym Anne Zoltan and titled *Annie: The Female Experience,* the author experiences a series of destructive relationships with men, whom she describes as "not-persons." After, in her words, "Jeffery had done me in," she spends a period alone, in an unstructured and unfamiliar relationship to the world. She struggles to see the world without the preconceived assumptions that have kept her from living. It is only at the end of this period of self-imposed isolation that she develops a relationship with a man who is "not a not-person":

> But now, without tricks or fancy style, but because he was clear-sighted and appreciated my state, I learned something—in or out of bed was not germane—for the first time for years.
> *I learned, because George Marshall was not a not-person.* Somehow, after all these years, he released in me the glimmerings of understanding. I lost my other virginity—my psychological virginity, that sealed aspect of myself which had eluded me for so long, not so that I got out of the bed in any way noticeably different, but so that I knew—to actualize later—that dimly but deep, I had been rejoined to myself.[65]

The experience of sharing oneself totally with another is often credited with helping the hero to find herself. Florida Scott-Maxwell writes,

> The intimacy that exists between men and women can seem the confrontation between good and evil, the place where there is the greatest chance of their being resolved by compassion and insight. It is here that souls are bared. Here in the welter of complete exposure we meet our glories and our sins, and we can see when we should have accused ourselves, not the other: here too we may find the mutual support to enable us to say, "I see myself."[66]

One cannot, of course, meet with "bared souls" when striving to fulfill stereotyped images of what men and women should be. For this and other reasons, women writers and characters often protest the convention that women must hide their talents so as to not threaten their mates. Alta, in poem "#19," writes to a lover, "don't go away from me." Her fear is that he will be threatened by her abilities as a writer. She refuses to be less than she is, and promises him that without any masks, she will try to remain close and accessible to him.[67]

Literature by women often expresses a yearning (as we have seen in Chapter 2) to cast off the roles both of the inferior who validates the lover's pretensions to superiority and of the courtly lady who pretends reluctance to confer her queenly favors on a man. Mary Elizabeth Coleridge in her poem "Regina" expresses her high regard for the woman who lays aside her queenly garments because she understands that the only true nobility is to be found in "nakedness": "In her nakedness was she / Queen of the world, herself and me." The stanza that follows suggests, moreover, that the experience of appearing bare gives the woman strength to put back on her royal garments and accomplish an unspecified but daring and heroic deed.[68]

Writers who celebrate the clarifying and strengthening power of love stress not only the absence of masks, but also the lack of patterns of dominance and submission expected in traditional sex-role patterns. Paula Reingold, in "And This Is Love," notes that lovers should be equally free and without ulterior motives, such as proving one's manhood or womanhood: "And this is love: two souls / That freely meet, and have / No need of proving anything."[69] Moreover, because the conventions of romantic love call for men and women to play prescribed roles, the hero is often happiest when she marries a man who was initially her friend, as in the case with George Eliot's Dorothea Brooke and Will Ladislaw. In some cases, the hero may work aggressively to dispel any romantic illusions herself in order to establish a genuine friendship with the potential marriage partner. Millamant, in William Congreve's *The Way of the World,* and Beatrice, in Shakespeare's *Much Ado about Nothing,* accomplish this with great flair.

Further, authors often try to redress the power imbalance between men and women to make an egalitarian relationship possible by creating a female character who is financially better off than the male, as well as his intellectual and moral superior. Such is the case with Dorothea Brooke and Will Ladislaw, and with the young Catherine and Hareton in *Wuthering Heights.* In Jane Austen's *Pride and Prejudice,* although Elizabeth Bennet does not become Darcy's equal in wealth or status before the wedding, she is clearly his moral and intellectual equal. The change in the power relationship between them is interpersonal, not economic. She was initially prejudiced against him because he is so wealthy and because he is something of a snob. When he is cured of his "pride" and begins to understand that he is only her equal and is not conferring a privilege on a woman to show interest in her, she gives up her prejudice against him. Their marriage proves to be one of mutually respecting equals.

In the most traditional literature, the lovers approximate equality by dividing up functions. In Samuel Richardson's *Pamela,* for example, Mr. B is Pamela's superior in wealth and social position, but she is his superior in the moral and spiritual realm. This separate-but-equal division of functions, however, has caused personal and cultural schizophrenia and does not address the continuing inequity that results from men's collective power over women. Thus, in *Through the Flower,* Judy Chicago argues that in the public realm as well as the private, women must stop playing the role of goddess and must reveal their true identities. To do so seems to threaten women's power base in relationships with men (for men in general still continue to maintain economic and social primacy), yet only when women take off the masks of femininity and men the masks of masculinity will it be possible to heal the false dichotomy between man and woman, and thus develop egalitarian social, political, and economic institutions; only then will people discover their true identities and develop honest relationships between the sexes. In Chicago's words,

> We can change and mold our environment, but only if we can
> be ourselves and express our real points and views. Moving

"through the flower" is a process that is available to all of us, a process that can lead us to a place where we can express our humanity and values as women through our work and in our lives and in so doing, perhaps we can also reach across the great gulf between masculine and feminine and gently, tenderly, but firmly heal it.[70]

Robin Morgan, in *Going Too Far,* links the public with the private relationships between women and men. She explores the tension between her love for her husband and son and her awareness that, as men, they are oppressors. In the prose poem that ends the work, she calls for both men and women to move past the mutually alienating roles of victim and victimizer to embark on a journey as loving and heroic equals: "*I love you.* I am my people. *I am come into my power,* I am the mirror-blastula reflected in the newest nova. *I love you, Blake,* My son, my son. . . . Here is my hand. Breathe in me. We are dancing in the still-warm ashes of our burnt-away selves, *endlessly birthing.* Insurrection. *Resurrection.* Come along now, *you too,* don't you think it's time we started?"[71] There will be no true revolution until we are all heroes, Morgan says; "Greatness is simply a way of life, and it must become so for everyone, that is the meaning of revolution" (p. 313).

The true hero—whether male or female—moves past hierarchical ways of interacting with other people and recognizes everyone's heroic potential. Don Juan, in Carlos Castaneda's *Tales of Power,* for example, explains that the warrior is humble but "the humbleness of a warrior is not the humbleness of a beggar. The warrior lowers his head to no one, but at the same time, he doesn't permit anyone to lower his head to him. The beggar, on the other hand, falls to his knees at the drop of a hat and scrapes the floor for anyone he deems to be higher; but at the same time, he demands that someone lower than him scrape the floor for him. . . . I know only the humbleness of a warrior, and that will never permit me to be anyone's master."[72] In another conversation with Castaneda, Don Juan makes it clear that the community of equal heroes includes women. In fact, he notes that women are more likely than men to undertake the heroic journey. The male hero is a pretender, rather than a true warrior, if he becomes a woman's lord and master, for the true hero always recognizes the heroism or heroic potential of each person he or she meets.

A danger for women is that they will delay their journey, waiting for men to embark with them. Adrienne Rich, in *Of Woman Born,* warns women against such delays, summarizing a story by Alice Schreiner, called "Dreams," published in 1890: "A woman is trying to cross a deep, fordless river into the land of freedom. She wants to carry with her the male infant sucking at her breast, but she is told, No, you will lose your life trying to save him; he must grow into a man and save himself, and then you will meet him on the other side."[73]

Because the journey requires men to renounce their birthright of ascribed superiority to women and of relative economic and political privilege, they are less likely to depart on the heroic journey than women are. In many cases, therefore, the community that is the female hero's reward is primarily composed of other women. In others, the male counterpart of the hero is on a similar quest. Encountering his female counterpart often jars him out of traditional assumptions about sex roles and accelerates his development. Such is the case in Bette Greene's children's story *Philip Hall Likes Me, I Reckon Maybe.* Beth Lambert is a strong, intelligent girl whose ingenuity, leadership, and superior performance in school alienate her from her best friend, Philip Hall. When he becomes cold and aloof because she wins over him so consistently, she hears herself saying, "I should have let you win." He, of course, notes that he is not "some baby other folks have to let win," and he argues that "all you been doing lately is winning, and that ain't hard to live with. Hard thing is losing." She does not give in and devalue her own accomplishments, but she does admit how hard it is to lose, and finally asks sympathetically if he is getting used to it.

> Philip nodded his head. "I ain't no baby."
> "Reckon I know that," I told him, "cause I can see you growing." When I saw on his face the makings of a smile, I said, "Come on, we still have time to enter the square-dancing contest."
> He stopped short. "I'm not about to enter no more contests with you, leastways not today."
> "You don't understand, Philip. This contest is for partners. Win together or lose together."
> "Sometimes I reckon I likes you, Beth Lambert," he said.[74]

In this case, and in such relationships as that between Lord Peter Wimsey and Harriet Vane of Dorothy Sayers's *Gaudy Night* and *Busman's Honeymoon,* two lovers and friends mutually aid each other's journey, and the result is a closer bond between them. Sayers's works, however, emphasize the importance of supportive noninterference in another's journey. In *Gaudy Night,* Harriet Vane has refused to marry Lord Peter Wimsey for years because, as the man who saved her from the gallows, he is her superior. She must first be allowed the experiences that teach her she is his heroic equal. She finally agrees to marry him when he knows she is in danger and does nothing, because he thereby demonstrates his belief in her ability to fight her own battles.

The sequel, *Busman's Honeymoon,* turns the tables. On their honeymoon, Peter Wimsey begins to face the realization that as a detective he is guilty of the execution of many criminals. In his eyes, he is a murderer, and not good enough for her. He begins to hide his feelings behind British reserve, and, rather than blithely reassuring him of his innocence, she wisely waits while he works out his sense of guilt. At the end of the book, he comes to her room and openly and honestly allows her to see him as he is, without the masks of lord and detective. Thus, both Harriet and Peter face and share with one another their strengths and their weaknesses, their beauty and their participation in evil. For Harriet, beginning with a clear sense of guilt and ineptitude, her task is to own her strength; for Peter, who begins with a strong knowledge of his own abilities, the journey includes a recognition of his weakness and guilt. Their reward is the happy ending of wholeness and of the sharing possible only between two souls courageous enough to appear psychologically naked before one another.

As we see here, heroic action that supports another's journey may involve waiting—but waiting supportively with faith that others are capable of undertaking the quest. One must not take it for them. While waiting for others, however, the hero may feel lonely and impatient. Zenna Henderson's science fiction classic *Pilgrimage: The Book of The People,* symbolically explores the dilemma faced by the hero who is ahead of her time and thus has insights and powers that are far beyond those of most of her neighbors and potential friends. In this case, the heroes come from another planet, which had the same potential as Earth; while on Earth people settled for "gadgets," "The People" from the other planet opt for "power." They can communicate telepathically, are capable of psychokinesis, and can fly (or "lift," as they call it). They hide their powers from their human neighbors because they are afraid of being killed as demons or witches.

They come to Earth because their planet died, and during the landing, the mother ship explodes. Many of The People are killed, and most are scattered. In the first generation on Earth, then, many of them know they had extraordinary talents, and they know they should conceal them to survive. By the first generation born on Earth, many do not know of their origins and not only feel alone and alienated, but believe they are freaks. Repressing their powers, they are, of course, extremely unhappy. Even when these beings have no faith that others like themselves exist, they are caught in a double bind. They are afraid to show their powers, but if they do not do so, they never find out whether others exist. Thus, each yearns for a place to go where he or she would feel at home and resemble other people, but it is only through desperation or accident that they reveal who they are and thus make a connection with The People.

Finding others with whom they can be fully themselves is their first experience of coming home. Collectively, however, the group still yearns to go back to their planet—to a "Home" populated entirely by people like themselves. Yet when the chance arises, through the agency of a spaceship sent to take them to the planet that The People have taken over, they begin to have second thoughts. Most of the group were, in fact, born on Earth. Some are half human. Further, they have begun to discover that some people of Earth are developing qualities like theirs. Bram, the member of The People who has been most vocal in yearning to go away from Earth to their real home, decides he cannot leave Earth. He loves it, and it is his home. He argues that The People should take over Earth and "use" it "instead of submitting to it," for the people of Earth had "forfeited their rights to the planet" by their ineptitude and inhumanity. If they cannot take over and save it, he argues, they should leave. The Old Ones, however, say no. They must wait until the "earth ones . . . develop along our lines someday."[75]

The pioneering effort of The People, then, is one of nurturing the humans of the Earth who are evolving superior wisdom and abilities, so that they will use their powers, not in anger against the others who do not understand them and not in "little sideshow" tricks, but in "miracles that really count" (p. 69). Further, by their very presence, they fight the despair that cripples so many of Earth's people and hampers the evolutionary process. The frame for the stories of various of The People is the situation of Lea, a woman with no extraordinary powers, who feels so little hope for herself or for humankind that she attempts suicide. She is saved by Karen, one of The People, and through hearing the stories of other such courageous and powerful beings, she gains hope in the future and in the potential for love, so that she can persevere in her own life and discover her own place in the design of Earth's evolution.

Through such Earth-people as Lea (who is able to understand the implications of The People's existence), and through the humans who have developed powers analogous to those of their more highly evolved visitors, the pilgrims learn that the worldwide community they seek is implicit on Earth now. Their home is not elsewhere, but here—now and potentially. To use Bram's metaphors, the Home in the sky the spaceship offers them is not "the promised land"; Earth is: "For our Jordan was crossed those long years ago. My trouble was that I thought that wherever I looked, just because I did the looking, was the goal ahead. But all the time, the Crossing, shimmering in the light of memory, had been something completed, not something yet to reach. My yearning for the Home must have been a little of the old hunger for the flesh pots that haunts any pioneering efforts" (p. 255). The work ends with Bram, Salla, and Obla in the spaceship on a visit to the other planet so that Obla's dismembered body can be healed and regenerated. Even aboard the ship, however, they long for the "sights and sounds, the smell and tastes, the homeness of Earth," and in Bram's words, only when "Earth will swell in the portholes again" will they "truly be coming home" (p. 255).

Thus, the hero does not have to wait for realization of the utopian dream implicit in the present society to feel happy and at home. Simply by embarking on the heroic journey herself, and by consciously promoting life against Holdfast, the dragon of the status quo, whenever possible, she is fulfilling her vocation and therefore she finds her true "place," her true home. Ella Price, in Dorothy Bryant's *Ella Price's Journal*, gets a hint of this feeling for the first time when she participates in an antiwar march. She has previously never written a letter to her congressman, "never worked to elect someone who'd change things." At the beginning of the rally, she is frightened and "sheepish," but as the march begins, she feels "calm and peaceful. And pure. Pure in the sense of being concentrated, free of distractions and anxieties. I felt right—not self-righteous, not smugly correct, not right while others were wrong; I don't mean that. Just right, like a piece of tile dropped into place, perfectly fitting its place in a design. And warm with closeness, something more. Something I had missed all my life without knowing it existed."[76]

In some works, the sense of coming home that follows the discovery of one's vocation is explained in terms of a preordained design. In Zenna Henderson's *Pilgrimage,* for example, Karen chides Lea for taking a job just to tide her over. Lea says, "It'll do," and Karen replies, "Nothing will *do* . . . if it's just a make-do, a time-filler, a drifting. If you won't fill the slot you were meant to, you might as well just sit and count your fingers. Otherwise you just interfere with everything."[77] A calm and peaceful sense of appropriate action comes from being true to one's own vision. Bonanza Jellybean, in Tom Robbins's *Even Cowgirls Get the Blues,* realizes,

> I just said "fantasy" and "struggle" in the same sentence, and on one level, at least, I guess that's what it's all about. That's what it's about for cowgirls, and maybe everybody else. A lot of life boils down to the question of whether a person is going to be able to realize his fantasies, or else end up surviving only through compromises he can't face up to. The way I figure it, Heaven and Hell are right here on Earth. Heaven is living in your hopes and Hell is living in your fears. It's up to each individual which he chooses.[78]

In either case, the hero begins to experience "heaven" or to feel at home as soon as she makes the decision to promote life in herself and in others. That is why, in the utopian novels, which form the basis for the final chapter of this work, so many heroes do not travel to the new world in a spaceship, but merely awaken there the instant they fully reject the old society.

While not immune to the restraints of the old world, the hero already enjoys many aspects of the new one. Suffragists, for example, were persecuted and imprisoned in Holloway prison; and although Holloway was notorious for brutal treatment of suffragists, the poetry written by women incarcerated there speaks of the pride and joy they experienced as a result of heroically standing up for their beliefs and of spending time—even while in prison—with their sister heroes. One such poem includes the line, "And the handgrip of true friendship—that is the prize."[79]

Similarly, Louisa May Alcott's Christie, in *Work: A Story of Experience,* feels community with other feminists, and she also has the sense of being at home that comes with finding one's vocation. She has worked at a variety of occupations and has found satisfaction in them, but in accepting the "role of speaker for the feminist cause," she, like Ella Price, feels that she has found her place. Her reward, there-fore, is inherent in her task—the satisfaction of knowing she is doing the work she should be doing, and the love of her sisters. She says,

> I accept the task, and will do my share faithfully with words or work, as shall seem best. We all need much preparation for the good time that is coming to us, and can get it best by trying to know, to help, love and educate one another,—as we do here!
>
> With an impulsive gesture Christie stretched her hands to the friends about her, and with one accord they laid theirs on hers, a loving league of sisters, old and young, black and white, rich and poor, each ready to do her part to hasten the coming of the happy end.[80]

While all heroes help to slay Holdfast and hence to aid in the birthing of the new, transformed kingdom, it is the hero who fearlessly and publicly shares her truth that most radically undermines Holdfast's grip on others, and hence who most noticeably undermines the foundations of the old repressive systems. Muriel Rukeyser, in her poem "Käthe Kollwitz," writes, "What would happen if one woman told the truth about her life? / The world would split open."[81]

This is why wise and honest women are so threatening to the repressive system's authorities. When G. B. Shaw's Joan of Arc speaks the truth that she learns from her voices, the archbishop insists that she is being "proud and disobedient." Because she speaks her truth, not his conventional one, he accuses her of the au-dacious crime of telling "the Archbishop in his cathedral that he lies." Charles, the Dauphin, admits that her power is compelling, saying, "I could follow her to hell when the spirit rises in her like that," and concludes the conversation by saying, "If only she would keep quiet, or go home!"[82] Rather than listening to her and learning from her truth, they are so frightened of her that they burn her at the stake.

Angela Davis, in *With My Mind on Freedom,* writes about her own discovery of how frightened prison officials are of truth when she begins sharing her ideas with other inmates. The officials are so upset that they put her in solitary confinement, and a court later declares this is a violation of her constitutional rights: "The court was all but saying that Commissioner of Corrections George McGrath and Jessie Behagan, the superintendent of the Women's House of D.C., were so fearful of letting the women in jail discover what communism was that they preferred to violate my most basic constitutional rights."[83]

The hero's ultimate weapon against the dragon myths is the sword of truth, yet many women believe that women's truth has been so obscured by patriarchal myths that new forms, new styles, and a new language must be developed to express women's heroic knowledge. In Robin Morgan's "Art and Feminism: A One-Act Whimsical Amusement on All That Matters," in *Going Too Far,* Plymnia gives the final, summary speech calling on her sisters to destroy the oppressive system by articulating the inexpressible:

> Let it be sung, this new word. . . . Think, Sisters. Think, Daughters: The power of spiritual frenzy is sufficiently threatening all unto itself, but think of the danger to every enforced system of order should such a mystery again be *reunited with intelligent expression*—and wake and stretch and move and come alive in a form that is intricate and beautiful, even as it was of old. There are words not even we can understand until they have been spoken. Not until we—any of us—recognize that we have said precisely what we mean do we know what we meant, after all.[84]

Adrienne Rich's poem "Planetarium" develops a similar theme. The speaker creates new images and new myths that will free her and other women. She tries "to translate pulsations / into images for the relief of the body / and the reconstruction of the mind." She begins with a recognition of the influence of heavenly bodies on her, so that she writes about them as a partly external and partly internal phenomenon. She is thus both inside and outside the reality she describes. In alliance with the monster-woman in the constellation, it is she "whom the moon ruled" and who is influenced by "the radio impulse pouring in from Taurus," and conversely she who "translates" their and her own "pulsations" into language.[85]

Rich's stance as a writer is one of a cooperating participant in the universe. Contemporary writing by women (and by some men) tends to emphasize the interrelatedness of self and others and the impossibility of seeing the world clearly without confronting one's own participation in the world. From this perspective, divisions between personal issues and political or social ones are artificial. To understand political or cosmic issues, the writer first explores the inner world—or the inner and the outer simultaneously. Thus, when Adrienne Rich writes of "diving into the wreck" of her own consciousness to find "the thing itself and not the myth,"[86] and when Muriel Rukeyser calls for "no more masks,"[87] the journey they trace has personal, cosmic, *and* political implications.

When the hero correctly names her own experience, she aids others in doing the same, and thus supports their journeys. One of the underlying messages of Erica Jong's *Fear of Flying* is the destructive and isolating effect of lying to oneself and to others. Isadora Wing vows that she will be totally honest with herself and write what she feels. Part of that honesty is admitting how much she has denied feelings and experiences in the past: "I censored myself. I refused to let myself write about what really moved me: my violent feelings about Germany, the unhappiness in my marriage, my sexual fantasies, my childhood, my negative feelings about my parents. . . . I had pasted imaginary oak-tag patches over certain areas of my life and steadfastly refused to look at them."[88] The capacity of certain authors to write honestly about taboo subjects serves as a lifeline to isolated readers lost in a morass of falsehoods and half-truths. The confessional school of writing creates a community of author, protagonist, and reader. Similarly, in Kurt Vonnegut, Jr.'s *Sirens of Titan*, the protagonist writes a letter to himself before he undergoes a lobotomy by the social authorities. After the operation, he discovers a letter from a heroic person who inspired him to believe in his own secret sense of self-worth, and only later does he find out that the heroic person is his previous, presocialized self. The hero in literature may likewise provide the needed encouragement to propel the reader on his or her own quest. Vonnegut describes the letter as "literature in its finest sense, since it made Unk courageous, watchful, and secretly free. It made him his own hero in very trying times."[89] When a woman is totally isolated from anyone who shares her perceptions, reading may provide the fictional community that keeps her sane. Katherine Mansfield, for example, refers to Jane Austen as a "secret friend."[90] Every hero liberates by exploding outmoded myths. In the comic, the hero may appear to be a fool, and her childlike comment that the emperor is naked provokes the liberating laughter of relief. At the same time, by showing the emperor to be ridiculous and not to be feared, she liberates the readers from his tyranny.

Often the fool acts quietly in line with her own vision, and explains that vision in public only when she is threatened with punishment for deviating from convention. Benjamin Franklin's Polly Baker declares to the assembled Puritan magistrates that she should not be punished for having her fifth illegitimate child: "The duty of the first and great command of nature and nature's God, *increase and multiply;* a duty, from the steady performance of which nothing has been able to deter me, but for its sake I have hazarded the loss of the public esteem, and have frequently endured public disgrace and punishment; and therefore ought, in my humble opinion, instead of a whipping, to have a statue erected to my memory."[91] Polly's speech "influenced the court to dispense with her punishment, and . . . induced one of her judges to marry her the next day—by whom she had fifteen children" (p. 155). As in John Davidson's "A Ballad of Hell," the fool may simply refuse to accept the "inevitable consequences" of her actions. In doing so, she and the reader discover that those consequences are not inevitable. In Davidson's poem, a young woman, tricked by a lover into killing herself, awakens to find herself in hell. Realizing that she has been duped, she does something unthinkable: she simply refuses to remain in hell and sets off for heaven. The Seraphs and Saints "Welcomed that soul that knew not fear. / Amazed to find it could rejoice, / Hell raised a hoarse, half-human cheer."[92] The world splits open, therefore, when its most sacred assumptions are challenged.

When consciously exploding patriarchal categories, the hero is likely to be portrayed as a witch. Mary Daly, in *Gyn/Ecology: The Metaethics of Radical Feminism,* explains the importance of the witch, hag, or crone as the symbol of female power:

> For women who are on the journey of radical be-ing, the lives of the witches, of the Great Hags of our hidden history are deeply intertwined with our own process. As we write/live our own story, we are uncovering their history, creating Hagography and Hagology. Unlike the "saints" of christianity, who must, by definition, be dead, Hags live. Women traveling into feminist time/space are creating Hagocracy, the place we govern. To govern is to steer, or pilot. . . . The point is that they should be governed by the Witch within—the Hag within.[93]

The invitation to the life of the witch is often the call to begin flying. In her poem "Invitation to Miss Marianne Moore," Elizabeth Bishop invites her sister poet to fly over the Brooklyn Bridge one morning for a celebration. The one poet imagines the other sailing through the air, rising "above the accidents, above the malignant moves" of the conventional world below, and listening to "a soft uninvented music," on which she floats up, "mounting the sky with natural heroism."[94] As Daly and Bishop both suggest, the witch's flight is governed by an inner power or music, unaided by external rules, conventions, or maps. This concept is implicit in Kate Millett's *Flying* and in Erica Jong's *Fear of Flying*, and it is explicit in a number of modern poems, such as Jean Tepperman's "Witch," Robert Frost's "Two Witches," and Anne Sexton's "Her Kind."

In becoming a witch, the hero makes the forbidden decision to value herself as an individual and a woman and to vent her rage not against herself and other women, but against the system and the individuals who oppress her and other women. Susan Sutheim, in "For Witches," begins by noting that women are not supposed to lose their tempers. Breaking the cultural taboo against the angry woman, she writes, "today i found my temper." Although she has been trained for twenty-seven years to excuse the clumsiness of others who "step on my head," she determines today to "prefer my head to your clumsiness."[95]

Whether as revolutionary, fool, bard, or witch, the hero transforms the kingdom through the power of true naming. Madeleine L'Engle's science fiction classic *A Wind in the Door* (the sequel to *A Wrinkle in Time*) gives this power cosmic dimensions; in so doing, she clarifies the way that the hero can aid in the transformation of the kingdom without dominating others or interfering with their journeys. The metaphysical assumption behind the novel is that everything in the universe, no matter how small or large, is alive; the unfolding of the universe depends on each element's successfully completing its journey. In this way, everything is interdependent. The hero, Meg Murray, witnesses the birth of a star and learns that when the star takes its rightful place in the universe, its journey is "a dance, a dance ordered and graceful, and yet giving an impression of complete and utter freedom, of ineffable joy."[96]

The evil forces of the universe, the Echthroi, disrupt the pattern and "X" things, keeping stars, planets, and people from knowing their true identities and hence their part in this universal dance. The concept of the "farandolae" emphasizes L'Engle's idea of universal interdependence. Within each human cell is a little organism called a mitochondrion—a totally independent creature with its own DNA and RNA. The human cell is totally dependent on these beings to process oxygen. Inside the mitochondrion is the farandola, a being that has the same relationship to the mitochondrion that the mitochondrion has to the human cell. Meg discovers that her beloved brother, Charles Wallace, is dying because his farandolae have been convinced by the Echthroi that they need not take their journeys, need not "deepen" because they "are [already] the greatest beings in the universe" (p. 177).

When the farandolae deepen, Meg learns, they sing with the stars and their song "orders the rhythm of creation" (p. 176). Afflicted with hubris, the young farandolae refuse to deepen, and thus not only will Charles Wallace die, but the whole balance of the universe will be disrupted. As Meg tells Mr. Jenkins, "Remember . . . you're great on Benjamin Franklin's saying, 'We must all hang together, or assuredly we will all hang separately.' That's how it is with human beings and mitochondria and farandolae—and our planet, too, I guess, and the solar system. We have to live together in—in harmony, or we won't live at all" (p. 147).

Meg is aided by a cherub named Proginoskes, who explains to her that the Echthroi are responsible for Black Holes in the sky as well as for war, alienation, and crime: "War and hate are their business, and one of their chief weapons is un-Naming—making people not know who they are. If someone knows who he is, really knows, then he doesn't need to hate. That's why we still need Namers, because there are places through the universe like your planet Earth. When everyone is really Named, the Echthroi will be vanquished" (p. 97).

In the course of the narrative, Meg discovers her vocation. Her job, as Namer, is to make humans and farandolae "feel alive, but more fully themselves," just as her friend Dalvin makes her feel more herself when she is with him because "love . . . makes people know who they really are" (p. 99). Named, they experience both their individuality and their oneness with the universe. Meg names Mr. Jenkins, the elementary school principal, and then the farandolae. The Echthroi, however, have Mr. Jenkins in their grasp. To save him, she recognizes that she must "do as Mr. Jenkins had done when he had broken through the mad circle of whirling farandolae and held her. She must hold the Echthroi and name them." She begins a litany of naming of stars, of farandolae, of her friends, which includes "I hold you! I love you, I name you. I name you, Echthroi. You are nothing. You are. . . . I fill you with Naming. Be!" The author notes that her song is the same as that of the deepening farandolae and of the stars. She concludes, "Echthroi! You are named! My arms surround you. You are no longer nothing. You are. You are filled. You are me. You are Meg" (p. 205). When named and fully claimed, the Echthroi are transformed into a positive part of the wholeness of self and universe. Thus, when the hero finds her own true name and her wholeness, she becomes a namer who aids others in successfully completing their journeys. Both individual and microcosm of the universe, her reward is a community that paradoxically exists only when beings are most themselves and hence most individual and different.

As demonstrated in this chapter, when the hero claims the treasure of her true identity, the kingdom is transformed and she experiences community with herself, with others, and with the cosmos. The concluding chapter of this book, "The Kingdom Transfigured," explores visions of political and social community that reflect the consciousness of the returned hero.

Chapter 8
The Kingdom Transfigured

"Toto, I don't think we are in Kansas anymore."
Dorothy in L. Frank Baum's *The Wizard Of Oz*

At the end of her quest, the female hero returns to enjoy a new community with herself, with the natural and spiritual worlds, and frequently with other people. To some degree, she also embodies the power necessary to revitalize the entire kingdom—to rid it of dragons as her classical predecessor did. No matter how alienated she is from the larger society, the hope present in the description of her experience is that if one woman has made that particular journey beyond convention, so can others. Each is a role model to another, and so on, until eventually the myths and institutions of the entire society are altered. Diane Di Prima in "Revolutionary Poem #19" reminds her reader that the transformed world imagined by all reformers *is* a possibility: "you can have what you ask for."[1]

In many works, the respiritualized community to which the hero returns is portrayed symbolically. At the end of D. H. Lawrence's *The Rainbow*, Ursula Brangwen's emerging heroism is likened to the discovery of a new world: "It was the unknown, the unexplored, the undiscovered upon whose shore she had landed, alone, after crossing the void."[2] At the last, she awaits the impending cultural transformation, which Lawrence likens to "a new generation" in an old dead husk: "In everything she saw she grasped and groped to find the creation of the living God, instead of the old, hard barren form of bygone living. . . . She saw in the rainbow the earth's new architecture, the old, brittle corruption of houses and factories swept away, the world built up in a living fabric of Truth, fitting to the overarching heaven" (pp. 494–495).

Even when the narrative ends with the promise of a kingdom transfigured, however, the author usually fails to include any detailed account of the world that the new vision promises. Detailed descriptions of the transfigured kingdom—the last stage of the archetypal heroic journey—tend to be the subject of a separate set of stories, collectively referred to as feminist utopias. These stories recount the nature and, in many cases, the origin of an ideal society in which the values of the female hero are the norm. For example, Mary Bradley Lane's *Mizora: A Prophecy*[3] and Charlotte Perkins Gilman's *Herland,*[4] which grew out of the nineteenth-century women's movement, and Joanna Russ's contemporary novel *The Female*

Man[5] describe ideal societies made up exclusively of women. Five other utopian stories, all contemporary American, tell of societies in which men and women live together as equals—Dorothy Bryant's *The Kin of Ata Are Waiting for You,*[6] Mary Staton's *From the Legend of Biel,*[7] Ursula Le Guin's *The Dispossessed,*[8] Ernest Callenbach's *Ecotopia,*[9] and Marge Piercy's *Woman on the Edge of Time.*[10] Whether the story is told from a mystical, a psychological, a sociological, or a political point of view, the new world being celebrated is always one in which women are strong and autonomous, and exert direct political, economic, and social power.[11]

William Morris's late-nineteenth-century utopian novel *News from Nowhere* prefigures many of the standard elements of the feminist utopian novel. The author envisions an anarchistic, pastoral community of artists who provide all the community's needs and who work for the love of their art rather than for money. Social and class discrimination have been eliminated, and women and men are considered to be equally free and equally able: "The idea (a law-made idea) of the woman being the property of the man . . . vanished with private property, as well as certain follies about the 'ruin' of women for following their natural desires in an illegal way, which of course was a convention caused by the laws of private property."[12]

Utopian works such as Morris's are in a feminist, romantic, revolutionary tradition, in which stratification, alienation, dominance, and crime are considered products of industrialization and of the split between mind and body, head and heart. The utopian vision involves a return to nature and to a faith in the human power to change our destiny. In this pastoral world of respiritualized matter, knowledge and virtue, independence and community are no longer antithetical, because all things are God and therefore are One. This belief, expressed in Arthur C. Clarke's contemporary work *Childhood's End,* is that "the whole human race will reach the same beatitude."[13] Charles Reich, in *The Greening of America,* calls this state "consciousness three."[14] Theodore Roszak, in *Where the Wasteland Ends: Politics and Transcendence in Post-Industrial Society,* describes a "visionary commonwealth."[15] Marshall McLuhan, in *Understanding Media: The Extension of Man,* writes of the "new tribalism."[16] The adjectives that all three theorists use to describe this new world are similar: "celebrative," "active," and "intuitive."

Many utopian writers associate the new consciousness with female qualities, while the present, repressive system is associated with male qualities. According to Roszak, the major quality of the modern world is "a compulsive masculine drive to demonstrate toughness, expel sentiment, and to get things under heavy-handed control" (p. 242). In contrast to feminist utopias are the dystopias of the late nineteenth century and the first half of the twentieth century, which prophesy a future in which the values of the modern world are carried to their logical conclusion. They frequently include a judgmental father figure, such as Aldous Huxley's "Our Ford" in *Brave New World* and the Well-Doer in Eugene Zamiatin's Russian dystopia, *We,* whose powerful, dominating, oppressive, egotistical, and destructive qualities pervade the society.

Women in dystopian novels frequently represent the humanizing influence in an impersonal, competitive, masculine world. In Sinclair Lewis's *Babbitt,* which might be described as a realistic dystopia, women are dissociated from the values of the regulated "male" world; Babbitt himself comments, "Trouble with women is, they never have sense enough to form regular habits."[17] Babbitt, who ironically neither finds true community nor freedom within the he-man world of Zenith, denigrates women for their values, which suggest an alternative to his miserable life. In his fantasy life, however, the values of the postindustrial dream are realized through his relationship with a female fairy child, to whom he escapes in his sleep: "Instantly he was in the magic dream. He was somewhere among unknown people who laughed at him. He slipped away, ran down the paths of a midnight garden, and at the gate the fairy child was waiting. Her dear and tranquil hand caressed his cheek. He was gallant and wise and well-beloved; warm ivory were her arms; and beyond perilous moors the brave sea glittered" (p. 86).

Babbitt has the ability to act communally and lovingly, but he is ashamed when he does because he sees emotion as female and therefore unmanly. He captures the emotion associated with the fairy child once while loafing on the edge of a wharf in the backwoods of Maine with his best friend, Paul Reisling.

> The immense tenderness of the place sank into Babbitt, and he murmured, "I'd just like to sit here—the rest of my life—and whittle—and sit. And never hear a typewriter. Or Stan Graff fussing in the phone. Or Rone Ted scrapping. Just sit. Gosh!"
>
> "Oh, it's darn good, Georgie. There's something sort-of eternal about it."
>
> For once, Babbitt understood him. . . .
>
> "Well, you know what it means to me, Georgie. Saved my life." The shame of emotion overpowered them; they cursed a little, to prove they were good rough fellows. (p. 125)

In that moment of simultaneous communion and freedom, Babbit feels "as though he had cleansed his veins of poisonous energy and was filling them with wholesome blood" (pp. 125–126). He discovers the healing experience of "female" consciousness as an antidote to the sterility of a masculine, dehumanizing society: "What did he [Babbitt] want? Wealth? Social position? Travel? Servants? Yes, but only incidentally. . . . He did know that he wanted the presence of Paul Reisling; and from that he stumbled into the admission that he wanted the fairy girl—in the flesh. If there had been a woman whom he loved, he would have fled to her, humbled his forehead on her knees" (p. 219).

The belief that male society needs to be "saved" by women or by female qualities has become a cliché of the American patriarchy. In the nineteenth century, women were seen as saviors because of their greater spirituality and purity; in contemporary society, they are more often seen as representatives of the unconscious. The poet Robert Bly, for example, has run several conferences on "mother consciousness," which emphasizes the necessity for modern men and women to free their repressed "female" energy.

The association of women with suppressed and underrated values is not limited to English and American culture. In Eugene Zamiatin's dystopia, women are denigrated as the "irrational component"; they are believed to be incapable of thinking abstractly and are sacrificed to the Well-Doer.[18] I-330 is the female leader of the spiritualized, organic utopian society behind the Green Wall, which is endeavoring to take over the spaceship *Integral*. She makes friends with D-530, the builder of the spaceship, and lives with him above the Earth in the wind.

Like Babbitt, D-530 associates his love for a woman with the nonutilitarian life of freedom and true community. The novel's symbolic association of I-330 with

Christ, moreover, suggests that she might save him. D-530 wants "to transfuse my whole being into hers through a contact with her shoulder or through our interwoven fingers" (p. 102). His joyful anticipation of joining with her and with the cosmic unity is described in the transcendental image of flying, organically, like birds fly: "Everything seems to have wings, to fly; the day flies; and our *Integral*, too, already has wings" (p. 10). When he is faced with the painful fact that I-330 may have cared about him only as the builder of the *Integral*, he runs away from the Well-Doer's machine, crying, "Save me from it—save me!" In his despair he associates the suppression of female qualities in the culture with the absence of mothering: "If only I had a mother as the ancients had—my mother, *mine*, for whom I should be not the Builder of the *Integral*, and not D-530, not a molecule of the United States, but merely a living human piece, a piece of herself" (pp. 201–202).

As we have seen, the female heroic pattern must be delineated before a truly human, heroic archetype can be defined. Feminist utopias provide a corrective. Traditional utopias and dystopias often speak of sexual equality, but portray a society in which men are primary and women secondary. Although female imagery and characteristics suggest hope for a utopian alternative, the female characters are not presented as primary beings. Robert Heinlein's *Stranger in a Strange Land* is an example of the inconsistency of philosophy and dramatization. In this novel, everyone, including the grasshopper, is theoretically God, yet the women characters are beautiful, sexually uninhibited "handmaidens."[19] As Dorothy Bryant puts it, somewhere "in the middle of a scene, the women get up and serve food."[20]

In feminist utopias, on the other hand, women save themselves and, in some cases, save men also, when they seize direct political and economic power—that is, when they become active, strong, courageous heroes. Such heroes, however, differ from the traditional symbolic female savior and from the "macho" hero because they are not seen as superior to other people. The female hero is neither the traditional helpmate rescuer, who "saves" others by immolating herself, nor is she like the male superhero seen in such works as Frank Herbert's *Dune* and Heinlein's *Stranger in a Strange Land*, who leads while others only follow. She saves by teaching others that they have the power to become heroic. They do not become her followers, but are coequals in a community of heroes.

The novels and legends that explain the origins of feminist utopias parallel the stages of the hero's journey. The society kills the dragon of patriarchal consciousness, achieves reconciliation with the mother, and experiences the treasure of full humanity. In *Mizora, Herland,* and *The Female Man*, patriarchal consciousness is seen as innately male, so that women slay the dragon by killing all the men. In each, however, the bloody revolution has occurred long before the action of the novel and is more symbolic than realistic. In Russ's *The Female Man*, the citizens of utopian Whileaway have forgotten the war between the sexes and believe that a plague wiped out the male sex.

The novels by Piercy, Le Guin, Bryant, Staton, and Callenbach identify as the dragon not men, but primitive, patriarchal ways of seeing. The vanquishing of the dragon often includes a violent conflict. In most cases, the confrontation is not entirely resolved. Piercy's future utopian community in *Woman on the Edge of Time* carries on a protracted war with an alternative, dystopian future (where the class structure has become inhumanly rigid, men are fast turning into robots, and women—"biologically improved" to be more sexy—are glorified prostitutes). In *The Dispossessed*, Ursula Le Guin's utopia, Anarres, emerges out of a revolution, but the revolutionaries do not defeat the patriarchal Urrasti; they only create such a continued threat that they are given the planet's moon to live on, provided they do not interfere with Urrasti life.

Sometimes the revolution is relatively peaceful. Callenbach's Ecotopia is formed when the female-dominated Survivalist Party becomes the majority of the electorate. Ecotopia secedes from the United States, and although some violence ensues, it is minor and temporary. Both Ecotopia and Le Guin's Anarres experience a "cold war," which helps unify the country. In *From the Legend of Biel*, the revolution is "bloodless and thorough." Xitr-Bielen kills the dragon of the "syntax of Despair" and discovers the treasure of "the infinite capacities of any human brain-system." By changing "language," "reality was transformed" (p. 176). The syntax of despair, another metaphor for patriarchal consciousness, is connected to the idea that it is possible to "own" or control anything. Freedom from the sickness of owning, however, liberates the true self: "A person's natural involvement is in the self. It is focused on the pleasurable discovery of the possibilities in selfness. It means doing, not possessing" (p. 176). Slaying the syntax of despair and affirming the infinite potential of each individual creates the "more precisely human posture" (p. 177) underlying the utopian society. Dorothy Bryant's "kin" of Ata awaken the utopian community when their consciousness changes. The new utopia is not then so much a geographical space as a state of mind, a way of relating to other people and to the natural world.

Whether the utopian communities originate from violent confrontation or not, they all include a series of emperor's-new-clothes situations that reveal the bankruptcy of patriarchal assumptions. For example, male explorers often assume that women are weak and in need of protection. The narrator of *Herland*, for example, wonders how the women fared without men to protect them, but then realizes, "These stalwart virgins had no men to fear and therefore no need of protection" (p. 128).

The liberation of women follows the growing consciousness that women need not be cloistered if men no longer rape. In the majority of the utopian communities, men are not eliminated or punished for their past violence; rather, they are converted to a gentler, more humane way of living. Only Callenbach in *Ecotopia* suggests that men will have a continuing desire to be violent. "Young men, especially, needed a chance to combat 'the others,' to charge and flee, to test their comradeship, to put their beautiful resources of speed and strength to use, to let their adrenalin flow, to be brave and to be fearful" (p. 195). Ecotopia provides young men with ritual war games, in which about fifty young men die every year. This siphons off men's violent impulses so that the society can be peaceful.

Released from the constant fear of rape or assault, women exult in their newfound freedom and mobility. Luciente in *Woman on the Edge of Time* explains, " 'I've never actually known of a case of rape, although I've read about it. It seems . . . particularly horrible to us. Disgusting, like cannibalism. . . . It seems unbelievable. . . .' [Connie, the time traveler] imagined herself taking a walk at night under the stars. She imagined herself ambling down a country road and feeling only mild curiosity when she saw three men coming toward her. She imagined hitching a ride with anyone willing to give her a ride. She imagined answering the door without fear, to see if anyone needed help" (p. 200). In *The Female Man*, the narrator explains, "There's no being out too late in [the all-female world] Whileaway, or *up too early*, or *in the wrong part of town or unescorted*. You cannot fall out of the kinship web and become sexual prey for strangers, for there is no prey and there are no strangers—the kinship web is world-wide. In all of Whileaway there is no one who can keep you from going where you please" (p. 81). Freed from male protection as well as oppression, women in *Mizora* and *Herland* exult in their newly discovered competence. Because there are no men to run the government or the economy, women discover they can do it, and do it well.

In all these works, the metaphor for liberation is rebirth. The protagonist becomes reconciled with the mother by giving birth to a new, heroic conscious-ness. Joanna Russ's protagonist gives birth to a new self through fantasy, and Russ describes the rise of the new hero from earth and sky as distinctly female. "Janet," she notes, "comes from the place where the Labia of ship and horizon kiss each other so that Whileawayans call it The Door and know that all legendary things come therefrom." Born of Joanna's imaginings, Janet is "the Mightbe of our dreams, living as she does in a blessedness no one will ever know, she is nonethe-less Everywoman" (p. 213). In order to give birth to the embryonic Janet who can transform the world, Russ's protagonist allows herself to imagine Jael, an allegori-cal figure of women's rage against patriarchal oppression. Jael kills an aggressively sexist male with her fingernails and teeth, and confesses that she enjoyed doing it. The narrator suggests that when women stop denying their power and their anger, they will give birth to their true selves and to a new society: "We will all be changed. In a moment, in the twinkling of an eye, we will all be free. I swear it on my own head. . . . We will be ourselves" (p. 213).

A male protagonist typically experiences the liberation and rebirth of his repressed "female" self only after meeting (and often falling in love with) a strong, liberated woman. When William Weston, the protagonist of *Ecotopia,* falls in love with Marissa, "a powerful, and remarkable person," he marvels at the contrast between her strength, wisdom, and honesty and the artificiality and manipulative-ness of the patriarchal women he has loved. He feels liberated by Marissa, because she is not dependent or manipulative, but even more because with her he experi-ences "feelings I never knew were there: a deep, overwhelming, scary sharing of our whole beings" (p. 88). When he discovers a natural woman, he learns that the male as well as the female sex role is an artificial, alienating convention: He is reborn to himself in response to liberated female power.

The reclaiming of the self is often associated with coming home to mother. However, authors such as Charlotte Perkins Gilman in *Herland* take pains to define that mother as fully human, free, and independent, in contrast to the stereotype of a fluffy, smothering, dependent woman. The male explorer who decides to marry one of the women in *Herland* explains that loving a powerful, liberated woman is a very good sensation after all.

> It gave me a queer feeling, way down deep, as of the stirring of some ancient dim prehistoric consciousness, a feeling that they were right somehow—that this was the way to feel. It was like—coming home to mother. I don't mean the wide-flannels and doughnuts mother, the fussy person that waits on you and spoils you and doesn't really know you. I mean the feeling that a very little child would have, who had been lost—for ever so long. It was a sense of getting home; of being clear and rested,

of safety and yet freedom, of love that was always there, warm like sunshine in May, not hot like a stove or a feather bed, a love that didn't irritate and didn't smother. (p. 323)

In *Ecotopia*, Weston notes, "Something peculiar is going on in this place. Don't yet exactly locate the source of the feeling. It's like waking up after a dream and not being quite able to remember what it was about. The way people deal with each other—and with me—keeps reminding me of something—but I don't know what" (p. 36). Like the protagonist of *Herland,* Weston particularly values the society's reconciliation of the need for security and adventure. In Ecotopia, people are adventurous precisely because they have extended families with many people to love and care for them; they do not have to cling to one another or be dependent, because love is always there. As in early childhood, an atmosphere of love and concern frees individuals to experiment and to be adventurous.

The birth of an Ecotopian, feminist consciousness is associated with rebirth from a symbolic mother. Near the end of the work, Weston goes to soak in the baths and loses "all sense of horizon, of place—all sense of everything except the steady gurgling of the water coming to me from deep inside the warm earth" (p. 221). Having entered this symbolic womb, he is reborn an Ecotopian and determines to remain in the country: "I begin to see that I have fallen in love with her country as much as with Marissa. A new self has been coming to life within me here, thanks to both her and her people. This new me is a stranger, an Ecotopian, and his advent fills me with terror, excitement, and strength" (p. 212).

Feminist utopian works assume that patriarchy is not natural and does not create an environment conducive to the maximization of human potential. In discovering a sexually egalitarian utopian society, each narrator has a sense of coming home to a nurturing, liberating environment. The explorer who discovers the utopian community initially assumes that he or she will be alienated in the public world and will have to repress or deny vital parts of the self, such as emotion, vulnerability, or spontaneity, in order to function. In fact, having traveled to the alternative society, the hero *stops* repressing valuable human qualities and feels rejoined to the self. When Howard Scott, in *From the Legend of Biel,* discovers a structure made by the utopian Thoacdiens, "he felt that if he could stay here, in this room, he would come together with that in himself which was not realized. What was lost would be found. The pieces of the shattered mosaic which was himself would come naturally, easily together, matching edge to edge, and click into a whole" (p. 46). He "wept because he was no longer afraid. He wept because he was no longer alone, even though that to which he had been joined was hidden" (p. 47).

In many cases, a male protagonist gives birth to a new self only when he stops repressing his buried female characteristics. Shevek, in Le Guin's *The Dispossessed,* comes to realize that the men from the sexist, class-ridden society of Urras dominated and oppressed others because they "contained a woman, a suppressed, silenced, bestialized woman, a fury in a cage. He had no right to ease them. They knew no relation but possession. They were possessed" (p. 60). The central character of Dorothy Bryant's *The Kin of Ata* has achieved the macho ideal of a man of his culture. He is rich, famous, and attractive to women. He is also alienated, unhappy, and misogynistic. At the beginning of the novel, he kills a lover in a frenzy of sexual disgust. He awakens after his act of violence to a nonsexist world where he is forced to confront and overcome his hostility toward women. He does so first by falling in love with a woman whom he acknowledges to be superior to him, and second by a vision in which he liberates the repressed woman inside himself. His first reaction is not to free but to kill her: "I had to destroy her. I tried every way I could think of, but she anticipated my every move. Then she grabbed the initiative and I was defensive until I could get it back. But I was so tired. Finally I stopped doing anything but defensive, complementary moves. I let her dictate the dance . . . her movements became great sweeps of grace, or joy, that I followed in perfect simultaneity" (p. 129). When he stops repressing the woman within, he discovers his full human power.

Le Guin's and Russ's works provide interesting variations on this theme. In *The Dispossessed,* Shevek is initially impatient with the poverty and provincialism of anarchistic Anarres, but after actually seeing for himself the repression and oppression that characterize Urras, he returns to his mother country. Before leaving Urras he makes a speech, exposing the patriarchal lie that it is possible to own anyone or anything:

> We know that there is no help for us but from one another, that no hand will save us if we do not reach out our hand. And the hand that you reach out is empty, as mine is. You have nothing. You possess nothing. You own nothing. You are free. All you have is what you are, and what you give. . . . If it is Anarres you want, if it is the future you seek, then I tell you that you must come to it with empty hands. You must come to it alone, and naked, as the child comes into the world, into his future, without any past, without any property, wholly dependent on other people for his life. You cannot take what you have not given, and you must give yourself. You cannot buy the Revolution. You cannot make the Revolution. You can only be the Revolution. (pp. 214, 242)

The voyager is like a child, born to the nurturing mother, Anarres. Howard Scott, the explorer from Earth in *From the Legend of Biel,* is literally reborn into a new world and a new time. The work ends with Thoacdien's announcement that "we are deviating from the standard birthing schedule of 1,000 infants each five sets of seasons in order to receive on the earth a human who was able to find his way here through much darkness. Howard Scott, male, will be born in the next season of the sun" (p. 332).

The new heroic men and women and the new culture and institutions, these works suggest, do not spring full-blown from a deity's head. As children come from a woman's body, the utopian future, like the novel itself, is an outgrowth of women's actual experience. The authors labor to transcend the limitations of that experience and to bring to life new institutions and new ways of seeing, which are based on women's experience in patriarchy without being bound by that experience. Furthermore, each utopian society is in process, and its citizens are always altering it, discovering new, freer, more humane ways to live. In Staton's novel, the people of Lir go beyond the premises of the Thoacdiens and become even more liberated than the original society. Le Guin demonstrates how the tyranny of the majority limits Anarres and notes that people have to fight continually for their freedom: Anarres is not perfect; it is merely preferable to patriarchal Urras. Russ ends her novel, "her daughter," with the recognition that it is a product of a still limited vision. She counsels the novel to seek her fortune "bravely on book racks of bus terminals and drugstores," but not to "get glum when you are no longer understood. . . . For on that day, we will be free" (p. 214). These works, then, do not pretend to outline a static social goal. Instead, they explore the implications for consciousness and for institutions of the massive rebirth of female power in men and women as one step in a process toward fuller humanity.

Often the reconciliation with the mother is symbolically associated with a mother-god. Although the citizens of feminist utopias do not worship an external theistic "god," their societies are more religious than secular in feeling. Their reverence for all life and their feeling of unity with nature in some cases find symbolic expression in a vision of an earth-mother goddess. The association of women with nature has been used in patriarchal society to justify and perpetuate the oppression of women. Yet these writers see in this association the basis for potential strength, which will develop when both men and women recognize their dependence on nature. Unlike the judgmental patriarchal god, who reigns above nature and above humankind in opposition to evil, the mother-goddess represents life in all its fluidity and contradictions. Russ describes a statue of the Whileawayan deity as "awful as Zeus," and also as comic trickster: "Her cheekbones are too broad, Her eyes set at different levels. . . . She becomes in turn gentle, terrifying, hateful, loving, 'stupid' (or 'dead') and finally indescribable" (p. 103). Because she embraces all of life, she does not judge or deny people or qualities. The idea of the mother-god also emerges from men's and women's historical experience (or at least the myth of such experience) of nurturance and acceptance in the arms of a loving mother. In *Herland,* the "mother love . . . was a Religion. . . . All they did related to this power" (p. 266).

Turn-of-the-century works frequently sentimentalize motherhood and assert the moral superiority of women over men. The narrator of *Herland* notes that the women of the utopian society "had no enemies; they themselves were all sisters and friends" (p. 129) because they are all mothers. In them, "the power of mother love, that maternal instinct we so highly lauded," is developed to the fullest and is complemented by "a sister love . . . we found it hard to credit" (p. 128). The women of *Herland* themselves explain their success in creating a perfect society as a product of mother love: "The children in this country are the one center and focus of all our thoughts. Every step of our advance is always considered in its effect on them—on the race. You see we are *mothers,* she repeated, as if in that she had said it all" (p. 152).

More recent works see women's socialization and the nurturing capacities that are developed through parenting—rather than an innate mothering instinct —as responsible for women's success in developing nurturing institutions. Piercy makes it possible for men to be positive contributors to a feminist utopia by making them mothers, and hence enabling them to develop qualities traditionally reserved for women.

> It was part of Women's long revolution. When we were break-
> ing all the old hierarchies. Finally, there was that one thing we
> had to give up too, the only power we ever had, in return for
> no more power for anyone. The original production: the
> power to give birth. Cause as long as we were biologically
> enchained, we'd never be equal. And males never would be
> humanized to be loving and tender. So we all became
> mothers. Every child had three. (p. 96)

In Piercy's work, scientific advances make it possible for both men and women to nurse their babies. In other works, men do not give birth or nurse children, but they do share equally in child care.

Only in Callenbach's Ecotopia is the parenting role of men not entirely equal to that of women. Callenbach explains:

> Ecotopian life is strikingly equalitarian in general—women hold responsible jobs, receive equal pay, and of course they also control the Survivalist Party. The fact that they also exercise absolute control over their own bodies means that they openly exert a power which in other societies is covert or nonexistent: the right to select the fathers of their children. "No Ecotopian woman ever bears a child by a man she has not freely chosen," I was told sternly. And in the nurturing of children while they are under two, women continue this dominance; men participate extensively in the care and up-bringing of the very young, but in cases of conflict the mothers have the final say, and mince no words about it. (p. 82)

These utopian writers, however, do not assume that the patriarchal form of the mother-daughter bond is always positive. In *Herland, Mizora,* and *From the Legend of Biel,* the love between mother and child is the pattern for all other relationships, but it is a bond significantly altered from its patriarchal form.

No illegitimacy exists, because all children have mothers, and children are not seen as the property of their parents. Perhaps most important, the mother is not dependent on a father, but is a free, independent person. The idea of having two parents is presented as ludicrous in *Mizora*. When asked about her father, or "other parent," a young girl laughs, "You have a queer way of jesting. I have but one mother, one adorable mother. How could I have two? And she laughed again" (p. 2). As we have seen, the "mother" may even be male.

In *From the Legend of Biel,* we learn that the nuclear family must, by its very nature, be destroyed, because it is always made up of captor parents and a captured child. "The whole object of the family is to repeat itself, to create the future in the image of the past. Consequently it is a very effective obstacle to change because it keeps all children within the boundaries of cultural tradition. In the family, learning is a process of psychological brutality at the end of which a child knows nothing but what is permissible to the tribe" (p. 219). The patriarchal parents entrap the children because they depend on them for justification of their own sacrifices. The parent who lives her own life, in contrast, does not need to live through her child.

To avoid the parental desire to achieve immortality through their children, the actual biological link between parent and child is severed or deemphasized. Women no longer give birth naturally to children in *Woman on the Edge of Time* or in *From the Legend of Biel.* The period of childhood in both works is quite short. Children are liberated from their mothers' care at age twelve in *Woman on the Edge of Time:* The young child goes into the wilderness alone to prove his or her self-sufficiency. When the child returns, the three mothers acknowledge the newly gained independence by refraining from giving advice. In *The Female Man,* children leave their mothers at age five. These child-rearing practices are consistent with the goal of promoting autonomy and individuality and in discouraging dependence and the limitation of freedom of action for both children and adults.

The dissolution of the nuclear family and the de-emphasis on the biological link between mother and child leads to a redefinition of the parent-child relationship. The central myth that informs Thoacdien culture, in *From the Legend of Biel,* is the story of the love between Mikkran and her young charge, Biel. Unlike the traditional parent-child relationship, "the mentor/charge relationship is based on mutual sovereignty—not on imitation. The one truth in the Federation which has maintained equilibrium in the absence of prescribed morality, in the absence of unquestioned basic tenets, is the relationship which teaches that two persons of relaxed and curious mind who learn and share together, who confront the unknown, also create joy" (p. 22). Furthermore, no person bears total responsibility for child care except in Russ's Whileaway. There, mothers get a five-year vacation after giving birth, to enjoy themselves and to play with the child. Even so, professionals care for the child's physical needs, and after the child is five, the mother's responsibility is shared by the community.

In Bryant's *The Kin of Ata,* communal responsibility begins with childbirth. The narrator (a visitor from a patriarchal culture) is told, "giving birth is a very hard thing. We all try to help." He watches a young girl go into labor assisted in the preliminary stages by the fathers (the three men who might have conceived the child). When she is nearing delivery, the entire community crowds around to help. One explains, "We try to take some of the pain on ourselves, to share it. We try to give some of our strength for the hard work. We try to make the girl feel happy that, once she has done this she need no longer carry the burden of the child alone. Then she will labor in joy. At the least, we give the warmth of our bodies surrounding her" (p. 149).

Although the mother-child bond is celebrated, good child rearing is the responsibility of professionals. Even the women of Herland, who so emphasize the overriding power of mother love, turn their children at a young age over to trained teachers. When the male explorers express shock that they abandon their children, the women explain that a mother's filling her child's teeth herself, instead of taking the child to a dentist, is not a demonstration of love.

The reconciliation with the mother in these societies includes a renewed appreciation of the mother-child role; it also calls for ridding the female experience of patriarchy. Often activities denigrated by patriarchal society—and associated with women—are particularly valued in these feminist utopias. Thus, although there is characteristically no difference in income and consequently no class structure in any of these feminist societies, the narratives often emphasize the particular importance of certain traditionally feminine occupations. The citizens of Mizora, for example, have particular respect for cooks, while one of the most valued occupations in Herland is teaching. The ready capacity for feeling associated with women in patriarchy is valued in feminist societies. Indeed, the stoicism so valued by patriarchy is viewed as the source of its social problems.

These novels also note that women's roles in patriarchal society have enabled them to see truths denied to men, who have undergone socialization to prepare them for public, dominant, and competitive roles. Callenbach explains that the Survivalist Party is dominated by women because women's heritage is consistent with the "basic cooperation—and biology—oriented policies of the party" (p. 3). Because women have not traditionally earned salaries for their work as housewives, creators of feminist utopias understand that it is natural for people to work for love, pride, or duty. Men, blinded by their experience in the competitive marketplace, are often oblivious to the many evidences around them that people will work without being paid. Shevek in *The Dispossessed* contrasts concepts of work in patriarchal Urras with those of the utopian Anarres, patterned after the ideas of the great woman philosopher, Odo:

> Here you think that the incentive to work is finances, need for money or desire for profit, but where there's no money the real motives are clearer, maybe. People like to do things. They like to do them well. People doing them, they can—egoize, we call it—show off?—to the weaker ones. Hey, look, little boys, see how strong I am! You know? A person likes to do what he is good at doing. . . . But really, it is the question of ends and means. After all, work is done for the work's sake. It is the lasting pleasure of life. The private conscience knows that. And also the social conscience, the opinion of one's neighbors. There is no other reward, on Anarres, no other law. One's own pleasure, and the respect of one's fellows. That is all. (p. 121)

In these societies, everyone works, and no group (or sex) has "special" duties. If the work is worth doing, then it is worth everyone's time and effort. Luciente, in Piercy's *Woman on the Edge of Time*, explains that the goal of work is the satisfaction of human needs, rather than an ever-increasing gross national product. Therefore, technology is used only for the work that no one wants to do. This does not mean, however, that no one works at jobs patriarchal society judges to be menial labor. The "kin" of Ata find that cultivating the soil enriches their dreams. Everyone on Le Guin's Anarres engages in tasks that directly meet people's material needs. Work itself is not seen as degrading or as drudgery, and therefore people do not have to be rewarded with money to do it. Instead, they work for intrinsic satisfaction and for the good of the group.

Only in Callenbach's Ecotopia do people still get paid for their work, but even in this society work is envisioned differently. No one is hired to work for anyone else. Everyone is hired as a partner and is actively engaged in the decision-making process of the factory, business, or school. The protagonist is amazed that workers often shut down plants to take a sauna or hold a party, and they are equally likely to come in on their own time to fix a broken machine. "Perhaps because of their part ownership of them, they seem to regard the plants as home, or at least as their own terrain" (p. 189).

Feminist utopias, therefore, not only challenge the division between the inhumane marketplace (the traditional male sphere) and the humane hearth (the traditional female sphere); they also reject the values of the patriarchal public sphere, in which human lives are sacrificed for abstract ideals or for the production of material goods. Utopian communities are human centered, like the home. Authors of these works, furthermore, make the continuity with the female experience explicit by comparing these societies to ideal families. Herland, for example, is "like a pleasant family—an old established, perfectly-run country place" (p. 238).

Just as they redefine the mother-child bond, the authors of these works create new family units, replacing the biologically based, hierarchical nuclear family with families of equals. These are not claustrophobic nuclear families, but relatively large extended families made up of people who freely choose to live together. Ecotopians still speak of "families," but they mean by that term "a group of between five and 20 people, some of them actually related and some not, who live together" (p. 82). Further, these families do not divide functions and roles into male and female roles. The narrator of Bryant's *The Kin of Ata* notes that there are words for male and female, but they are almost never used. Everyone is called simply "kin." Gender, in these works, is simply not an important differential between people. The narrators of *The Kin of Ata* and *Woman on the Edge of Time* have difficulty determining the sex of individuals. The explorers of Herland are shocked to realize that the women "don't seem to notice our being men. . . . They treat us well—just as they do one another. It's as if our being men was a minor incident" (p. 69).

These sexually, ethnically, and economically egalitarian families are the basic social unit. The communities are so small that everyone knows one another, or people live in a number of small groups, which function like extended families. In Russ's *The Female Man*, the groups consist of approximately thirty people. Often, as in Le Guin's *The Dispossessed* and Piercy's *Woman on the Edge of Time*, people live in small villages. Kinship networks between the families form the basic pattern of the larger social organization. There are no cities and no central governments; villages are deurbanized and decentralized. Odo, the female founder and planner of Le Guin's Anarres, saw "decentralization" as the "essential element."

> Though she suggested that the natural limit to the size of the community lay in its dependence on its own immediate region of essential food and power, she intended that all communities be connected by communication and transportation networks, so that goods and ideas could get where they were wanted, and the administration of things might work with speed and ease, and no community should be cut off from change and interchange. But the network was not to be run from the top down. There was to be no controlling center, no capital, no establishment for the self-perpetuating machinery of bureaucracy and the dominance of individuals seeking to become captains, bosses, chief of state. (p. 77)

In Piercy's novel, people rotate jobs every few years so that a person doing an "important" job will not begin to feel innately superior to anyone else. On Anarres, everyone, including brilliant scientists, perform the "menial" tasks necessary to survival; and in Ecotopia, people who plan to use a large quantity of wood work in the forest for a time to promote the growth of additional trees and to renew their awareness of the sacredness of the trees they use.

Except for Callenbach's Ecotopia, these societies are all cooperative anarchies, and Callenbach's society moves in an anarchist direction. Russ's Whileaway has "no government . . . [and] no place from which to control the entire activity of Whileaway." The utopian society described in *From the Legend of Biel* has a central unit, called Thoacdien: "Thoacdien suggests procedures. It does not give orders. It figures out the sanest possible course of action in a given situation by shuffling the circumstances with the possibilities. Then it offers conclusions and helps to articulate probability and ramification. It does not create law" (p. 28).

A citizen of Mizora notes, "In a country like ours, where civilization has reached that state of enlightenment that needs no laws, we are simply guided by custom" (p. 28). Ursula Le Guin writes in "Is Gender Necessary?" "To me the 'female principle' is, or at least historically has been, anarchic. It makes order without constraint, rule by custom, not by force. It has been the male who enforces order, who constructs power-structures, who makes, enforces, and breaks laws."[21] In *The Dispossessed,* she comments, "I think men mostly have to learn to be anarchists. Women don't have to learn" (p. 43).

Within small family units, decisions are made, when possible, by consensus. In Herland, decisions are made by a community family council. When faced with the threat of poverty and hunger because of overpopulation, the citizens call a meeting and agree by consensus to have only one child each in the future. When the people in Piercy's utopia do not agree, they keep talking until they do. Decisions are made by a town planning council, chosen by lot every year. In this ecologically conscious society, the town council also includes an "Earth Advocate" and an "Animal Advocate," which are chosen not "by lot, but by dream" (p. 143). Individuals are expected to practice civil disobedience if council decisions conflict with their values.

Order is kept in such societies not by the use of force, but by persuasion. And the enforcers act not as kings and legislators, but as mothers. Traditionally, mothers have been given the responsibility for caring for children and husbands; it has been their responsibility to socialize the children, and to guide the husband socially, emotionally, and spiritually. Except in the case of very young children, the mother cannot force her family to be guided by her perceptions; instead she convinces them that her advice is in their best interest.

In contrast to patriarchs, moreover, women have been socialized to rule not for their own benefit, but for the families they govern and serve. Trained to be nurturing helpmates, women find it easier than men to envision societies in which people cooperate, instead of compete, and nurture, instead of dominate one another. These positive aspects of traditional female conditioning cannot be maximized, however, until they have been separated from the negative aspects of female socialization, which encourage women to be dependent, passive, and self-sacrificing. Citizens of feminist utopias learn to be cooperative and nurturing, but not at the sacrifice of their own fulfillment or growth. All citizens—including mothers—are loved and nurtured as children ideally are, but they also are expected to be independent and responsible, and to nurture others.

The development of citizens in these feminist, anarchist societies is characterized by an almost total lack of restraints. The basic rule governing the mentors in *From the Legend of Biel* is noninterference. The mentor is to guide the charge without altering the basic, organic development of the child's potential. The plot of the novel centers on the difficulty Mikkran has in protecting her charge from harm without interfering with her journey. Biel takes off on a journey that includes, among other adventures, a trek through a desert and a confrontation with a hostile patriarchal tribe. Mikkran initially plays the martyr in order to avoid interfering with Biel's quest, but after she almost dies (from saving all the water and food for Biel during the journey), she learns that it is possible to give guidance without disrupting a child's natural growth and that she can best do so as an equal rather than as a master or a martyr. The mothers of Herland see the creation of children's games as one of the supreme achievements of the society, for children learn entirely through playing. In this way, the adults provide direction without limiting the children's natural exploration and experiment, and the children learn to be wise and productive adults by doing exactly what they wish. Time after time, explorers who discover feminist utopias marvel that they never heard a baby cry.

Such child-rearing practices result from the belief that the good of the individual and that of the group are not in conflict. Educated self-interest results in behavior that is nurturing to the individual and to others. The children of Ata, for example, are encouraged by example and by discussion to grow and experiment, but they are cautioned to avoid actions that could destroy or damage them. Their goal is to live according to their dreams; certain actions are not taboo, they are "denagdeo"—that is, "not productive of good, valuable, or enlightening dreams" (p. 67). Children in Piercy's utopia are schooled in both "inknowing" and "outknowing" (p. 103), for only when people have the skills to understand their own deepest needs does an anarchist ethic produce a nurturing and free society. Luciente notes, "We were born screaming Ow and I! The gift is in growing to care, to connect, to cooperate. Everything we learn aims to make us feel strong in ourselves, connected to all living. At home" (p. 241).

Although these works assume the romantic hypothesis that people prefer to be ethical beings, they do not romanticize human behavior. The kin of Ata have a low birthrate because children "are pure desire. And they must not be thwarted, for if they are they will never grow. . . . They must try everything, have everything—too many would destroy our way of life faster than any invasion from outside" (p. 152). People learn as much from their negative acts as from their positive ones. The narrator of *The Kin of Ata* learns that sexual love and commitment is preferable to lust by experiencing both. Contemporary feminist utopias are totally free of sexual taboos, except rape, yet Le Guin, Bryant, and Callenbach celebrate genuine and long-term relationships of intimacy and trust; and Piercy, Russ, and Staton clearly demonstrate a preference for sexuality based on respect and intellectual and emotional intimacy. Casual sex is seen as a lesser good.

People who commit acts of violence or thievery are assumed to be troubled rather than evil. The narrator of *Herland* expects punishment for violating the customs of Herland and finds he is treated as a "truant" and cared for by women who seem sympathetic to his truancy. The protagonist of *The Kin of Ata* accidentally kills a much revered old man (he has earlier killed a young woman) and discovers, to his surprise, that he is not punished. The kin perform a rite of purification over him and ask his forgiveness for wanting to hit him. However amazing such charitableness may seem, it appears to be good psychology in the novel, for the narrator chooses thereafter to avoid "denagdeo" acts. The citizens of Le Guin's Anarres are not quite so saintly. They have set up hospitals to help people who have committed violent acts, but in certain cases (such as rape) friends of the victim have been known to attack the criminal. *Woman on the Edge of Time* focuses on the relationship of the criminal to the victim. If one person hurts another, he or she is expected by custom to meet with the victim (or the family in the case of murder) and work out a way to atone. But if a person kills twice, he or she is executed.

Such approaches are based on the assumption that crime is bad for the perpetrator as well as for the victim and that people learn to avoid behavior that is damaging to them only by experimentation. Each utopia discussed here rejects the patriarchal view of the world as a battle ground in which opposing forces struggle for dominance. Instead of "conquering" or denying qualities that are seen as unproductive or evil, citizens in feminist works allow them to exist and by doing so dissipate the energy behind them. This is more than a manipulative way to make "sin" lose its appeal. Instead, it is based on a philosophical rejection of dualistic thinking. Le Guin asserts that the central problem of patriarchy that will spell its destruction is

> the problem of exploitation—exploitation of the woman, of the weak, of the earth. Our curse is alienation, the separation of Yang from Yin. Instead of a search for balance and integration, there is a struggle for dominance. Divisions [are] insisted upon, interdependence is denied. The dualism of value that destroys us, the dualism of superior/inferior, ruler/ruled, owner/owned, user/used, might give way to what seems to me, from here, a much healthier, sounder, more promising modality of integration and integrity.[22]

When Ecotopians stop seeing internal and external traits as "bad," "inferior," or in need of "taming" or "conquering," they must radically change their attitudes toward work. The first act of the Survivalist government is to institute a twenty-four hour work week. "What was at stake, informed Ecotopians insisted, was nothing less than the revision of the Protestant work ethic upon which America has been built." The economic consequences are immediate and severe. The gross national product declines sharply and consumption is curtailed, but the quality of life improves. "But the profoundest implications of the decreased work week were philosophical and ecological." People discovered that they were "not meant for production, as the 19th and early 20th centuries had believed. Instead, humans were meant to take their modest place in a seamless, stable-state web of living organisms, disturbing the web as little as possible." This goal becomes "an almost religious objective, perhaps akin to earlier doctrines of 'salvation.' People were to be happy not to the extent they dominated their fellow creatures on the earth, but to the extent they lived in balance with them" (p. 55).

Rather than repressing valuable human qualities in order to dominate nature and to increase production rates, citizens of feminist utopias strive to be fully human. The people in Lir, in Staton's *From the Legend of Biel,* develop an ethic based on becoming fully and freely themselves. They do not try to avoid disease; rather they "try to stay in balance": "We desire to be synchronized with ourselves, with each other, and with all that is neither." To accomplish this, they have learned that "equilibrium is a natural state for persons, and ultimately inevitable, once the screen of systems has been removed." Systems are "Basic Tenets, Constitutions, Morals, Law, Belief, Ethics—any construct which presumes to decide what is appropriate human behavior" (p. 297). Systems also dictate appropriate behavior to those who believe they design and control these systems.

> Since the dawn of human consciousness some persons have been in control of others—is the definition of a system. If, for whatever reason or end—paradise or nightmare—you are living in a system, you are either controlled or in control and therefore foolish, because you are essentially dead, unable even to recognize your own desire and capability to be positive and whole. In every system there are only slaves, because only slaves will maintain a system." (p. 298)

Coming home to the self, then, is based on an organic, anarchistic ethic of growth rather than a dualistic pattern of ownership, denial, and repression. The mothers of Herland, for example, "had no theory of the essential opposition of good and evil; life to them was Growth; their pleasure was in growing and their duty also" (p. 240). The people of the village of Lir *(From the Legend of Biel)* have no laws. Their morality is based on one question: "How do we manifest potential?" (p. 300). Process, accordingly, is as important as product. Shevek, in *The Dispossessed,* comes to recognize that "there was process: process was all. You could go in a promising direction or you could go wrong, but you did not set out with the expectation of ever stopping anywhere" (p. 268).

"How things are done" is seen as more important in *Woman on the Edge of Time* than what is done or how quickly it is done. Scurrying around to finish the dishes as quickly as possible to get it over with, the visitor from America stops short when he is told, "Our point of view is that if something's worth doing, it ought to be done in a way that's enjoyable—otherwise it can't really be worth doing." When he argues that washing dishes isn't fun, the others tell him, "Almost anything can be, if you keep your eye on the process and not on the goal" (p. 87). They tell stories, give back rubs, and joke with each other while doing the dishes. When the protagonist learns not to "focus on the task" and not to "blot out" the other people, he enjoys dishwashing perhaps for the first time in his life (p. 86). Connie is amazed at how much time is "wasted" on working through people's feelings and relationships between people. Luciente explains to her that the concern for human interaction and human feelings is efficient because "many actions fail because of inner tensions. To get revenge against someone an individual thinks wronged her, individuals have offered up nations to conquest. Individuals have devoted whole lives to pursuing vengeance. . . . The social fabric means a lot to us" (p. 189). Blotting out the human context for the sake of efficiency, she learns, is notably inefficient.

The citizens of such utopian communities learn to work without trying to short-circuit the processes of life. Shevek and Takver, in *The Dispossessed,* recognize that "the thing about working with time, instead of against it, is that it is not wasted. Even pain counts" (p. 269). The pain they feel about their long separation is part of the organic process of the development of their individual lives and their love for each other. If they were unwilling to experience this pain, they could not grow. The commitment to growth and to process counters an impulse to abstraction. The kin of Ata avoid writing down their sacred myths because they have discovered that to abstract "truth" out of experience freezes or kills it. Accordingly, they prefer an oral tradition, so that the myths might be enriched and altered by the dreams and interpretations of each storyteller.

The elimination of hierarchies and the reliance on an ethic of growth changes the spatial metaphors used to aid people in understanding the world. Shevek, the protagonist of Le Guin's *The Dispossessed,* visualizes the world differently from the patriarchal Urrasti. He wonders about "this curious matter of superiority and inferiority. Shevek knew that the concept of superiority, of relative height, was important to the Urrasti; they often used the word 'higher' as a synonym for 'better' in their writings, where the Anarressi would use 'more central' " (p. 12). The kin of Ata lay out their village in a spiral pattern and their buildings are circular; the communities of Anarres are cellular in organization. In *From the Legend of Biel,* the sacred symbol is a vertical infinity sign. The space enclosed symbolizes "what you know"; the space outside represents the unknown. The sign represents the capacity of the human brain "to embrace all concepts and all reality" (p. 174) when it frees itself from a belief in human power to "own mates, progeny, land, knowledge, or emotions" (p. 176).

Citizens of feminist utopias typically reject the assumptions behind terms like "abstract" and "objective." To know a phenomenon fully, people must recognize their interaction with the world. Further, they come to know outer phenomena best by combining reasoned analysis with intuitive understanding. Again, women's experience in patriarchal society undoubtedly contributes to this emphasis. Women have not been encouraged to abstract themselves out of experience and consequently have often developed the intuitive skills that patriarchal society denigrates as "women's intuition." The narrator of Russ's *The Female Man* comments that Jeannine (the traditional, oppressed woman) "is on very good terms with her ailanthus tree. Without having to reflect on it, without having to work at it, they both bring into human life the breath of magic and desire" (p. 108). The citizens of Ecotopia are emotional and playful, and do not dissociate intellect and emotion, mind and body. The reporter visiting the society notes that the Ecotopians "seem to enjoy their bodies tremendously" (p. 38); and they cry, laugh, and shout at one another in the most natural way.

The technology of feminist utopian societies is advanced, but unlike patriarchal science, it does not reflect opposition between people and nature, or mind and heart. Howard Scott, in Staton's novel, enters the "cerebral cortex" of the Thoacdien dome and feels beneath him "a large, benevolent heart which was glad he was here, and in beating, spoke to him" (p. 47). Technology resulting from a consciousness that fuses thought and feeling is also designed to work with natural processes. Citizens of Piercy's utopia explain, "our technology did not develop in a straight line from yours." Because they have no sense of either inner or outer as "Other," nothing is seen as foreign or different. "We have limited resources. We plan cooperatively. We can afford to waste nothing. You might say our—you'd say religion?—ideas make us see ourselves as partners with water, air, birds, fish, trees" (p. 118). Ecotopians "feel a little as the Indians must have felt: that the horse and the teepee and the bow and arrow all sprang, like the human being, from the womb of nature, organically." Their technology is more advanced than that of the Indians, but "they treat materials in the same spirit of respect, comradeship." The reporter visiting from America watches some carpenters mark and saw wood "lovingly." "They seemed almost to be collaborating with the wood, rather than forcing it into the shape of a building. . . . The Ecotopians do not feel 'separate' from their technology" (p. 60).

Thus, the holistic principles that enable people to use technology to work with the natural world rather than to conquer it produce societies that seem more pastoral and Edenic than futuristic. When Connie visits the utopian future in *Woman on the Edge of Time,* she is disappointed at seeing small, old-fashioned buildings and cows grazing. "You sure we went in the right direction? into the future?" (p. 62) she asks. Russ writes, "Whileaway is so pastoral that at times one wonders whether the ultimate sophistication may not take us all back to a kind of pre-Paleolithic dawn age, a garden without any artifacts except for what we would call miracles" (p. 14).

These societies seem familiar to the hero because they are patterned after the nurturing and humane institutions of the home, and because the hero experiences the change from patriarchy to feminist utopia not as a linear progress, but as a centering in. The focus of the society shifts from goals "out there" to the growth of each person. Both the male and the female hero discover that in reclaiming human values—and specifically in rejecting the macho denigration of female qualities —they are rejoined to the natural world and to each other. The transformation of the kingdom promised by the hero's return creates a macrocosmic family in which the hero feels, finally, at home.

Notes

Chapter 1: The Female Hero

1. See Joseph Campbell, *The Hero with a Thousand Faces* (New York: World Publishing Co., 1970); Lord Raglan, *The Hero: A Study in Tradition, Myth and Drama* (New York: Oxford Univ. Pr., 1937); Jessie Weston, *From Ritual to Romance* (Garden City, NY: Doubleday, 1957); and Dorothy Norman, *The Hero: Myth/Image/Symbol* (New York: New Amer. Lib., 1969).
2. Norman, *The Hero,* p. 12.
3. Carl Jung, *Man and His Symbols* (New York: Dell, 1968), p. 168.
4. Campbell, *The Hero with a Thousand Faces.*
5. Sigmund Freud, "On the Sexual Theories of Children" in *Standard Edition of the Complete Psychological Works of Sigmund Freud,* ed. by James Strachey, vol. 9 (London: Hogarth, 1964).
6. Campbell, *The Hero with a Thousand Faces,* p. 136. Note that Campbell's use of italics underscores his stereotyped assumptions about sex roles.
7. Herman Melville, *Moby Dick or, The Whale,* ed. by Charles Feidelson, Jr. (Indianapolis: Bobbs-Merrill, 1964), p. 221.
8. Norman, *The Hero,* p. 11.
9. Campbell, *The Hero with a Thousand Faces,* p. 337.
10. Bertolt Brecht, "Mother Courage and Her Children," in *Classics of the Modern Theater: Realism and After,* ed. by Alvin B. Kernan (New York: Harcourt, Brace and World, 1965), p. 356.
11. Alta, "#29," in *Theme and Variations* (San Lorenzo, CA: Shameless Hussy Pr., 1975), n.p.
12. Sheryll Patterson-Black, "Women Homesteaders on the Great Plains Frontier," *Frontiers* 1, no. 2 (Spring 1976): 68.
13. Lenore J. Weitzman and Diane M. Rizzo, "Images of Males and Females in Elementary School Textbooks in Five Subject Areas." (Old Westbury, NY: Feminist Pr., 1974), pp. 4–6.
14. Molly Haskell, *From Reverence to Rape: The Treatment of Women in the Movies* (Baltimore: Penguin, 1974), p. 370.
15. George Meredith, *The Egoist* (Boston: Houghton, 1958), p. 93.
16. Elizabeth Barrett Browning, "Aurora Leigh," in *The Complete Works of Elizabeth Barrett Browning,* ed. by Charlotte Porter and Helen A. Clarke, vol. 4 (New York: Crowell, 1900), p. 52.
17. Charlotte Brontë, *Shirley* (New York: Putnam, n.d.), p. 256.
18. Mary Daly, *Beyond God the Father: Toward a Philosophy of Women's Liberation* (Boston: Beacon, 1973), pp. 44–68, 47, 51.

19. Charles Portis, *True Grit* (New York: New Amer. Lib., 1968), p. 13.
20. Eliot Fremont-Smith, "Two Cheers for Mattie Ross," *New York Times,* June 12, 1968.
21. Haskell, *From Reverence to Rape,* p. xiv.
22. Portis, *True Grit,* p. 148–149.
23. Margaret Atwood, *The Edible Woman* (New York: Popular Lib., 1969), pp. 40–42.
24. Annis V. Pratt, "The New Feminist Criticism: Exploring the History of the New Space," in *Beyond Intellectual Sexism,* ed. by Joan Roberts (New York: McKay, 1976), pp. 182–183.
25. Isabella Bird, *A Lady's Life in the Rocky Mountains* (New York: Ballantine, 1960).
26. Joanna Russ, "What Can a Heroine Do? or, Why Women Can't Write" in *Images of Women in Fiction,* ed. by Susan Koppelman Cornillon (Bowling Green, OH: Bowling Green Univ. Popular Pr., 1972), p. 9.
27. Mary Wilkins Freeman, "The Revolt of Mother," in *The Revolt of Mother and Other Stories* (Old Westbury, NY: Feminist Pr., 1974), p. 122.
28. Florida Scott-Maxwell, "The Measure of My Days," in *Revelations: Diaries of Women,* ed. by Mary J. Moffat and Charlotte Painter (New York: Random, 1975), p. 363.
29. Virginia Woolf, *A Room of One's Own* (New York: Harcourt, Brace and World, 1929), p. 72.
30. George Gissing, *The Odd Women* (New York: Norton, 1971), p. 87.
31. Norman, *The Hero,* p. 23.
32. Campbell, *The Hero with a Thousand Faces,* pp. 337, 398.
33. Weston, *From Ritual to Romance,* pp. 113–136.
34. Germaine Greer, *The Female Eunuch* (New York: Bantam, 1971). Greer explains the deleterious effects on women of the idea that they are castrated men.

Chapter 2: The Mirror and the Cage

1. Joseph Campbell, *The Hero with a Thousand Faces* (Cleveland and New York: Meridian, 1956), p. 337.
2. Pearl Epstein, in *Monsters: Their Histories, Homes and Habits* (Garden City, NY: Doubleday, 1973), defines the monsters encountered in fairy tales as "guardians of cosmic secrets": "The hero must always conquer the symbolic [outer] beast and the one within himself [or herself] in order to gain the secret" (p. 18).
3. Doris Lessing, *The Four-Gated City* (New York: Bantam, 1970), p. 516.
4. Maya Angelou, *I Know Why the Caged Bird Sings* (New York: Bantam, 1971), p. 231.
5. Alfred Lord Tennyson, *The Princess: A Medley,* ed. by Charles Townstend Copeland and Henry Milnor Rideout (Chicago: Scott, Foresman, 1899), p. 121.
6. Emily Brontë, *Wuthering Heights: Text, Sources, Criticisms,* ed. by V. S. Pritchett (Boston: Houghton, 1956), p. 20.
7. Edna Stumpf, "You're Beautiful When You're Scared," *Metropolitan,* April 1974, p. 14.
8. D. H. Lawrence, *Women in Love* (New York: Modern Lib., 1920), pp. 168, 169–170.

9. Joan Didion, *Play It as It Lays* (New York: Bantam, 1971), pp. 22, 157.

10. Henry James, *The Portrait of a Lady* (New York: Norton, 1975), p. 367.

11. Tom Robbins, *Even Cowgirls Get the Blues* (Boston: Houghton, 1976), p. 130.

12. Samuel Richardson, *Clarissa; or, History of a Young Lady,* vol. 1 (London: Whittingham & Rowland, 1810), p. 80.

13. John Ruskin, "Of Queen's Gardens" in *Sesames and Lilies* (New York: Homewood, 1902), p. 143–144.

14. George Eliot, *Daniel Deronda* (New York: Harper and Brothers, 1876), p. 244.

15. Charlotte Brontë, *Jane Eyre* (New York: Harper, 1965), p. 104.

16. Marge Piercy, "A Work of Artifice," in *Liberation Now* (New York: Dell, 1971), p. 209.

17. Jean-Jacques Rousseau, *L'Emile: A Treatise on Education,* ed. by W. H. Payne (Boston: Ginn, Heath, 1906), p. 263.

18. Alta, "#74," in *Theme and Variations* (San Lorenzo, CA: Shameless Hussy Pr., 1975), n.p.

19. Erica Jong, "Alcestis on the Poetry Circuit," in *Half-Lives* (New York: Holt, 1973), p. 25.

20. Margaret Atwood, *Surfacing* (New York: Popular Lib., 1974), p. 194.

21. Mary Elizabeth Coleridge, "The Other Side of a Mirror," in *The World Split Open: Four Centuries of Women Poets in England and America, 1552–1950,* ed. by Louise Bernikow (New York: Vintage, 1974), p. 136.

22. Agnes Smedley, *Daughter of Earth* (Old Westbury, NY: Feminist Pr., 1973), pp. 15, 12.

23. George Eliot, *The Mill on the Floss* (New York: New Amer. Lib., 1965), pp. 69, 50.

24. Alice Munro, *Lives of Girls and Women* (New York: New Amer. Lib., 1974), p. 16.

25. Margaret Drabble, *The Ice Age* (New York: Knopf, 1977), p. 295.

26. Joanna Russ, *The Female Man* (New York: Bantam, 1975), p. 119.

27. Florida Scott-Maxwell, *The Measure of My Days* (New York: Knopf, 1968), p. 101.

28. Bram Dijkstra, "The Androgyne in Nineteenth-Century Art and Literature," *Comparative Literature* 26, no. 1 (Winter 1974): 62–73.

29. Charles Dickens, *The Old Curiosity Shop and Hard Times* (Boston: Estes and Laurait, 1953), pp. 596–597.

30. Quoted in George H. Ford, *Dickens and His Readers* (New York: Norton, 1965), p. 55. (Originally quoted in Heskell Pearson, *Oscar Wilde* [New York, 1946], p. 208.)

31. Jane Austen, *Emma* (New York: Airmont, 1966), p. 17.

32. Emily Dickinson, "What Soft, Cherubic Creatures," in *The Poems of Emily Dickinson,* ed. by Thomas H. Johnson (Cambridge, MA: Harvard Univ. Pr., 1955) p. 314.

33. Virginia Woolf, *A Room of One's Own* (New York: Harcourt, Brace and World, 1929), p. 51.

34. Jane Austen, *Pride and Prejudice & Sense and Sensibility* (New York: New Amer. Lib., 1950), p. 234.

35. Munro, *Lives of Girls and Women,* p. 147.

36. George Meredith, *The Egoist* (Boston: Houghton, 1958), p. 34.

37. James, *The Portrait of a Lady,* pp. 475, 451.

38. Margaret Drabble, *Thank You All Very Much* (New York: New Amer. Lib., 1965), p. 121.

39. R. D. Laing, *The Divided Self: An Existential Study in Sanity and Madness* (Baltimore: Penguin, 1972), p. 176.

40. Eliot, *The Mill on the Floss*, p. 305.

41. Elizabeth Gaskell, *Sylvia's Lovers* (New York: Dutton, 1971), p. 426.

42. Mary Daly, *Beyond God the Father: Toward a Philosophy of Women's Liberation* (Boston: Beacon, 1973), p. 77.

43. Elizabeth Tanfield Cary, "Chorus from Mariam," in *The Tragedie of Mariam, The Faire Queen of Jewrie*, Act 2 (London: Oxford Univ. Pr., 1914), n.p.

44. Nathaniel Hawthorne, "The Birthmark," in *The Portable Hawthorne* (New York: Viking, 1965), p. 169.

45. Munro, *Lives of Girls and Women*, p. 36.

46. Thomas Hardy, *Tess of the D'Urbervilles: A Pure Woman* (New York: Modern Lib., 1951), p. 126.

47. Oliver Goldsmith, *The Vicar of Wakefield* (New York: Houghton, 1901), p. 164.

48. Kate Millett, *Flying* (New York: Ballantine, 1974), pp. 10–11.

49. Angelou, *I Know Why the Caged Bird Sings*, p. 68.

50. Russ, *The Female Man*, p. 193.

51. Munro, *Lives of Girls and Women*, p. 100.

52. Joyce Carol Oates, *Wonderland* (Greenwich, CT: Fawcett, 1973), p. 295. See Germaine Greer, *The Female Eunuch* (New York: Bantam, 1971), for a full discussion of the connection between the myth of female inferiority and negative feelings about female genitalia.

53. Munro, *Lives of Girls and Women*, p. 138.

54. Thomas Hardy, *Jude the Obscure* (New York: Harper, 1966), p. 300.

55. Gen. 3:16, King James Version.

56. Donald Barthelme, *Snow White* (New York: Bantam, 1967), p. 70.

57. Faith Wilding, "Waiting," quoted in *Through the Flower: My Struggle as a Woman Artist*, by Judy Chicago (Garden City, NY: Doubleday, 1977), pp. 214–215.

58. Sylvia Ashton Warner, "Myself," in *Revelations: Diaries of Women*, ed. by Mary J. Moffat and Charlotte Painter (New York: Random, 1974), pp. 207–208, 212.

59. Angelou, *I Know Why the Caged Bird Sings*, p. 63.

60. Marge Piercy, *Small Changes* (Greenwich, CT: Fawcett, 1974), p. 36.

61. Erica Jong, *Fear of Flying* (New York: Holt, 1974).

62. Samuel Richardson, *Pamela; or, Virtue Rewarded*, vol. 1 (Stratford-upon-Avon: Shakespeare Head Pr., 1929), p. 45

63. Charlotte Brontë, *Jane Eyre*, p. 265.

64. Emily Carr, *Hundreds and Thousands* (Toronto: Clarke, Irwin, 1966), p. 223.

65. Joan Didion, *Slouching toward Bethlehem* (New York: Delta, 1968), pp. 29–30.

66. Barthelme, *Snow White*, pp. 69, 169, 180.

67. Jong, *Fear of Flying*, p. 101.

68. Charlotte Brontë, *Jane Eyre*, p. 423.

69. Denis de Rougemont, *Love in the Western World* (New York: Pantheon, 1959), p. 21.

70. Anne Finch, "The Unequal Fetters," in *Poems of Anne, Countess of Winchelsea*, ed. by Myra Reynolds (Chicago: Univ. of Chicago Pr., 1903), p. 22.

71. Alix Kates Shulman, *Memoirs of an Ex-Prom Queen* (New York: Bantam, 1973), p. 256.

72. Dorothy Parker, "Story of Mrs. W——," in *Not So Deep as a Well* (New York: Viking, 1943), p. 28.
73. Sylvia Plath, "The Applicant," in *Ariel* (New York: Harper, 1966), p. 5.
74. Robbins, *Even Cowgirls Get the Blues*, p. 63.
75. Elizabeth Bowen, *The Death of the Heart* (New York: Vintage, 1968), p. 317.
76. Smedley, *Daughter of Earth*, p. 189.
77. Erica Jong, *How to Save Your Own Life* (New York: Holt, 1977), p. 94.
78. Daniel Defoe, *Moll Flanders* (New York: Washington Square, 1966), p. 76.
79. James, *The Portrait of a Lady*, p. 407.
80. Jane Lazarre, *The Mother Knot* (New York: Dell, 1977), p. 24.
81. John Steinbeck, *The Grapes of Wrath* (New York: Viking, 1958), p. 619.
82. Virginia Woolf, *To the Lighthouse* (New York: Harcourt, Brace and World, 1927), p. 25.
83. Henry James, *The Sacred Fount* (London: Methuen, 1901), p. 34.
84. Woolf, *To the Lighthouse*, p. 59.
85. Anaïs Nin, *Diary of Anaïs Nin*, vol. 1, (New York: Harcourt, Brace and World, 1966), p. 27.
86. Russ, *The Female Man*, p. 47.
87. Drabble, *Thank You All Very Much*, p. 68.
88. Quoted in Clement Shorter, *The Brontës: Life and Letters*, vol. 1 (New York: Haskell House, 1964), p. 130.
89. Alta, *Momma: A Start on All the Untold Stories* (New York: Time Change Pr., 1974), pp. 30–31.
90. Lazarre, *The Mother Knot*, p. 118.
91. Elizabeth Stuart Phelps, "The Angel over the Right Shoulder" (Andover, MA: Propor, 1868), pp. 20–30.
92. Rebecca Harding Davis, "The Wife's Story," *Atlantic Monthly* 14 (July 1864): 172.
93. Phelps, "The Angel over the Right Shoulder," p. 6.
94. Alta, *Momma*, p. 8.
95. Grace Paley, "A Subject of Childhood," in *The Little Disturbances of Man* (New York: Doubleday, 1959), p. 145.
96. Nathaniel Hawthorne, *The Scarlet Letter* (New York: New Amer. Lib., 1959), pp. 112, 114, 200.
97. Tillie Olsen, "Tell Me a Riddle," in *Tell Me a Riddle and Other Stories* (Philadelphia and New York: Lippincott, 1961), p. 117.
98. Olsen, "I Stand Here Ironing," in *Tell Me a Riddle*, p. 88.
99. Margaret Drabble, *The Realms of Gold* (New York: Knopf, 1976), p. 4.
100. George Bernard Shaw, "Major Barbara," in *Drama in the Modern World: Plays and Essays*, ed. by Samuel A. Weiss (Boston: Heath, 1964), p. 133.
101. Shulman, *Memoirs of an Ex-Prom Queen*, p. 256.
102. Sophia Tolstoy, *The Diary of Tolstoy's Wife, 1860–1891*, trans. by Alexander Werth (London: Gollancz, 1928), p. 47.
103. Drabble, *The Realms of Gold*, p. 123.
104. Joyce Carol Oates, *Expensive People* (Greenwich, CT: Fawcett, 1968), p. 203.
105. Oates, *Wonderland*, p. 424.
106. Doris Lessing, "To Room Nineteen," in *To Room Nineteen: Collected Stories* (London: Jonathan Cape, 1978), p. 306.
107. Piercy, *Small Changes*, p. 28.
108. Charlotte Brontë, *Villette* (Philadelphia: Ashmead, n.d.), p. 80.

109. Dorothy Bryant, *Ella Price's Journal* (New York: New Amer. Lib., 1972), pp. 62, 72.
110. Eliot, *Daniel Deronda,* p. 241.
111. Lessing, *The Four-Gated City,* p. 4.
112. Defoe, *Moll Flanders,* p. 76.
113. Elizabeth Janeway, *Man's World, Woman's Place* (New York: Dell, 1972), p. 209.
114. Meredith, *The Egoist,* p. 163.
115. Emily Dickinson, "She Rose to His Requirement," in *The Poems of Emily Dickinson,* ed. by Thomas H. Johnson (Cambridge, MA: Harvard Univ. Pr., 1955), pp. 558–559.
116. Anne Sexton, "The Farmer's Wife," in *To Bedlam and Part Way Back* (Boston: Houghton, 1960), p. 27.
117. Evangeline Walton, *The Children of Llyr* (New York: Ballantine, 1971), p. 14.
118. George Bernard Shaw, *Arms and the Man* (New York: Bantam, 1968), p. 70.
119. Jane Howard, *A Different Woman* (New York: Dutton, 1973), p. 413.
120. Scott-Maxwell, *The Measure of My Days,* p. 102.
121. Nin, *Diary of Anaïs Nin,* p. 326.
122. Note that Daisy's husband Tom Buchanan, who also achieved mythic status as an athlete, is similarly portrayed as "careless" and even ruthless. In his case, however, the reader is not called on to join in the celebration of his mythic qualities. Indeed, we wonder what Daisy sees in him besides his wealth and confidence. Both Daisy and Tom are irresponsible because they simply act out the expected sex-role definition. That they are able to do so, of course, results from upper-class leisure.
123. F. Scott Fitzgerald, "The Last of the Belles," in *The Bodley Head Scott Fitzgerald,* vol. 2 (London: Bodley Head, 1959), p. 429.
124. Georgia Douglas Johnson, "A Paradox," in *The World Split Open: Four Centuries of Women Poets in England and America, 1552–1950,* ed. by Louise Bernikow (New York: Vintage, 1974), p. 264.
125. M. Esther Harding, *The Way of All Women* (New York: Harper, 1970), p. 17.
126. Adrienne Rich, "Snapshots of a Daughter-in-law," in *Poems: Selected and New, 1950–1974* (New York: Norton, 1975), p. 49.
127. Djuna Barnes, *Nightwood* (New York: New Directions, 1961), p. 121.
128. Nin, *Diary of Anaïs Nin,* p. 21.
129. Jong, *Fear of Flying,* p. 135.
130. John Fowles, *The French Lieutenant's Woman* (New York: New Amer. Lib., 1971), p. 354.
131. Meredith, *The Egoist,* pp. 167–168.
132. Joanna Field, *A Life of One's Own* (London: Chatto & Windus, 1934), p. 65.
133. Tolstoy, *The Diary of Tolstoy's Wife,* p. 43.
134. Piercy, *Small Changes,* p. 35.
135. Anaïs Nin, *House of Incest* (Denver: Swallow Press, 1958), p. 497.
136. Kate Wilhelm, *Abyss* (Garden City, NY: Doubleday, 1971), p. 22.
137. Edith Wharton, *The House of Mirth* (New York: Holt, 1962), p. 33.
138. Charlotte Perkins Gilman, *The Yellow Wallpaper* (Old Westbury, NY: Feminist Pr., 1973), p. 10.
139. This story is autobiographical. Instead of going mad, however, Gilman left her husband and pursued her writing.
140. Harriet Arnow, *The Dollmaker* (New York: Avon, 1974), p. 48.

141. Ruth Benedict, Journal entry October 1912, in *Revelations: Diaries of Women,* ed. by Mary J. Moffat and Charlotte Painter (New York: Random, 1974), p. 150.
142. Emily Carr, *Hundreds and Thousands* (Toronto: Clarke, Irwin, 1966), p. 223.
143. Nin, *House of Incest,* p. 497.

Chapter 3: Slaying the Dragon

1. Doris Lessing, *The Four-Gated City* (New York: Bantam, 1970) p. 375.
2. Doris Lessing, *The Golden Notebook* (New York: Simon & Schuster, 1962), p. 557.
3. Joanna Russ, *The Female Man* (New York: Bantam, 1975), p. 212.
4. Joanna Russ, lecture on *The Female Man,* delivered to Martin Bickman's class on science fiction at the University of Colorado, Boulder, Spring 1976.
5. Ursula Le Guin, *The Left Hand of Darkness* (New York: Ace Books, 1976), p. 147.
6. L. Frank Baum, *The Wizard of Oz* (Chicago: Reilly and Lee, 1966), p. 12. *The Wizard of Oz* is not explicitly a feminist work although Baum was influenced by the suffragist beliefs of his mother-in-law, Matilda Joselyn Gage. Its continued popularity with both children and adults, however, is undoubtedly due, in part, from the story's archetypal elements and from its satiric approach to patriarchal society. Accordingly, the Oz books "were banned in New York City during the McCarthy era and prohibited in the Detroit Public Library until 1973" (Washington *Post,* June 30, 1977).
7. Dorothy Sayers, *Gaudy Night* (New York: Avon, 1968), p. 383.
8. Margaret Atwood, *Lady Oracle* (New York: Simon & Schuster, 1976), p. 345.
9. Ibid., p. 169.

Chapter 4: The Exit from the Garden

1. Paul Roche, "What Makes Her Special?" in *To Tell the Truth* (London: Duckworth, 1967), pp. 52–53.
2. Vita Sackville-West, *All Passion Spent* (Garden City, NY: Doubleday, Doran, 1931), p. 58.
3. Constance Beresford-Howe, *The Book of Eve* (New York: Avon, 1973), p. 189.
4. May Sarton, *As We Are Now* (New York: Norton, 1973), p. 116.
5. Erica Jong, *How to Save Your Own Life* (New York: Holt, 1977), p. 189.
6. Mary Staton, *From the Legend of Biel* (New York: Ace Books, 1975), p. 298.
7. Vita Sackville-West, *The Edwardians* (Garden City, NY: Doubleday, Doran, 1930), p. 229.
8. Charlotte Perkins Gilman, *The Living of Charlotte Perkins Gilman: An Autobiography* (New York: Harper, 1963), p. 34.
9. Charlotte Brontë, *Jane Eyre* (New York: Harper, 1965), p. 254.
10. Marge Piercy, *Small Changes* (Greenwich, CT: Fawcett, 1974), p. 313.
11. Lewis Carroll, *Alice's Adventures in Wonderland and Through the Looking Glass* (New York: New Amer. Lib., 1960), p. 47.
12. Margaret Mead, *Blackberry Winter* (New York: Pocket Bks., 1975), n.p.
13. Anaïs Nin, *House of Incest* (Denver: Swallow Press, 1958), pp. 21–32.
14. Gilman, *The Living of Charlotte Perkins Gilman,* p. 97.

15. Adrienne Rich, "Prospective Immigrants Please Note," in *Adrienne Rich's Poetry*, sel. and ed. by Barbara Charlesworth Gelpi and Albert Gelpi (New York: Norton, 1975), p. 21.

16. Hilda Doolittle, "The Walls Do Not Fall," Part 43, *Trilogy: The Walls Do Not Fall; Tribute to the Angels; The Flowering of the Rod* (New York: New Directions, 1973), p. 59.

17. Jong, *How to Save Your Own Life*, p. 173.

18. Margaret Drabble, *The Realms of Gold* (New York: Knopf, 1976), p. 104.

19. Annie Dillard, *Pilgrim at Tinker Creek* (New York: Bantam, 1975), p. 35.

20. Beresford-Howe, *The Book of Eve*, p. 5.

21. Charlotte Brontë, *Villette* (London: Everyman's Lib., 1974), p. 37.

22. Rita Mae Brown, *Rubyfruit Jungle* (Plainfield, VT: Daughter, 1973), pp. 139, 167.

23. Anne Tyler, *Earthly Possessions* (New York: Popular Lib., 1978), p. 41.

24. Erica Jong, *Fear of Flying* (New York: New Amer. Lib., 1974), p. 47.

25. Brown, *Rubyfruit Jungle*, pp. 119–120.

26. Nin, *House of Incest*, p. 70.

27. Sylvia Plath, "Stings," in *Ariel* (New York: Harper, 1966), pp. 61–63.

28. Plath, "Lady Lazarus," in *Ariel*, p. 9.

29. Joseph Heller, *Catch-22* (New York: Dell, 1955), p. 414.

30. Dorothy Bryant, *Miss Giardino* (Berkeley, CA: Ata Books, 1978), p. 8.

31. Tom Robbins, *Even Cowgirls Get the Blues* (Boston: Houghton, 1976), p. 72.

32. Ibid., p. 41. According to a famous Buddhist parable, a Master of Kennin temple provided his protegé with a koan, asking him to meditate on the sound of one hand clapping. "For almost a year the student pondered what the sound of one hand might be," until he collected so many possible sounds he "could collect no more." Then he "entered true meditation and transcended all sounds," having found "the soundless sound" (Robert Sohl and Audrey Carr, eds., *The Gospel according to Zen: Beyond the Death of God* [New York: New Amer. Lib., 1970]).

33. Lisa Alther, *Kinflicks* (New York: New Amer. Lib., 1977), p. 1.

34. May Sarton, *Joanna and Ulysses* (New York: Norton, 1963), p. 113.

35. R. D. Laing, *The Politics of Experience* (New York: Pantheon, 1967), p. 75.

36. Sarton, *Joanna and Ulysses*, p. 127.

37. Evangeline Walton, *The Children of Llyr* (New York: Ballantine, 1971), p. 102.

38. Anaïs Nin, *Diary of Anaïs Nin*, vol. 1, ed. by Gunther Stuhlman (New York: Swallow Press, 1966), p. 40.

39. Boston Women's Health Collective, *Our Bodies, Ourselves: A Book by and for Women*, 2nd ed. (New York: Simon & Schuster, 1976), p. 20.

40. Molly Haskell, *From Reverence to Rape: The Treatment of Women in the Movies* (Baltimore: Penguin, 1974), p. 220.

41. Dorothy Bryant, *Ella Price's Journal* (New York: New Amer. Lib., 1972), p. 103.

42. Louisa May Alcott, *Work: A Story of Experience* (Boston: Little, n.d.), p. 425.

43. Bryant, *Ella Price's Journal*, p. 15.

44. Agnes Smedley, *Daughter of Earth* (Old Westbury, NY: Feminist Pr., 1973), p. 37.

45. Gilman, *The Living of Charlotte Perkins Gilman*, p. 34.

46. Doris Lessing, *The Four-Gated City* (New York: Bantam, 1970), p. 284.

47. Margaret Drabble, *Jerusalem the Golden* (New York: Popular Lib., 1977), p. 5.

48. Kate Millett, *Flying* (New York: Ballantine, 1974), p. 293.

49. Anne Sexton, "The Division of Parts," in *To Bedlam and Part Way Back* (Boston: Houghton, 1960), p. 37.

50. Anne Sexton, "The Double Image," in *To Bedlam and Part Way Back*, p. 55.
51. Alix Kates Shulman, *Memoirs of an Ex-Prom Queen* (New York: Bantam, 1973), p. 23.
52. Henry James, "Daisy Miller," in *The Great Short Novels of Henry James*, ed. with introd. by Philip Rahv (New York: Dial, 1974), p. 132.
53. Jane Austen, *Pride and Prejudice* (New York: Rinehart, 1949), p. 3.
54. Jane Austen, *Sense and Sensibility* (London: Martin Decker, 1930), p. 38.
55. Jacqueline Lapidus, "Coming Out," *Amazon Quarterly* 3, no. 2 (1975).
56. Marge Piercy, *Woman on the Edge of Time* (New York: Knopf, 1976), p. 41.
57. Tyler, *Earthly Possessions*, p. 200.
58. Alther, *Kinflicks*, p. 511.
59. Adrienne Rich, "Re-Forming the Crystal," in *Poems: Selected and New, 1950–1974* (New York: Norton, 1975), pp. 227–228.
60. Adrienne Rich, *Of Woman Born: Motherhood as Experience and Institution* (New York: Norton, 1976), p. 225.
61. Nancy Hardin, "An Interview with Margaret Drabble," *Contemporary Literature* 14, no. 3, p. 278.
62. Muriel Rukeyser, "More Clues," in *Breaking Open* (New York: Random, 1973), p. 23.
63. Millett, *Flying*, pp. 263–264.
64. Radicalesbian Collective, "The Woman-Identified Woman," in *Liberation Now* (New York: Dell, 1971), pp. 291–292.
65. Kate Chopin, *The Awakening* (New York: Avon, 1972), p. 16.
66. Bryant, *Ella Price's Journal*, p. 172.
67. Jane Lazarre, *The Mother Knot* (New York: Dell, 1977), p. 78.
68. Iris Murdoch, *The Unicorn* (New York: Avon, 1963), p. 67.
69. Jane Austen, *Emma* (New York: Airmont, 1966), p. 17.
70. Marilyn French, *The Women's Room* (New York: Harcourt, 1978), p. 5.
71. Doris Lessing, *The Summer before the Dark* (New York: Knopf, 1973), p. 178.
72. Nin, *Diary of Anaïs Nin*, vol. 1, pp. 52, 76.
73. Maya Angelou, *I Know Why the Caged Bird Sings* (New York: Bantam, 1971), p. 45.
74. Nathaniel Hawthorne, "Rappacini's Daughter," in *Great Short Works of Nathaniel Hawthorne*, ed. by Frederick C. Crews (New York: Harper, 1967), p. 350.
75. Emily Carr, *Hundreds and Thousands* (Toronto: Clarke, Irwin, 1966), p. 86.
76. Sylvia Plath, "The Colossus," in *The Colossus and Other Poems* (New York: Knopf, 1962), p. 20.
77. Plath, "Daddy," in *Ariel*, p. 51.
78. Mary Shelley, *Frankenstein or, The Modern Prometheus* (New York: Dell, 1974), p. 131.
79. Madeleine L'Engle, *A Wrinkle in Time* (New York: Dell, 1978), pp. 52–53.
80. Erica Jong, *How to Save Your Own Life* (New York: Holt, 1977), p. 56.
81. Piercy, *Small Changes*, p. 41.
82. Margaret Atwood, *The Edible Woman* (New York: Popular Lib., 1976), p. 277.
83. Jong, *How to Save Your Own Life*, p. 106.
84. Doris Lessing, *Martha Quest*, in Children of Violence, vol. 1 (New York: Simon & Schuster, 1964), p. 243.
85. Bryant, *Ella Price's Journal*, p. 99.
86. Henrik Ibsen, *A Doll's House: Six Plays by Henrik Ibsen*, trans. by Eva LeGallienne (New York: Modern Lib., 1957), p. 77.

87. George Eliot, *Middlemarch*, ed. with introd. and notes by Gordon S. Haight (Boston: Houghton, 1968), p. 21.
88. George Meredith, *The Egoist* (Boston: Houghton, 1958), pp. 164, 250.
89. Joyce Carol Oates, *Wonderland* (Greenwich, CT: Fawcett, 1973), p. 476.
90. Lessing, *The Four-Gated City*, p. 405.
91. William Faulkner, *Light in August* (New York: Modern Lib., 1950), p. 100.
92. Dylan Thomas, "Ballad of the Long-Legged Bait," in *The Collected Poems of Dylan Thomas* (New York: New Directions, 1957), p. 170.
93. Robert Browning, "Porphyria's Lover," in *Shorter Poems* (New York: Crofts, 1934), pp. 29–30.
94. Norman Mailer, "The Time of Her Time," in *Advertisements for Myself* (New York: Putnam, 1969), p. 465.
95. French, *The Women's Room*, p. 41.
96. Lessing, *The Summer before the Dark*, p. 52.
97. Alice Munro, *Lives of Girls and Women* (New York: New Amer. Lib., 1974), p. 150.

Chapter 5: The Emperor's New Clothes

1. Alix Kates Shulman, *Memoirs of an Ex-Prom Queen* (New York: Bantam, 1973), p. 80.
2. Charlotte Brontë, *Villette* (Philadelphia: Ashmead, n.d.), p. 48.
3. Margaret Atwood, *Surfacing* (New York: Popular Lib., 1974), p. 23.
4. Tom Robbins, *Even Cowgirls Get the Blues* (Boston: Houghton, 1976), p. 227.
5. Doris Lessing, *The Golden Notebook* (New York: Ballantine, 1971), p. 302.
6. Ellen Glasgow, *Barren Ground* (New York: Hill & Wang, 1957), p. 1.
7. Willa Cather, *O Pioneers* (Boston: Houghton, 1938), p. 8.
8. George Gissing, *The Odd Women* (New York: Norton, 1971), p. 37.
9. Alice Munro, *Lives of Girls and Women* (New York: New Amer. Lib., 1974), pp. 169, 171.
10. Doris Lessing, *The Four-Gated City* (New York: Bantam, 1970), p. 302.
11. Muriel Rukeyser, "Mortal Girl," in *The American Tradition of Literature*, 3rd ed., ed. by Sculley Bradley, Richmond C. Beatty, and E. Hudson Long (New York: Norton, 1967), pp. 1834–1835.
12. Munro, *Lives of Girls and Women*, p. 181.
13. Thomas Pynchon, *The Crying of Lot 49* (New York: Bantam, 1967), p. 5.
14. Emily Brontë, *Wuthering Heights* (Boston: Riverside Pr., 1956), p. 70.
15. Munro, *Lives of Girls and Women*, p. 168.
16. Samuel Richardson, *Clarissa; or, The History of a Young Lady*, 8 vols. (London: Whittingham & Rowland, 1810), p. 80.
17. Leslie Fiedler, *Love and Death in the American Novel* (Cleveland: World, 1962), p. 45.
18. Thomas Hardy, *Tess of the D'Urbervilles: A Pure Woman* (New York: Modern Lib., 1951), p. 18.
19. Charlotte Brontë, *Jane Eyre* (New York: Houghton, 1959), p. 429.
20. Kate Chopin, *The Awakening* (New York: Avon, 1972), p. 16.
21. Anne Zoltan, *Annie: The Female Experience* (New York: Julian, 1973), p. 90.
22. Carolyn Heilbrun, "The Woman as Hero," *Texas Quarterly* 8, no. 4 (1965): 136
23. John Barth, *The End of the Road* (New York: Grosset, 1969), p. 187.

24. Ken Kesey, *Sometimes a Great Notion* (New York: Viking, 1964), p. 62.
25. Erica Jong, *Fear of Flying* (New York: New Amer. Lib., 1973), p. 39.
26. Adrienne Rich, "Re-forming the Crystal," *Poems: Selected and New 1950–1974* (New York: Norton, 1975), pp. 227–228.
27. Geoffrey Chaucer, "The Canterbury Tales" in *The Works of Geoffrey Chaucer*, ed. by F. N. Robinson (Boston: Houghton, 1957), p. 80.
28. George Bernard Shaw, *Mrs. Warren's Profession* (New York: Brentano's, 1913), pp. 33–34.
29. Thomas Hardy, "The Ruined Maid," in *Collected Poems* (New York: Macmillan, 1925), p. 132.
30. D. H. Lawrence, *The Rainbow* (New York: Viking, 1964), p. 493.
31. M. Esther Harding, *Woman's Mysteries: Ancient and Modern* (New York: Bantam, 1971), p. 121.

Chapter 6: A Woman is Her Mother

1. Joseph Campbell, *The Hero with a Thousand Faces* (New York: The World Publishing Co., 1979), p. 136. "When the child outgrows the popular idyll of the mother breast and turns to face the world of specialized adult action, it passes, spiritually, into the sphere of the father—who becomes, for his son, the sign of the future task, and for his daughter, of the future husband. Whether he knows it or not and no matter what his position in society, the father is the initiating priest through whom the young being passes on into the larger world. And just as, formerly, the mother represented the 'good' and 'evil,' so now does he, but with this complication—that there is a new element of rivalry in the picture: the son against the father for the mastery of the universe, and the daughter against the mother to be the mastered world."
2. Kurt Vonnegut, Jr., *Breakfast of Champions or Goodbye, Blue Monday* (New York: Delacorte Pr., Seymour Lawrence, 1973), p. 263.
3. Fanny Burney, *Evelina; or, The History of a Young Lady's Entrance into the World* (New York: Norton, 1965), p. 354.
4. Adrienne Rich, *Of Woman Born: Motherhood as Experience and Institution* (New York: Norton, 1976), pp. 237–238.
5. Evangeline Walton, *The Children of Llyr* (New York: Ballantine, 1971), p. 185.
6. Joanna Russ, "The Autobiography of My Mother," *Epoch*, Fall 1975, p. 87.
7. Jane Howard, *A Different Woman* (New York: Dutton, 1973), p. 413.
8. Jessamyn West, *The Woman Said Yes: Encounters with Life and Death* (New York and London: Harcourt, 1976), p. 5.
9. Joanna Russ, "Daddy's Girl," *Epoch* 24, no. 2 (Winter 1975): 151.
10. Doris Lessing, *Memoirs of a Survivor* (New York: Bantam, 1976), p. 49.
11. Charles Moulton, *Wonder Woman*, introd. by Gloria Steinem (New York: Holt, 1972), n.p.
12. Erica Jong, *Fear of Flying* (New York: New Amer. Lib., 1974), p. 20.
13. Charlotte Brontë, *Jane Eyre* (New York: Harper, 1965), p. 309.
14. Sylvia Plath, "The Moon and the Yew Tree," in *Ariel* (New York: Harper, 1966), p. 41.
15. Doris Lessing, *The Golden Notebook* (New York: Ballantine, 1962), pp. 403–404.
16. Jong, *Fear of Flying*, p. 198.

17. Carolina Maria de Jesus, *Child of the Dark: The Diary of Carolina Maria de Jesus,* trans. by David St. Clair (New York: Dutton, 1962), p. 57.
18. Elizabeth Gurley Flynn, *The Rebel Girl: An Autobiography* (New York: International, 1974), p. 266.
19. George Meredith, *The Egoist* (Boston: Houghton, 1958), p. 154.
20. Daniel Defoe, *Moll Flanders* (New York: Washington Square, 1966), pp. 274–349.
21. Adrienne Rich, "Like This Together," in *Adrienne Rich's Poetry,* sel. and ed. by Barbara Charlesworth Gelpi and Albert Gelpi (New York: Norton, 1975), pp. 26–27.
22. Charlotte Brontë, *Shirley* (New York and London: Harper, 1900), p. 229.
23. Maya Angelou, *I Know Why the Caged Bird Sings* (New York: Bantam, 1971), p. 50.
24. Maxine H. Kingston, *The Woman Warrior: Memoirs of a Girlhood among Ghosts* (New York: Vintage, 1977), p. 24.
25. Jong, *Fear of Flying,* p. 147.
26. Tillie Olsen, "Tell Me a Riddle," in *Tell Me a Riddle and Other Stories* (New York: Dell, 1965), p. 146.
27. Lisa Alther, *Kinflicks* (New York: New Amer. Lib., 1977), pp. 430–431.
28. Margaret Drabble, *Jerusalem the Golden* (New York: Popular Lib., 1977), p. 241.
29. Celia Fremlin, "Don't Be Frightened," in *Ms. Mysteries,* ed. by Arthur Lieberman (New York: Washington Square, 1976), p. 58.
30. Alice Brown, "The Way of Peace," in *Tiverton Tales* (Boston and New York: Houghton, 1899), p. 180.
31. George Bernard Shaw, *Mrs. Warren's Profession* (New York: Brentano's, 1913), p. 82.
32. Russ, "The Autobiography of My Mother," p. 87.
33. Anne Sexton, "Housewife," in *All My Pretty Ones* (Boston: Houghton, 1962), p. 48.
34. Jong, *Fear of Flying,* p. 147.
35. Russ, "The Autobiography of My Mother," p. 95.
36. Joan Didion, *Play It as It Lays* (New York: Bantam, 1971), p. 61.
37. Marge Piercy, *Woman on the Edge of Time* (New York: Knopf, 1976), p. 56.
38. Jong, *Fear of Flying,* p. 46.
39. Dorothy Bryant, *Ella Price's Journal* (New York: New Amer. Lib., 1972), p. 157.
40. Jong, *Fear of Flying,* p. 46.
41. Nathaniel Hawthorne, *The Scarlet Letter* (New York: New Amer. Lib., 1959), p. 159.
42. Margaret Drabble, *Thank You All Very Much* (New York: New Amer. Lib., 1965), p. 9.
43. Rich, *Of Woman Born,* p. 64.
44. Jane Lazarre, *The Mother Knot* (New York: Dell, 1977), p. 159.
45. Marge Piercy, *Small Changes* (Greenwich CT: Fawcett, 1974), p. 511.
46. Besmilr Brigham, "Tell Our Daughters," in *31 New American Poets,* ed. by Ron Schreiber (New York: Hill & Wang, 1969), p. 17.
47. Anne Sexton, "Little Girl, My String Bean, My Lovely Woman," in *Live or Die* (Boston: Houghton, 1966), p. 62.
48. Judy Chicago, *Through the Flower: My Struggle as a Woman Artist* (Garden City, NY: Doubleday, 1977), p. 139.

49. Lazarre, *The Mother Knot,* p. 24.

50. Margaret Atwood, *Surfacing* (New York: Popular Lib., 1976), p. 124.

51. See Adrienne Rich, *Of Woman Born,* for a discussion of obstetrics and the resulting sense of alienation of the mother from the childbearing process.

52. Atwood, *Surfacing,* p. 173.

53. Margaret Drabble, *The Realms of Gold* (New York: Knopf, 1976), p. 121.

54. Virginia Woolf, *To the Lighthouse* (New York: Harcourt, Brace and World, 1927), p. 29.

55. Nancy Reeves, *Womankind* (Chicago: Aldine, 1971), p. 29.

56. Chicago, *Through the Flower,* pp. 205–206.

57. Evelyn Hinz, "The Creative Critic," *Celebration with Anaïs Nin,* ed. by Valerie Harms (Riverdale, CT: Magic Circle Pr., 1973), p. 59.

58. Claudia Van Gerven, "Virginia Woolf: The Style of Contextuality" (Paper written for Carol Pearson's seminar on women writers, University of Colorado, Boulder, Spring 1976).

59. Virginia Woolf, *Mrs. Dalloway* (New York: Harcourt, Brace, 1925), p. 54.

60. Anaïs Nin, *Diary of Anaïs Nin,* vol. 2 (New York: Swallow Press, 1966), p. 174.

61. Virginia Woolf, *A Room of One's Own* (New York: Harcourt, Brace and World, 1929), p. 4.

Chapter 7: The New Family

1. Florida Scott-Maxwell, *The Measure of My Days* (New York: Knopf, 1968), pp. 76–77.

2. Joanna Field, *A Life of One's Own* (London: Chatto & Windus, 1934), p. 87.

3. Virginia Woolf, *A Writer's Diary,* ed. by Leonard Woolf (New York: Harcourt, 1954), p. 230.

4. R. D. Laing, *The Divided Self: An Existential Study in Sanity and Madness* (Baltimore: Penguin, 1972), p. 205.

5. Anne Sexton, "Kind Sir: These Woods," in *To Bedlam and Part Way Back* (Boston: Houghton, 1960), p. 5.

6. Marge Piercy, *Small Changes* (Greenwich, CT: Fawcett, 1974), p. 47.

7. Jean Tepperman, "Witch," in *Who Am I This Time? Female Portraits in British and American Literature,* ed. by Carol Pearson and Katherine Pope (New York: McGraw-Hill, 1976), p. 297.

8. Ben L. Reitman, *Sister of the Road: The Autobiography of Box-Car Bertha,* as told to Dr. Ben L. Reitman (New York: Harper, 1937), p. 280.

9. Iris Murdoch, *Flight from the Enchanter* (New York: Viking, 1956), p. 305.

10. Ann Spencer, "Letter to My Sister," in *The World Split Open: Four Centuries of Women Poets in England and America, 1552–1950,* ed. by Louise Bernikow (New York: Vintage, 1974), pp. 265–266.

11. Margaret Drabble, *The Realms of Gold* (New York: Knopf, 1976), p. 29.

12. Grant Allen, *The Woman Who Did* (Boston: Roberts Bros., 1895), p. 219.

13. Louisa May Alcott, *Little Women* (Boston: Little, 1911), p. 236.

14. George Eliot, *Middlemarch,* ed. with introd. and notes by Gordon S. Haight (Boston: Houghton, 1968), pp. 612–613.

15. Erica Jong, *Fear of Flying* (New York: New Amer. Lib., 1973), pp. 25–26.

16. Field, *A Life of One's Own*, p. 65.
17. Katherine Mansfield, *Letters of Katherine Mansfield to John Middleton Murray* (New York: Knopf, n.d.), p. 104.
18. Anaïs Nin, *Diary of Anaïs Nin*, vol. 1 (New York: Harcourt, Brace and World, 1966), p. 8.
19. Anaïs Nin, *House of Incest* (Denver: Swallow Press, 1958), pp. 70–71.
20. Emily Brontë, "No Coward Soul Is Mine," in *Emily Brontë: Her Life and Work*, ed. by Muriel Spark and Derek Stanford (London: Peter Owen, 1960), pp. 227–228.
21. Loran Hurnscot, *A Prison, A Paradise*, vol. 2 (New York: Viking, 1959), p. 47.
22. May Sarton, *Mrs. Stevens Hears the Mermaids Singing* (New York: Norton, 1965), p. 169.
23. Joan Didion, *Play It as It Lays* (New York: Bantam, 1971), pp. 22, 157.
24. Annie Dillard, *Pilgrim at Tinker Creek* (New York: Bantam, 1975), p. 278.
25. Eudora Welty, "A Worn Path," in *Women and Fiction: Short Stories by and about Women*, ed. by Susan Cahill (New York: New Amer. Lib., 1975), p. 100.
26. Emily Carr, *Hundreds and Thousands* (Toronto: Clarke, Irwin, 1966), p. 50.
27. Robert Graves, "The Great Grandmother," in *Collected Poems (1914–1947)*, (London: Cassell, 1948), p. 166.
28. Ursula Le Guin, "The Day before the Revolution," in *More Women of Wonder*, ed. by Pamela Sargent (New York: Vintage, 1976), p. 301.
29. Scott-Maxwell, *The Measure of My Days*, p. 65.
30. Helen Hunt Jackson, "Emigravit," in *The World Split Open*, p. 211.
31. Ednah D. Cheney, *Louisa May Alcott: Her Life, Letters and Journals* (Boston: Little, 1919), p. 36.
32. Scott-Maxwell, *The Measure of My Days*, p. 24.
33. Dorothy Richardson, *Pilgrimage*, vol. 1 (New York: Knopf, 1967), p. 149.
34. Virginia Woolf, *To the Lighthouse* (New York: Harcourt, Brace and World, 1927), pp. 97–98.
35. Mary Wilkins Freeman, "A New England Nun," in *Best Stories of Mary Wilkins Freeman* (New York: Harper, 1927), p. 79.
36. Kate Chopin, "The Story of an Hour," in *The Complete Works of Kate Chopin*, vol. 1, ed. by Per Seyersted (Baton Rouge, LA: Louisiana State Univ. Pr., 1969), pp. 352–354.
37. Charlotte Brontë, *Villette* (Philadelphia: Ashmead, n.d.), p. 520.
38. Carolina Maria de Jesus, *Child of the Dark: The Diary of Carolina Maria de Jesus*, trans. by David St. Clair (New York: Dutton, 1962), p. 35.
39. Katherine Mansfield, *Journal of Katherine Mansfield*, ed. by John Middleton Murray (New York: Knopf, 1927), pp. 251–255.
40. Sarton, *Mrs. Stevens Hears the Mermaids Singing*, p. 182.
41. Carolyn Rodgers, "i have changed so much in this world," in *how i got ovah: new and selected poems* (Garden City, NY: Doubleday, 1976), p. 4.
42. Tom Robbins, *Even Cowgirls Get the Blues* (Boston: Houghton, 1976), p. 172.
43. Margaret Atwood, *Surfacing* (New York: Popular Lib., 1974), pp. 222–223.
44. William Faulkner, *Light in August* (New York: Modern Lib., 1950), p. 480.
45. Willa Cather, *My Mortal Enemy* (New York: Vintage, 1954), p. 76.
46. Thomas Carlyle, *On Heroes, Hero Worship and the Heroic in History*, vol. 5, in the *Works of Thomas Carlyle*, 30 vols., ed. by H. D. Traill (New York: AMS Pr., 1969), p. 69.
47. Woolf, *To the Lighthouse*, p. 98.

48. Thomas Hardy, *The Return of the Native* (London: Macmillan, 1975), p. 58.
49. Tennessee Williams, "The Mattress by the Tomato Patch," in *Hard Candy* (New York: New Directions, 1967), pp. 147–161.
50. Henry James, "The Beast in the Jungle," in *The Turn of the Screw and Other Novels*, ed. by William Thorp (New York: New Amer. Lib., 1962), p. 450.
51. Somerset Maugham, "The Colonel's Lady," in *W. Somerset Maugham: Four Short Stories* (Kansas City, MO: Hallmark, 1970), pp. 34–62.
52. Edwin Arlington Robinson, "The Tree in Pamela's Garden," in *The American Tradition in Literature*, 3rd ed., ed. by Sculley Bradley, Richmond C. Beatty, and E. Hudson Long (New York: Norton, 1967), p. 1370.
53. Robbins, *Even Cowgirls Get the Blues*, p. 120.
54. Adrienne Rich, *Women and Honor: Some Notes on Lying* (Pittsburgh: Motheroot Publns., 1977), pp. 7–9.
55. May Sarton, *Kinds of Love* (New York: Norton, 1970), p. 563.
56. Alta, "#35," in *Theme and Variations* (San Lorenzo, CA: Shameless Hussy Pr., 1975), n.p.
57. Kate Millett, *Flying* (New York: Knopf, 1974), p. 211.
58. George Meredith, *The Egoist* (Boston: Houghton, 1958), p. 291.
59. Angela Davis, *With My Mind on Freedom: An Autobiography* (New York: Bantam, 1975), p. 54.
60. Robbins, *Even Cowgirls Get the Blues*, p. 350.
61. Margaret Drabble, *Thank You All Very Much* (New York: New Amer. Lib., 1965), p. 96. Originally published as *The Millstone*.
62. Lucille Clifton, "Sister," in *An Ordinary Woman* (New York: Random, 1974), p. 5.
63. Louisa May Alcott, *Little Women* (Boston: Little, 1915), p. 505.
64. Doris Lessing, *The Golden Notebook* (New York: Ballantine, 1968), p. 450.
65. Anne Zoltan, *Annie: The Female Experience* (New York: Julian, 1973), p. 151.
66. Scott-Maxwell, *The Measure of My Days*, p. 102.
67. Alta, "#19," in *Theme and Variations*, n.p.
68. Mary Elizabeth Coleridge, "Regina," in *The World Split Open*, p. 140.
69. Paula Reingold, "And This Is Love," in *I Hear My Sisters Saying*, ed. by Carol Konek and Dorothy Walters (New York: Crowell, 1976), p. 36.
70. Judy Chicago, *Through the Flower: My Struggle as a Woman Artist* (Garden City, NY: Doubleday, 1977), p. 219.
71. Robin Morgan, *Going Too Far: A Personal Chronicle of a Feminist* (New York: Random, 1977), p. 314.
72. Carlos Castaneda, *Tales of Power* (New York: Simon & Schuster, 1974), p. 27.
73. Adrienne Rich, *Of Woman Born: Motherhood as Experience and Institution* (New York: Norton, 1976), pp. 59–62.
74. Bette Greene, *Philip Hall Likes Me, I Reckon Maybe* (New York: Dial, 1974), pp. 134–135.
75. Zenna Henderson, *Pilgrimage: The Book of The People* (New York: Avon, 1950), p. 209.
76. Dorothy Bryant, *Ella Price's Journal* (New York: New Amer. Lib., 1972), p. 107.
77. Henderson, *Pilgrimage*, p. 221.
78. Robbins, *Even Cowgirls Get the Blues*, p. 357.
79. "Poems from Holloway Prison," in *The World Split Open*, p. 147.
80. Louisa May Alcott, *Work: A Story of Experience* (New York: Schocken, 1977), p. 442.

81. Muriel Rukeyser, "Käthe Kollwitz," in *No More Masks: An Anthology of Poems by Women,* ed. by Florence Howe and Ellen Bass (Garden City, NY: Doubleday, 1972), p. 103.

82. George Bernard Shaw, *Saint Joan* (Baltimore: Penguin, 1951), pp. 110–113.

83. Davis, *With My Mind on Freedom,* p. 48.

84. Morgan, *Going Too Far,* p. 289.

85. Adrienne Rich, "Planetarium," in *Adrienne Rich's Poetry,* sel. and ed. by Barbara Charlesworth Gelpi and Albert Gelpi (New York: Norton, 1975), p. 46.

86. Adrienne Rich, "Diving into the Wreck," in *Adrienne Rich's Poetry,* p. 67.

87. Muriel Rukeyser, "The Poem as Mask," in *By a Woman Writ: Literature from Six Centuries by and about Women,* ed. by Joan Goulianos (Baltimore: Penguin, 1974), p. 379.

88. Jong, *Fear of Flying,* p. 67.

89. Kurt Vonnegut, Jr., *Sirens of Titan* (New York: Delacorte Pr., 1959), p. 132.

90. Katherine Mansfield, *Novels and Novelists,* ed. by J. Middleton Murray (Boston: Beacon, 1959), p. 302.

91. Benjamin Franklin, "The Speech of Polly Baker," in *The American Tradition in Literature,* p. 157.

92. John Davidson, "A Ballad of Hell," in *How Does a Poem Mean?* ed. by John Ciardi (Boston: Houghton, 1959), pp. 700–702.

93. Mary Daly, *Gyn/Ecology: The Metaethics of Radical Feminism* (Boston: Beacon, 1978), p. 15.

94. Elizabeth Bishop, "Invitation to Miss Marianne Moore," in *The Complete Poems* (New York: Farrar, 1969), pp. 94–96.

95. Susan Sutheim, "For Witches," in *No More Masks: An Anthology of Poems by Women,* ed. by Florence Howe and Ellen Bass (Garden City, NY: Doubleday, 1973), p. 297.

96. Madeleine L'Engle, *A Wind in the Door* (New York: Dell, 1978), p. 148.

Chapter 8: The Kingdom Transfigured

1. Diane Di Prima, "Revolutionary Poem #19," *Revolutionary Letters* (San Francisco: City Lights, 1971), n.p.

2. D. H. Lawrence, *The Rainbow* (New York: Viking, 1964), p. 493. *The Rainbow* is Lawrence's best treatment of a female protagonist and lacks the sexism that characterizes many of his other works, for example, *Lady Chatterley's Lover.*

3. Mary Bradley Lane, *Mizora: A Prophecy* (Boston: Gregg, 1975).

4. Charlotte Perkins Gilman, *Herland,* serialized in *The Forerunner* 6 (1915).

5. Joanna Russ, *The Female Man* (New York: Bantam, 1975).

6. Dorothy Bryant, *The Kin of Ata Are Waiting for You* (New York: Random, 1976). Originally published as *The Comforter* (New York: Moon Books, 1971).

7. Mary Staton, *From the Legend of Biel* (New York: Ace Books, 1975).

8. Ursula Le Guin, *The Dispossessed* (New York: Avon, 1975).

9. Ernest Callenbach, *Ecotopia: The Notebooks and Reports of William Weston* (New York: Bantam, 1975).

10. Marge Piercy, *Woman on the Edge of Time* (New York: Knopf, 1976).

11. Since feminist utopias are attempts to envision societies where all people can be more fully themselves, it is no surprise that the issues they address are those that have concerned social reformers and utopian theorists since the last half of

the eighteenth century. Communalism was perhaps the most important ideal of the nineteenth century. The true community, which was seen as dynamic rather than static, was expected to encourage individual freedom. Group cooperation was to occur not through dominance and control but through the voluntary support of its citizens, who were to see its goals as synonymous with their own. The present chapter does not discuss works such as Thomas Berger's *A Regiment of Women,* which feature sex-role reversal and the oppression of men by women. It focuses rather on works that either present all-female worlds or advocate complete equality between the sexes.

Many of the ideas and examples in this chapter appeared in Carol Pearson, "Women's Fantasies and Feminist Utopias," *Frontiers: A Woman Studies Journal* 2, no. 3 (Fall 1977): 50–61, and also in "Coming Home: Feminist Utopias and Patriarchal Experiences," in *Alternative Future,* ed. by Marlene Barr (Bowling Green, OH: Popular Press, 1979). Another portion of this chapter is based on Katherine Pope's paper "Utopia and Human Nature," which was presented at the 1974 Modern Language Association Convention.

12. William Morris, *News from Nowhere* (New York: Harper, 1953), p. 25.
13. Arthur C. Clarke, *Childhood's End* (New York: Ballantine, 1953), p. 167.
14. Charles Reich, *The Greening of America* (New York: Random, 1970).
15. Theodore Roszak, *Where the Wasteland Ends: Politics and Transcendence in Post-Industrial Society* (Garden City, NY: Doubleday, 1973).
16. Marshall McLuhan, *Understanding Media: The Extension of Man* (New York: New Amer. Lib., 1964).
17. Sinclair Lewis, *Babbitt* (New York: New Amer. Lib., 1961), p. 78.
18. Eugene Zamiatin, *We* (New York: Dutton, 1959), p. 21.
19. Robert Heinlein, *Stranger in a Strange Land* (New York: Berkley, 1961).
20. Unpublished interview by Elaine Chernoff.
21. Ursula Le Guin, "Is Gender Necessary?" in *Aurura: Beyond Equality,* ed. by Vonde N. McIntyre and Susan Janice Anderson (Greenwich, CT: Fawcett, 1976), pp. 134–135.
22. *Ibid.* p. 138.

Bibliography

Alcott, Louisa May. *Little Women*. Boston: Little, 1911.

————. *Work: A Story of Experience*. New York: Schocken, 1977.

Allen, Grant. *The Woman Who Did*. Boston: Roberts Bros., 1895.

Alta. *Momma: A Start on All the Untold Stories*. New York: Time Change Pr., 1974.

————. *Theme and Variations*. San Lorenzo, CA: Shameless Hussy Pr., 1975.

Alther, Lisa. *Kinflicks*. New York: New Amer. Lib., 1977.

Angelou, Maya. *I Know Why the Caged Bird Sings*. New York: Bantam, 1971.

Arnow, Harriet. *The Dollmaker*. New York: Avon, 1974.

Atwood, Margaret. *Lady Oracle*. New York: Simon & Schuster, 1976.

————. *The Edible Woman*. New York: Popular Lib., 1976.

————. *Surfacing*. New York: Popular Lib., 1974.

Austen, Jane. *Emma*. New York: Airmont, 1966.

————. *Pride and Prejudice*. New York: Rinehart, 1949.

————. *Sense and Sensibility*. London: Martin Decker, 1930.

Barnes, Djuna. *Nightwood*. New York: New Directions, 1961.

Barth, John. *The End of the Road*. New York: Grosset, 1969.

Barthelme, Donald. *Snow White*. New York: Bantam, 1967.

Baum, L. Frank. *The Wizard of Oz*. Chicago: Reilly & Lee, 1966.

Beresford-Howe, Constance. *The Book of Eve*. New York: Avon, 1973.

Bernikow, Louise, ed. *The World Split Open: Four Centuries of Women Poets in England and America, 1552–1950*. New York: Vintage, 1974.

Bird, Isabella. *A Lady's Life in the Rocky Mountains*. New York: Ballantine, 1960.

Bishop, Elizabeth. "Invitation to Miss Marianne Moore." In *The Complete Poems*. New York: Farrar, 1969.

Boston Women's Health Collective. *Our Bodies, Ourselves: A Book by and for Women,* 2nd ed. New York: Simon & Schuster, 1976.

Bowen, Elizabeth. *The Death of the Heart*. New York: Vintage, 1968.

Brecht, Bertolt. "Mother Courage and Her Children." In *Classics of the Modern Theater: Realism and After,* ed. by Alvin B. Kernan. New York: Harcourt, Brace and World, 1965.

Brigham, Besmilr. "Tell Our Daughters," in *31 New American Poets,* ed. by Ron Schreiber. New York: Hill & Wang, 1969.

Brontë, Charlotte. *Jane Eyre*. New York: Harper, 1965.

————. *Shirley*. New York and London: Harper, 1900.

————. *Villette*. Philadelphia: Ashmead, n.d.

Brontë, Emily. *Wuthering Heights: Text, Sources, Criticisms,* ed. by V. S. Pritchett. Boston: Houghton, 1956.

————. "No Coward Soul Is Mine." In *Emily Brontë: Her Life and Work,* ed. by Muriel Spark and Derek Stanford. London: Peter Owen, 1960.

Brown, Alice. "The Way of Peace." In *Tiverton Tales.* Boston and New York: Houghton, 1899.

Brown, Rita Mae. *Rubyfruit Jungle.* Plainfield, VT: Daughter, 1973.

Browning, Elizabeth Barrett. "Aurora Leigh." In *The Complete Works of Elizabeth Barrett Browning,* ed. by Charlotte Porter and Helen A. Clarke. New York: Crowell, 1900.

Browning, Robert. "Porphyria's Lover." In *Shorter Poems.* New York: Crofts, 1934.

Bryant, Dorothy. *Ella Price's Journal.* New York: New Amer. Lib., 1972.

————. *The Kin of Ata Are Waiting for You.* New York: Random, 1976.

————. *Miss Giardino.* Berkeley, CA: Ata Books, 1978.

Burney, Fanny. *Evelina; or, The History of a Young Lady's Entrance into the World.* New York: Norton, 1965.

Callenbach, Ernest. *Ecotopia: The Notebooks and Reports of William Weston.* New York: Bantam, 1975.

Campbell, Joseph. *The Hero with a Thousand Faces.* Cleveland and New York: Meridian Books, 1956.

Carlyle, Thomas. *On Heroes, Hero Worship and the Heroic in History.* In the *Works of Thomas Carlyle,* vol. 5, ed. by H. D. Traill. New York: AMS Pr., 1969.

Carr, Emily. *Hundreds and Thousands.* Toronto: Clarke, Irwin, 1966.

Carroll, Lewis. *Alice's Adventures in Wonderland and Through the Looking Glass.* New York: New Amer. Lib., 1960.

Carey, Elizabeth Tanfield. "Chorus from Mariam." In *The Tragedie of Mariam, The Faire Queen of Jewrie.* London: Oxford Univ. Pr., 1914.

Castaneda, Carlos. *Tales of Power.* New York: Simon & Schuster, 1974.

Cather, Willa. *My Mortal Enemy.* New York: Vintage, 1954.

————. *O Pioneers.* Boston: Houghton, 1938.

Chaucer, Geoffrey. "The Canterbury Tales." In *The Works of Geoffrey Chaucer,* ed. by F. N. Robinson. Boston: Houghton, 1957.

Cheney, Ednah D. *Louisa May Alcott: Her Life, Letters and Journals.* Boston: Little, 1919.

Chicago, Judy. *Through the Flower: My Struggle as a Woman Artist.* Garden City, NY: Doubleday, 1977.

Chopin, Kate. *The Awakening.* New York: Avon, 1972.

————. "The Story of an Hour." In *The Complete Works of Kate Chopin.* ed. by Per Seyersted, vol. 1. Baton Rouge, LA: Louisiana State Univ. Pr., 1969.

Clarke, Arthur C. *Childhood's End.* New York: Ballantine, 1953.

Clifton, Lucille. "Sister." In *An Ordinary Woman.* New York: Random, 1974.

Daly, Mary. *Beyond God the Father: Toward a Philosophy of Women's Liberation.* Boston: Beacon Pr., 1973.

————. *Gyn/Ecology: The Metaethics of Radical Feminism.* Boston: Beacon, 1978.

Davidson, John. "A Ballad of Hell." In *How Does a Poem Mean?,* ed. by John Ciardi. Boston: Houghton, 1959.

Davis, Angela. *With My Mind on Freedom: An Autobiography.* New York: Bantam, 1975.

Davis, Rebecca Harding. "The Wife's Story." *Atlantic Monthly* 14 (July 1864): 172.

Defoe, Daniel. *Moll Flanders.* New York: Washington Square, 1966.

de Jesus, Carolina Maria. *Child of the Dark: The Diary of Carolina Maria de Jesus,* trans. by David St. Clair. New York: Dutton, 1962.

de Rougemont, Denis. *Love in the Western World.* New York: Pantheon, 1959.

Dickens, Charles. *The Old Curiosity Shop and Hard Times.* Boston: Estes and Laurait, 1953.

Dickinson, Emily. "What Soft, Cherubic Creatures." In *The Poems of Emily Dickinson,* ed. by Thomas H. Johnson. Cambridge, MA: Harvard Univ. Pr., 1955.

_____. "She Rose to His Requirement." In *The Poems of Emily Dickinson,* ed. by Thomas H. Johnson. Cambridge, MA: Harvard Univ. Pr., 1955.

Didion, Joan. *Play It as It Lays.* New York: Bantam, 1971.

_____. *Slouching toward Bethlehem.* New York: Delta, 1968.

Dijkstra, Bram. "The Androgyne in Nineteenth-Century Art and Literature." *Comparative Literature* 26, no. 1 (Winter 1974): 62–73.

Dillard, Annie. *Pilgrim at Tinker Creek.* New York: Bantam, 1975.

Di Prima, Diane. "Revolutionary Poem #19." In *Revolutionary Letters.* San Francisco: City Lights, 1971.

Doolittle, Hilda. *Trilogy: The Walls Do Not Fall; Tribute to the Angels; The Flowering of the Rod.* New York: New Directions, 1973.

Drabble, Margaret. *The Ice Age.* New York: Knopf, 1977.

_____. *Jerusalem the Golden.* New York: Popular Lib., 1977.

_____ *The Realms of Gold.* New York: Knopf, 1976.

_____ *Thank You All Very Much.* New York: New Amer. Lib., 1965.

Eliot, George. *Daniel Deronda.* New York: Harper and Brothers, 1876.

_____. *Middlemarch,* ed. with introd. and notes by Gordon S. Haight. Boston: Houghton, 1968.

_____. *The Mill on the Floss.* New York: New Amer. Lib., 1965.

Epstein, Pearl. *Monsters: Their Histories, Homes and Habits.* Garden City, NY: Doubleday, 1973.

Faulkner, William. *Light in August.* New York: Modern Lib., 1950.

Fiedler, Leslie. *Love and Death in the American Novel.* Cleveland: World, 1962.

Field, Joanna. *A Life of One's Own.* London: Chatto & Windus, 1934.

Finch, Anne. "The Unequal Fetters." In *Poems of Anne, Countess of Winchelsea,* ed. by Myra Reynolds. Chicago: Univ. of Chicago Pr., 1903.

Fitzgerald, F. Scott. "The Last of the Belles." In *The Bodley Head Scott Fitzgerald.* vol. 2. London: Bodley Head, 1959.

Flynn, Elizabeth Gurley. *The Rebel Girl: An Autobiography.* New York: International, 1974.

Ford, George H. *Dickens and His Readers.* New York: Norton, 1965.

Fowles, John. *The French Lieutenant's Woman.* New York: New Amer. Lib., 1971.

Freeman, Mary Wilkins. "A New England Nun." In *Best Stories of Mary Wilkins Freeman.* New York: Harper, 1927.

_____. "The Revolt of Mother." In *The Revolt of Mother and Other Stories.* Old Westbury, NY: Feminist Pr., 1974.

Fremlin, Celia. "Don't Be Frightened." In *Ms. Mysteries,* ed. by Arthur Lieberman. New York: Washington Square, 1976.

Fremont-Smith, Eliot. "Two Cheers for Mattie Ross." *New York Times,* June 12, 1968, p. 45.

French, Marilyn. *The Women's Room.* New York: Harcourt, 1978.

Gaskell, Elizabeth. *Sylvia's Lovers.* New York: Dutton, 1971.

Gilman, Charlotte Perkins. *Herland.* Serialized in *The Forerunner* 6 (1915). Reprint. New York: Pantheon, 1979.

————. *The Living of Charlotte Perkins Gilman: An Autobiography.* New York: Harper, 1963.

————. *The Yellow Wallpaper.* Old Westbury, NY: Feminist Pr., 1973.

Gissing, George. *The Odd Women.* New York: Norton, 1971.

Glasgow, Ellen. *Barren Ground.* New York: Hill & Wang, 1957.

Goldsmith, Oliver. *The Vicar of Wakefield.* New York: Houghton, 1901.

Graves, Robert. "The Great Grandmother." In *Collected Poems (1914–1947).* London: Cassell, 1948.

Greene, Bette. *Philip Hall Likes Me, I Reckon Maybe.* New York: Dial, 1974.

Greer, Germaine. *The Female Eunuch.* New York: Bantam, 1971.

Hardin, Nancy. "An Interview with Margaret Drabble." *Contemporary Literature* 14, no. 3, p. 278.

Harding, M. Esther. *The Way of All Women.* New York: Harper, 1970.

————. *Woman's Mysteries: Ancient and Modern.* New York: Bantam, 1971.

Hardy, Thomas. "The Ruined Maid." In *Collected Poems.* New York: Macmillan, 1925.

————. *Jude the Obscure.* New York: Harper, 1966.

————. *The Return of the Native.* London: Macmillan, 1975.

————. *Tess of the D'Urbervilles: A Pure Woman.* New York: Modern Lib., 1951.

Haskell, Molly. *From Reverance to Rape: The Treatment of Women in the Movies.* Baltimore: Penguin, 1974.

Hawthorne, Nathaniel. "The Birthmark." In *The Portable Hawthorne.* New York: Viking, 1965.

————. "Rappacini's Daughter." In *Great Short Works of Hawthorne,* ed. by Frederick C. Crews. New York: Harper, 1967.

————. *The Scarlet Letter.* New York: New Amer. Lib., 1959.

Heilbrun, Carolyn. "The Woman as Hero." *Texas Quarterly* 8, no. 4 (1965): 136.

Heinlein, Robert. *Stranger in a Strange Land.* New York: Berkley, 1961.

Henderson, Zenna. *Pilgrimage: The Book of The People.* New York: Avon, 1950.

Heller, Joseph. *Catch-22.* New York: Dell, 1955.

Hinz, Evelyn. "The Creative Critic." In *Celebration with Anaïs Nin,* ed. by Valerie Harms. Riverdale, CT: Magic Circle Pr., 1973.

Howard, Jane. *A Different Woman.* New York: Dutton, 1973.

Hurnscot, Loran. *A Prison, A Paradise,* vol. 2. New York: Viking, 1959.

Ibsen, Henrik. *A Doll's House: Six Plays by Henrik Ibsen,* trans. by Eva LeGallienne. New York: Modern Lib., 1957.

James, Henry. "Daisy Miller." In *The Great Short Novels of Henry James,* ed. with introd. by Philip Rahv. New York: Dial, 1974.

————. *The Portrait of a Lady.* New York: Norton, 1975.

————. *The Sacred Fount.* London: Methuen, 1901.

————. "The Beast in the Jungle." In *The Turn of the Screw and Other Novels,* ed. by William Thorp. New York: New Amer. Lib., 1962.

Janeway, Elizabeth. *Man's World, Woman's Place.* New York: Dell, 1972.

Jong, Erica. *Fear of Flying.* New York: Holt, 1974.

————. "Alcestis on the Poetry Circuit." In *Half-Lives.* New York: Holt, 1973.

————. *How to Save Your Own Life.* New York: Holt, 1977.

Jung, Carl. *Man and His Symbols.* New York: Dell, 1968.

Kesey, Ken. *Sometimes a Great Notion.* New York: Viking, 1964.

Kingston, Maxine H. *The Woman Warrior: Memoirs of a Girlhood among Ghosts.* New York: Vintage, 1977.

Laing, R. D. *The Divided Self: An Existential Study in Sanity and Madness.* Baltimore: Penguin, 1972.

————. *The Politics of Experience.* New York: Pantheon, 1967.

Lane, Mary Bradley. *Mizora: A Prophecy.* Boston: Gregg, 1975.

Lapidus, Jacqueline. "Coming Out." *Amazon Quarterly* 3, no. 2 (1975).

Lawrence, D. H. *The Rainbow.* New York: Viking, 1964.

————. *Women in Love.* New York: Modern Lib., 1920.

Lazarre, Jane. *The Mother Knot.* New York: Dell, 1977.

L'Engle, Madeleine. *A Wind in the Door.* New York: Dell, 1978.

————. *A Wrinkle in Time.* New York: Dell, 1978.

Le Guin, Ursula. "The Day before the Revolution." In *More Women of Wonder*, ed. by Pamela Sargent. New York: Vintage, 1976.

————. *The Dispossessed.* New York: Avon, 1975.

————. "Is Gender Necessary?" In *Aurura: Beyond Equality*, ed. by Vonde N. McIntyre and Susan Janice Anderson. Greenwich, CT: Fawcett, 1976.

————. *The Left Hand of Darkness.* New York: Ace Books, 1976.

Lessing, Doris. *Children of Violence*, vol. 1. New York: Simon & Schuster, 1964.

————. *The Four-Gated City.* New York: Bantam, 1970.

————. *The Golden Notebook.* New York: Simon & Schuster, 1962.

————. "To Room Nineteen." In *A Man and Two Women and Other Stories.* New York: Simon & Schuster, 1958.

————. *Memoirs of a Survivor.* New York: Bantam, 1976.

————. *The Summer before the Dark.* New York: Knopf, 1973.

Lewis, Sinclair. *Babbit.* New York: New Amer. Lib., 1961.

McLuhan, Marshall. *Understanding Media: The Extension of Man.* New York: New Amer. Lib., 1964.

Mailer, Norman. "The Time of Her Time." In *Advertisements for Myself.* New York: Putnam, 1969.

Mansfield, Katherine. *Journal of Katherine Mansfield*, ed. by John Middleton Murray. New York: Knopf, 1927.

————. *Letters of Katherine Mansfield to John Middleton Murray.* New York: Knopf, n.d.

————. *Novels and Novelists*, ed. by J. Middleton Murray. Boston: Beacon, 1959.

Maugham, Somerset. "The Colonel's Lady." In *W. Somerset Maugham: Four Short Stories.* Kansas City, MO: Hallmark, 1970.

Mead, Margaret. *Blackberry Winter.* New York: Pocket Bks., 1975.

Melville, Herman. *Moby Dick; or, The Whale*, ed. by Charles Feidelson, Jr. Indianapolis: Bobbs-Merrill, 1964.

Meredith, George. *The Egoist.* Boston: Houghton, 1958.

Millett, Kate. *Flying*. New York: Ballantine, 1974.

Moffat, Mary J., and Painter, Charlotte. *Revelations: Diaries of Women*. New York: Random, 1974.

Morgan, Robin. *Going Too Far: A Personal Chronicle of a Feminist*. New York: Random, 1977.

Morris, William. *News from Nowhere*. New York: Harper, 1953.

Moulton, Charles. *Wonder Woman*. New York: Holt, 1972.

Munro, Alice. *Lives of Girls and Women*. New York: New Amer. Lib., 1974.

Murdoch, Iris. *Flight from the Enchanter*. New York: Viking, 1956.

————. *The Unicorn*. New York: Viking, 1963.

Nin, Anaïs. *Diary of Anaïs Nin*. Vol. 1, New York: Harcourt, Brace and World, 1966. Vol. 2, New York: Swallow Pr., 1966.

————. *House of Incest*. Denver: Swallow Pr., 1958.

Norman, Dorothy. *The Hero: Myth/Image/Symbol*. New York: New Amer. Lib., 1969.

Oates, Joyce Carol. *Expensive People*. Greenwich, CT: Fawcett, 1968.

————. *Wonderland*. Greenwich, CT: Fawcett, 1973.

Olsen, Tillie. *Tell Me a Riddle and Other Stories*. Philadelphia and New York: Lippincott, 1961.

Paley, Grace. "A Subject of Childhood." In *The Little Disturbances of Man*. New York: Doubleday, 1959.

Parker, Dorothy. "Story of Mrs. W—." In *Not So Deep as a Well*. New York: Viking, 1943.

Patterson-Black, Sheryll. "Women Homesteaders on the Great Plains Frontier." *Frontiers* 1, no. 2 (Spring 1976): 68.

Pearson, Carol, and Pope, Katherine. *Who Am I This Time? Female Portraits in British and American Literature*. New York: McGraw-Hill, 1976.

Phelps, Elizabeth Stuart. "The Angel over the Right Shoulder." Andover, MA: Propor, 1868.

Piercy, Marge. "A Work of Artifice." In *Liberation Now*. New York: Dell, 1971.

————. *Small Changes*. Greenwich, CT: Fawcett, 1974.

————. *Woman on the Edge of Time*. New York: Knopf, 1976.

Plath, Sylvia. *Ariel*. New York: Harper, 1966.

————. *The Colossus and Other Poems*. New York: Knopf, 1962.

Portis, Charles. *True Grit*. New York: New Amer. Lib., 1968.

Pratt, Annis V. "The New Feminist Criticism: Exploring the History of the New Space." In *Beyond Intellectual Sexism*, ed. by Joan Roberts. New York: McKay, 1976.

Pynchon, Thomas. *The Crying of Lot 49*. New York: Bantam, 1967.

Radicalesbian Collective. "The Woman-Identified Woman." In *Liberation Now*. New York: Dell, 1971.

Raglan, Lord. *The Hero: A Study in Tradition, Myth and Drama*. New York: Oxford Univ. Pr., 1937.

Reeves, Nancy. *Womankind*. Chicago: Aldine, 1971.

Reich, Charles. *The Greening of America*. New York: Random, 1970.

Reingold, Paula. "And This Is Love." In *I Hear My Sisters Saying*, ed. by Carol Konek and Dorothy Walters. New York: Crowell, 1976.

Reitman, Ben L. *Sister of the Road: The Autobiography of Box-Car Bertha.* As told to Dr. Ben L. Reitman. New York: Harper, 1937.

Rich, Adrienne. *Adrienne Rich's Poetry,* sel. and ed. by Barbara Charlesworth Gelpi and Albert Gelpi. New York: Norton, 1975.

_____. *Of Woman Born: Motherhood as Experience and Institution.* New York: Norton, 1976.

_____. *Poems: Selected and New, 1950–1974.* New York: Norton, 1975.

_____. *Women and Honor: Some Notes on Lying.* Pittsburgh: Motheroot Pubns., 1977.

Richardson, Dorothy. *Pilgrimage,* vol. 1. New York: Knopf, 1967.

Richardson, Samuel. *Clarissa; or, History of a Young Lady,* vol. 1. London: Whittingham & Rowland, 1810.

_____. *Pamela; or, Virtue Rewarded,* vol. 1. Stratford-upon-Avon: Shakespeare Head Pr., 1929.

Robbins, Tom. *Even Cowgirls Get the Blues.* Boston: Houghton, 1976.

Robinson, Edwin Arlington. "The Tree in Pamela's Garden." In *The American Tradition in Literature,* ed. by Sculley Bradley, Richmond C. Beatty, and E. Hudson Long, 3rd ed. New York: Norton, 1967.

Roche, Paul. "What Makes Her Special." In *To Tell the Truth.* London: Duckworth, 1967.

Rodgers, Carolyn. "i have changed so much in this world." In *how i got ovah: new and selected poems.* Garden City, NY: Doubleday, 1976.

Roszak, Theodore. *Where the Wasteland Ends: Politics and Transcendence in Post-Industrial Society.* Garden City, NY: Doubleday, 1973.

Rousseau, Jean-Jacques. *L'Emile: A Treatise on Education,* ed. by W. H. Payne. Boston: Ginn, Heath, 1906.

Rukeyser, Muriel. "More Clues." In *Breaking Open.* New York: Random, 1973.

_____. "The Poem as Mask." In *By a Woman Writ: Literature from Six Centuries by and about Women,* ed. by Joan Goulianos. Baltimore: Penguin, 1974.

_____. "Käthe Kollwitz." In *No More Masks: An Anthology of Poems by Women,* ed. by Florence Howe and Ellen Bass. Garden City, NY: Doubleday, 1972.

_____. "Mortal Girl." In *The American Tradition in Literature,* ed. by Sculley Bradley, Richmond C. Beatty, and E. Hudson Long, 3rd ed. New York: Norton, 1967.

Ruskin, John. "Of Queen's Gardens." In *Sesames and Lilies.* New York: Homewood, 1902.

Russ, Joanna. "The Autobiography of My Mother." *Epoch,* Fall 1975, p. 87.

_____. "Daddy's Girl." *Epoch* 24, no. 2 (Winter 1975): 151.

_____. *The Female Man.* New York: Bantam, 1975.

_____. "What Can a Heroine Do? or, Why Women Can't Write." In *Images of Women in Fiction,* ed. by Susan Koppelman Cornillon. Bowling Green, OH: Bowling Green Univ. Popular Pr., 1972.

Sackville-West, Vita. *All Passion Spent.* Garden City, NY: Doubleday, Doran, 1931.

_____. *The Edwardians.* Garden City, NY: Doubleday, Doran, 1930.

Sarton, May. *As We Are Now.* New York: Norton, 1973.

_____. *Joanna and Ulysses.* New York: Norton, 1963.

————. *Kinds of Love.* New York: Norton, 1970.

————. *Mrs. Stevens Hears the Mermaids Singing.* New York: Norton, 1965.

Sayers, Dorothy. *Gaudy Night.* New York: Avon, 1968.

Scott-Maxwell, Florida. *The Measure of My Days.* New York: Knopf, 1968.

Sexton, Anne. "Housewife." In *All My Pretty Ones.* Boston: Houghton, 1962.

————. "Little Girl, My String Bean, My Lovely Woman." In *Live or Die.* Boston: Houghton, 1966.

————. *To Bedlam and Part Way Back.* Boston: Houghton, 1960.

Shaw, George Bernard. *Arms and the Man.* New York: Bantam, 1968.

————. "Major Barbara." In *Drama in the Modern World: Plays and Essays,* ed. by Samuel A. Weiss. Boston: Heath, 1964.

————. *Mrs. Warren's Profession.* New York: Brentano's, 1913.

————. *Saint Joan.* Baltimore: Penguin, 1951.

Shelley, Mary. *Frankenstein or, The Modern Prometheus.* New York: Dell, 1974.

Shorter, Clement. *The Brontës: Life and Letters,* vol. 1. New York: Haskell House, 1964.

Shulman, Alix Kates. *Memoirs of an Ex-Prom Queen.* New York: Bantam, 1973.

Smedley, Agnes. *Daughter of Earth.* Old Westbury, NY: Feminist Pr., 1973.

Sohl, Robert, and Carr, Audrey, eds. *The Gospel according to Zen: Beyond the Death of God.* New York: New Amer. Lib., 1970.

Staton, Mary. *From the Legend of Biel.* New York: Ace Books, 1975.

Steinbeck, John. *The Grapes of Wrath.* New York: Viking, 1958.

Stumpf, Edna. "You're Beautiful When You're Scared." *Metropolitan,* April 1974, p. 14.

Sutheim, Susan. "For Witches." In *No More Marks: An Anthology of Poems by Women,* ed. by Florence Howe and Ellen Bass. Garden City, NY: Doubleday, 1973.

Tennyson, Alfred Lord. *The Princess: A Medley,* ed. by Charles Townstend Copeland and Henry Milnor Rideout. Chicago: Scott, Foresman, 1899.

Thomas, Dylan. "Ballad of the Long-Legged Bait." In *The Collected Poems of Dylan Thomas.* New York: New Directions, 1957.

Tolstoy, Sophia. *The Diary of Tolstoy's Wife, 1860–1891,* trans. by Alexander Werth. London: Gollancz, 1928.

Tyler, Anne. *Earthly Possessions.* New York: Popular Lib., 1978.

Vonnegut, Kurt, Jr. *Breakfast of Champions or Goodbye, Blue Monday.* New York: Delacorte Pr., Seymour Lawrence, 1973.

————. *Sirens of Titan.* New York: Delacorte Pr., 1959.

Walton, Evangeline. *The Children of Llyr.* New York: Ballantine, 1971.

Weitzman, Lenore J., and Rizzo, Diane M. "Images of Males and Females in Elementary School Textbooks in Five Subject Areas." Old Westbury, NY: Feminist Pr., 1974.

Welty, Eudora. "A Worn Path." In *Women and Fiction: Short Stories by and about Women,* ed. by Susan Cahill. New York: New Amer. Lib., 1975.

West, Jessamyn. *The Woman Said Yes: Encounters with Life and Death.* New York and London: Harcourt, 1976.

Weston, Jessie. *From Ritual to Romance.* Garden City, NY: Doubleday, 1957.

Wharton, Edith. *The House of Mirth.* New York: Holt, 1962.

Wilding, Faith. "Waiting." In *Through the Flower: My Struggle as a Woman Artist* by Judy Chicago. Garden City, NY: Doubleday, 1977.

Wilhelm, Kate. *Abyss.* Garden City, NY: Doubleday, 1971.

Williams, Tennessee. "The Mattress by the Tomato Patch." In *Hard Candy.* New York: New Directions, 1967.

Woolf, Virginia. *Mrs. Dalloway.* New York: Harcourt, 1925.

————. *A Room of One's Own.* New York: Harcourt, Brace and World, 1929.

————. *To the Lighthouse.* New York: Harcourt, Brace and World, 1927.

————. *A Writer's Diary,* ed. by Leonard Woolf. New York: Harcourt, 1954.

Zamiatin, Eugene. *We.* New York: Dutton, 1959.

Zoltan, Anne. *Annie: The Female Experience.* New York: Julian, 1973.

Index